Confounding Powers

Nearly a decade and a half after 9/11, the study of international politics has yet to address some of the most pressing issues raised by the attacks, most notably the relationships between Al Qaeda's international systemic origins and its international societal effects. This theoretically broad-ranging and empirically far-reaching study addresses that question and others, advancing the study of international politics into new historical settings while providing insights into pressing policy challenges. Looking at actors that depart from established structural and behavioral patterns provides opportunities to examine how those deviations help generate the norms and identities that constitute international society. Systematic examination of the Assassins, Mongols, and Barbary powers provides historical comparison and context to our contemporary struggle, while enriching and deepening our understanding of the systemic forces behind, and societal effects of, these confounding powers.

William J. Brenner is a national security analyst based in Washington, D.C. His work has been published in the journal *Security Studies* and the *European Journal of International Relations* (*EJIR*), where his co-authored article received the award for best article published in *EJIR* between 2007 and 2009 from the European Consortium for Political Research. He received his PhD from the Department of Political Science at Johns Hopkins University in 2008, and his work there on the effects of 9/11 on international relations theory was recognized in 2005 with the inaugural Graduate Student Paper Award given by the International Security Studies Section of the International Studies Association.

Confounding Powers
*Anarchy and International Society from
the Assassins to Al Qaeda*

William J. Brenner

CAMBRIDGE
UNIVERSITY PRESS

University Printing House, Cambridge CB2 8BS, United Kingdom

One Liberty Plaza, 20th Floor, New York, NY 10006, USA

477 Williamstown Road, Port Melbourne, VIC 3207, Australia

314-321, 3rd Floor, Plot 3, Splendor Forum, Jasola District Centre, New Delhi - 110025, India

79 Anson Road, #06-04/06, Singapore 079906

Cambridge University Press is part of the University of Cambridge.

It furthers the University's mission by disseminating knowledge in the pursuit of
education, learning and research at the highest international levels of excellence.

www.cambridge.org
Information on this title: www.cambridge.org/9781107521605

© William J. Brenner 2016

This publication is in copyright. Subject to statutory exception
and to the provisions of relevant collective licensing agreements,
no reproduction of any part may take place without the written
permission of Cambridge University Press.

First published 2016
First paperback edition 2020

A catalogue record for this publication is available from the British Library

Library of Congress Cataloging in Publication data
Brenner, William J., author.
Confounding powers : anarchy and international society from the Assassins
to Al Qaeda / William J. Brenner.
Cambridge, United Kingdom : Cambridge University Press, [2016] | Includes
bibliographical references and index.
LCCN 2015031741 | ISBN 9781107109452 (alk. paper)
LCSH: International relations | Non-state actors (International relations) |
Non-state actors (International relations) – Case studies. | Assassins
(Ismailites) – History. | Mongols – History. | Pirates – Africa,
North – History. | Qaida (Organization) – History.
LCC JZ4059 .B74 2016 | DDC 327.1–dc23
LC record available at http://lccn.loc.gov/2015031741

ISBN 978-1-107-10945-2 Hardback
ISBN 978-1-107-52160-5 Paperback

Cambridge University Press has no responsibility for the persistence or
accuracy of URLs for external or third-party internet websites referred to in
this publication, and does not guarantee that any content on such websites is,
or will remain, accurate or appropriate.

Contents

List of figures		vi
List of maps		vii
List of tables		viii
Preface and acknowledgments		ix
	Introduction	1
1	International society and the logics of anarchy	23
2	Confusion in the hearts of men: the Nizari Ismailis and the Assassin legends	70
3	*"A furore Tartarorum libera nos"*: the Mongol eruption and aftermath	107
4	Out of the shadow of God: power and piracy along the Barbary Coast	151
5	In the shadow of the spears: Al Qaeda's clash with civilization	199
	Conclusion	243
	Index	268

Figures

4.1 Cinque-tetes, or the Paris Monster (1798)
Image reproduced by permission of The Huntington Library,
San Marino, California   193
C.1 Identity and functional uncertainty   255

Maps

2.1 Abbasid successor states (late tenth century CE)	73
2.2 Seljuk Empire (late eleventh century CE)	75
2.3 Major Nizari Ismaili fortifications in Persia	80
2.4 Major Nizari Ismaili fortifications in Syria	88
3.1 Sedentary states and steppe tribes	111

Tables

I.1	Cases and contexts	18
1.1	Logics of concealment	36
1.2	Systemic to system change	38
1.3	System change to international society	68

Preface and acknowledgments

There are times when we experience events that confound expectations and rattle our cognitive foundations as they exceed anticipated bounds of possibility. The study of international politics has long grappled with the perils of possibilities, fashioning dangers into patterns by applying theory and engaging with history, making them more fathomable. September 11, 2001, was the first day of classes of my second year in the graduate program in political science at Johns Hopkins University. R.W. Apple captured, as much as one could, not only the enormity of the acts but also the confusion they generated, writing that "mere words were inadequate vessels to contain the sense of shock and horror that people felt. As Washington struggled to regain a sense of equilibrium, with warplanes and heavily armed helicopters overhead, past and present national security officials earnestly debated the possibility of a Congressional declaration of war – but against precisely whom, and in what exact circumstances?"[1] From that point on, my intellectual trajectory was set, and frustration with how international relations theory fell short in accounting for these seminal events drove this work from its conception.

While propelled by that dissatisfaction, further examination showed that some answers could be found in existing theory, and later contributions added to the tools we can use to try to make more sense of these ultimately senseless events. What became very clear is that none of those ideas or frameworks alone could suffice in explaining a phenomenon so rooted in the variety and complexity of the contemporary international system. Still clearer was the recognition that the modern international system offered few new insights into a transforming global landscape and a more expansive examination of world history would be essential.

Though this work was spurred by September 11, it has evolved to provide insights into a broader scope of international phenomena,

---

[1] R.W. Apple, "Nation Plunges into Fight with Enemy Hard to Identify," *New York Times*, September 12, 2001, A1.

x   Preface and acknowledgments

demonstrating the creative power of events in advancing our knowledge and the field. Progress in the face of uncertainty requires both determination and humility given that we are in the midst of the change we seek to understand. Flexibility is also a necessity as stark departures from expected patterns make our thought not only a function of professional practice but a means to cope. "Nothing creates intellectual confidence like catastrophe," Leon Wieseltier wrote of the attacks. "After the mind breaks, it stiffens; in the aftermath of grief, it lets in only certainty."[2] Uncertainty is a driving force in this analysis and should also shape how we approach the study of international politics. The ability of theory to increase our capacity to navigate the complexity and ambiguity of international politics demands greater pliability, including enhanced collaboration and engagement within and outside of the field as well as a willingness to question our assumptions. We have come a long way since Apple's reaction to the attacks in understanding the events and actors that brought them about. Applying these lessons and fully focused on those goals, this book, hopefully, will prove to be a step toward further comprehension, and perhaps spark additions and corrections that move us closer to full understanding.

Many people were instrumental in helping me through what, despite its often thrilling spells, was at times a long, hard slog. This book is based on a much revised and condensed version of my doctoral dissertation. My dissertation advisers at Hopkins were Professors Steven David and Daniel Deudney. Beyond setting the fine example of balancing academic excellence and unceasing decency, Professor David made it clear that some of my initial theoretical arguments were too abstruse and required translation into more plain English. Professor Deudney also helped correct some of my early errors. My zeal in responding to the events and dissatisfaction with existing theory led to some fairly embarrassing efforts to rethink the theory more than a little too deeply. Many would have seen this failed attempt and dismissed any future potential. Instead, gently chiding my overreaching, he pointed out the errors and encouraged me to challenge but to do so more wisely. I hope that the ultimate results justify that confidence.

Beyond the guidance they provided, each set examples in their work that I have endeavored to follow. Professor David once faced the misfit of neorealist theory to the context of the developing world. What resulted was not falsification but theoretical innovation and progress. Professor Deudney taught me through his work that often the best way to critique a theory is to look at its founding assumptions. Extending those

---

[2] Leon Wieseltier, "The Catastrophist," *New York Times*, April 27, 2008.

Preface and acknowledgments

assumptions to their logical ends can yield propositions that expand and improve rather than upend and discard inadequate theories. His work also demonstrated to me that the necessities of international politics generate possibilities in addition to limitations on world order. I have tried to apply these key lessons throughout my work.

I also had the good fortune to work with other major scholars. Participating in the Dartmouth Workshop on Hierarchy and Balance in International Systems was a remarkable opportunity for a graduate student. I am particularly grateful to Professors William Wohlforth, Stuart Kaufman, and Richard Little. Working on a project similar in methodology and emphasis on world history provided me with experiences and lessons that I applied throughout this study. I do not believe I would have had the confidence, or hubris, to attempt to tackle such a broad historical scope in this project without this formative experience.

Working on diverse and largely unfamiliar historical contexts also necessitated interactions with scholars outside of the field. I cannot attest to whether there is any tension between political science and other fields, as I witnessed none. Practically every (mostly "cold call") e-mail I sent to various scholars was met with a helpful and often lengthy response. For guidance concerning sources and other questions on the Mongols, a number of scholars were extremely helpful. The list is long and represents a "who's who" in that field, including Denis Sinor, Christopher Atwood, Timothy May, Hok-lam Chan, and Nicola Di Cosmo. Donald Wagner was very helpful in my initial investigation into the potential role of lapsed iron embargoes in the rise of the Mongols. This argument did not pan out but was engaging and interesting nonetheless. William Honeychurch introduced me to a much valued anthropological and archaeological perspective that influenced the early formation of my arguments. Regarding a still missing piece of the puzzle concerning Edmund Burke and the Assassins, both David Armitage and Richard Bourke were quite accommodating. Nathan Citino provided critical scholarship concerning the early attitudes of US administrations toward Islam during the Cold War. Of course, any errors and all of the views expressed in this book are mine alone.

I need to acknowledge the excellence of the Johns Hopkins University Library system. This study was very research intensive, often requiring obscure articles that would have been impossible to find and retrieve without the diligence and efficiency of the interlibrary loan and other library staff. As much as I tried, I could never stump them. Accessing a library in Baltimore while residing in Washington, D.C. presented a special challenge. Given the patience and professionalism of the library staffs at the Hopkins Milton S. Eisenhower and School of Advanced

xii   Preface and acknowledgments

International Studies libraries, I was able to overcome that boundary. The staffs at the Library of Congress, British Library, and George Camp Keiser Library at the Middle East Institute were also quite helpful.

Many thanks to John Haslam for recognizing the potential in my thesis, even as I stumbled through the first phases of the book proposal, and for his patience as the time for revision extended well past the normal. I would like to extend my gratitude to the readers whose mix of praise, incisive criticism, and concrete recommendations helped me push through to the later phases of publication. I also truly appreciate the hard work, patience, and professionalism of the editorial and production staffs at CUP in helping ensure the quality of the final product.

In my personal life I am grateful for the support of my parents, my mother Catherine and late father William Brenner, who have always been behind me in achieving my goals. Heartfelt thanks to the extended Schulman, Kaiserman, and Earn families for their kindness and support. I would like to express my thanks to my wife, Alissa, who has been my partner and dearest friend through what at times has been an ordeal. It was more than enough to ask you to deal with years of lonely dissertation work, only to then lose many more weekends together and take the extra share of work raising a child while I grinded out the revision. But you endured, making me able to do the same. Only your love and support made this possible and worthwhile. I look forward to making up for that lost time.

I found out that those efforts would result in this book while on a family picnic on the Mall in Washington, D.C. Our son, Dan, was running joyously pointing to the airplanes taking off and landing at the airport nearby. It later struck me and brought some relief that he never had to witness and live through the time that so shook us during and after the attacks. He will learn about them in part from books, and that this would be one of them is both deeply gratifying and humbling.

Introduction

> The life of all thought is to effect a junction at some point of the new and the old, of deep sunk customs and unconscious dispositions, that are brought to the light of attention by some conflict with newly emerged directions of activity. Philosophies which emerge at distinctive periods define larger patterns of continuity which are woven in, effecting enduring junctions of a stubborn past and an insistent future.
>
> —John Dewey, *Philosophy and Civilization*

The response to September 11 in the study of international politics encompassed claims of epochal change as well as dismissals that the event was a mere aberration. Both positions reinforce the atypicality of the events, but neither is sustainable. Nearly a decade and a half later, international relations theory has yet to engage the full range of questions raised by September 11, particularly those at the levels of the international system and society. This study addresses two of those questions. First, how and when do new, dissimilar kinds of political actors appear on the international stage and not only survive but have significant effects on international politics, and, second, how do these novel actors affect the development of international society?[1] Existing theory has tended to focus on the likening constraints of the material underpinnings of the international system, or to emphasize the emancipatory, creative energies of agency and their fostering of variety. Neither adequately captures the mixture and interaction of constraints and opportunities that emerging actors face as they seek security and survival in international systems. Moreover, the international societal effects associated with these actors go well beyond the violence that accompanies their quest for existence and influence, making purely actuarial accounts of their significance all the more wanting,[2] and cannot be captured by theories that devalue the non-material elements of international politics.

---

[1] Novelty in this case refers to newness to the actors that compose the system, as well as them having system-spanning scope and effects.

[2] Arguments that seek to dismiss the significance of Al Qaeda have been couched in crudely quantitative dismissals of the overall impact of terrorism on US national security. Unfortunately, they have too often relied on sophistic comparisons (deaths from attacks to slipping in a bathtub) and *ad hominem* (labeling those who focus on terrorist threats as at

2   Introduction

Due to their atypicality, these actors confound the system's composition, the actors with which they contend, and as a result, existing theories of international relations. The systemic origins of these actors (including the timing and conditions of their emergence) and their societal effects (including both material and non-material impacts) are interrelated due to their peculiar and highly disruptive character. This makes addressing each of these areas in concert necessary to capture the mechanisms and processes that underlie these episodes.[3] Al Qaeda is an actor of strikingly distinct composition from the major actors in the international system, challenging the system's predominant power, evoking and provoking a reaction both domestically and internationally that belies claims of insignificance. How did this happen, and what can accounts of similarly dissimilar historical actors tell us about their international systemic origins and international societal effects?

Argument and key concepts

I argue the decline of once-dominant powers enables expanded agency for marginal political organizations to exert themselves as systemic actors rather than subsystemic adjuncts. These actors may take on novel forms, in part due to distinct sets of constraints, or "opportunity structures," that affect their tendency to adhere to predominant developmental pathways.

---

best "deluded" and at worst seeking gain). Even more unfortunate is that the central message of these analyses has merit: the United States *has*, at times, both overreacted and clumsily responded to the threat. The exclusive focus on US casualties, moreover, when the vast majority of the deaths from Al Qaeda's actions have happened to Muslims abroad, is another aspect that should discount this analysis when accounting for the group's significance. For an example of the demotion of the significance of Al Qaeda, see John Mueller and Mark G. Stewart, "The Terrorism Delusion: America's Overwrought Response to September 11," *International Security* 37, no. 1 (summer 2012): 81–110. While body counts are problematic as a measure of relative significance, among democratic peace theorists 1,000 fatalities is offered as a benchmark for determining what constitutes a war, defined as "large-scale institutionally organized lethal violence." Bruce Russett, *Grasping the Democratic Peace* (Princeton: Princeton University Press, 1993), 12. Although large-scale institutions may be more amenable to study, they have not maintained their monopoly on large-scale lethal violence.

[3] According to Charles Tilly: "Mechanism- and process-based accounts explain salient features of episodes, or significant differences among them, by identifying within those episodes robust mechanisms of relatively general scope." Distinguishing these, Tilly explains that mechanisms "form a delimited class of events that change relations among specified sets of elements in identical or closely similar ways over a variety of situations. . . ." while processes "are frequently occurring combinations or sequences of mechanisms." Episodes, he adds, "are bounded streams of social life." Charles Tilly, "Mechanisms in Political Processes," *Annual Review of Political Science* 4 (2001): 24–26. While recognizing these distinctions this study uses the labels "mechanisms" and "processes" interchangeably or as a compound.

Argument and key concepts

In so doing they avoid the likening pressures of international systems, most prominently emphasized in neorealism, which have been highlighted to explain how international systems over time have tended toward rough structural homogeneity among units. It is the interaction of expanded opportunities and often severe constraints that creates conditions that foster structural and behavioral dissimilarity in systemic circumstances that might otherwise favor isomorphic outcomes. Systemic change (change *within* the system and its power distribution) in the form of the decline of dominant actors sets in motion mechanisms and processes that lead to system change (change *of* the system and its composition).[4]

The actors highlighted in this study – the Nizari Ismailis (Assassins), Mongols, Barbary powers, and Al Qaeda – each deviated structurally in their development leading to dissimilar unit outcomes compared to their more powerful challengers. The mechanisms and processes underlying this deviation are captured under the label "logic of dissimilation." These structural deviations most often accompanied behaviors that enhanced the chances of survival for the weaker of those challengers. Because of their precarious environments these actors adopt strategies including hiding from their more powerful competitors, deceiving others about their intentions, and, at times, masking their true identity. The Mongols were an exception among these systemic exceptions, given that they amassed enough power to make these strategies – labeled here "logics of concealment" – adjunct rather than core behaviors. But in their deviation from these deviations, the Mongols provide further insight into how these logics realize.

The actors' growing relevance combined with their marked departure from expected patterns, in turn, create a climate of uncertainty that helps spur the development of international society. This happens in response to normative development associated with coping with uncertainty, and the interrelated effects on identity formation from encounters with unlike "others." The interaction of these processes is best understood through engagement with the concept of "ontological security." "Ontological security," Bill McSweeney writes, "relates to the self, its social competence, its confidence in the actor's capacity to manage relations with others. It is a security of a social relationship, a sense of being safely in cognitive control of the interaction context."[5] Confounding these relationships, these actors unsettle stable patterns, setting off reactions in their times that manifest in the form of the components of

---

[4] "Dominant" actors refers to those that have the greatest power in the system as well as to the dominant mode of organization.

[5] Bill McSweeney, *Security, Identity, and Interests: A Sociology of International Relations* (Cambridge: Cambridge University Press, 1999), 157.

4   Introduction

international society. Eventually the historical dissimilar actors became symbols for illegitimate political institutions and conduct, and helped draw the boundaries between civilization and barbarism. These mechanisms and processes help account for principles of legitimacy, rightful membership and conduct, most recognizably in the form of standards of civilization. In this way, these actors have played a significant role in the development of norms and identities that constitute international society. Those boundaries include those that Al Qaeda rudely transgressed, and which it continues to help define.

The use of the label "dissimilar" is intended to draw a distinction between dissimilarity and difference, and to avoid some of the traps associated with the discussion of "like" and "unlike" units. Distinguishing between "like" and "unlike" units is limited by the difficulty operationalizing this distinction. The Russian Federation and France are "like" as sovereign states, but "unlike" as a patchwork empire and a highly centralized nation-state. Were early modern England and Venice "like" actors because they fielded militaries and controlled territory from a capital, or were they an "unlike" composite monarchy and republican maritime city-empire?[6] Focusing on similarities stifles appreciation of variety and understanding of its effects, while focusing on variety can inhibit generalization and determination of important patterns.[7]

"Similarity" and "dissimilarity" here refer primarily to convergence with, or divergence from, the organization of political space in any given international system, and most importantly, how these traits affect the edges of that space and interactions with other actors. The novelty or distinctiveness of political units is the primary factor in distinguishing this phenomenon, rather than the heterogeneity or homogeneity of the preexisting system. However, a higher degree of homogeneity in a system is likely to provide our best measure of the manifestation and impact of a dissimilar form. Paradoxically, by this definition in a more diverse system – containing larger numbers of dissimilar types – actors overall may be more similar given their conformity to plural types. Another benefit of examining largely homogeneous and less diverse systems is that greater similarity among actors would also place increased pressures on actors to imitate, through the processes of emulation and socialization, improving

---

[6] These comparisons and characterizations were helpfully provided during an exchange with an anonymous reader of the book's typescript.

[7] Georg Sørenson points to the presence of weak states in the European state system as evidence that "unlike units" may not be subject to the Darwinian pressures posited in neorealism. Georg Sørenson, "'Big and Important Things' in IR," in *Realism and World Politics*, ed. Ken Booth (London and New York: Routledge, 2011), 111. Without complete homogeneity of shape, size, and relative power of actors in a system, however, one can always find some distinctions, which are not necessarily indicative of true variety.

Argument and key concepts

clarity concerning circumstances that may allow or compel resistance to those pressures. We would also expect that the juxtaposition of a dissimilar actor to more similar, homogeneous rivals would amplify the international societal effects, making them more observable. For those reasons the preexisting systems examined here are primarily composed of roughly similar types of dominant actors, a condition that makes the emergence of a dissimilar form all the more unlikely and confounding.

Dissimilar units have important features of their spatial organization that deviate from expected or established patterns. The relationship between authority and territory differs markedly among political communities, but this is not sufficient to determine dissimilarity as a condition of a system.[8] France and the Ottoman Empire had quite a bit in common despite having clear distinctions in their internal structures. They interacted as major powers of an extended European state system that was continuing to form with the territorial consolidation that would create the modern international system. The Barbary powers, in contrast, competed in that emerging system as city-states, when that form was moving toward effective extinction, making the distinctions between France and the Ottomans less salient than their similarities in that systemic context. Like neorealism, dissimilarity here is not concerned with the internal characteristics of the unit, like modes of governance. Deviations in internal spatial relations may help define the edges of political spaces, influencing the form or shape of the actor in its interactions with other actors, but they are not enough in themselves to establish dissimilarity.[9]

Having outlined the main argument and clarified some key concepts, it is also important to specify what this study does not claim or attempt. There is no effort to provide a broadly generalizable theory of the origins of all kinds of structurally dissimilar actors nor the sources of heterogeneous systems across history.[10] The variety of such systems and

---

[8] Barry Buzan and Richard Little, while embracing a more expansive view of the varieties of international systems and actors, point out that "[i]t is not at all clear where one should stop differentiating once the idea of domestic structure is opened up," noting that distinctions among what are seen as quite similar units can be pronounced. Barry Buzan and Richard Little "Reconceptualizing Anarchy: Structural Realism Meets World History," *European Journal of International Relations* 2, no. 4 (December 1996): 426.

[9] The edges may indeed be inside the unit, the interstices of authority and not the gaps between distinct, adjacent authorities. Nesting, according to Yale Ferguson and Richard Mansbach, refers to the "phenomenon in which some polities are encapsulated by others and embedded within them." See Yale H. Ferguson and Richard W. Mansbach, *Polities: Authorities, Identities, and Change* (Columbia: University of South Carolina Press, 1996), 48.

[10] For a more ambitious effort along those lines, see Barry Buzan and Richard Little, *International Systems in World History: Remaking the Study of International Relations* (Oxford: Oxford University Press, 2000).

6   Introduction

overdetermined nature of their origins would almost certainly doom such an effort. Rather, the study focuses on a subset where actors emerge into systems of rough homogeneity, thwart existing modes of spatial organization and behavior, survive for some extended period of time, and have distinct systemic and societal effects. Nor is there an effort to account for the full lifecycle of these actors, though observations of their duration and viability can provide insight concerning the neorealist premise that the logic of emulation reinforces similarity among units.

One would expect actors to exploit major power decline to establish themselves as actors of systemic import. Few manage to do this, and still fewer take on distinctive forms and survive. Neorealism considers that outcome to be the least likely – if not impossible for any extended duration – due to the effects of competition and the advantages of imitating successful practices. Other theories allow for plural systems but emphasize opportunities over constraints.[11] The emphasis in this study on systemic and structural forces does not exclude agency in explaining these rare but highly disruptive episodes. Relatively few episodes of decline spawn marked departures in structural form, particularly in systems still populated by other powerful actors. Where severe constraints, including powerful and hostile competitors and material deprivation, make innovation a prerequisite for survival, one would expect key leaders to play an important role in recognizing and taking advantage of these constraints and opportunities. The question of how some actors survive despite severe disadvantages, and in at least one instance (the Mongols) go on to dominate their adjoining systems, also requires digging into their relationships with dominant powers prior to their emergence as systemic players.

Like its bounded scope for international systemic outcomes, this study does not offer a general theory for the development of international society, but it should help deepen our understanding of forces behind its unfolding. Barry Buzan's observation of the functional drivers behind the development of international society provides a departure point, as does his extension of structural realism to explain outcomes that go beyond that theory's purview.[12] This study takes advantage of these episodes to examine how additional logics of anarchy bring about

---

[11] Granted, this is mostly in order to correct structural arguments that overemphasize constraints. See Philip G. Cerny, "Political Agency in a Globalizing World: Toward a Structurational Approach," *European Journal of International Relations* 6, no. 4 (December 2000): 435–63.

[12] Barry Buzan, "From International System to International Society: Structural Realism and Regime Theory Meet the English School," *International Organization* 47, no. 3 (Summer 1993): 334.

Theoretical approach

functional societal adaptations *and* spur processes of identity formation. In concert, functional and identity-based responses act and interact to provide building blocks for international society in these systems and beyond.

By expanding our understanding of divergent systemic forces, and systemic and societal outcomes, there is no effort here to "dethrone" the logic of anarchy.[13] Indeed, the study is founded initially on the central assumption that unitary actors under anarchy compete in conditions of uncertainty and self-help that make international systems inherently conflictual. Where it departs is in examining how additional logics of anarchy rooted in those conditions make international systems less predictable in terms of their composition and behaviors than previously appreciated. It also recognizes that existing theory tells us little about the relationships between the international systemic and societal phenomena that emerge when formative and behavioral expectations are dashed, like during the shock and confusion that occurred following September 11.

Theoretical approach

In one of my articles I noted Al Qaeda's status as not only an international societal misfit but also a paradigmatic one.[14] Just as the actor rudely flouts conventions, it transgresses paradigmatic divisions involving a broad range of frameworks: transnational relations (dealing with a non-state actor), constructivism (the high profile of ideas including religious ideology), international society (with the overt challenge to international societal norms), and realism (concerning power and violence in the international system).[15] Because of its heterodox nature, no one of these frameworks is capable of explaining the phenomenon in full.

---

[13] See Ken Booth, "Dare Not to Know: International Relations Theory versus the Future," in *International Relations Theory Today*, ed. Ken Booth and Steve Smith (University Park: Pennsylvania State University Press, 1995), 330.

[14] See William J. Brenner, "In Search of Monsters: Realism and Progress in International Relations Theory after September 11," *Security Studies* 15, no. 3 (July–September 2006): 496–528.

[15] High-quality work has followed in, and across, most of these areas. For an examination of violent transnational actors, see Oded Löwenheim, *Predators and Parasites: Persistent Agents of Transnational Harm and Great Power Authority* (Ann Arbor: University of Michigan Press, 2007). Among the number of works on the role of religion in world politics is the collection Jack Snyder, ed., *Religion and International Relations Theory* (New York: Columbia University Press, 2011). The role of religious devotion in the duration of conflicts is investigated in Michael C. Horowitz, "Long Time Going: Religion and the Duration of Crusading," *International Security* 34, no. 2 (Fall 2009): 162–93. The intersection of transnational networks and religious ideology are treated in-depth in Daniel H. Nexon, *The Struggle for Power in Early Modern Europe: Religious Conflict, Dynastic Empires, and International Change* (Princeton: Princeton University Press,

8   Introduction

Accordingly, claims of proprietary explanatory power, particularly to the exclusion of other paradigms, ring hollow.[16] "Theoretical pluralism," K.J. Holsti writes, "is the only possible response to the multiple realities of a complex world." Establishing orthodoxies, or tumbling them with "intellectual knockouts," he notes, misses opportunities for expanding knowledge.[17]

The move in the study of international relations toward employing theoretical constructs from multiple research programs, or analytic eclecticism, has become increasingly prevalent and sophisticated.[18] Rudra Sil and Peter Katzenstein have provided useful guidelines for judging the substance and merit of theoretically eclectic work. "The distinctiveness of analytic eclecticism," they write, "arises from its effort to specify how elements of different causal stories might coexist as part of a more complex argument that bears on problems of interest to both scholars and practitioners."[19] While the pluralist posture of this study was primarily compelled by the nature of the phenomenon, the more intensive

2009), and John M. Owen, IV, *The Clash of Ideas in World Politics: Transnational Networks, States, and Regime Change, 1510–2010* (Princeton: Princeton University Press, 2010). The functioning of international society in reaction to the spread of transnational jihadism is investigated in Barak Mendelsohn, *Combating Jihadism* (Chicago: University of Chicago Press, 2009), while challenges to world order, including from radical Islamism, are covered in Andrew Phillips, *War, Religion, and Empire: The Transformation of International Orders* (Cambridge: Cambridge University Press, 2011) and Mendelsohn, "God vs. Westphalia: Radical Islamist Movements and the Battle for Organizing the World," *Review of International Studies* 38, no. 3 (July 2012): 589–613.

[16] Realism was quickly singled out for exclusion following the attacks. See Daniel Philpott, "The Challenge of September 11 to Secularism in International Relations," *World Politics* 55, no. 1 (October 2002): 66. While it is true that other paradigms have fared better in approaching the broad problem set presented by Al Qaeda, the presumptive exclusion of realism would be self-defeating, particularly when trying to examine the group's systemic origins and impact.

[17] Events that contravene paradigmatic boundaries, Holsti notes, may cause crises or even revolutions within an analytic framework, spawning "new research programs, themes, [and] sets of new questions" for theory to address. See Kalevi J. Holsti, "Mirror, Mirror on the Wall, Which Are the Fairest Theories of All?" *International Studies Quarterly* 33, no. 3 (September 1989): 255–61. On the value of observed deviation in advancing scientific knowledge, see Imre Lakatos, *Proofs and Refutations: The Logic of Mathematical Discovery* (Cambridge: Cambridge University Press, 1976), 96. I previously highlighted that the very deviation in structure and behavior by Al Qaeda presents an opportunity for progress. See Brenner, "In Search of Monsters."

[18] For justification, elaboration, and exemplars of analytic eclecticism, see Rudra Sil and Peter J. Katzenstein, eds., *Beyond Paradigms: Analytic Eclecticism in the Study of World Politics* (Basingstoke; New York: Palgrave Macmillan, 2010). Patrick Jackson grounds the approach in the philosophy of science in *The Conduct of Inquiry in International Relations: Philosophy of Science and Its Implications for the Study of World Politics* (New York: Routledge, 2010).

[19] Rudra Sil and Peter J. Katzenstein, "Analytic Eclecticism in the Study of World Politics: Reconfiguring Problems and Mechanisms across Research Traditions," *Perspectives on Politics* 8, no. 2 (June 2010): 414.

Theoretical approach 9

examination and definition of analytic eclecticism can help provide a more refined explanation of the goals and means employed here.

Sil and Katzenstein identify three characteristics that distinguish analytically eclectic work, each exemplified in this study. First, analytically eclectic work "proceeds at least implicitly on the basis of a pragmatist ethos."[20] This study was born of the analytic disorientation following the real-world disorientation after the attacks of September 11. It also aims to bring the focus back on the real-world problem of coping with Al Qaeda and its offshoots. Second, analytically eclectic work "addresses problems of wide scope that ... incorporate more of the complexity and messiness of particular real-world situations." Here, examination of the origins, behavior, and international societal impact are woven to present a narrative that accounts for the stages of the emergence of these types of actors, the disruption they produce, and reactions of contemporary and future observers. Third, in order to account for such a multifaceted inquiry, Sil and Katzenstein explain, some parsimony is lost in favor of "complex causal stories that incorporate different types of mechanisms as defined and used in diverse research traditions."[21] In order to address the scope of this problem, in this study a range of mechanisms and processes from diverse research traditions are applied, adapted, and combined. Each stage of the theoretical narrative could be treated in greater depth, but not without compromising the ability to address a fuller scope of factors behind the rupture Al Qaeda brought about in the international system and society.

It would be sufficient to justify this pluralist approach by emphasizing its match with the problem set, but there are further benefits for the advancement of theory among and within paradigms. Mark Blyth observed that the field, despite its numerous rifts, advances in both an intra- and inter-paradigmatic fashion, in both a linear and a dialectical manner.[22] Much of that inter-paradigmatic progress may have resulted from the "gladiatorial contests" among paradigms that dominated the field in the past.[23] This study will provide little help to resolve those struggles as no major debate, for instance over the import of norms in international systems, is made the focus let alone settled. With this problem-focused theory, such persistent rifts are dangerous distractions, the main progress being found in areas of theoretical convergence among

---

[20] Ibid., 412.   [21] Ibid., 419.

[22] Mark Blyth, "Structures Do Not Come with an Instruction Sheet: Interests, Ideas, and Progress in Political Science," *Perspectives on Politics* 1, no. 4 (December 2003): 695–706.

[23] See Christopher Reus-Smit, "The Constructivist Challenge after September 11," in *International Society and Its Critics*, ed. Alex J. Bellamy (Oxford: Oxford University Press, 2005), 82.

10   Introduction

paradigms, with clear benefits accruing within individual research programs as well.

The overarching emphasis in this study, how systemic developments rooted in the logics of anarchy may engender international society, is one opening for a progressive inter-paradigmatic exchange between neorealists and members of the English School. Within the English School there has been not only extensive discussion of the social factors operating in international politics, but also a greater appreciation of the variety of systems and actors across time. While the opposition to realist explanations is visceral in many segments of the field, this is not the case with a sizeable subset of the English School.[24] The English School and those whom Richard Little termed "American realists" do have differences. Realists have not been as enthusiastic about the English School, pointing to what they see as the methodological and theoretical deficiencies of treatments of international society.[25] Realism's relative ahistorical content, English School theorists argue, particularly with respect to its understanding of the composition and structure of international systems, neglects both the varieties of systems and their social elements.[26]

Originating this study's argument from Buzan's insight concerning the effects of anarchy, and its materially driven roots, on the development of international society could be seen as shutting out those in the English School who emphasize shared identity. An interpretation starting with materialist presumptions may suggest that the elements of international society (norms, rules, legitimacy) are wholly instrumental, more fitting with Robert Gilpin's model where the dominant power(s) determine the system's rights and rules.[27] But societal outcomes in this study are not

---

[24] The affinities of classical realism and the English School are discussed in Richard Little, "The English School vs. American Realism: A Meeting of Minds or Divided by a Common Language?" *Review of International Studies* 29 (2003): 443–60. In works like *The Logic of Anarchy* and *International Systems in World History* the debt to realism, particularly Waltz's structural variant, and its foundational role are recognized. See Barry Buzan, Charles Jones, and Richard Little, *The Logic of Anarchy: Neorealism to Structural Realism* (New York: Columbia University Press, 1993); and Buzan and Little, *International Systems in World History*.

[25] See Dale C. Copeland, "A Realist Critique of the English School," *Review of International Studies* 29, no. 3 (July 2003): 427–41.

[26] Little, "The English School vs. American Realism," 458. Paul Schroeder made the observation that the assumption of structurally induced sameness in neorealism, focusing on policy behavior, makes it "unhistorical, perhaps anti-historical." Paul Schroeder, "Historical Reality vs. Neo-Realist Theory," *International Security* 19, no. 1 (Summer 1994): 148. Advances in expanding the historical purview to enrich international relations theory include Stuart J. Kaufman, Richard Little, and William C. Wohlforth, eds., *The Balance of Power in World History* (Basingstoke: Palgrave Macmillan, 2007).

[27] Robert Gilpin, *War and Change in World Politics* (Cambridge: Cambridge University Press, 1981).

Theoretical approach

based solely in the desire of actors to reduce instability and uncertainty in the system. They are also rooted in identity formation resulting from encounters with these unfamiliar actors, adding to the systemic underpinnings of international society a component that eludes realist frameworks. It is especially in understanding the interaction of these functional and identity-based drivers, which elude each research program alone, where progress can be made. While the question of how those societal elements impact the behavior of actors is not the focus here, a better understanding of the diverse elements that compose and constitute international society can only enrich that discussion.

While neorealists are likely to remain steadfast in their demotion of the effects of non-material social forces in international politics, this study provides additional benefits through the empirical enrichment of examining less familiar actors and systems. I have argued elsewhere that September 11 presented an opportunity for both theoretical and empirical progress for realism.[28] Years later, great powers still remain the near-exclusive focus for neorealists, at the expense of widening the theoretical and empirical breadth of the research program. Studies of unipolarity, for instance, focus on the concentration of power and the competition that engenders from similar forms that aspire to check it, each acting with predictable patterns and behaviors.[29] As valuable and relevant as those discussions are, they capture only a portion of the system-spanning competition we have witnessed over the last decade and a half. This study focuses on declining powers and the competition that manifests in diverse forms and behaviors. Al Qaeda's emergence, I argue, can be traced not primarily to the concentration of US power, but to the decline of the Soviet Union and the opportunities that presented for an actor of systemic scope but distinct form to challenge the system's predominant power. A more fully realized neorealism, relieved of its state-centricity, could inform each facet of that competition.

Enriching the interaction between neorealism and constructivism is another benefit of this theoretically eclectic posture. Studiously ignoring what may be considered core incompatibilities is one way to flush out theoretical affinities. Samuel Barkin has observed that the interaction of

---

[28] Brenner, "In Search of Monsters."

[29] One exception is found in Daniel H. Deudney, "Unipolarity and Nuclear Weapons," in *International Relations Theory and the Consequences of Unipolarity*, ed. G. John Ikenberry and Michael Mastanduno (Cambridge: Cambridge University Press, 2011), 282–316. Deudney's emphasis on non-state actors' potential possession of nuclear weapons tilts toward the tendency to need to make these actors more state-like in their modes and means for them to be conceived as real challengers. See also Mendelsohn, *Combating Jihadism*, 135–60. While those capabilities might be a sufficient characteristic to rate these groups as competitors, they are not necessary for a group to be considered as such.

12   Introduction

neorealism (particularly Kenneth Waltz's brand) and constructivism is limited by the methodological individualism of the former and intersubjectivity of the latter.[30] He also notes that Waltz's structural realism explains that states are socialized into a system, which implies the existence of intersubjective norms, though they are driven by the system rather than socially constructed. State socialization, a process that is linked hand-in-hand with emulation in Waltz's model, is driven by the system and, Barkin emphasizes, "therefore norms can be expected to remain constant over time."[31] That assumes, however, a relative consistency in structure and behavior among the system's constituents. This study examines the effects of inconstancy in the constitution of international systems, when actors do not emulate, on the socialization rooted in functional and identity-based drivers from encounters with unfamiliar patterns of organization and behavior.

How these drivers reinforce each other is a key puzzle. In his examination of the foundations and transition of international orders, Andrew Phillips notes that while "the search for physical and ontological security draws us together to form communities beyond the limits of intimate familiars, several powerful constraints limit the possibility of sociability among strangers."[32] I highlight circumstances where systemic constraints lead to greater variety in organization and intimacy with violence in unfamiliar forms, each leading to greater sociability among actors who seem less strange in the face of deviation by common enemies. Understanding how the needs of physical and ontological security interact, and indeed may be indistinguishable, is critical for appreciating how the functional requirements of maintaining international systems and identity-based foundations of international society are intertwined. In a bounded set of conditions I examine the roles and interaction of both physical and ontological security seeking. The functional uncertainty brought about by system change – defined here as compositional change, in this case the nature of the actors – interacts with identity-based forces that are affected by, but not wholly rooted in, systemic inputs. A greater understanding of how those functional, systemically induced drivers interact with the identity-based, intersubjective factors is one benefit of transgressing this set of analytic boundaries.

Approaching the problem set with foreknowledge of the limits on ontological compatibility and methodological commensurability, rather than being an invitation to incomprehensibility, promotes what Patrick

---

[30] Samuel Barkin, *Realist Constructivism: Rethinking International Relations Theory* (Cambridge: Cambridge University Press, 2010), 41.
[31] Ibid.   [32] Phillips, *War, Religion, and Empire*, 17.

Methodology 13

Jackson characterized as "dialogical *encounters* between arguments," which then may be transformed by the interaction.[33] Jackson points out that there is a translation issue that prevents simply cobbling together elements of different methodologies.[34] He argues that this lack of a "methodologically neutral metalanguage" argues for a more "abstract and spare delineation of methodological stances."[35] For the purposes of this study that means not trying to cobble together incommensurable approaches into a single, seamless methodological stance capturing both the material and intersubjective elements or stages of the argument. There are risks in tilting toward the settled (perhaps too much so) ontology and methodology of neorealism or the pluralist (not settled enough) universe of English School methodologies. This study embraces elements of each and recognizes that this ecumenism will leave some readers wanting, but, hopefully, that unease will end up being a source of fruitful contention.

Methodology

This study combines comparative process analysis and discourse analysis to explain the regularities of a particular form of irregularity in the formation of international systems and its effects on international society. Jackson and Daniel Nexon explain that comparative process analysis focuses on mechanisms and processes and "seeks to understand how similar processes unfold differently in different contexts."[36] Here, the mechanisms associated with security seeking and coping with uncertainty, previously tied to narrowing outcomes in neorealism, lead to a wider range of forms and behaviors, resulting in both international systemic and societal outcomes. Security seeking under uncertainty instead of leading to more uniformity, through processes of emulation and socialization, leads to processes (or logics) of dissimilation and concealment. In each case the same broad systemic context (an anarchic system characterized by competition and uncertainty) leads to outcomes that are different from those considered most likely due to combinations of opportunities and constraints: systemic opportunity in the form of dominant power decline combined with opportunity structures (sets of constraints) particular to each actor. These structural

---

[33] Jackson, *Conduct of Inquiry*, 210–11.   [34] Ibid., 210.   [35] Ibid., 211.
[36] Patrick T. Jackson and Daniel H. Nexon, "Globalization and the Comparative Method," in *Constructivism and Comparative Politics*, ed. Daniel Green (New York: M.E. Sharp, 2002), 105. A mechanisms- and processes-based approach, as Charles Tilly observed, allows for greater appreciation of the interaction of environmental, relational, and cognitive mechanisms. Tilly, "Mechanisms in Political Processes," 22.

14   Introduction

contexts lead similarly across the cases to deviation but not necessarily to similar deviations, as each case examined is distinct. The cases, as explained below, also provide a large measure of variety in historical, geographical, and cultural contexts, which increases confidence that the posited mechanisms and processes are not the result of idiosyncratic features.

Considering the argument concerning international system change, these logics serve as guideposts to gauge the operation and effects of the posited mechanisms and processes. The *systemic* propositions build off of more developed theories of how actors respond to the constraints of anarchy under uncertainty. Repeated observations within and across cases increase our confidence, but since we are looking at rare episodes they do not allow for the development of fully generalizable, predictive theory. This study does not aim at establishing a generalized theory of systemic, structural dissimilarity, but can extend the web of explanation to some infrequent, highly significant episodes.[37] In the *societal* phase of the explanation, where the foundational theories are less developed, the theory building is supported by offering a number of propositions derived from the literature concerning the functional roots of systemic norms and rules, and another set that focuses on identity formation. Those provisional propositions serve as markers to help investigate the relationships between these sets of drivers in response to acute conditions of uncertainty, and ultimately to formulate and refine our understanding of which of, and how, these mechanisms operate and interact. These posited mechanisms and processes are not intended as testable propositions, where an up or down judgment for each proves or disproves a causal story, but rather as building blocks for constructing explanations of how similar processes may effect similar outcomes across diverse contexts.[38] Accordingly, some may be supported, others rejected, and some refined to provide a richer explanation of the phenomena. Theoretical synthesis, informed by close examination of the cases, is reserved for the concluding chapter.

[37] This approach recalls Timothy McKeown's characterization of a "pattern model of explanation, in which the research task is viewed as akin to extending a web or network, while being prepared to modify the prior web in order to accommodate new findings." Timothy J. McKeown, "Case Studies and the Limits of the Quantitative Worldview," in *Rethinking Social Inquiry: Diverse Tools, Shared Standards*, ed. Henry E. Brady and David Collier (Lanham, Md.: Rowman & Littlefield, 2004), 167.

[38] For a delineation of types of theory building, see Alexander L. George and Andrew Bennett, *Case Studies and Theory Development in the Social Sciences* (Cambridge: MIT Press, 2005), 75–76. They explain that "'building block' studies of particular types or subtypes of a phenomenon identify common patterns or serve a particular type of heuristic purpose. These studies can be component parts of larger contingent generalizations and typological theories."

Methodology

Sil and Katzenstein argue that "[f]or most substantive problems that have greater scope than those formulated within research traditions, useful causal stories are likely to incorporate the interactive effects of mechanisms operating across levels of social reality."[39] Tracing the development of norms and formation of identities is challenged by the extended time frames examined, the evidentiary bases afforded, limitations on interpreting a vast range of foreign and historical actors, and the lack of one static identity group to examine over any one discrete time or place for each case. Rather than narrowing the problem set, and losing value in what useful stories to tell, the pragmatist ethos suggests adopting whatever analytic leverage, whether positivist or interpretivist, with a conscious disregard of the broader methodological implications. One point of analytic leverage is language, which, despite some reliance on secondary sources, allows insight into how these actors were viewed by contemporaries facing an inscrutable adversary, and by later chroniclers who provided enduring, though often obscuring, depictions.

The use of identity as a variable, as elaborated by a group of scholars, emphasizes its content, which includes *constitutive norms* defining group membership, *social purposes* shared by an identity group, *relational comparisons* concerning views and beliefs of other groups, and *cognitive models* of political and material conditions and interests.[40] In this study the latter two categories are the most relevant, and the dynamics between them resulting from confrontations with dissimilar actors, past and present, provide the most valued observations. Among the methods they outline is discourse analysis, which "is the qualitative and interpretive recovery of meaning from the language that actors use to describe and understand social phenomena." They continue: "discourse is usually understood as a collection of related texts, constituted as speech, written documents, and social practices, that produce meaning and organize social knowledge." Discourse analysis, they note, is particularly useful in studying the relational content of identity, which is at the core of a key question in this study, the relationship between functional and identity-based drivers in the unfolding of international society.[41]

---

[39] Sil and Katzenstein, "Analytic Eclecticism," 421.
[40] Rawi Abdelal, Yoshiko M. Herrera, Alastair Iain Johnston, and Rose McDermott, "Identity as a Variable," *Perspectives on Politics* 4, no. 4 (December 2006): 696.
[41] Above, Ibid., 698; 702. This method is not without its challenges and limitations. "Unlike statistics, programming, or modeling," the authors note, "discourse analysis requires deep social knowledge, interpretive skills, and a familiarity with a body of interrelated texts in order for scholars to recover meanings from a discourse."

16   Introduction

Case selection

Cases examined in this study include structurally dissimilar actors emerging into systems populated with roughly similar dominant actors. These are necessarily rare episodes, particularly if we accept neorealism's emphasis on the likening forces of international competition, as opposed to other more common instances of systemic heterogeneity where a wider array of actors may operate. Selection bias is a risk mitigated by the probabilistic nature of the predictions. There is no claim that the mechanisms and processes will yield the expected systemic outcomes all or even most of the time. The study examines variations that may yield important exceptions to previously posited generalized mechanisms that suggest the likelihood of sameness in system composition. Another way to state this is to characterize the study as a *correction* of long-standing selection bias: the near-exclusive examination of structurally homogeneous systems and the analytic marginalization of dissimilar units by overlooking them or their differences. Choices are made that distinguish actors based on a key differentiating factor, the way the unit is configured in space. The degree of homogeneity across cases is, somewhat paradoxically, their degree of heterogeneity from other actors in the system.

One challenge of this problem set concerns the requirements for "actorhood." What constitutes a unit or an actor in an international system? Since this study deals with structural variation, liberal standards for inclusion could open up what Buzan and Little characterized as a Pandora's Box, where all manner of actors would be considered relevant.[42] What extent of central direction is necessary to be considered an actor, rather than simply a phenomenon demoted to an environmental condition?[43] Reference to the concept of "conflict groups," defined as "imperatively coordinated associations," helps address some of these concerns.[44] In each of the cases there is some measure of central coordination, which in addition to increasing general coherence enables us to

---

[42] Buzan and Little, "Reconceptualizing Anarchy," 426.

[43] Robert Axelrod defines a "new political actor" as having effective control over subordinates, collective action, and recognition by other actors. Robert Axelrod, *The Complexity of Cooperation: Agent-Based Competition and Collaboration* (Princeton: Princeton University Press, 1997), 126. This definition is less useful when considering actors who may – due in part to structural constraints and opportunities – take forms that allow for autonomy of component elements and receive no affirmative recognition from established actors.

[44] Ralf Dahrendorf, *Class and Class Conflict in Industrial Society* (Stanford: Stanford University Press, 1959), 172. The use of this term is advocated by a range of international relations theorists, including neorealists. See Robert Gilpin, "The Richness of the Tradition of Political Realism," in *Neorealism and Its Critics*, ed. Robert O. Keohane (New York: Columbia University Press, 1986), 305; and Randall L. Schweller, "The Progressiveness of Neoclassical Realism," in *Progress in International Relations Theory*, ed.

Case selection 17

conceive of decisions and outcomes as derived from largely unitary, though perhaps at times fractious, actors.[45]

Another important consideration when selecting cases is the significance of the actor. What qualifies the actor to be considered as part of a system rather than a peripheral figure or adjunct? The first requirement is that the actor is *autonomous*. Actors that remain dependent on dominant actors may present interesting puzzles for other studies, but the concern here is how such actors break free of such dependence and survive on their own. It should be noted that the actor need not be autarkic, and may maintain symbiotic (including parasitic) relationships with other actors, but these cannot be situations of dominance and subordination. The British East India Company would be limited as a potential case by its dependence and the restraints placed on it by the Crown. Another instance with a lack of sufficient autonomy is the Maltese corsairs who maintained both a sacral-legitimating and material dependence on the papacy and their Christian state sponsors.[46] This relationship is in contrast with the Barbary powers, their contemporaries, whose dependent relationship with the Ottomans was broken at a key juncture.

The second element of significance is the *overall impact* of the actor on a given system. This study gauges impact by a combination of the duration of the actor and the reaction of other actors in the system. Concerning the duration of the actor, we can look at the actor's life span and its ratio to the duration of the system, though it may be tricky to find a clear start and end point of either actor or system. Duration alone cannot be a reliable measure of significance, however, especially if the actor had no effect on the other actors in the system. Hedley Bull's definition of an international system where "there is interaction between them sufficient to make the behavior of each a necessary element in the calculation of the other"

Colin Elman and Miriam Fendius Elman (Cambridge: MIT Press, 2003), 325–26. See also Nexon, *Struggle for Power in Early Modern Europe*, 21.

[45] This requirement could be relaxed and this would enable the inclusion of a broader range of actors, including cases like the Thugs of colonial India. The initial insight of a potential link between systemic (positional) change and system (compositional) change came from reading a study of Thuggee. Historian Stewart Gordon's structural explanation of the phenomenon's emergence looked at the British consolidation of power on the Subcontinent and its effects on the constraints in that system. See Stewart Gordon, *Marathas, Marauders, and State Formation in Eighteenth-Century India* (Delhi: Oxford University Press, 1994). Cautious of problems with actorhood, another borderline case was American Western outlaw bands after the Civil War, which emerged in the wake of major systemic changes following the war. See T.J. Stiles, *Jesse James: Last Rebel of the Civil War* (New York: Alfred A. Knopf, 2002); and Robert R. Mackey, *The Uncivil War: Irregular Warfare in the Upper South, 1861–1865* (Norman: University of Oklahoma Press, 2004).

[46] See Joseph Busuttil, "Pirates in Malta," *Melita Historica* 5 (1971): 310.

18   Introduction

Table I.1 *Cases and contexts*

	Topographic	Sociocultural	Temporal
Nizari Ismailis (Assassins)	Variegated: mountains; plains	Intra-Islamic (Shia, Sunni, and sub-sects); Christian	Late 11th to mid-13th centuries CE
Mongols	Steppes	Multiple: nomadic, Chinese, Islamic, Christian	1206–1260 CE
Barbary powers	Variegated: sea; coastal enclaves; desert	Fault-line (Islamic, Christian)	16th to early 19th centuries CE
Al Qaeda	Variegated: urban; rural; mountains	Islamic; multiple, global/ secular	Late 20th to early 21st centuries CE

provides a reference point.[47] In some cases this judgment is easy, as with the Mongols. For others it requires gauging their impact through the available evidence to assure that the actor generated sufficient attention and reactions to merit system-level status. In one case, the Nizari Ismailis, the very means they employed (stealthy targeted killing) led to the amplification of their importance by observers, and similar assessments have been made concerning Al Qaeda. But in each of those cases, as in the others, a sufficient level of sustained interaction, reaction, and impact is evident to negate claims of concocted significance.[48]

Each case has a distinctive geography and topography, and also a distinct sociocultural setting (see Table I.1). Particular topographic settings could potentially have causal import, allowing for deviating organizational and behavioral outcomes, adding value to presenting a variety of contexts. One example where a sociocultural explanation has been argued to be germane is the concept of *taqiyya*. Taqiyya refers to the dissimulation of religious beliefs in the face of predominant power and is most closely associated with Shia Islam. If the argument is that structural deviation is associated with dissimulative behavior, then it is significant to see it in contexts where that ideational input is absent. Similarly, observers have pointed to Shi'ism's association with martyrdom as causally associated with suicide attacks, with the Nizari Ismailis supposedly

---

[47] Hedley Bull, *The Anarchical Society: A Study of Order in World Politics* (New York: Columbia University Press, 1977), 10.

[48] See note 2 above for a refutation of arguments demoting Al Qaeda's significance. The overall duration of Al Qaeda cannot yet be measured, though its impact on other actors in the system, particularly given the overhaul of the US national security apparatus, would seem obvious.

Case selection   19

providing historical precedent.[49] Disaggregating these behaviors from their purported cultural sources is one potential benefit of comparison over multiple contexts. In addition, while some of the cases overlap, there is considerable temporal variation. This variation can help control for system change brought about by major shifts in the material environment that allow for divergent patterns of organization.

One factor that jumps out when taking even a cursory look at the selected cases is individual leadership. In these cases key figures are closely associated with the founding and emergence of the groups. While individual leadership has been demoted elsewhere as an explanatory variable, as the "great man" approach to history, there have been moves back toward appreciating the role of individuals in driving events.[50] Were these leaders producers or a product of their circumstances? The manner in which some relevant earlier histories were composed, focusing on charismatic (often exotic) figures, may favor the former interpretation. Improvements in historiography, however, provide sufficient material for a more balanced accounting. Emphasis on structural factors in this study may bias in favor of the latter conclusion that these individuals were products of their particular times. But, as Waltz notes, actors need not respond well to structural cues.[51] Accordingly, the role of capable, charismatic leaders in making the most of their circumstances does not contradict and likely complements the structural explanations offered.

The Mongols depict that puzzle most clearly, but that case is also valuable due to its variance concerning systemic outcomes. Unlike the other cases, the Mongols came to dominate and expand the system into which they emerged. They did not just hold their own, and this divergence from the other cases allows additional leverage for the assessment. In this sense, the Mongols function as a "deviant case." Deviant cases, Alexander George and Andrew Bennett explain, assist in the development of contingent generalizations "that identify the conditions under which alternative outcomes occur."[52] This deviant among deviants aids in improving the theory by helping explain how it reached its status before it too succumbed.[53]

---

[49] See Assaf Moghadam, *The Globalization of Martyrdom: Al Qaeda, Salafi Jihad, and the Diffusion of Suicide Attacks* (Baltimore: Johns Hopkins University Press, 2008), 18–20.

[50] See Daniel L. Byman and Kenneth M. Pollack, "Let Us Now Praise Great Men: Bringing the Statesman Back In," *International Security* 25, no. 4 (Spring 2001): 107–46; and Robert Jervis, "Do Leaders Matter and How Would We Know?" *Security Studies* 22, no. 2 (April 2013): 153–79.

[51] Kenneth N. Waltz, *Theory of International Politics* (New York, N.Y.: McGraw-Hill, 1979), 77.

[52] George and Bennett, *Case Studies and Theory Development*, 216.

[53] George and Bennett explain that when deviant cases are explained through process tracing, and "explanations for the outcome of individual cases vary, the results can be

20   Introduction

While there are clear benefits to expanding the empirical scope of international relations theory to under-examined historical contexts, it does present challenges for researchers. One of those is the time and effort it takes to master new cases.[54] Of all of the historical cases examined, only one, the Barbary powers, is associated with a well-known systemic context in international relations. Even then it lies on the fringes of early modern Europe, requiring substantial additional research to orient and inform. Much effort is needed simply to identify the systems, their actors, and the major events marking these settings. Due to the vast investment it would take to master languages for even one of the cases (the Mongols case involves Chinese, Mongolian, Persian, Latin, and others), there is significant reliance on secondary sources.[55] Some primary sources are also available in translation, such as contemporary or near contemporary accounts. As Alexander George and Timothy McKeown highlight, a familiarity with the historian's craft is often necessary, including the use of multiple weak rather than single strong inferences to support conclusions.[56]

The nature of the actors further compounds these challenges. Given that these actors did not conform with prevailing practices, we should not expect their historical footprint to match familiar investigatory expectations. For actors characterized by mobility or concealment, records are not likely to be as comprehensive and accessible as those of sedentary and centralized (i.e., bureaucratized) actors. In addition, each of these actors was to an unusual degree dependent on others to register its presence and nature. Indigenous records, to the extent they existed, may not be extensive or available. For instance, the Nizari Ismaili library in their fortress at Alamut was destroyed by the Mongols. On the other hand, the Barbary powers were fairly well documented, though largely by captives or consuls. Negative and faulty representations are common to each of the

---

cumulated and contribute to the development of a rich, differentiated theory about that phenomenon." Ibid., 16.

[54] See Ian Lustick, "History, Historiography, and Political Science: Multiple Historical Records and the Problem of Selection Bias," *American Political Science Review* 90, no. 3 (September 1996): 606–7.

[55] The conditions described above, however, differ only by degree with established practices in international relations theory. Ian Lustick has argued that limitations of historical evidence exist even for the most well documented cases. He suggests a number of strategies to overcome the problem of the reliance on secondary sources, which have their own ingrained biases and competing narratives. These strategies include acknowledging the differing interpretations, discussing potential biases, and triangulation with multiple sources. Ibid., 615–16.

[56] Alexander L. George and Timothy J. McKeown, "Case Studies and Theories of Organizational Decision Making," in *Advances in Information Processing in Organizations, Vol. 2*, ed. Robert J. Coulam and Richard A. Smith (Greenwich, Conn.: JAI Press, 1985), 47.

Plan of study 21

historical cases.[57] In the case of the Nizari Ismailis, the very naming of the actor, the Assassins, is tied to their representation by outsiders. While this does present a challenge to sort out the good from the bad information, there is also a benefit to having these depictions. The nature of the representation itself provides evidence, particularly when identity formation is examined. While the first portion of the study (focusing on systemic outcomes) would be burdened by these depictions without proper care, they provide the second (focusing on societal outcomes) with a significant amount of its evidence and content.

Plan of study

I first develop theory concerning the episodically protean nature of international systems under anarchy, and the relationship between this change and the development of international society. Case studies, three historical and one contemporary, are then presented to observe whether the mechanisms and processes are operative, and to aid in further developing and refining the theory.

Chapter 1, "International society and the logics of anarchy," spells out the mechanisms and processes that lead to these episodes of system change (changes in composition), and outlines the forces most likely to be behind the structural and behavioral deviations' effects on the development of international society. The sets of guideposts allow for examination of whether these were evident, and in the concluding chapter any confirmation, rejection, or alteration of the posited mechanisms and processes are offered, as well as any further insight into their interaction.

Chapter 2, "Confusion in the hearts of men," is the first case study and examines the Nizari Ismailis of medieval Persia, otherwise known as the Assassins. The Nizaris vexed the Seljuk Turk protectors of the Sunni orthodoxy beginning in the eleventh century. Their ability to establish what was essentially a "state within a state," their methods, and, later,

---

[57] Fortunately for both the scope and fidelity of the evidence, each of these cases has received increased and improved attention from historians. The Nizari Ismailis have experienced vast improvements in their historical record by those seeking to correct pervasive distortions. Mongol historiography continues to improve its textual and archaeological foundations, including contributions from Mongolian historians. The Barbary powers have a relatively good historical record in terms of both consistency and fidelity, and studies continue from historians who focus on the Mediterranean, the Ottomans, Africa, and Europe. The case of Al Qaeda, being a mostly clandestine organization, may be among the most challenging in terms of reliable information. This is due to the murkiness of the current history of its origins and development, as well as having only the beginnings of cumulative scholarship that adds to and corrects our initial examinations.

22   Introduction

their interactions with the crusaders had a decided impact on their system and beyond.

The main title of Chapter 3, "'*A furore Tartarorum libera nos*,'" evokes a prayer that Christian Europe hoped would ward off the Mongol menace. In this case the actor, the Mongol polity united under Chinggis Khan in 1206 and his immediate successors, not only persisted but ended up encompassing the system and encroaching on others before succumbing to its own internal contradictions. It fell apart, though, not before shaking and in many ways shaping parts of the Middle East and Europe.

Chapter 4, "Out of the shadow of God," examines the Barbary powers, whose raiding and captive taking imperiled European societies and commerce from the sixteenth to early nineteenth centuries. The status of these sea-raiding city-states, in an era favoring territorial consolidation and centralization, was debated by jurists as the more dominant powers acceded to and abetted their extortive practices. The centralized territorial states of Europe, as well as the new American republic, would sort out the membership and rules of the system and international society, and whether the Barbary powers could possibly be accommodated within them.

Chapter 5, "In the shadow of the spears," examines the emergence of Al Qaeda and looks at its effects on the development of international society. The material under examination for this chapter is limited in the respect that the events are either relatively new or underway. There is enough material to help determine whether the proposed systemic forces and conditions contributed to its emergence, but less longitudinal evidence concerning its impact on international society. Nevertheless, enough time has passed to sense some trends and track certain outcomes concerning its societal effects, even as the group and its offshoots evolve.

The study concludes with an assessment of the posited mechanisms and processes and their operation within each case, along with observations of their impact across cases. Synthesis of the observations, particularly the initially less developed societal side of the puzzle, is offered. Questions concerning the relationship between functional and identity-based drivers, benefiting from examination of the cases, receive particularly close attention. Consistent with the problem set and pragmatist posture, the conclusion discusses topics related to the ongoing challenges Al Qaeda and its offshoots pose, as well as lessons to better respond to future challenges from a rapidly changing and uncertain international environment.

1 International society and the logics of anarchy

> Environment and circumstance do not always make a prison, wherein perforce the organism must either live or die; for the ways of life may be changed, and many a refuge found, before the sentence of unfitness is pronounced and the penalty of extermination paid.
>
> —D'Arcy Wentworth Thompson, *On Growth and Form*

> It is thus a fundamental error of the *a priori* or deductive political economy that it takes no cognizance of the cardinal fact that the movement of the economic world has been one from simplicity to complexity, from uniformity to diversity, from unbroken custom to change, and therefore from the known to the unknown.
>
> —T.E. Cliffe Leslie, "The Known and the Unknown in the Economic World"

International society and possibility

In his essay "How is Society Possible?" Georg Simmel wrote, "Society is a structure of unlike elements."[1] That different sorts of units occupy and interact in the international system is well established. Neorealists demote the importance of these differences, emphasizing factors that reinforce sameness among the system's significant actors. Competition and socialization in this view operate to reduce the variety of outcomes, with competition the predominant factor spurring actors to "accommodate their ways."[2] The two major components of the puzzle examined in this chapter are the circumstances under which actors may not respond uniformly to systemic constraints in terms of their structure and behavior, and how the resulting changes in the patterns of interactions in international systems may affect international societal outcomes.

Highlighting the functional logics underlying international society, Barry Buzan explained that with increased interaction "international

[1] Georg Simmel, "How is Society Possible?" *The American Journal of Sociology* 16, no. 3 (November 1910): 387.
[2] Kenneth N. Waltz, *Theory of International Politics* (New York, N.Y.: McGraw-Hill, 1979), 77.

24   International society and the logics of anarchy

society could evolve functionally from the logic of anarchy without preexisting cultural bonds."[3] Buzan's formulation provides one basis for international society in the struggle for security and survival, resulting not only in comportment but in self-regulation in the form of norms and rules. How international society may be rooted in some of the dynamics of anarchic competition is a central question here. To fully address that question, however, the elaboration of multiple logics of anarchy is necessary. In this scenario irregularly structured and comported actors emerge into systems of dominant, roughly structurally similar units, with that similarity highlighted when viewed in comparison with new and distinct rivals. That functional imperatives can propel interacting actors toward international society absent common culture does not remove identity as a motive force. Indeed, identity plays an important role in actors coping with the uncertainty that emerges when faced with unfamiliarity.

Here, systemic change (change *within* the system and its power distribution) in the form of the decline of dominant actors sets in motion mechanisms and processes that lead to system change (change *of* the system and its composition) through the interaction of constraints and opportunities present to emerging actors.[4] These developments create conditions of uncertainty and spur processes of identity formation that help foster the development of international society. The theory offered here initially operates in a similar theoretical space as neorealism, with most of the same fundamental assumptions – namely that anarchy creates circumstances of self-help and that international systems are characterized by necessity and uncertainty. The make and shape of the actors in the system most often tend toward isomorphism, but this is not a predetermined outcome and is subject to exception. Moving beyond this conception of international systems, this chapter considers how a wider range of unit-structural, behavioral and, accordingly, systemic and societal outcomes may obtain.

Circumstances are examined where structurally dissimilar actors, those distinct in key ways in which they interact with their environment and

---

[3] Barry Buzan, "From International System to International Society: Structural Realism and Regime Theory Meet the English School," *International Organization* 47, no. 3 (Summer 1993): 334.

[4] The distinction between "systemic" and "system" change is borrowed and adapted from Robert Gilpin. Systemic change in Gilpin's schema concerns the dominant power in the system, and "changes in the international distribution of power, the hierarchy of prestige, and the rules and rights embodied in the system." System(s) change, the most fundamental type of change, concerns change in the "nature of the types of the actors or diverse entities that compose the international system." Robert Gilpin, *War and Change in World Politics* (Cambridge: Cambridge University Press, 1981), 39–43.

other actors, emerge and overcome systemic constraints that normally prevent such challenges. This sequence does not overturn the basic logics of the international system, where competition and socialization create strong incentives to imitate. It does provide a systemic explanation as to why imitation is not a necessary outcome of competition. Given a system composed of dominant, structurally similar actors, as certain dominant actors decline, the changing circumstances provide opportunities for systemically subordinate actors to assert themselves on a system-wide scale. Differential access to means shapes these responses, at times compelling innovations that deviate from channeled and expected structures and behaviors. This is realized through what are termed the "logic of dissimilation" and "logics of concealment," affecting the form and behaviors of the actors, respectively. Prior relationships with dominant actors help these emergent deviants to overcome early organizational imperatives and the "liability of newness."[5] In all, this set of systemic forces and effects suggests a larger role for distributional elements in shaping the composition of international systems, rather than just conditioning behavioral outcomes. Rather than replacing the logic of anarchy, focusing on a system's ecology in *addition* to its economy supplements our understanding of a wider range of logics of anarchy.

With this increase in systemic diversity, two spurs toward the development of international society are emphasized: increased uncertainty and common identity formation. While the former suggests functional roots and affinities with neorealism, identity-based explanations are more consistent with constructivist approaches. Neither can explain the posited societal outcomes alone. Increased uncertainty and enhanced identities both trigger very similar requirements (categorization and discrimination) that yield similar, complementary outcomes. Engaging the implications of the relationship between ontological security and threats to physical security, each magnified by conditions of uncertainty, helps us appreciate the complementary nature of these goals or conditions, and how the needs for coping with uncertainty and the drives toward identity formation interact and overlap. Examination of the case studies will help further define and refine these relationships.

In the shorter term, norms and rules develop in response to systemic exigencies, while common identity formation contributes to the establishment of in- and out-groups. Over the longer term, in some measure in

---

[5] Arthur Stinchcombe coined the term the "liability of newness" to highlight advantages new organizations lack: familiarity with their new roles, established relationships with other actors, stability of internal relations, and standardized routines. See Arthur Stinchcombe, "Social Structure and the Founding of Organizations," in *Handbook of Organizations*, ed. James G. March (Chicago: Rand McNally, 1965), 148–49.

26   International society and the logics of anarchy

response to these irregular actors, norms develop and establish certain modes and behaviors as illegitimate. "Standards of civilization" communicate principles of membership that indicate rightful association with international society, extending the mantle of "civilization" to those who comport and denying it to those who do not. Together, these shorter-term actor- and context-specific inputs and the longer-term diffusion and cumulation of norms and identities contribute to the establishment of principles of legitimacy, understood in terms of rightful membership and conduct in international society.

Proceeding through the theoretical discussion, I first outline arguments concerning the expected forms of actors in international systems and discuss how under certain circumstances they may deviate in shape and behavior. I then examine how processes of socialization posited in neorealism do not adequately account for deviations that fall outside of an expected range of structural outcomes, and how functional needs for coping with uncertainty drive some foundational elements of international society. This is followed by a discussion of processes of identity formation that drive the creation of "others," and how a greater appreciation of ontological security helps elide distinctions between functional and identity-based responses to uncertainty.

Emulation, socialization, and the logic of anarchy

The international system, according to neorealism, contains forces that reinforce similarity, in structure and behavior, among the system's constituents. To survive and preserve their autonomy, actors may imitate successful practices but may also fail to do so and succumb to the selective pressures of anarchy. The result of competition, according to Kenneth Waltz, is that "the units that survive come to look like one another," and failing to adopt the most successful practices makes actors vulnerable to annihilation or subjugation.[6] Waltz maintains a great deal of autonomy for reactions to systemic pressures, and his discussion of emulation and like units focuses initially on the unit's autonomy rather than structural similarity. His emphasis on imitation among actors as subject to Darwinian selective processes rendering the survivors similar in key structural features and behaviors, however, has led many scholars to

---

[6] Waltz, *Theory of International Politics*, 77. Waltz contends that "competition spurs the actors [firms] to accommodate their ways to the most acceptable and successful practices. Socialization and competition are two aspects of a process by which the variety of behaviors and outcomes is reduced." For the role of emulation and socialization in the "competitive realm" of international politics, see pages 127–28.

Emulation, socialization, and the logic of anarchy 27

interpret his theory as making unit-structural isomorphism a necessary outcome of an international system.[7]

Waltz's "powerful homogenizing argument," in Buzan's characterization, is used to explain "the striking isomorphism of the 'like units' of the international system."[8] Changes in the types of units that compose the system will occur, but in Richard Little's casting of Waltz's argument, "states will be remarkably similar [in terms of their configuration] at any point in time [though] ... their common structures will vary across time."[9] Despite its foundational importance, the systemic determination of unit-structural likeness through emulation and socialization – affecting the units' configuration in space rather than military or organizational imitation alone – remains underspecified in neorealist theory.[10] Whether one accepts strict structural isomorphism as a necessary outcome or not, it is clear that neorealism considers rough similarity among units in a system to be the likely outcome. Emulation and socialization are *at least* the most likely way out of extinction or effective marginalization, the latter being the equivalent of extinction in a world defined by great powers. Waltz's metaphor of the firm is problematic when considering the potential for variety in international systems. Given perfect information and resource allocation, imitation and gravitation toward a most efficient practice would seem likely to lead to a single dominant organizational form.[11] Perfect information and

---

[7] This interpretation of likening forces in Waltz's model is accepted by a number of international relations theorists. See Barry Buzan, Charles Jones, and Richard Little, *The Logic of Anarchy: Neorealism to Structural Realism* (New York: Columbia University Press, 1993), 41; 43; 50; 74–75. See also Alexander Wendt, *Social Theory of International Politics* (Cambridge: Cambridge University Press, 1999), 103; 151. Andres Osiander notes, however, "such a possibility [of heterogeneous systems] is precluded in Waltz only by the context of his remarks, not explicitly," leaving room for interpretation that variety is not so constrained in Waltz's model. Andres Osiander, *Before the State: Systemic Political Change in the West from the Greeks to the French Revolution* (Oxford: Oxford University Press, 2007), 13.

[8] Barry Buzan, *From International to World Society? English School Theory and the Social Structure of Globalisation* (Cambridge: Cambridge University Press, 2004), 61.

[9] Richard Little, "International Relations and Large-Scale Historical Change," in *Contemporary International Relations: A Guide to Theory*, ed. A.J.R. Groom and Margot Light (London: Pinter, 1994), 18.

[10] For examinations of military emulation, as opposed to the general structural likening in international systems, see João Resende-Santos, *Neorealism, States, and the Modern Mass Army* (New York: Cambridge University Press, 2007). Other useful discussions of emulation as a theory of military innovation and diffusion can be found in Emily O. Goldman and Richard B. Andres, "Systemic Effects of Military Innovation and Diffusion," *Security Studies* 8, no. 4 (Summer 1999): 79–125; and Michael C. Horowitz, *The Diffusion of Military Power: Causes and Consequences for International Politics* (Princeton: Princeton University Press, 2010).

[11] "Organizational form" is one feature of the firm and has been described as "a functional relationship between the state of the world ... and the firm's actions." Sidney G. Winter,

28 International society and the logics of anarchy

uniform or sufficient distribution of human and material resources are not necessary conditions of international systems; far from it.[12] The unevenness of those may lead to differences not only in the distribution of power, but in its configuration as well.

The need for innovation is pronounced for entities that arrive late to the contest for power, in part due to previous conditions of domination. "Without dynamic innovation," João Resende-Santos argues, "selection will only lead to the dominance of those institutions and states that started the contest."[13] Competition need not lead to military emulation but to innovation, according to Resende-Santos, mediated through socialization understood as structural adjustment or adaptive learning.[14] The very straitening of choices, faced by some actors more than others, may be a spur for innovation.[15] This innovation, however, may not take place within uniform resource bases or follow established developmental pathways.[16] Emulation as military imitation may not be possible, leading to structural deviation as actors seek alternative pathways to survival, ultimately challenging established members of a system. The international system presents opportunities along with constraints. Opportunities may be found within the functioning of the international system (outcomes of competition) and exogenous factors like technical change. Rather than adopting "best practices," innovation takes form in novel practices, while neorealism suggests necessity is the mother of conformity, not of invention.

Jr., "Economic 'Natural Selection' and the Theory of the Firm," *Yale Economic Essays* 4 (1964): 237. Factors such as geography, time of entry, size, and distribution of resources lead to outcomes in organizational forms that are more in line with ecological theories' emphases on "the multilineal and probabilistic nature of evolution." See Glenn R. Carroll, "Organizational Ecology," *Annual Review of Sociology* 10 (1984): 72.

[12] Perfect information in the pitched competition of an international system would entail access to various technological bodies of knowledge.

[13] João Resende-Santos, "Anarchy and the Emulation of Military Systems: Military Organization and Technology in South America, 1870–1930," in *Realism: Restatements and Renewal*, ed. Benjamin Frankel (London and Portland, Or.: Frank Cass, 1996), 207–8.

[14] Ibid., 208.

[15] Frederick Barth emphasizes this connection between constraint and choice: "[T]he unfortunate circumstance of a gross disadvantage of power does not mean that strategy is unavailing – indeed it may be all the more pervasive in shaping . . . behavior." Frederick Barth, *Process and Form in Social Life: Selected Essays of Frederick Barth* (London: Routledge & Kegan, 1981), 89.

[16] See Leslie C. Eliason and Emily O. Goldman, "Introduction: Theoretical and Comparative Perspectives on Innovation and Diffusion," in *The Diffusion of Military Technology and Ideas*, ed. Goldman and Eliason (Stanford: Stanford University Press, 2003), 8.

Opportunity, constraint, and variety

Whether and in what form new actors emerge into international systems is affected by two distinct types of political opportunity. Expectations that such actors would follow established pathways as they rise in systemic status and capability – from adjuncts to actors – may be dashed by the interaction of each dimension of opportunity. Philip Cerny discusses opportunity understood as greater access and a sort of systemic entrepreneurship, which allow agents to experiment "with new ways to conceptualize and organize their activities."[17] These "transnational opportunity structures," in Cerny's characterization, "provide vital structural space for key agents to act in potentially transformational ways ... [and change] will be determined primarily by which actors can most effectively manipulate, utilize and steer changing patterns of opportunities and constraints." Change may occur in a "structure-bound, adaptive, or strategic/transformational fashion" with the potential for "effective political and institutional entrepreneurs [emerging] to exploit the manifest and latent structural resources available to them in a period of flux."[18] While illustrative of some modes of change, this characterization of political opportunity presents an incomplete picture by bounding situations that are either structure-bound *or* transformational.[19] The transformational capacity of opportunities *and* constraints in tandem is underrepresented.

Transformation may inhere in systems characterized by severe constraints, requiring our appreciation of another dimension of political opportunity. Under certain circumstances such constraints may make transformation more likely. In order to better understand the role of constraints as generative, it is useful to apply the concept of opportunity structure as it was originally developed by sociologist Robert Merton. Merton's focus was on "how some social structures *exert a definite pressure* upon certain persons in the society to engage in nonconformist behavior

---

[17] Philip G. Cerny, "Political Agency in a Globalizing World: Toward a Structurational Approach," *European Journal of International Relations* 6, no. 4 (December 2000): 441. See also Philip G. Cerny, *Rethinking World Politics: A Theory of Transnational Pluralism* (Oxford: Oxford University Press, 2010), 15.

[18] Cerny, "Political Agency," 441.

[19] Another limitation is the broad application of the concept of the "structure of political opportunities." The term in social movement literature can mean just about anything that makes social action more possible. Doug McAdam states what constitutes a change in the structure of political opportunities: "The point is that *any* event or broad social process that serves to undermine the calculations and assumptions on which the political establishment is structured occasions a shift in political opportunities." Doug McAdam, *Political Process and the Development of Black Insurgency, 1930–1970* (Chicago: University of Chicago Press, 1982), 41.

30   International society and the logics of anarchy

rather than conformist conduct."[20] Merton isolated two elements of social structure. These are "culturally defined goals, purposes, and interests" and structurally defined, regulated, and controlled "acceptable modes of achieving these goals."[21] He emphasized the relationship between socially determined goals and institutionalized means, associating this with the idea of "differential access to opportunities" and what Max Weber referred to as "life-chances."[22] The match or mismatch of these may lead to a number of outcomes. Acceptance of cultural goals and institutionalized means leads to conformity, while acceptance of the goals and rejection of the social limitations on the means may lead to innovation.

The main insight borrowed from Merton is the idea that diverse systemic outcomes come from the interaction of goals and the availability of means; change results not only from the absence of constraints but their existence. "If the social structure restrains some dispositions to act," Merton noted, "it creates others."[23] The extent to which the means are "institutionalized" is a reflection of the existing structure of the system. Following neorealist tenets, the distribution of power in an international system is a function of the distribution of capabilities. Emphasis should not only be placed on the accumulation of capabilities as an outcome but also on the availability of means. Power is not simply an exogenously dispersed property, but a commodity demanded and contested by dominants and aspirants alike. Large-scale change in technology, posited by those who emphasize globalization, may lead to a change in the availability of certain means if that change is sufficiently diffused. But such expansive exogenous change is not the only spur to innovation and potential disruption of the existing international order. Outcomes may significantly deviate from what Merton characterized as "canalized modes of striving," or society's chosen paths to success.[24] "Success" in

---

[20] Robert K. Merton, "Social Structure and Anomie," *American Sociological Review* 3, no. 5 (October 1938): 672. Discussion of the evolution of the concept is found in Robert K. Merton, *On Social Structure and Social Science* (Chicago: University of Chicago Press, 1996), 153–61.

[21] Merton, "Social Structure and Anomie," 672–73.

[22] Merton, *On Social Structure*, 155. Merton is careful to note that "differential access is a probabilistic, not a deterministic concept ... structural constraints and opportunities provide for individual variations in choices among socially structured alternatives." Robert K. Merton, "Opportunity Structure: The Emergence, Diffusion, and Differentiation of a Sociological Concept, 1930s–1950s," in *The Legacy of Anomie Theory: Advances in Criminological Research, Volume 6*, ed. Freda Adler and William S. Laufer (New Brunswick and London: Transaction Publishers, 1995), 8.

[23] Merton, "Opportunity Structure," 17.

[24] Merton, "Social Structure and Anomie," 674.

Systemic change and the logic of dissimilation 31

realizing systemically induced goals of security and survival may result from dissimilar modes of advancing those goals.

Structural changes that present opportunities may intersect with limitations on material capabilities leading to increased variety. Kyriakos Kontopoulos characterizes constraint as "the limitation applied on the possibility spaces of a set of phenomena, a restriction of the expression of possibilities ... favoring the production of a particular structured subset out of the larger set of all combinatorial possibilities."[25] As far as international systems are concerned, favored pathways may not be available, leading actors to resort to other modes that defy expectations and broaden the set of combinatorial possibilities. Anthony Giddens has distinguished between types of constraint: "material constraints," derived from the character of the material world; "[negative] sanctions," derived from punitive responses of some agents toward others; and "structural constraints," derived from the contextuality of action vis-à-vis other actors.[26] All three of Giddens' senses of constraint are considered in the framework offered in this study, but particularly material and structural constraints. In the context of international systems such constraints have productive, and potentially transformative, capacity through the compulsion of innovation. In terms of opportunities, the deep structure of the system may be stable (anarchy), but cracks or gaps in the surface structure of competing actors (power distribution) may allow for novel combinations. Those innovations, in turn, may translate into challenges to, or at least disruptions of, world order and the actors maintaining it.

Systemic change and the logic of dissimilation

Change in the distribution of power is a primary generator of systemic outcomes in neorealism as it is here, though the ultimate ranges of likely outcomes diverge. Systemic change acts as a trigger for system change; positional change leads to compositional change. The structural constraints in the system compel actors to seek security and survival. Material constraints disallow certain pathways, making innovation toward those goals more likely for certain actors not content to remain on the margins of the system. The decline of major powers alters the calculations and expectations of actors concerning their current position in the international system, compelling or allowing their assertion and expansion to

---

[25] Kyriakos M. Kontopoulos, *The Logics of Social Structure* (Cambridge: Cambridge University Press, 1993), 27.

[26] Anthony Giddens, *The Constitution of Society: Outline of the Theory of Structuration* (Berkeley and Los Angeles: University of California Press, 1984), 174–79.

32   International society and the logics of anarchy

system-level status. Given a certain opportunity structure, specific to each actor, alternate pathways of development result in dissimilar organizational forms, affecting the composition of the system. This is a probabilistic rather than deterministic outcome and how prevalent this is can only be appreciated if some of the logics that may bring it about are outlined.

The relationship between the pre-emergent actors and the dominant actors in the system is assumed to be one of effective and perhaps formal dominance. When dominant actors decline, calculations of opportunity may change accordingly. It is important to distinguish between opportunities (as "moments" of potential transformation based on decreased constraints) and opportunity structure (relating to the availability of resources that shape responses to those opportunities). To reinforce that distinction, the term "opportunity structure" will be reserved for the version of Merton's relationship between "culturally defined goals, purposes, and interests" and institutionalized (i.e., available and legitimate) means. The relationship between systemic (positional) change and system (compositional) change is not limited to disintegrating empires (i.e., severe cases of decline where hierarchy dissolves to anarchy) or system fragmentation.

Whether actors take advantage of opportunities is uncertain, and how the opportunities are acted on will be conditioned by the actor's opportunity structure. That opportunity structure may allow for following established developmental pathways, or may compel some deviation from the dominant modes of organization and behavior.[27] Whether these outcomes occur depends, like neorealism, on the ability of agents to perceive and respond to their conditions effectively. Systemic change in this sequence creates flux by disrupting power relations, calculations, and expectations. Actors take into account changes in the major contenders in the system and their relationships, assessing how these changes might affect their prospects. But this does not necessarily lead to variety as an outcome. The actors could very well do nothing, accept their subordinate position, establish similarly subordinate relationships with other actors, or overtake the unit structures of those actors in decline. In general, though, these actors should be expected to prefer action to inaction and greater autonomy to subordination. This is not a determinate outcome in neorealism, however, and there is the possibility of a sort of bandwagoning: a permanent status of subordination in exchange for a measure of

---

[27] This conception of opportunity structure is consistent with agent-based models where actors face local rules that help determine outcomes. See Robert Axelrod, *The Complexity of Cooperation: Agent-Based Competition and Collaboration* (Princeton: Princeton University Press, 1997), 126.

Systemic change and the logic of dissimilation 33

security. Nevertheless, at least some and perhaps most will equate more power with more security and better prospects for survival.[28]

The opportunity structure faced by the emergent actor will present a set of means matched with a certain set of societal goals. What are the "cultural" or societal goals of an anarchic system? At their most basic, these are security, survival, and autonomy, in varying levels of importance.[29] To simplify, these are treated as the primary cultural goals and are constant when considering the relational concept of opportunity structure. For those actors who have achieved those aims, greater levels of consolidation afford (adopting offensive realist tenets) greater amounts of those basic goals. What then are the means that are central to survival in an international system? The factors of production are land, labor, and capital. Following neorealist assumptions, the capacity for survival and security is a function of protection. What then would be considered, in a sense, the factors of *protection*?[30]

Land in this case is most closely associated with territory. Territory is essential for the generation of other resources, provides protected space, and offers a base for actions intended to protect and sustain its inhabitants. The identification of territory with closed, contiguous, clearly bordered land is natural. Political space more generally, however, may provide the base for action and may itself be the product of innovation. This could involve the transformation of spaces free of excessive levels of coercion to serve the purposes of territory listed above. Labor involves both unskilled or semi-skilled labor, the human beings that become the soldiers and other individuals that help produce action, and highly skilled labor. The latter involves technical know-how to produce, arrange, and employ the technics

---

[28] One might expect these actors to be motivated not by *animus dominandi* – Hans Morgenthau's concept of desire for power rooted in human nature – but by a clear animus toward being dominated. Hans Morgenthau, *Scientific Man vs. Power Politics* (Chicago: University of Chicago Press, 1946).

[29] As Randall Schweller emphasizes, "security" is a murky concept. See Randall L. Schweller, "Neorealism's Status-Quo Bias: What Security Dilemma?" *Security Studies* 5, no. 3 (Spring 1996): 90–121. Schweller notes that for Kenneth Waltz security is understood as the minimum power to assure survival, while autonomy (independence coupled with functional integrity) is considered a goal consistent with greater security and prospects for survival.

[30] This overall approach owes much to Daniel Deudney's usage of "modes of destruction" in his discussion of the viability of certain sociopolitical forms given a particular material context (the relationship between geography and technology). While the capacity for protection entails a capacity for destruction, it cannot be reduced to it, which is why the former is favored here. See Daniel H. Deudney, "Regrounding Realism: Anarchy, Security, and Changing Material Contexts," *Security Studies* 10, no. 1 (Autumn 2000): 1–42.

34   International society and the logics of anarchy

that encompass capital, which then combine to form the technology available to actors.[31]

Together, the combination of limitations and availability may shape unit-structural outcomes of emergent systemic aspirants. Initially actors are limited by their presence in highly constrained systems of dominant units. Then they are presented with a change in the power distributional elements that allow or compel their action.[32] One pathway is to imitate the other actors in the system, while another, driven by systemic constraints, is to seek alternative modes to maximize their prospects for meeting the system's primary goals. Opportunity structure is a condition but not a constant. Changes in the distribution of power may affect the availability of means (e.g., the diffusion of skilled labor or freeing of territory). While systemic change may affect opportunity structure, it does not constitute its primary cause. There may be no effects of systemic change on opportunity structure and system change will still occur. In examining the case studies it will be useful to see whether this freeing up of resources represents more than a secondary effect on outcomes, and constitutes a necessary cause. In the meantime, the effects of systemic change on opportunity structure will be assumed to be secondary.

The systems into which new and structurally dissimilar actors emerge are inherently perilous places. Neorealists are correct to emphasize the scarcity of security and the jealous control and aggrandizement of resources. What has been overlooked is the plasticity of power, and the distinct arrangements that may be brought about in the fulfillment of certain functions. Anarchic systems are characterized by constraints on all of their actors, particularly those new arrivals, and even more so if those actors deviate from established developmental pathways. Nevertheless, these systems may end up being populated not only by defensive positionalists or power maximizers but also by defensive contortionists and offensive opportunists. How emergent actors escape the pressures of the system and avoid being selected out, especially when their arrival is late and the constraints so severe, remains a key part of the puzzle. The condition of emergent actors, particularly structurally dissimilar ones,

---

[31] The distinction between technics and technology is noted in Daniel H. Deudney, "Geopolitics and Change," in *New Thinking in International Relations Theory*, ed. Michael W. Doyle and G. John Ikenberry (Boulder, Colo.: Westview Press, 1997), 106. Technics concerns artifacts, while technology involves know-how. For the sake of simplicity, "technology" will be used to describe both facets.

[32] Kyriakos Kontopoulos discusses circumstances where "higher structures *avail* to the lower ones a labyrinthine web of unexplored opportunities, the 'gray areas' of imaginative and exploratory, sometimes even counterintuitive, invention of new structuring logics . . . or improvised strategies." Kontopoulos, *Logics of Social Structure*, 235.

Systemic change and the logic of dissimilation   35

may be compromised by late entry and first-mover advantages.[33] How then do such actors overcome the liability of newness to survive and persist in these conditions?

The answer to why these particular actors may be more suited to survive may be found, at least in part, in their prior collaborative relationships with dominant actors. Other explanations may be found in unit-level characteristics, such as individual leaders whose skills and charisma may be essential to overcome early collective-action and organizational challenges. The international system, however, has not been so lacking in the human capital necessary to produce effective leaders. Resorting to unit-level explanations, while likely necessary to fully account for the success of such actors, is not sufficient to explain why more marginal actors do not increase their power and effects in international systems more often.

In neorealism the sensitivity of states to relative gains explains limitations on collaboration, as each state measures the gains of its possible adversaries against its own potential gains. According to Waltz, states conduct their affairs "in the brooding shadow of violence," presenting impediments to cooperation.[34] Actors do cooperate when their core interests are at stake, but this is constrained by anticipation of potential future conflict.[35] This would explain why dominant actors may be preoccupied with relative gains when interacting with other dominant actors, but seem far less constrained when collaborating with marginal actors in the system. The possibility of harmful capabilities or intentions among these weak and marginal actors would likely not be as distressing. Collaboration may take the form of material assistance, including shelter and access to technology, as well as the conferring of legitimacy. Leaders accumulate further legitimacy by garnering such resources on behalf of their constituents and translating them into initial successes.[36]

---

[33] Robert Gilpin notes the closing of opportunities as systems advance in age and the "once empty space around the centers of power in the system is appropriated [and e]xploitable resources begin to be used up." Gilpin, *War and Change*, 201.

[34] Waltz, *Theory of International Politics*, 102.

[35] See Robert Powell, "Absolute and Relative Gains in International Relations Theory," *American Political Science Review* 85, no. 4 (December 1991): 1303–20.

[36] Organizational ecologists have focused on the lack of legitimacy for new organizations when they enter an environment, particularly a crowded and competitive one. See Mark A. Hager, et al., "Structural Embeddedness and the Liability of Newness among Nonprofit Organizations," *Public Management Review* 6, no. 2 (2004): 164. See also Michael T. Hannan and Glenn R. Carroll, *Dynamics of Organizational Populations: Density, Legitimation, and Competition* (New York: Oxford University Press, 1992). This legitimacy conferred primarily at the unit level, with some measure of recognition by other actors, should be distinguished from the legitimacy at the level of the international system and society that is subsequently denied due to their deviation.

36   International society and the logics of anarchy

Shifts in political opportunities may effect a change in the roles and associated expectations concerning marginal actors who acted in previous conditions of dominance. It is not only the potential violence of the system that casts a shadow, but also the distribution of power in the system itself. The distribution of power shapes some relationships and commitments that expire as that distribution alters. Subordinate actors may take on new roles and commit actions that contravene the expectations and interests of their former sponsors, a phenomenon that has been referred to as "blowback." The shadow of violence may compel certain behavior, just as the shadow of power may obscure future actions. Brooding in those shadows may be actors both compelled and constrained by the distribution of power and resources in the system, which influence their configuration and in some critical respects their behavior.

Logics of concealment: skulking in the shadows of power

Weighing the benefits of imitation against their constraints, deviators from accepted and successful practices may emerge attempting to ascend to the top, or at least rise from the depths, of relative power.[37] Distinct disadvantages incurred through the imitation of behaviors proven successful for others result in behaviors that do not conform with institutionalized means or accepted practices, captured here under the category of "logics of concealment" (see Table 1.1). The first of these is *hiding*, concealment of physical presence. Daniel Deudney associates this behavior with small, vulnerable republics who resort to physical isolation.[38] Here, hiding involves concealment of physical presence by either concealing location or using social or physical environments to make detection and accessibility difficult.

The second logic is *deception*, concealment of intentions. The concept of "denial and deception" has been employed in strategic studies, with denial referring "to the attempt to block information that could be used

Table 1.1 *Logics of concealment*

Hiding	Physical presence (location and insulation)
Deception	Intentions
Dissimulation	Identity

[37] According to Kenneth Waltz, actors "may perceive the structure that constrains them and understand how it serves to reward some kinds of behavior and to penalize others." Waltz, *Theory of International Politics*, 92.

[38] Daniel H. Deudney, *Bounding Power: Republican Security Theory from the Polis to the Global Village* (Princeton: Princeton University Press, 2007), 57.

Logics of concealment 37

by an opponent to learn some truth. Deception by contrast refers to a nation's effort to cause an adversary to believe something that is not true."[39] Those concepts are conflated here under deception, whether achieved through concealment of information or intentional misrepresentation, and focused on intentions, while the concealment of capabilities is captured under hiding and dissimulation. Concealment of intentions is commonplace among actors competing under anarchy. What would distinguish these actors is routinized deception that constitutes a core element of their interactions. When deception is necessary for physical survival, rather than used to secure competitive advantage, this represents a qualitative difference. The more vested an actor becomes in an international system, the less deception is necessary, becoming an adjunct behavior rather than an essential one. When a state deceives (e.g., the use of rubber tanks and planes by the Allies prior to the Normandy invasion) it may have implications for survival; for some weaker actors deception is a foundation for survival.

The logic of *dissimilation* can also lead to the logic of *dissimulation*. This third logic of concealment concerns concealment of identity and combines elements of the first two. It provides the protection of hiding with the misdirection of deception by cloaking one's identity or adopting the identity of another. This, in turn, enables both hiding and deception behaviors more broadly. These behaviors may be evident in some measure among more established actors, such as in the employment of intelligence operatives. But the degree to which they are used may constitute a distinct behavioral trait. Norms concerning military uniforms, for instance, communicate the importance of identifying friend and foe among established actors. In other circumstances such recognition would spell doom.

When faced with more powerful enemies this "skulking way of war" may be the only available set of behaviors consistent with survival.[40] Asymmetry is not merely a function of the distribution of power but also of how power is configured, affecting the nature (i.e., pace, intensity, regularity) of interactions. This may result in advantages as well as disadvantages in relationships with other actors in the system. Behaviors that deviate from the norm may be beneficial, though the question remains

---

[39] See Roy Godson and James J. Wirtz, "Strategic Denial and Deception," in *Strategic Denial and Deception: The Twenty-First Century Challenge*, ed. Godson and Wirtz (New Brunswick, N.J.: Transaction, 2002), 1–2.

[40] The term is derived from Patrick Malone's study of Native American warfare, where "skulking" was used by Europeans to describe unconventional tactics and the use of concealment. Patrick M. Malone, *The Skulking Way of War: Technology and Tactics among the New England Indians* (Baltimore: Johns Hopkins University Press, 1991).

38   International society and the logics of anarchy

Table 1.2 *Systemic to system change*

Systemic to System Change: The emergence of dissimilar actors is preceded by the decline of a dominant actor(s) in the system, providing opportunities for expansion and ascension from subordinate (or subsystemic) to systemic status.
Opportunity Structure: Each actor faces a specific opportunity structure: a particular resource base that provides the means to fulfill its functional requirements, allowing or constraining its patterns of interaction with other actors in the system.
Logic of Dissimilation: The mixture of opportunities and constraints may result in actors that are qualitatively different in terms of organizational form, determined by a distinct relationship with space.
Logics of Concealment: In order to overcome both structural and material constraints these actors adopt behaviors – hiding, deception, and dissimulation – that deviate from accepted practices, increasing the level of uncertainty in the system.
Blowback: Prior relationships with dominant actors in the system allow highly vulnerable emergent actors to overcome organizational challenges, material constraints, and initial competition with actors as they ascend to system-level status. The actors then may act against their initial sponsor's interests.

how long actors who retain this vulnerability and employ these tactics can persist. If such actors can survive and effectively maintain these behaviors (based in logics of concealment) the result would be a greater level of uncertainty, perhaps one that is seen as untenable to other actors in the system. To say that structures affect outcomes, behavior in this instance, is not to say that they determine them. Actors may misread the strategic environment and the constraints in the system through faulty learning or distortive ideas. Aberrant behavior may not be conducive to survival in either its initial effectiveness, sustainability, or responses it evokes. The resulting maladaptive behavior may affect their already precarious prospects for survival by provoking negative sanctions.

Before moving on to examine the societal forces that result from these systemic developments, the posited mechanisms and processes behind system change are summarized in Table 1.2. Each is bundled to ease assessment of how they match observations from the case studies. It is important to emphasize the probabilistic nature of the ultimate outcome – dissimilarly shaped and comported actors of systemic significance – as well as the contingent nature of these generalizations. As Daniel Nexon highlighted concerning the study of complex historical phenomena: "To the extent that specific formal properties of relational contexts endure across time and space, we should expect to see similar mechanisms and processes at work. But these dynamics will concatenate with other factors – differences in content, agent-level decisions, adjacent processes, other nested relational structures – to produce historically variable outcomes."[41] We should expect to observe this first set of systemic mechanisms and processes, it follows, but not be surprised when they manifest in decidedly non-uniform ways.

Error making, uncertainty, and society

Socialization of roughly similar actors through selective mechanisms has been at the core of neorealism's limited allowance for a social element of international politics. Evolution by selection, however, requires both divergent and convergent processes, variation *and* selection. These processes bring about forms that vie for the resources and power that underpin their survival. The state of nature both proposes and disposes. Robert Dodgshon notes that there are two fundamentally different types of selection. "The first is the initial creation of information through the development, intentionally or unintentionally, of new or variant codes, strategies, forms, structures and solutions: this is a creative, divergent process, one that leads to diversity."[42] This process creates "error makers" or "stochasts" that do not respond in predictable patterns "to the information about the present returns on effort."[43] According to Dodgshon, "[w]here society is able to absorb such deviation or noise as part of its ongoing selection, it leads to morphogenesis and real change." Neorealism has largely ignored this stage of selection in favor of the second type. "The second is the selection made by the sifting and sorting of what is viable or successful from what is not: this represents a convergent process, one that works to conserve dominant forms." This morphostatic process maximizes potential redundancy and predictability, reducing possibilities.[44]

The sparseness of the theory concerning how competition and socialization narrow the range of outcomes in neorealism has been widely noted by critics.[45] Cameron Thies has attempted to fill in some of the blanks as far as state socialization goes, emphasizing roles and the adjustment of state behavior. Roles are associated with expectations of behavior, and

---

[41] Daniel H. Nexon, *The Struggle for Power in Early Modern Europe: Religious Conflict, Dynastic Empires, and International Change* (Princeton: Princeton University Press, 2009), 65.

[42] Robert A. Dodgshon, *Society in Time and Space: A Geographical Perspective on Change* (Cambridge: Cambridge University Press, 1998), 175.

[43] Peter M. Allen, "Evolution, Innovation, and Economics," in *Technical Change and Economic Theory*, ed. Giovanni Dosi, et al. (London: Pinter, 1998), 117; Dodgshon, *Society in Time and Space*, 175.

[44] Dodgshon, *Society in Time and Space*, 176.

[45] See Cameron Thies, "State Socialization and Structural Realism," *Security Studies* 19, no. 4 (October 2010): 689–717.

40 International society and the logics of anarchy

within these roles, borrowing from William Wentworth, Thies defines socialization as "the activity that confronts and lends structure to the entry of nonmembers into an already existing world or a sector of that world."[46] Thies points out that some deviance is tolerated in the short run, but ultimately punished "in accordance with neorealism's logic of selection."[47] He is referring to behavioral deviation among actors within a certain bounded range of organizational form. What happens, though, when the deviation extends to fundamental configuration – interactions in space to the point where these represent structural properties – rather than aberrant behavior of otherwise familiar, and largely predictable, actors? States that look like other states but act aberrantly have been labeled "rogues"; actors that deviate in behavior *and* unit structure have a still more marginal position from which to contend.

Waltz cautioned against including outcomes where "[t]he rich variety and wonderful complexity of international life would be reclaimed at the price of extinguishing theory."[48] This false choice between variety and theory constrains the malleability and applicability of theory that is supposed to be highly attuned to the effects of necessity and uncertainty. Actors in international systems face distinct situational logics, some which may lead to morphogenetic rather than morphostatic outcomes.[49] In this study's sequence, change is rooted in the interaction of the deep structure (anarchic and non-differentiated) and the surface structure (power and resource distribution) of the system. The surface structure not only conditions outcomes, it contributes to shaping actors and their responses to the system. Rather than extinguishing theory, this provides it with a greater measure of realism and explanatory power over a wider range of circumstances and contexts, and imbues it with the insight that changes in the economy of a system may have effects on its ecology as well.

The emphasis on constancy leaves neorealism's formulation of socialization ill-suited for anything other than deviations that fall within an accepted and, not coincidentally, expected range of transgression. Socialization of state behavior involving the amelioration of deviation through punishment by established actors presumes a level of continuity and predictability in the behavior of nonconformists. When the deviation is more severe, of functioning *and* form, the effects may go well beyond the adjustment of state (or dominant unit) behavior. "Uncertainty is a synonym for life," Waltz asserted, "and nowhere is uncertainty greater

[46] Quoted in Ibid., 694.   [47] Ibid., 697.
[48] Kenneth N. Waltz, "Realist Thought and Neorealist Theory," *Journal of International Affairs* 44, no. 1 (Summer 1990): 32.
[49] See Margaret S. Archer, *Realist Social Theory: The Morphogenetic Approach* (Cambridge: Cambridge University Press, 1995), 216–18.

International society, anarchy, and identity 41

than in international politics."[50] While he was arguing against the prospects for economic competition to trump security concerns, the metaphor is apt and the reasoning may be reversed. In order to regulate observation it is not necessary to expel all life out of the system.[51] Truly appreciating uncertainty means more fully accounting for outcomes that diverge from expectations. Allowing a little life back into the composition of the system, and allowing that life to deviate in form, expands our appreciation of not only the presence but also the interaction of necessity and uncertainty. Due to those conditions, that life and the unfolding of the social life of international systems under certain circumstances may also be more tightly bound.

International society, anarchy, and identity

In Hedley Bull's oft-cited definition, international society "exists when a group of states, conscious of certain common interests and common values, form a society in the sense that they conceive themselves bound by a common set of rules in their relations with one another, and share in the working of common institutions."[52] Buzan has offered a refinement of the definition, dividing what he terms "interstate society" (which comports with the classical English School usage) and a narrowed definition of international society. Interstate society concerns "the institutionalization of shared interest and identity amongst states, and puts the creation and maintenance of shared norms, rules and institutions at the center of IR theory." His definition of international society is developed "to indicate situations in which the basic political and legal frame of international social structure is set by the states-system, with individuals and [transnational actors] being given rights by states within the order defined by interstate society."[53] An additional concept, "world society," involves non-state actors and individuals; while some see a transcendence of the state system, for Buzan the three domains are "all are in play together."[54]

---

[50] Kenneth N. Waltz, "The Emerging Structure of International Politics," *International Security* 18, no. 2 (Autumn 1993): 60. For a neorealist statement on the limiting aspects of uncertainty, see Dale Copeland, "A Realist Critique of the English School," *Review of International Studies* 29, no. 3 (July 2003): 427–41.

[51] In his mock interview with an imaginary Kenneth Waltz, Hans Mouritzen poses the question as to why Waltz can't "blow some more life into [his] theory by adding more structural attributes." See Hans Mouritzen, "Kenneth Waltz: A Critical Rationalist Between International Politics and Foreign Policy," in *The Future of International Relations: Masters in the Making?* ed. Iver B. Neuman and Ole Waever (London and New York: Routledge, 1997), 78.

[52] Hedley Bull, *The Anarchical Society: A Study of Order in World Politics* (New York: Columbia University Press, 1977), 13.

[53] Buzan, *From International to World Society*, xvii.   [54] Ibid., xviii.

42   International society and the logics of anarchy

Each of these definitions is predicated on an advanced level of development, wherein systems of powerful states have interacted sufficiently over a long-enough period to have developed institutions and other manifestations of society. Domains of interacting states and non-state actors, where this distinction is clear and accepted, involve circumstances where rights and recognition are conveyed by the former to the latter. This may describe certain international societies, including the modern international system, but applies only to highly developed systems. The search here is for some of the foundations of international society in interactions where a variety of units are "all in play together." Since this involves systems where such advanced development is mostly absent, the division between states and non-state actors cannot be considered as a conceptual distinction. To do so would prejudge membership, status, and barriers for entry, which are all parts of the puzzle.

The appreciation of the development of norms and rules from which actors may deviate and that may exclude actors from good standing requires a definition of international society that does not include stratification in its premise. For that reason a less restrictive definition of international society, offered by Bull and Adam Watson, is preferred:

By international society [it is meant] a group of states (or more generally, a group of independent political communities) which not merely form a system, in the sense that the behavior of each is a necessary factor in the calculation of others, but also have established by dialogue and consent common rules and institutions for the conduct of their relations, and recognize their common interest in maintaining these arrangements.[55]

Determining what is meant by institutions is important. Buzan identifies two characteristics of institutions as the term is used in the English School: "they are relatively fundamental and durable practices, that are evolved more than designed; and ... they are constitutive of actors and their patterns of legitimate activity in relation to each other."[56] The emphasis in this study is on patterns of practices and legitimate activity. To the extent we can examine institutions, particularly in historical contexts where explicit regimes are not as common, again a less restrictive definition is preferred. One suitable definition of institution offered by Buzan is "an established custom, law, or relationship in a society or community," which relies less on identifying specific organizations common to a more formal definition.[57]

---

[55] Hedley Bull and Adam Watson, "Introduction," in *The Expansion of International Society*, ed. Bull and Watson (Oxford: Clarendon Press, 1984), 1.
[56] Buzan, *From International to World Society*, 167.
[57] Ibid., 164. The definition is drawn from *Collins Dictionary of the English Language*, as quoted by Buzan.

International society, anarchy, and identity   43

Central to these understandings is the functional role of institutions, and the norms and rules that compose them, in establishing expectations concerning behavior. Norms have been defined by Stephen Krasner as "standards of behavior defined in terms of rights and obligations." Rules are defined as "specific prescriptions or proscriptions for action."[58] Buzan observes that norms and rules are not easily disentangled, even by assessing the degree of formality. He settles on the following distinction where "norms represent the customary, implicit end of the authoritative social regulation of behavior, and rules the more specific, explicit end," though maintains that these are not always distinguishable.[59]

Norms will be defined here in Peter Katzenstein's terms as "collective expectations for the proper behavior of actors with a given identity ... [that] either define (or constitute) identities or prescribe (or regulate) behavior, or they do both."[60] This formulation includes the instrumental use of norms, where "actors construct and conform to norms because norms help them get what they want."[61] But the constitutive role of these norms goes beyond intentionality and utility. While certain identities help distinguish expected behaviors, identities cannot be reduced to those expectations, nor to those norms. Examining the effects of norms and rules on agents, Friedrich Kratochwil identifies as an important function of norms and rules "the reduction in the complexity of the choice situations in which actors find themselves."[62]

Critical to our understanding of international society is the principle of legitimacy. Ian Clark emphasizes legitimacy as not only a feature of international society but constitutive of it. Clark argues that legitimacy itself specifies key requirements for international society in the form of rightful membership and conduct.[63] "Legitimacy draws substance

---

[58] Stephen D. Krasner, "Structural Causes and Regime Consequences: Regimes as Intervening Variables," in *International Regimes*, ed. Krasner (Ithaca: Cornell University Press, 1983), 2.

[59] Buzan, *From International to World Society*, 164. See also Adam Watson, *The Evolution of International Society: A Comparative Historical Analysis* (London: Routledge, 1992), 311.

[60] Peter J. Katzenstein, "Introduction: Alternative Perspectives on National Security," in *The Culture of National Security: Norms and Identity in World Politics*, ed. Katzenstein (New York: Columbia University Press, 1996), 5.

[61] Martha Finnemore and Kathryn Sikkink, "International Norm Dynamics and Political Change," *International Organization* 52, no. 4 (Autumn 1998): 912.

[62] Friedrich V. Kratochwil, *Rules, Norms, and Decisions: On the Conditions of Practical and Legal Reasoning in International and Domestic Affairs* (Cambridge: Cambridge University Press, 1989), 10. Rules are often treated interchangeably with norms, and no effort will be made in this study to draw clear boundaries. Following Kratochwil, it is understood that all rules are norms, but not all norms have "rule-like characteristics."

[63] Ian Clark, *Legitimacy in International Society* (Oxford: Oxford University Press, 2005), 6. See also Jean-Marc Coicaud, "Deconstructing International Legitimacy," in *Fault Lines*

44   International society and the logics of anarchy

from ... norms," he writes, "but is distinct from them."[64] Norms and rules also have a co-constitutive relationship with membership in international society. Those actors that comport to norms are considered to be members in good standing, while actors who do not are left outside of the fold.

The distinctions between the "pluralist" and "solidarist" interpretations of international society were first introduced by Bull. According to Christian Reus-Smit, the distinction is between "those who see international society as bound together in solidarity by common values and purposes and those who hold that states have a plurality of different purposes and that international society rests solely on the observance of common rules of existence."[65] Pluralism, Buzan explains, "stresses the instrumental side of international society as a functional counterweight to the threat of excessive disorder."[66]

Solidarist conceptions of international society go beyond the collective regulation of self-interested actors, depending on a measure of collective agreement on principles and values. According to Buzan, this has to involve a certain amount of "we-feeling," a common "package of values" that is necessary as a precursor for the development of international society and world order. This may involve a common set of political structures, but also a realized level of convergence among the "norms, rules, institutions, and goals, of the states concerned." A pluralist conception of international society, in contrast, "does not require that [states] agree on anything beyond the basics, or that they hold any common values other than an interest in survival and the avoidance of unwanted disorder." Pluralist international society does not rule out common identity among actors in a system, but it does not prerequire it.[67] Buzan characterizes pluralist international societies as "thin" and solidarist international societies as "thick," reframing the conceptions not as contrary positions but as degrees of difference. The thickness is based on the extent to which common values underpin the pursuit of the minimal goals of coexistence and more expansive goals of collective regulation of common problems.[68]

---

of International Legitimacy, ed. Hilary Charlesworth and Jean-Marc Coicaud (Cambridge: Cambridge University Press, 2010), 36.

[64] For Clark, norms are an object of international society while legitimacy "refers to international society as the subject." Clark, *Legitimacy in International Society*, 7. That distinction is not adopted here.

[65] Christian Reus-Smit, "The Constructivist Challenge after September 11," in *International Society and Its Critics*, ed. Alex J. Bellamy (Oxford: Oxford University Press, 2005), 86.

[66] Buzan, *From International to World Society*, 47.   [67] Above, Ibid., 145–47.

[68] Ibid., 59.

International society, anarchy, and identity 45

Another important distinction that Buzan makes is between international society based on functional logics that is more contractual and constructed than organic ("society") and international society based on bonds of common sentiment, experience, and identity ("community").[69] The functional logic has as its causal mechanism the necessities engendered due to sustained interaction. "Units that have no choice but to interact...," Buzan writes, "and that begin to accept each other as essentially similar types of sociopolitical organization, will be hard put to avoid creating some mechanisms for dealing with each other peacefully."[70] Among those agreements is the fundamental right to exist, which "adds importantly to the security of units by defining boundaries of legitimacy and order within which they function."[71]

While instrumental in its conception, Buzan seeks to demonstrate how anarchy can generate international society in ways that neorealism sees as short-lived or trivial. Though identifying with the functional side, Buzan sees a weakness in "that it omits the notion of common identity that is central to the concept of society." He identifies two ways in which functional logics of the system could reinforce common identity, which involves "a sense of 'we-ness' that comprises more than shared goals." One way this may happen involves the development of common identity based on similarity. Building on Waltz's systemic logic of the shaping effects of anarchy, Buzan posits that as "interaction makes units more similar, it becomes easier for each to accept that the other members of the system are in some important sense the same type of entity as itself." In this way a "collection of otherwise disparate actors" can consider themselves as part of a community.[72] Kratochwil and Yosef Lapid believe that these functional explanations cast identity "as little more than (sustained) membership in a set of interacting actors."[73] This may be seen to situate identity as epiphenomenal, a functional outgrowth of competition under anarchy. Reducing identity and international society to survival needs is not Buzan's intention, and he emphasizes that organic, identity-based forces and functional drivers – community and society, respectively – are

---

[69] Buzan, "From International System," 333. [70] Ibid., 343.

[71] Ibid., 347. For an overview of these distinctions, see Ole Waever, "Four Meanings of International Society: A Trans-Atlantic Dialogue," in *International Society and the Development of International Relations Theory*, ed. Barbara A. Roberson (London: Continuum, 1998), 80–144.

[72] Above, Buzan, "From International System," 335. See also Jörg Friedrichs, "The Meaning of New Medievalism," *European Journal of International Relations* 7, no. 4 (December 2001): 475–501.

[73] Yosef Lapid and Friedrich V. Kratochwil, "Revisiting the 'National': Toward an Identity Agenda in Neorealism?" in *The Return of Culture and Identity in IR Theory*, ed. Lapid and Kratochwil (Boulder, Colo.: Lynne Rienner, 1996), 120.

46 International society and the logics of anarchy

"nearly always linked but with little or no determinate causality in either direction."[74] There is a strong relationship between them, and they are "frequently collocated and nearly always interactive."[75] Despite this caveat, identity in Buzan's formulation can be seen as a secondary outcome of the functional roots of pluralist international society. The ways in which community (and its emphasis on identity) and society (with functional requirements as a driver) reinforce each other and interact require better specification.

Interactions with irregular (functionally similar, structurally dissimilar) actors provide an opportunity to examine how these functional and common identity roots of international society interact. Theoretical consideration and empirical examination will reveal how artificial these divisions are and describe a relationship that is co-constitutive, raising some key questions. How are difference and sameness determined and conceived in terms of both functional requirements and identity formation, and what are their effects? What is the relationship between the functional imperatives presented by the emergent actors and the development or reinforcement of common identity among established actors in the system? To begin to address these questions it is helpful to look at previous considerations of the relationship between homogeneity and international society.

Homogeneity and international society

The association of homogeneity with outcomes in international politics is longstanding.[76] Fred Halliday surveyed thinkers as diverse as Edmund Burke and Karl Marx and saw in each an emphasis on the importance of homogeneity among constituents of the international system. Burke saw an analogy with human relations based on "resemblances, by conformities, by sympathies" that extended to nations basing their amity on "correspondence in laws, customs, manners, and habits of life."[77] Marx recognized the spread of capitalism as not only transforming societies but creating a manner of international society, "a world after its own image."[78] Later, Raymond Aron emphasized the greater stability and limitation of violence in homogeneous systems, those composed of states of the same type. "A homogeneous system appears stable," he observed, "because it is foreseeable."[79] More recently, discussion of the effects of

---

[74] Buzan, *From International to World Society*, 128. [Emphasis added.]   [75] Ibid., 114.

[76] See Fred Halliday, "International Society as Homogeneity: Burke, Marx, Fukuyama," *Millennium: Journal of International Studies* 21, no. 3 (December 1992): 458.

[77] Ibid., 448.   [78] Quoted in Ibid., 452.

[79] Raymond Aron, *Peace and War: A Theory of International Relations* (Piscataway, N.J.: Transaction Publishers, 2003; 1966), 100.

institutional similarity on international outcomes is most developed in the debate on the democratic peace.[80] Competitive homogenization provides a basis, according to Halliday, for conceiving of "international society as homogeneity."[81] But how does "alikeness" translate into outcomes, and how might it affect behaviors and the development of the norms and identities that constitute international society?

In the pluralist conception of international society, according to Buzan, the institution of sovereignty serves as a form of shared identity by establishing mutual recognition as similar types with legal standing.[82] Similarity brought about by interaction and coexistence, and a mutual need for survival and aversion to disorder, engenders a level of cooperation to maintain certain modes of interaction and behavior.[83] That similarity, in a sense, is their common identity. According to Buzan, though, in order for international society to become further rooted, a level of convergence is necessary that involves a greater level of solidarity. Transformation beyond international society as *society* toward a level of *community* occurs as states "seek to reinforce the security and legitimacy of their own values by consciously linking with others who are likeminded, building a shared identity with them."[84] This provides a fairly clear functional account of the development of not only a pluralist but gradually a more solidarist international society. Similarity is necessary for generating momentum toward greater levels of cooperation and shared standards, which, in turn, provide the basis for further convergence toward greater levels of solidarity and shared identity. If homogeneity plays a role in fostering international society, though, what happens when interlopers of less familiar forms intrude?

These sorts of disruptions present circumstances that may be conducive to solidarism among "like" actors as they face unfamiliar and potentially threatening foes. This effect may be even more pronounced when the "unlike" actors have a lesser commitment to maintaining the existing order. The order may not promote their survival, leading to transgression of norms and rules in more advanced international societies, and helping to define those norms and rules in inchoate ones. An appreciation of the role of common identity beyond instrumental necessity, however, is necessary to explain why emergent, structurally dissimilar actors come

---

[80] John Owen sees common identity as a cause of peace among liberal states. Their commonality creates expectations of restraint and fair play that influence behavior. John M. Owen, *Liberal Peace, Liberal War: American Politics and International Security* (Ithaca: Cornell University Press, 1997). See also Mark Souva, "Institutional Similarity and Interstate Conflict," *International Interactions* 30, no. 3 (July–September 2004): 263–80.

[81] Halliday, "International Society as Homogeneity," 458.

[82] Buzan, *From International to World Society*, 145.   [83] Ibid.   [84] Ibid., 147–48.

48 International society and the logics of anarchy

to be seen not only as competitors but as systemic malefactors. These episodes involve not only disorders in a functional sense, of disturbed equilibria awaiting correction, but also disorders in a cognitive sense, making sense of jarred surroundings by distinguishing selves and others. Appreciating the mutually constitutive role of functional requirements of security and identity formation requires looking at conditions and processes emphasized by both neo-utilitarian and constructivist frameworks. The first element focuses on the level of uncertainty in a system, emphasized by neorealism, but looks deeper into its potential effects on the formulation of norms and rules. The second element will focus on identity formation and its contributions to establishing higher levels of solidarity. These processes, as it turns out, are not so discrete, blurring the effective distinction between the functional and solidarist roots of international society.

Bedeviling the strong: fear, uncertainty, and power

In neorealism the international system is rooted in mutual fear among great powers, with uncertainty acting as a brake on cooperation.[85] Assessments of factors like relative power, offensive capabilities, and intentions are all made under conditions of uncertainty. Developments related to the mitigation of uncertainty, though, may lead to outcomes that can be best understood outside of neorealism's highly proscribed allowance for socialization. Given their central role in neorealism in driving and limiting behaviors, the lack of distinction between different types of uncertainty and fear, and between uncertainty and fear themselves, is surprising. Drawing such distinctions is a key step in determining the difference between gradations and types of uncertainty and their links to the development of international society.

For John Mearsheimer, fear is a byproduct of anarchy and its intrinsic uncertainty and is determined in large part by capabilities. "Power considerations affect the intensity of fear."[86] Mearsheimer emphasizes characteristics that enhance conditions of fear in the international system: nuclear weapons, topography (namely oceans or a lack thereof), and the distribution of power (asymmetries in power and the number of actors).[87] As Mearsheimer employs it, fear may be understood in terms of the

---

[85] "Liberalism is rooted in appetite," Richard Ned Lebow writes, while "realism is rooted in fear." Richard Ned Lebow, "Constructive Realism," *International Studies Review* 6, no. 2 (June 2004): 348.

[86] John J. Mearsheimer, *The Tragedy of Great Power Politics* (New York: W.W. Norton, 2001), 43–44.

[87] Ibid., 44–45.

estimation of potential adverse outcomes in conditions of uncertainty. Inscrutability concerning intentions is constant while varying amounts of power introduce varying levels of fear. So the type of uncertainty that neorealists consider is, in effect, relatively constant.[88] Given changes in the nature of the units and their interactions, however, the level of impenetrability concerning intentions may be enhanced, as may the unfathomability of offensive capabilities.

As Mearsheimer treats them, the elements that contribute to fear may actually *decrease* uncertainty. Nuclear weapons may increase fears of annihilation but this risk is estimable: capabilities and vulnerabilities can be assessed, as well as the decision-making organizations and processes. Mearsheimer argues that nuclear weapons decrease uncertainty by increasing fear.[89] Topography is static, oceans expand but incrementally (for now), and adjacency or distance among major powers is mostly immutable. The number of actors may vary but not markedly or rapidly. This latter observation holds when considering great or major powers. It does not hold as strongly when considering the phenomenon of emergent actors.

The factors outlined by Mearsheimer affecting fear can be considered under broader categories: (1) specific capabilities and characteristics of violence capacity; (2) vulnerabilities resultant from spatial relationships; and (3) the distribution of power, which will be more widely conceived here to cover not only quantitative indices of power but its configuration in the system. Each of these indices is likely to be affected as structurally dissimilar actors begin to assert themselves in a system, a scenario affecting both the number and type of significant actors in the system. Changes in the character of the violence and means employed, and the spatial relationships these actors manifest, are likely to be distinct as they cope with differential resources and systemic pressures.

If "power affects fear," in the sense that the *amount* of power affects fear, then we should suppose that shifts in the *type* of power also affect fear. Neorealism states that power is reducible to material indices. But this leaves out that power manifests in different ways, which affect the likelihood that damage can be inflicted and are not reducible to static measures. While greater power may result in greater fear, an estimation derived in a condition of uncertainty, so too a lesser power may generate increased fear through a magnification of uncertainty. This is an

---

[88] For a discussion of the application of uncertainty in realism, see George W. Downs and David M. Rocke, *Optimal Imperfection: Domestic Uncertainty and Institutions in International Relations* (Princeton: Princeton University Press, 1995): 9–13.

[89] Mearsheimer, *Tragedy of Great Power Politics*, 43.

50   International society and the logics of anarchy

uncertainty characterized by inconstancy and unfamiliarity with the strategic environment, rather than mere unease concerning future capabilities.

Waltz hinted at this in his assessment of factors that work against systemic stability. "The powerful, out of their strength, influence and limit each other...," Waltz writes, "[t]he weak, on the other hand, bedevil the strong."[90] The weak may be less amenable to control, Waltz points out, because they have less to lose. The weak, or rather not as strong, can also be seen as having a more precarious existence that may incline toward taking risks. This is due not only to lesser constraints on actions due to lower costs, as emphasized by Waltz, but also to the costs of sustained weakness. Some actors may see inaction as more precarious than disruptive actions. Rather than having nothing to lose they may have more to lose by doing nothing.

The capacity to increase uncertainty is an overlooked element of relative power. Karl Deutsch proposed "the weight of the power or influence of an actor over some process is the extent to which he can change the probability of its outcome."[91] Going beyond the understanding of power that emphasizes the ability to control or effect outcomes, Manus Midlarsky associates power with the broader capacity to decrease uncertainty: "Power is here understood as a capability to effect a reduction of environmental uncertainty, while the exercise of power for the benefit of an actor is the actual reduction of that uncertainty."[92] It is in this regard that the type of actors focused on in this study may prove especially vexing to dominant powers, especially as they deviate from established forms and practices. If power can be understood as the capability to reduce uncertainty, then, considering the relative nature of power, any ability to increase the level of environmental uncertainty is in an unconventional sense power itself. This may not be enough power to exhibit any elevated status in the system or influence the overall structure of the system, but enough to compensate for their precarious condition in the system. The ability of actors to disrupt patterns is in contrast to the more powerful, which have an increasingly vested interest in predictability and order. Some weaker actors, especially those with marginal or highly dependent security, will prefer a system marked by stable patterns of interaction that

[90] Kenneth N. Waltz, "The Stability of a Bipolar World," *Daedalus* 93, no. 3 (Summer 1964): 887–88.
[91] Karl W. Deutsch, *The Analysis of International Relations* (Englewood Cliffs, N.J.: Prentice-Hall, 1968), 24. Quoted in Manus I. Midlarsky, "Power, Uncertainty, and the Onset of International Violence," *Journal of Conflict Resolution* 18, no. 3 (September 1974): 398.
[92] Midlarsky, "Power, Uncertainty," 395.

heighten their ability to navigate from their tenuous position. For others that take on dominant powers, and deviate from prevailing patterns, enhanced uncertainty may provide sufficient compensation for material weakness. The result may be systems characterized primarily not by fear of knowable outcomes, as neorealists emphasize, but by dominance coupled with deviance and dread toward the unknown.

Risk and uncertainty in international systems

The neorealist conceptions of uncertainty as an overarching condition, and fear as the result of an adverse estimation of relative power, overlook the elements of fear and anxiety that result not from estimation but from the condition of uncertainty itself. True uncertainty suggests a diminished capability to estimate outcomes or influence their probability. At the same time, wariness is not necessarily fearfulness. Being wary of a potential rival's future intentions is different from being unable to estimate the security environment effectively. To appreciate that difference, it is important to take into account the distinction between *risk* and uncertainty. Just as power can be accumulated and expressed in different modes, uncertainty has varying measures and distinct effects. While uncertainties may exist concerning familiar patterns of interaction, according to Daniel Ellsberg the "ambiguities surrounding the outcome of a proposed *innovation*, a departure from current strategy, may be much more noticeable."[93] The distinction between risk and uncertainty is essential in discerning how some uncertainty is accepted as a manageable condition of anarchy, while greater levels of uncertainty may be seen as inconsistent with security and, potentially, survival.

The differentiation between risk and uncertainty developed by economist Frank Knight provides a common reference point. Knight distinguished between types of uncertainty based on how measurable they are. Measurable uncertainty is "risk," while "true" uncertainty is of the "non-quantitative type."[94] Measurability and the objective or subjective nature of probabilities have been a focus of this distinction, with risk identified as having well-defined probabilities concerning possible outcomes and uncertainty lacking those.[95] Richard Langlois and Metin Cosgel emphasize the subjective nature of assessing probabilities, based on the problem of incomplete information and the challenges this presents for

---

[93] Daniel Ellsberg, "Risk, Ambiguity, and the Savage Axioms," *The Quarterly Journal of Economics* 75, no. 4 (November 1961): 666.

[94] Frank H. Knight, *Risk, Uncertainty, and Profit* (Boston: Houghton Mifflin, 1921), 20.

[95] Stephen F. LeRoy and Larry D. Singell, Jr., "Knight on Risk and Uncertainty," *Journal of Political Economy* 95, no. 2 (April 1987): 394–95.

52 International society and the logics of anarchy

classification.[96] The ability to classify instances is essential to the estimation of future probabilities. Knight focused on the problems of knowledge, making it clear that operating in an environment necessitates classification in order to discern and calculate probabilities.[97] Variety and combinatorial possibilities are vexatious when assessing potential outcomes. Limitations on variety and the fact that much change is relatively constant and ascertainable, according to Knight, make us able to function.[98] Given the inability to determine all the number of kinds of things, we are forced to rely on inferences concerning "a working number of properties or *modes of resemblance* between things," enabling us to move away from uncertainty toward measurable levels of risk.[99] The assessment of possible outcomes is linked not only to the stability of forms in a system, but also to the ability to determine a measure of homogeneity and to establish classifications of kind.

Concerning competition in international systems we may posit a relationship between increased variety and heightened levels of uncertainty. The uncertainty neorealists repeatedly mention should be considered more as estimable risk, a condition that may limit cooperation and increase the probability of conflict, but one also consistent with at least a measure of security and predictability. Crises may make uncertainty more pronounced and lead to adverse behaviors, but the level of risk still allows deliberation, planning, and organization around a relatively well-understood range of outcomes.

From these considerations it is not too difficult to see how the alternate logics of anarchy identified – logics of dissimilation and concealment – might affect the overall level of uncertainty in a system.[100] Novel

---

[96] Richard N. Langlois and Metin M. Cosgel, "Frank Knight on Risk, Uncertainty, and the Firm: A New Interpretation," *Economic Inquiry* 31 (July 1993): 458.
[97] Knight, *Risk, Uncertainty, and Profit*, 206.   [98] Ibid., 207.   [99] Ibid., 206; 231.
[100] Among the number of factors that may contribute to the level of uncertainty in a system are the following: (1) The *number of major powers* in the system, which is seen by Kenneth Waltz and others as a key index of how stable a system will be. See Waltz, *Theory of International Politics*, 134–36. (2) The *number of significant actors*. An increase in the number of actors that "matter" increases the potential for miscalculation and multiplies the number of combinations and outcomes possible. (3) The *number of types of actors*. Deviations from "best" practices may yield actors that are different in type. These differences translate into distinct modes of interaction and behavior. (4) *Power differential stability*. According to some neorealists, rising or declining power is a key source of uncertainty. See Dale C. Copeland, *The Origins of Major War* (Ithaca: Cornell University Press, 2000). (5) *Relational stability*: the solidity of relationships among actors. (6) *Role stability*. Role can be understood in terms of relative power (particularly in conditions of dominance and subordination) and qualitative relationships concerning specialization. (7) *Level of socialization*. This outcome is both predicted and proscribed in neorealism; deviations from accepted practices should lead to selecting out of the system. (8) *Level and extent of system regulation*. This includes the existence of norms and

relationships and characteristics affect the attributional confidence established actors hold concerning friends, rivals, and enemies. Novelty in this instance is a combination of deviance and relatively sudden relevance. Increase in the number of types and the lack of sustained interaction and learning present difficulties in assessing and reacting to threats. The emergence of structurally dissimilar actors, even when they do not rival dominant actors in material capacity, moves the system from estimable risk closer to true uncertainty. Actors in the system are wary of risk, but they dread uncertainty. At either end of the spectrum is fear, of the known and the unknown, from an imminent threat to survival or apprehension concerning inscrutable actors and outcomes. It is this intimacy with inestimable peril that the neorealist conception of uncertainty (as an overarching condition) fails to capture.

How might established, dominant actors respond to this shift? Offensive realists mention uncertainty about intentions as a cause behind states' relentless urge toward expansion.[101] Indeed, one fix in these circumstances would be to assert dominance either by subduing particular actors or expanding to dominate the system as a whole. Assuming systemic dominance is not feasible, eradication or forced submission might be preferable. Another option would be to allow time for socialization of behavior to take place, a period concurrent with an increase in knowledge concerning emergent and unfamiliar actors and their modes and means. That, however, would assume that uncertainty in the interim was considered tenable and consistent with security and survival. Moreover, as the next sections explain, the nature of these actors and the strategic environment may make any inclusion and accommodation less likely due to the necessary mediation of common identity formation as not only a result of but a requirement for security.

Regulation of the system is also an option for coping with and reducing uncertainty. The development and enforcement of norms and rules may be considered not only a brake on deviance but a power-maximizing behavior. This interpretation would suggest that the components of international society – the establishment of norms and rules, and the conference of rightful membership and means – were merely expressions of interests and power in the system. But these components are also conditioned, as are the interest themselves, by considerations more closely associated with identity formation. That interdependence is demonstrated through the confluence of common identity formation, in the face

---

rules, their institutionalization and internalization, and effective control over institutionalized means.

[101] Mearsheimer, *Tragedy of Great Power Politics*, 31.

54   International society and the logics of anarchy

of disruptions of homogeneity, with the fundamental needs for categorization and classification as essential processes for coping with uncertainty.

Identity, uncertainty, and society

Debates over identity in international relations theory include its nature as a fixed property or process, its conceptualization within causal models, and its overall commensurability with positivism.[102] Bill McSweeney criticizes treatments that interpret identity as a "fact of society." He argues that identity "is a process of negotiation among people and interest groups. ... We cannot decide the status, or even the relevance of identity *a priori*."[103] One way out of this bind, adopted here, is to distinguish between identity as a property or outcome and identity formation as a process. Working definitions of identity in international relations theory include "the understanding of oneself in relationship to others," and "varying constructions of nation- or state-hood."[104] Jan Stets and Peter Burke summarize Sheldon Stryker's assessment of the multiple views of identity found in sociological theory. Social identity theory "sees identity as embedded in a social group or category," while symbolic interactionism "takes into account individual role relationships and identity variability, motivation, and differentiation."[105] These views capture both the embeddedness and variability of identities, as well as the importance of categorization and expectations.

Alexander Wendt's breakdown of kinds of identity is also useful. For Wendt, "corporate identity" distinguishes difference, while "type identity" is based on common characteristics. "Role identity" is based on relationships and expectations, helping determine a "self" and "other," while "collective identity" blurs this distinction.[106] To simplify, in this

---

[102] For an overview of the development of identity as a concept in international relations theory, see Felix Berenskoetter, "Identity in International Relations," *International Studies Encyclopedia Online*, ed. Robert A. Denemark (Blackwell Publishing, 2010). See also Rawi Abdelal, Yoshiko M. Herrera, Alastair Iain Johnston, and Rose McDermott, "Identity as a Variable," *Perspectives on Politics* 4, no. 4 (December 2006): 695–711.

[103] Bill McSweeney, *Security, Identity, and Interests: A Sociology of International Relations* (Cambridge: Cambridge University Press, 1999), 73.

[104] Michael Barnett, "Culture, Strategy, and Foreign Policy Change: Israel's Road to Oslo," *European Journal of International Relations* 5, no. 1 (March 1999): 9; Katzenstein, "Introduction," 6.

[105] Jan E. Stets and Peter J. Burke, "A Sociological Approach to Self and Identity," in *Handbook of Self and Identity*, ed. Mark R. Leary and June Price Tangney (New York: Guilford Press, 2005), 133.

[106] Wendt, *Social Theory*, 221–30.

study role identity will be folded into corporate identity, with each distinguishing difference; type identity will collapse into collective identity, each stressing commonality. Together, corporate identity (emphasizing contrasts, "self" and "other" or "us vs. them") and collective identity (emphasizing commonalities, "we-feeling") will be considered here as "common identity." The processes that influence and reinforce common identity are essential to understanding the relationship between identity, identity formation, and international society. If changes in environment influence identity formation, where do these identities come from? Wendt emphasizes that identities have multiple sources, including unit-level characteristics and processes. These sources include history, language, and religion, mediated in processes at the unit level. He also points to the system level as an important source affecting identities and how they unfold. Similarity and its associated expectations root a basic identity, one founded on certain characteristics and routines that recognize and reinforce similarity through a series of interactions.[107]

The salience of the commonality among actors in the international system is likely to rise upon encountering actors who deviate from configurational and behavioral expectations. Ted Hopf affirms the functional role of identities. "Durable expectations between states," he writes, "require intersubjective identities that are sufficiently stable to ensure predictable patterns of behavior." He characterizes a world without such identities as a "world of chaos, a world of pervasive and irremediable uncertainty, a world much more dangerous than anarchy." In this regard identities serve as categories, "they tell you and others who you are and they tell you who others are."[108] The resulting categorization establishes a stable set of expectations concerning particular actors and courses of action. While uncertainty conditions the environment, the salience of identities cannot be reduced to the functional requirements brought about by increased uncertainty. The requirements of identity may converge with the functional requirements of security under uncertainty, but the relationship may be coincident rather than consequent. Uncertainty may condition the process of identity formation but does not determine the outcome. If identity could be reduced to reactions to uncertainty, then in more predictable circumstances there would be no need for identities or pronounced identities. The record includes many highly regularized, even ritualized, conflicts in which identities are both heightened and significant as either outcome or cause.

---

[107] Wendt discusses homogeneity as a source of collective identity in Ibid., 353–57.
[108] Ted Hopf, "The Promise of Constructivism in International Relations Theory," *International Security* 23, no. 1 (Summer 1998): 174–75.

56   International society and the logics of anarchy

Identity requires a contrary identity, whereas coping with uncertainty only requires a more ordered environment.[109] Collective identity formation, the establishment or increased salience of similarities, often goes hand-in-hand with corporate identity formation, the determination of difference with others. William Connolly's succinct statement captures the relational nature of identity formation. "An identity," he writes, "is established in relation to a series of differences that have become socially recognized. These differences are essential to its being." Differences are necessary for the solidity of identity, securing self-certainty. Maintaining identities, Connolly notes, at times "involves the conversion of some differences into otherness, into evil, or one of its numerous surrogates."[110] A process of determining one's place and the place of others (rather than "others") is common to each of Stryker's views of identity. Common principles of identity theory hold that:

1) behavior is dependent on a named or classified world and that these names carry meaning in the form of shared responses and behavioral expectations that grow out of social interactions; 2) among the named classes are symbols that are used to designate positions in the social structure; 3) persons who act in the context of social structure name one another in the sense of recognizing one another as occupants of positions and come to have expectations for those others; 4) persons acting in the context of social structure also name themselves and create internalized meanings and expectations with regard to their own behavior; and 5) these expectations and meanings form the guiding basis for social behavior.[111]

The overlap between the functional needs for discerning strategic environments and the requirements of identity is striking. Categorizing and discrimination characterize both processes, but for identity formation discrimination may take a distinct and more pronounced variety. Examining a strategic environment under uncertainty may often require crude calculations that distinguish friends and enemies, but it does not necessarily require an "other." Paul Kowert cites experiments in social psychology, noting that "[n]ot only are out-groups typically evaluated negatively, but they are also generally assumed to be more homogeneous

---

[109] That identity and identity formation cannot be understood except in relationship to contrary identities is known as the particularist thesis, which is widely employed in treatments of identity in international relations theory. See Arash Abizadeh, "Does Collective Identity Presuppose an Other? On the Alleged Incoherence of Global Solidarity," *American Political Science Review* 99, no. 1 (February 2005): 45.

[110] William E. Connolly, *Identity\Difference: Democratic Negotiations of Political Paradox*, Expanded Edition (Minneapolis: University of Minnesota Press, 2002), 64. On the forces behind the construction of "otherness," see Richard Kearney, *Strangers, Gods, and Monsters: Interpreting Otherness* (London: Routledge, 2003).

[111] Stets and Burke, "Sociological Approach," 133.

Ontological security and alterity 57

than in-groups."[112] Part of this phenomenon, Kowert notes, may result from an inability to discriminate and the imprecise nature of any social category, which lead to simplifying assumptions.[113]

The question of the transformation from out-groups to alterity remains: why do these simplifying assumptions impute varying levels of enmity? Why in certain circumstances is difference a somewhat mild contrast resulting in relatively benign rivalry, while in other conditions otherness leads to dehumanization and license for annihilation? The quantity of potential violence, it seems, may have less explanatory value than the quality of violence. Uncertainty influences the salience of certain identities due to the functional requirements of coping with uncertainty and novelty, including the need for categorization to bring true uncertainty closer to the status of estimable risk. Identity may also provide the basic associations that allow for functional responses to increased uncertainty, but that does not exhaust its effects. Beyond this functional role, identity formation allows for the enhancement of common identity among otherwise unlike actors that are more alike in the face of difference. Collective consciousness of similarities rises and common identity intensifies in reaction to encounters with the unfamiliar and uncertain. Mystification, enhanced by unfamiliarity, may lead to the magnification of similarities and differences. But the question of why these out-groups are sometimes subject not only to "othering" but also to attributions of enduring evil remains.

Ontological security and alterity

The transference from out-group to "other," and to "evil other," may be better understood by appreciating the interaction effects of uncertainty and identity, which is aided by the concept of ontological security. The situating of functional adaptation to uncertainty and identity formation as discrete intervening processes – between system change and the development of international society – should not occlude how each conditions and influences the other. In international systems an understanding of other actors occurs from sustained interaction over time. Waltz recognizes the importance of understanding actors and the environment, and the role of learning through sustained interaction: "Stable systems are

---

[112] Paul Kowert, "The Three Faces of Identity," in *The Origins of National Interests*, ed. Glenn Chafetz, et al. (London: Frank Cass, 1999), 17. Jonathan Mercer writes that "[i]t appears that the more we identify with our group, the more likely we are to discriminate against out-groups." Jonathan Mercer, "Anarchy and Identity," *International Organization* 49, no. 2 (Spring 1995): 251.

[113] Kowert, "Three Faces of Identity," 18.

58   International society and the logics of anarchy

self-reinforcing, moreover, because understanding others' behavior, making agreements with them, and policing the agreements become easier through continued experience."[114] Wendt affirms the relationship between homeostatic social tendencies and the requirements for stable social order, emphasizing the importance of knowledge in "making interaction relatively predictable." This "culture," in Wendt's vernacular, meets the "basic human needs for sociation and ontological security."[115]

The oversight of the importance of ontological security in the study of international relations was highlighted by Jef Huysmans. He noted that international relations has "concentrated on the mediation of relations between enemies rather than the mediation of relations with strangers."[116] Addressing that gap, Jennifer Mitzen scaled up the concept of ontological security from its origins in psychology, making it more amenable to system-level theory.[117] "Ontological *security*," Mitzen explains, "is the condition that obtains when an individual has confident expectations, even if probabilistic, about the means–ends relationships that govern her social life." This condition is not merely mental ease but underlies the ability of actors to function. "Ontological *in*security refers to the deep, incapacitating state of not knowing which dangers to confront and which to ignore, i.e. how to get by in the world." According to Mitzen, "[s]uch uncertainty can make it difficult to act, which frustrates the action–identity dynamic and thereby makes it difficult to sustain a self-conception."[118] Uncertainty affects routines that sustain identity, leading Mitzen to associate uncertainty with threats to identity: "the claim that ontological security is a basic need begins with the proposition that actors fear deep uncertainty as an identity threat."[119] Both physical and ontological security require routines, and changes that increase environmental uncertainty disrupt these. This casts identity not merely as a functional effect, but as part of the very fabric of the upturned order. "Attachment to routines and the social order they implicate," Mitzen explains, "is thus connected to, indeed a precondition for, identity and therefore the capacity for rational action."[120]

---

[114] Waltz, *Theory of International Politics*, 136.   [115] Wendt, *Social Theory*, 187.

[116] Jef Huysmans, "Security! What Do You Mean? From Concept to Thick Signifier," *European Journal of International Relations* 4, no. 2 (June 1998): 242–43.

[117] Jennifer Mitzen, "Ontological Security in World Politics: State Identity and the Security Dilemma," *European Journal of International Relations* 12, no. 3 (September 2006): 341–70. See also Brent J. Steele, "Ontological Security and the Power of Self-Identity: British Neutrality and the American Civil War," *Review of International Studies* 31, no. 3 (July 2005): 519–40. In sociology the concept of ontological security was cultivated by Anthony Giddens, who pointed to the need for "the reduction of uncertainties about the vagaries of nature and the reduction of uncertainties in respect to future events." Giddens, *Constitution of Society*, 271.

[118] Mitzen, "Ontological Security," 345.   [119] Ibid., 347; 345.   [120] Ibid., 349.

Ontological security and alterity

In some significant respects identity *is* security. "Ontological security-seeking," Mitzen writes, "is the drive to minimize hard uncertainty by imposing cognitive order on the environment."[121] Righting the cognitive order is not just a pretext for action in response to shifting environments but a constitutive necessity. This highlights the importance of identity for confirming or reestablishing stable routines based on regularity, familiarity, and attachment with others (not yet "others"). That involves the delineation of in- and out-groups that helps establish the requisite cognitive order. For Mitzen, the routines associated with prolonged conflict may provide a measure of ontological security, which can help explain continuing conditions of physical insecurity in ongoing ethnic conflicts. Conversely, and more relevant to its application here, severe disruptions of ontological security may be realized in conditions of uncertainty affecting stable expectations of physical security.

Huysmans notes that ontological security seeking strives to fix "social relations into a symbolic and institutional order."[122] Enhanced threats to ontological security may affect representations of actors and relationships, basing the symbolic orders on severe distinctions and stark categorizations. Jutta Weldes discusses the imperfect nature of encounters with uncertain environments and the importance of representations in constituting interests. Representations entail "situation descriptions and problem definitions – through which state officials and others make sense of the world around them."[123] These representations draw on "a wide array of already available cultural and linguistic resources," and serve "to populate the world with a variety of objects, including both the self . . . and others." This results in each of these "objects" being "given an identity; [and] endowed with characteristics which are sometimes precise and certain, at other times vague and unsettled."[124]

The greater the threat to ontological security, which threatens both physical security and identity, the more likely these categories will compensate for uncertainty with greater solidity and clarity. This "precision" in categorization may not comport with the objective environment, the assessment of which is compromised. If the needs for identity involve distinguishing "self" and "other," then uncertainty can only magnify that distinction. Uncertainty conditions the formation of identity by magnifying the contrast and valuation of others, which become "others." If the "self" is unsettled, and we assume a physical threat from the candidate "other" that precludes positive associations, then this results not only in

---

[121] Ibid., 346. [122] Huysmans, "Security! What Do You Mean?" 242.

[123] Jutta Weldes, "Constructing National Interests," *European Journal of International Relations* 2, no. 3 (September 1996): 280.

[124] Ibid., 281.

60   International society and the logics of anarchy

an "other," but potentially an "evil other." There can be no positive identification with such an "other," making the distinction severe and essential.

Ready-made categories serve the need to bring uncertainty to more manageable levels. Distinctions within the out-group are overlooked in favor of a singular characterization with an unambiguously negative valuation.[125] This, in turn, allows for "maximization" in response to these threats. Maximization here applies to the evaluation of the extent of the "other's" goals, their means to reach them, and the absence of restraints exhibited by the "other." This is not to say these actors may not match some of these expectations. A certain level of fidelity to type makes this negative identity formation plausible. These behaviors, though, are not seen as the outcome of fierce competition but as the outgrowth of some fundamental, psychosocial deviance. Irrationality or a racial or genetic predisposition to violence not only provide explanations for aberrant behavior but also buttress fundamental distinctions of "self" and "other." When in severe circumstances this process results in an "evil other," the normative deviance is seen as a reflection of a fundamental subhuman character rather than an outgrowth of systemic necessity. In this study's scenario, indeed, certain circumstances lead those bedeviling the strong to become seen as devils. It should be emphasized that this study looks, in part, at how norms are founded and formulated. With such norms emplaced one can validly judge the actions of these actors to be monstrous. This is a distinct process, however, from beginning with the proposition that these actors are monsters.

The socialization process posited by neorealism, bounding a set of behaviors and expectations, is strained in situations involving maximization and the construction of "others" or "evil others." The quality rather than the quantity of violence may make coexistence under anarchy untenable. Learning and signaling are further compromised by assigning values and expectations that reinforce the irremediable defects of an adversary. With negative identity formation, eradication rather than

---

[125] If a lack of familiarity contributes to "evil othering," why is this outcome so prevalent in ethnic conflicts where contending parties have long histories of interaction? Conditions posited for this study do not exhaust the sources for all possible similar outcomes. In the case of ethnic conflict this familiarity is likely to have been gained due to long-term experiences and interactions characterized by enmity that, contrary to decreased certainty, present an increased sense of certainty of ill-intentions. At the same time, ethnic conflict is often associated with state disintegration, where the state allowed for a measure of predictability in routines and physical security, at least for those groups not persecuted by the state or its ethnic compatriots. Even in cases where the physical security of a group(s) was directly threatened by the state, the patterns of that coercion were likely well known. This combination of factors leaves the potential for both uncertainty and familiarity to breed contempt.

International society: through thick and thin   61

accommodating violence, as actors often do under anarchy, is more defensible, especially if the actor is sufficiently vulnerable. Actual threats to the dominant powers' survival are not required. At the same time, strict and negative identity formation presents greater potential for the development of norms and rules, and for the process of system-wide delegitimization of actors and behaviors. Those norms and rules, in turn, reinforce common identities that provide an important basis for international society.

International society: through thick and thin

This section outlines mechanisms and processes, consistent with both the pluralist and solidarist conceptions of international society, by which the discussed conditions and drives may develop and shape international society. The additive content of norms is one way society thickens over time. So too is the constitutive route through the establishment of common identity. Both regulative and constitutive norms and identities develop and diffuse due to encounters with structurally dissimilar actors that spatially do not conform and behaviorally transgress. Principles of rightful membership and conduct, the core elements of legitimacy, are reformulated or reaffirmed in response to the deviation in structures and behaviors that disrupts equilibrium states of the system.[126] This response to disequilibrium can be understood as fulfilling functional requirements, as well as shaping and reinforcing identities. Functional requirements include reinforcing position and reestablishing stable equilibria, as well as the ability to cope with uncertainty more generally through distinguishing categorizations and valuations. After outlining these mechanisms deductively in this chapter, the case studies will enable us to examine how they appeared to operate, or not operate, allowing for further refinement in building theory.

Uncertainty, partiality, and society. John Ikenberry and Charles Kupchan see the confluence of domestic conditions and international change spurring socialization, as hegemons "seek to adjust to a new constellation of international power and to consolidate ... dominant position."[127] While hegemony is one mode for such reordering, another

---

[126] Rightful membership and conduct are reformulated, according to Ian Clark, at "great moments of international reordering." Clark, *Legitimacy in International Society*, 8. While great moments are associated with establishing those pillars of legitimacy, the implication of this study is that less momentous, yet still significant, episodes also play a role.

[127] G. John Ikenberry and Charles A. Kupchan, "Socialization and Hegemonic Power," *International Organization* 44, no. 3 (Summer 1990): 292.

62   International society and the logics of anarchy

may involve the actions of dominant actors that find it necessary to attempt to ameliorate the effects of what they no longer control. Structural and material constraints, in this scenario, move the system away from the equilibrium state by spurring innovation and deviation, which may lead to the imposition of negative sanctions to attempt to restore order. Norms and rules may provide justification for negative sanctions, but this does not exhaust their utility or significance.

These circumstances may result in "norms of partiality," norms that in Robert Axelrod's terms are either "disguised as equalitarian" or "blatantly hierarchical."[128] These are norms "which help perpetuate a *status quo* of inequality," according to Edna Ullmann-Margalit, who discusses circumstances where a "favorably placed party" seeks to maintain its relative position, while the unfavorably placed party seeks to improve its position.[129] In this study's scenario dominant actors, in terms of relative power vis-à-vis irregular emergents, may seek to regularize interactions in the system within a range consistent with their security, while diminishing the advantages of abnormal behavior. Ullmann-Margalit explains that both coercion in the form of force and norms of partiality are available options. These norms perpetuate conditions of inequality and, in effect, help maintain or restore position by "putting restraints on possible courses of conduct, [and restricting] the number of alternatives open for action."[130]

Functionally equivalent norms of partiality may be preferred over force, which is considered more costly, potentially less effective, and discriminatory rather than universal in its application.[131] Such norms may also enable the use of force. As applied to this study, compliance is served by setting ranges of acceptable behaviors that restrict the ability of structurally deviant actors to force claims or simply survive. Establishing out-groups reinforces the elaboration of these norms. By identifying out-groups and associating them with certain proscribed activities, dominant actors can then expand the range of acceptable activities used against deviators, which we will capture here under the label "enforcement thesis."

While norms may develop in circumstances related to positional and instrumental requirements, they need not take this specific form. Karl-Dieter Opp identified what he termed the "relief thesis" as an explanation for the emergence of norms.[132] Norms emerge in conditions of insecurity

---

[128] Axelrod, *Complexity of Cooperation*, 63. Axelrod emphasizes that "many norms obeyed and even enforced by almost everyone actually serve the powerful."

[129] Edna Ullmann-Margalit, *The Emergence of Norms* (Oxford: Clarendon Press, 1997), 173.

[130] Ibid., 187.   [131] Ibid., 170–72.

[132] Karl-Dieter Opp, "The Emergence and Effects of Social Norms: A Confrontation of Some Hypotheses of Sociology and Economics," *KYKLOS: International Review for Social Sciences* 32, no. 4 (1979): 781–82.

International society: through thick and thin 63

in order to increase the ability to anticipate outcomes. Opp cites Ursula Brandt and Bernd Köhler: "social norms have essentially a relieving function. They are a collection of codified behaviors which make it easy for the individual to inform and orient himself ... their function is to reduce uncertainty and ignorance."[133] These norms need not be specific to conditions of dominance, nor be expressed in terms of partiality, though the ultimate effects may be the same. They may also have similar effects in reducing both physical and ontological insecurity.

Axelrod identifies a number of ways that norms become stronger over time; among them are dominance, law, metanorms, and membership.[134] Dominance allows norms to become useful to a few major actors, and by extension types of actors, that seek to maintain their predominance. In game theory a norm of partiality is understood as a circumstance "in which an equilibrium with uneven asymmetric payoffs is established as the norm of behavior for a group of people and passed on as the status quo from generation to generation through a process of socialization."[135] Norms against weaker actors present clear advantages to dominant actors and modes of organization, reinforcing homogeneity across systems over time. Even without these advantages, norms resulting from interactions may become diffused and internalized, not reliant on the direct effects of positive or negative sanctions or particular situations. Opp refers to this as the "transmission thesis."[136] In this sense the norms may be additive, reinforced through a number of modes over time.

We should expect support for norms that serve to enhance the regularity of interactions by lowering the likelihood and benefits of surprise to within manageable bounds. Surprise in this instance is understood as any deviation that controverts stable expectations. Norms serve to lessen uncertainty and reinforce expectations of behavior within ranges that, though perhaps threatening security from time to time, are consistent with survival and ontological security. Metanorms require members of the society to enforce existing norms, while membership confers advantages to those members conforming to those norms.[137] How membership is conferred and defined, however, may be distinct in circumstances of severe deviation from expected modes of interaction. To understand this relationship it is necessary to examine how identity formation reinforces

---

[133] Ibid., 781.
[134] Robert Axelrod, "An Evolutionary Approach to Norms," *American Political Science Review* 80, no. 4 (December 1986): 1095–111.
[135] Andrew Schotter and Barry Sopher, "Social Learning and Coordination Conventions in Inter-Generational Games: An Experimental Study," Working Paper, New York University, November 2001, 3.
[136] Opp, "Emergence and Effects," 780–81.
[137] Axelrod, "Evolutionary Approach," 1102–3; 1105.

64   International society and the logics of anarchy

and may shape the character of functionally driven responses. Central to those considerations is how the principles and practices of legitimacy are developed as fundamental elements of international society.[138]

Thickening society: identity, solidarity, and civilization. International society thickens due to the accumulation of norms, rules, and identities. Encounters with difference increase the salience of certain identities. These effects are independent of, but also facilitate and alter, the formulation of instrumental norms and rules. In the functional sense, corporate identity allows for more coherence internally and collective identity allows for greater coordination among actors. At the same time identity aids the instrumental needs for order, it also reinforces the cognitive ordering that provides the basis for heightened distinctions between "self" and "other" (corporate identity) and increased "we-feeling" (collective identity). These common identities in turn found membership in an international society that is not solely functional but rooted in affective association and disassociation.

Unsettled identities in periods of heightened uncertainty are not likely to result in nuanced portrayals of unfamiliar outsiders. Maximization, dehumanization, and homogenization of the "other" have the effect of reinforcing common identities as they meet the needs for ontological security. The severity of difference is further enhanced by associating other actors and behaviors as monstrous and beneath contempt, placing greater emphasis on legitimated actors' common humanity. Denial of rightful membership and declaring certain behaviors as departing from rightful conduct, the central components of legitimacy, are complemented by the severity of these distinctions. Deviations from expectations help shape representations and firm the exaggeration of identities. Inclusion requires following what Jeffrey Alexander termed "the most basic rule for acquiring sociological citizenship ... 'no surprises.'"[139] Enduring typification of those who transgress (in the form of ingrained identity rather than contingent categorization) may affect the formation of interests, shaping threats to such an extent that incorporation into

---

[138] Ian Clark rejects the "imposition" of positivist interpretations on the "social property" of the practice of legitimacy. The "realm of the practice of legitimacy," he argues, is complex and indeterminate, and cannot be subject to rationalist paradigms. Clark, *Legitimacy in International Society*, 254. This represents one of the divisions within the English School that affects its interactions with neorealism and other neo-utilitarian frameworks. From the perspective of the latter set, represented in this study, complexity and indeterminacy are conditions that need to be addressed, even if it comes at the cost of descriptive fidelity.

[139] Jeffrey C. Alexander, *Action and Its Environments: Toward a New Synthesis* (New York: Columbia University Press, 1988), 313.

society by means of socialization (accommodation to accepted practices) is not an option.

The effects of common identity on international society may be fleeting. As Wendt notes, homogeneity among actors may lead to a narcissism of small differences.[140] These differences may reduce in salience due to the emergence of and encounters with greater difference. But one must assume in an anarchic system other conflicts will emerge and the solidarity effect may be minimized. Common identity based on a common enemy is a fairly regular occurrence in international politics and may be short-lived beyond initial interactions. Continued interaction with structurally dissimilar actors and their associated behaviors may sustain the sharp distinctions between "self" and "other." Alternatively, these actors, perilously situated on the margins of the system (materially and normatively), may indeed eventually succumb to systemic constraints, begin to emulate to a degree that mitigates differences, or become familiar even in their difference due to sustained interactions. The solidarity rooted in common identity in such circumstances could be expected to be more situational than enduring.

Over the longer term, however, these identity-based and uncertainty-enhanced portrayals, "invidious distinctions" to use Andrew Linklater's phrase, may diffuse.[141] Just as norms of partiality may jump generations of actors and transcend systems, so too may "standards of civilization" provide bases for logics of appropriateness.[142] A standard of civilization, according to Gerrit Gong, is "an expression of the assumptions, tacit and explicit, used to distinguish those that belong to a particular society from those that do not."[143] Logics of appropriateness allow for the development of international society "as a community of rule followers and role players with distinctive sociocultural ties, cultural connections, intersubjective understandings, and senses of belonging."[144] Membership in civilization becomes indicative of rule following, and rule following allows for membership in civilization.[145] Sociocultural ties may enhance this process, but they are as much a product, as civilization itself becomes

[140] Wendt, *Social Theory*, 355–56.

[141] Andrew Linklater, "Norbert Elias, The 'Civilizing Process' and the Sociology of International Relations," *International Politics* 41, no. 1 (March 2004): 9.

[142] See James G. March and Johan P. Olsen, "The Logic of Appropriateness," ARENA Working Papers, ARENA Centre for European Studies, University of Oslo, September 2004.

[143] Gerrit W. Gong, *The Standard of "Civilization" in International Society* (Oxford: Clarendon Press, 1984), 3.

[144] James G. March and Johan P. Olsen, "The Institutional Dynamics of International Political Orders," *International Organization* 52, no. 4 (Autumn 1998): 952.

[145] For Gong, "the continuing, self-conscious definition of international standards of civilization is a natural and necessary consequence of interaction among politically

66   International society and the logics of anarchy

disaggregated from its religious and national roots. Enduring effects on solidarity are realized through the provision of in-groups and out-groups associated with certain behaviors and traits.

As the scope of international society expanded, this process allowed for a gradual replacement of the distinction between Christian and non-Christian nations, with one based on "civilized" and "uncivilized" nations.[146] A plurality of standards of civilization was gradually replaced with a distinctly European one.[147] The division between civilized and uncivilized was necessary in the development of positive international law in order to exclude effectively sovereign entities from membership in international society.[148] While there were juridical outcomes to this process, its core was the establishment of common identity. "What the 'civilized' world had in common," Gong writes, "became apparent only when juxtaposed with the 'barbarous' and 'savage' worlds."[149] These comparisons also allowed for the establishment of separate sets of rules, including lessened constraints concerning actions by "civilized" against "uncivilized" peoples.[150] This "barbarian option," according to Gong, no longer existed in the contemporary international system, with the effective worldwide acquiescence to European modes of order.[151] But the lack of a "barbarian option" assumes the absence of "barbarians," determined in this study to be an equilibrium point rather than an end state.

and culturally diverse states in search of common interests, rules, values, and institutions." Gerrit W. Gong, "Standards of Civilization Today," in *Globalization and Civilizations*, ed. Mehdi Mozaffari (New York: Routledge, 2002), 7. Focusing on standards of civilization that help demarcate selves and others helps bring its usage here more in line with a process-oriented, pluralistic characterization of civilization as "a complex arrangement of habits, principles, and historical traditions of action on which people may draw in a variety of ways." See Patrick T. Jackson, "How to Think about Civilizations," in *Civilizations in World Politics: Plural and Pluralist Perspectives*, ed. Peter J. Katzenstein (London and New York: Routledge, 2010), 184.

[146] See Bernard V.A. Röling, *International Law in an Expanded World* (Amsterdam: Djambatan, 1960), 18–19; 27.

[147] Gong, *The Standard of "Civilization" in International Society*, 22–23. See also Hedley Bull, "The Emergence of a Universal International Society," in *The Expansion of International Society*, ed. Hedley Bull and Adam Watson (Oxford: Clarendon Press, 1984), 117–26; and David P. Fidler, "The Return of the Standard of Civilization," *Chicago Journal of International Law* 2 (2001): 140–41.

[148] Antony Anghie, *Imperialism, Sovereignty, and the Making of International Law* (Cambridge: Cambridge University Press, 2004), 56–59. See also Georg Schwarzenberger, "The Standard of Civilisation in International Law," *Current Legal Problems* 17 (1955): 212–34.

[149] Gong, *The Standard of "Civilization" in International Society*, 36.

[150] On considerations of the legitimacy of brutality by Western powers acting outside of their own areas, see Gil Merom, *How Democracies Lose Small Wars: State, Society, and the Failures of France in Algeria, Israel in Lebanon, and the United States in Vietnam* (Cambridge: Cambridge University Press, 2003), 73.

[151] Gong, *The Standard of "Civilization" in International Society*, 22–23.

Standards of civilization evolved from implicit assumptions about civilized behavior, derived from those "who wrestled with the natures of their own and foreign civilizations according to the cultural perceptions of their times."[152] These assessments included those made through encounters with dissimilar actors, contributing to the shaping of corporate and collective identities. In one mode of transference, enduring images of "evil others" help shape future identity formation by providing symbolic referents, facilitating in-group inclusion and out-group exclusion, and associating certain behavioral standards with in-group membership. Barbarity derives its normative import not only from objective outcomes but from cumulative historical content. Historical referents may be central components in the process of common identity formation. Earlier "others" are useful in transforming contemporary enemies into "others" themselves. The Germans in the First World War were not just an implacable enemy but "Huns." Delegitimization serves a functional role in marginalizing and allowing severe sanctions, as well as contributing to identity formation. Symbols and representations of "others" become important inputs for self-assessment. Savagery describes the quality of one kind of violence, while other types may be considered necessary or even virtuous. Common identity is heightened through adherence to these standards, and these effects may be cumulative in terms of expanding international society across space and time.

No surprises!: from international system to society

This study does not claim to explain system change or the development of international society as a whole. It seeks to explain the origins of some of the elements of international society in isolated systems, how these were spurred and shaped by episodes of system change, and how these societal outcomes diffused. Increased complementarity between neorealism and the English School does not require agreement over the centrality of international society, but presents the opportunity to benefit from the theoretical and empirical advances in each tradition, with the potential of conferring benefits to constructivist approaches as well.

Mechanisms and processes that help explain certain episodes of system change were outlined in a previous section. That part of the theory is based on a body of more developed theories this study is trying to expand and refine, while the theory linking those system changes with societal outcomes is more inchoate. Accordingly, while we have a greater expectation that the systemic mechanisms and processes outlined earlier (in

---

[152] Ibid., 35–36; xii.

68   International society and the logics of anarchy

Table 1.3 *System change to international society*

Functional adaptation	Identity formation
Relief Thesis: Interaction with irregular actors generates instrumental norms and rules that are intended to mitigate the effects of intensified or more pervasive uncertainty.	Collective Identity–Homogeneity: Interaction with irregular actors spurs collective identity formation that increases the salience of existing identities rooted in common structural properties (modes of organization and interaction).
Transmission Thesis: Regulative norms and rules associated with particular actors or their modes of behavior become generalized and applied to other actors, and through cumulation may take the form of customary or codified law.	Collective Identity–Cultural Bonds: Interaction with irregular actors spurs collective identity formation that increases the salience of existing identities rooted in common cultural bonds (common historical experience or shared values).
Enforcement Thesis: Categorization and valuation of actors allows for enforcement of norms that exceeds established norms for enforcement.	"Others": Corporate identity formation establishes a homogenized "other."
Norms of Partiality: Norms diffuse and become established as generalized, hierarchical norms of partiality.	"Evil Others": "Others" are characterized in terms of subhuman constitutions and evil natures.
Legitimation: Legitimacy is determined based on common identity (collective and corporate) and adherence to norms establishing rightful membership and conduct in international society.	
Standards of Civilization: Common identity based on adherence to accepted modes of behavior becomes established over the long term as standards of civilization, establishing and reinforcing rightful membership and conduct.	

Table 1.2) will be observed, the international societal elements of the theory will benefit most from deep engagement with the cases, further refining and developing the theory. Of particular interest for the international societal propositions is determining how functional and identity-based forces interrelate. The propositions above summarize the mechanisms and processes presented in the discussion concerning the development of international society. (See Table 1.3.) They are not intended as fully testable hypotheses but rather as reference points and potential building blocks for synthesis and theory building. Close examination of the case studies will allow for further refinement of our understanding of how these mechanisms and processes operate, if they are present at all, and how they may interact. We do not necessarily expect each type of norm or identity formation element to obtain in each case, but through multiple observations we can refine our

From international system to society   69

understanding of how international society is spurred through interactions with unfamiliar actors.

The requirements for coping with uncertainty (categorization and discrimination) are similar and may be indistinguishable from those concerning identity formation. Greater comprehension of how the regularity and intensity of interactions make international society a natural product rather than an ephemeral byproduct of anarchy requires investigation of both sets of processes, their origins, and interactions.[153] In so doing, uncertainty maintains its pride of place in this study, yet a fuller appreciation of uncertainty supports an understanding of international societal inputs and outcomes that are not wholly reducible to functional responses to anarchic conditions. Delving into a range of contexts where uncertainty was amplified by actors that did not comport to routine processes of emulation and socialization will aid in untangling and better defining the relationships between international society and the logics of anarchy.

---

[153] See Buzan, "From International System," 327; 334.

2 Confusion in the hearts of men
The Nizari Ismailis and the Assassin legends

> Although the affairs of kingdoms and nations, like the revolutions of day and night, are generally repeated in countless and continued successions, we, nevertheless, in our survey of the destinies of the human race, encounter single great important events, which, fertilizing like springs, or devastating like volcanoes, interrupt the uniform wilderness of history.
>
> —Joseph von Hammer-Purgstall, *History of the Assassins*

> Let those who shall come after this age and era know the extent of the mischief they wrought and the confusion they cast into the hearts of men.
>
> —'Ata-Malik Juvayni

Introduction

"In the midst of states held together by direct military power," one scholar observed, the Nizari Ismailis "formed a challenging exception."[1] The Nizari Ismailis, more popularly known as the Assassins, have gained some notice in the study of terrorism, but not in the systematic study of international relations. The group also presents a challenging exception within our understanding of how actors compose and comport themselves in international systems. The emergence and persistence of this actor were even more unlikely given its position within the Islamic world. Historian Bernard Lewis labeled the Nizari Ismailis a "heresy within a heresy," but this may understate their marginal position. The Nizari Ismailis were a sect of a sect of a sect, and this tenuousness in the community of believers was matched by their vulnerability in a system marked by hostile and powerful enemies. The survival strategies they innovated and the means they employed would have an impact not only on that system but well after their routing by the Mongols in 1256.

[1] Marshall G.S. Hodgson, "The Isma'ili State," in *The Cambridge History of Iran, Vol. 5, The Saljuq and Mongol Periods*, ed. John A. Boyle (Cambridge: Cambridge University Press, 1968), 422.

70

Introduction 71

The challenge posed by the Nizaris, Lewis argues, was "regarded as a profound threat to the existing order," and they had "no parallel" in their application of revolutionary violence.[2] "The Nizari Isma'ilis were not, then, a great territorial power...." David Morgan writes, "[b]ut the challenge they presented to the established Sunni order in society was out of all proportion to their numbers or the area they directly controlled." This impact, Morgan contends, was due in large part to "their idiosyncratic approach to warfare."[3] The means they employed – including the systematic use of targeted killing that would eventually be associated with the pejorative label attached to them, "*Hashishin*," later "Assassins" – created conditions of uncertainty that almost certainly magnified the threat they posed. This refraction itself serves to highlight the effects that irregular forms of warfare have on enhancing ontological as well as physical insecurity. The threat to the Sunni order Morgan refers to was not merely to those Sunnis who constituted that order, but to the ordering of Sunnis, Shia, and Muslims in general. Unorthodox threats to human bodies enhanced the threat to the body politic, as defined by the Sunni and Shia orthodoxy, provoking the use of force and leading to the alteration of identity.

In addition to contemporary distortions, imagination, myth, and legend further challenge the accurate recording of their history. The Nizaris' fractious development has been viewed primarily through prisms constructed by their enemies: first the hostility of the Islamic world, then the lenses of crusader fantasists and medieval chroniclers, and then a Europe not blessed with a learned appreciation of foreign cultures. The "intertextual parasitism," as one observer put it, made these legends take on the appearance of fact.[4] Fortunately, careful scholarship has corrected the compounded errors of previous centuries, though these revisions have yet to be thoroughly absorbed into the terrorism studies literature.

The beginning sections of this chapter describe the historical setting. This includes the system comprised of the Abbasid successor states and later – though only after the Nizaris' initial formation and development of their modes and means – their extension into the more plural system populated by Crusader states and orders in Syria. The decline of the Fatimid Empire spurred its former agents to act autonomously while their constrained circumstances, or opportunity structure, made their challenge to the established order stray from the norm. Analysis

---

[2] Bernard Lewis, *The Assassins: A Radical Sect in Islam* (New York: Oxford University Press, 1967), 139.

[3] David O. Morgan, *Medieval Persia, 1040–1797* (London: Longman, 1988), 45.

[4] Babak Nahid, "Review of Farhad Daftary, *The Assassin Legends*," accessed January 2, 2015, http://ismaili.net/Source/fd0328d.html.

72   The Nizari Ismailis and the Assassin legends

explaining the significance of the Nizaris is followed by a description of the reception and diffusion of the Assassin legends that emerged from encounters with their contemporaries. That discussion will provide context for assessing their effects on elements of international society, both in their own time and space and beyond, as opponents adapted to threats to physical and ontological security. Those outcomes and their transmission through interaction in the Levant transformed the political and identity challenges into enduring symbols that provided reference points for the firming of civilization well after their demise.

The system: Abbasid successor states

The system where the Nizaris originated resulted from the stunning expansion of Islam and the consolidation of a number of centralized states with contending claims for rightful leadership of the Muslim world. The starting point for this is the decline of the Abbasid Caliphate, which had extended from India to North Africa, and the emergence of successor states afterward. The Abbasid Caliphate had succeeded the Umayyad Caliphate as the center of Islamic power in 750 CE.[5] The Abbasids had been aided in their ascent by the Shia, with whom they had a common cause in revolt. They soon turned against the Shia who then spread throughout the empire, establishing a foothold in the Maghreb. The concentration of Shia power in North Africa and the decline of the Abbasids in the central Islamic lands would set the stage for a system of successor states.

The reasons for the decline of the Abbasids and the disintegration of the empire are too numerous to catalog, but include the reliance on military slave labor and the social disruptions it caused.[6] Local resistance to weakening central rule from Baghdad resulted in the devolution of power to provincial regimes including the Daylamites and Hamdanids. The recently converted Shia peoples of the mountainous Zagros region and northern provinces of Iran (Gilan and Daylam) filled the power vacuum, and later in the form of the Buyid Confederation they would rule much of Mesopotamia and Iran.[7] This rule by the Twelver Shia has

[5] Dates for dynastic rule vary across sources. Those listed here are drawn primarily from Ira M. Lapidus, *A History of Islamic Societies*, 2nd ed. (Cambridge: Cambridge University Press, 2002).

[6] See Ibid., 104–5; 111; and Hugh Kennedy, *The Prophet and the Age of the Caliphates: The Islamic Near East from the Sixth to Eleventh Century*, 2nd ed. (Harlow: Pearson Longman, 2004; 1986), 198–209.

[7] Lapidus, *History of Islamic Societies*, 108. See also Tilman Nagel, "Buyids," *Encyclopaedia Iranica* Online Edition (hereafter EIr), December 15, 1990, www.iranica.com/articles/buyids.

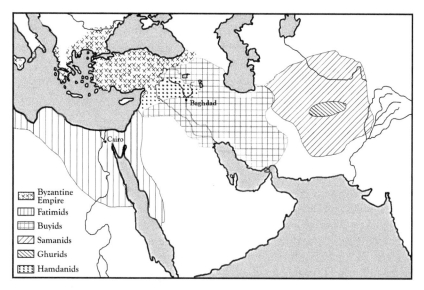

Map 2.1 Abbasid successor states (late tenth century CE)
Source: Ira Lapidus, *A History of Islamic Societies* (Cambridge University Press, 2002)

been labeled the "Iranian Intermezzo" and represents a little over a century of Iranian rule between the periods of Arab and Seljuk Turk domination.[8] While supplanting Abbasid rule, the Buyids maintained caliphs as nominal heads of state to bolster their legitimacy, a pattern later repeated with the advent of Seljuk rule.[9]

To the east, inner Asia around present-day Afghanistan, the Samanids ruled for over a century (875–999) until they were overtaken by the Ghaznavids, former slave warriors who in the early eleventh century pushed the Buyids back to the area of modern Iraq and southwestern Iran.[10] To the west, the Umayyad Emirate emerged from the remnants of that dynasty to rule over southern Spain and North Africa.[11] The latter area was contested with the expanding reach of the Shia Fatimids, who

---

[8] Clifford E. Bosworth, "Minorsky, Vladimir Fed'orovich (1877–1966)," EIr, July 20, 2004, www.iranica.com/articles/minorsky-vladimir.

[9] Claude Cahen, "Buwayhids or Buyids," *Encyclopaedia of Islam Online*, ed. P. Bearman, et al., Brill Online, 2006 (hereafter EIs); Lapidus, *History of Islamic Societies*, 116.

[10] On the Ghaznavids, see Clifford E. Bosworth, "The Early Ghaznavids," in *The Cambridge History of Iran, Vol. 4, The Period from the Arab Invasion to the Saljuqs*, ed. R.N. Frye (Cambridge: Cambridge University Press, 1975), 162–98.

[11] See Richard Fletcher, *Moorish Spain* (Berkeley and Los Angeles: University of California Press, 1993), 53–79.

74   The Nizari Ismailis and the Assassin legends

themselves struggled not only with the Abbasids and their Seljuk successors, but also with the Byzantine Empire. Byzantine pressure on Syria was at first checked by the Hamdanids, whose power center was around Mosul and Syria. Pressure from the Byzantines led the Hamdanids to convert to Shia Islam and seek protection from the Fatimids, who in due course absorbed them into their burgeoning empire.

Dominant actors: Fatimids and Seljuks

Out of this competition, two powers emerged in a pitched rivalry over material and sacral dominance. The Fatimids and Seljuks continued the contest following the waning of the Abbasids and the interim ascendancy of Shia power. The Fatimids have their roots in the Ismaili movement. The Ismailis accepted the succession from Muhammad through the sixth imam, Ja'far al-Sadiq. From there, a split emerged over Ja'far's successor with one group following the late Ismail, breaking away from what became known as Twelver Shi'ism.[12] They considered Ismail, or his son Muhammad, to be the last true imam.[13] Followers dispersed throughout the Islamic world and spread their doctrines through a missionary network called the *da'wa*.[14] The Fatimids drew their name from their claimed succession through Fatima, daughter of Muhammad. From their base in North Africa (present-day Tunisia), through both missionary- and military-based expansion, the Fatimids established a rival caliphate in 909 and conquered Egypt in 969.[15]

The Fatimid Empire rose in military power and through its missionary network propagated its claim to rule the Islamic world.[16] Fatimid grand strategy sought dominance of the western Mediterranean and its eventual control over the eastern part, through military expansion, proselytization,

---

[12] An overview of the Ismaili schism is provided in John J. Saunders, *A History of Medieval Islam* (New York: Barnes & Noble, 1965), 125–40. The broad sweep of Ismaili history is treated in Farhad Daftary, *The Isma'ilis: Their History and Doctrines* (Cambridge: Cambridge University Press, 1990).

[13] Kennedy, *Prophet and the Age of the Caliphates*, 285. The office of imam in Shia Islam concerns the "supreme leadership" of the *Umma* (community of believers) after the death of the Prophet.

[14] On the origins of the Ismaili-Fatimid da'wa, see P.J. Vatikiotis, "The Syncretic Origins of the Fatimid Da'wa," *Islamic Culture* 28, no. 4 (1954): 475–91.

[15] These events are covered in detail in Michael Brett, "The Fatimid Revolution (861–973) and Its Aftermath in North Africa," in *The Cambridge History of Africa, Vol. 2, c. 500 B.C. to A.D. 1050*, ed. John D. Fage (Cambridge: Cambridge University Press, 1978), 589–636.

[16] See Paula Sanders, "The Fatimid State, 969–1171," in *The Cambridge History of Egypt, Vol. 1, Islamic Egypt, 640–1517*, ed. Cary F. Petry (Cambridge: Cambridge University Press, 1998), 151–74.

Dominant actors: Fatimids and Seljuks

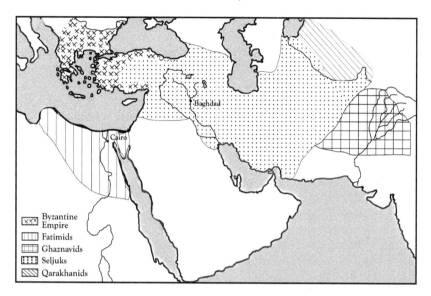

Map 2.2 Seljuk Empire (late eleventh century CE)
Source: Ira Lapidus, *A History of Islamic Societies* (Cambridge University Press, 2002)

and attempted domination of trade routes.[17] The Fatimids spread their influence and rule throughout North Africa, tenuously in Syria, and in the Mediterranean through its naval power.[18] Their expansion brought them into contact, and often conflict, with a number of powers: the Umayyads, Byzantines, and Nubians, among others.[19] A cold peace, and never-consummated alliance, kept the Fatimids and Buyids (rival claimants of Shia ascendancy) from either clashing or combining forces against common rivals.[20] The expansion peaked with the proclamation of the Fatimid caliph, by a Turkish general, in Mosul and then Baghdad. This brief period of Ismaili control (1057–1059) was ended by their ejection by the Seljuks.

The Seljuks were Turkic peoples who had converted to Sunni Islam, in part due to military service by these nomadic warriors as Islam spread into

---

[17] Bernard Lewis, "An Interpretation of Fatimid History," *Colloque internationale sur L'histoire du Caire (1969)* (Cairo, 1972), 291–92.

[18] On Fatimid naval power and its Mediterranean rivalries, see Yaacov Lev, "The Fatimid Navy, Byzantium, and the Mediterranean Sea, 909–1036," *Byzantion* 54 (1984): 220–52.

[19] Concerning Fatimid relations with the Byzantines, see Abbas Hamdani, "Byzantine–Fatimid Relations before the Battle of Manzikert," *Byzantine Studies* 1, no. 2 (1974): 169–79.

[20] See Shainool Jiwa, "Fatimid–Buyid Diplomacy during the Reign of Al-'Aziz Billah," *Journal of Islamic Studies* 3, no. 1 (January 1992): 57–71.

76   The Nizari Ismailis and the Assassin legends

Central Asia. They expanded into a Persia occupied by the remnants of Abbasid power, ejecting the Buyids and Ghaznavids. Toghril Beg, the founder of the Seljuk dynasty, marched on Baghdad in 1055. The arrival of a Sunni power resulted in the restoration of the Abbasid caliphs, but the Seljuks gave them little more authority than the Buyids did.[21] The Seljuks' legitimacy was rooted in their role as deliverers of the Abbasid Caliphate, but they were also seen as interlopers by local populations and religious authorities. The Seljuks not only took control over a vast territory, they also took up the cause of Sunni resistance to the Fatimids. The extent of Seljuk control varied across the empire, with conditions of direct and indirect (particularly around the Caspian area) control.[22]

Under the successors of Toghril Beg, Alp Arslan (r. 1063–1072) and Malik Shah (r. 1072–1092), the empire expanded. Their vizier, Nizam al-Mulk, was instrumental in the construction and expansion of the empire.[23] Beneficiaries of reforms during this period included the army, which enjoyed a more stable revenue base and consisted of both standing forces and mercenaries from a variety of nations. The powerful army advanced westward, coming into conflict with the Byzantines, culminating in the Battle of Manzikert (1071), which hastened the decline of the Byzantine Empire and helped usher in the Crusades.[24] The Seljuk-ruled domains and the Fatimid Empire would struggle for control over Syria. Their contest was, on the surface at least, the dominant land power versus the dominant sea power. It would also take place, though, on a different plane as the Fatimids attempted to spread their influence and undermine Abbasid and Seljuk control.

Fatimid propaganda and decline

As the Fatimids conquered Egypt they established their capital in what they named al-Qahira (Cairo).[25] Their growth into a great power was

---

[21] The division between caliph and sultan, including their sources of authority, was a prominent topic in Islamic jurisprudence. See Clifford E. Bosworth, "The Political and Dynastic History of the Iranian World (A.D. 1000–1217)," in *Cambridge History of Iran, Vol. 5*, 48.

[22] See Morgan, *Medieval Persia*, 34–37; and Richard Bulliet, "Local Politics in Eastern Iran under the Ghaznavids and Seljuks," *Iranian Studies* 11, nos. 1–4 (1978): 35–56.

[23] See Harold Bowen, "Nizam al-Mulk," EIs; and Antony Black, *The History of Islamic Political Thought: From the Prophet to the Present* (New York: Routledge, 2001), 90–96.

[24] The expansion of the Seljuk Turks into the areas of Byzantine and Fatimid control is covered in Claude Cahen, "The Turkish Invasion: The Selchukids," in *A History of the Crusades, Vol. I, The First Hundred Years*, ed. Kenneth M. Setton and Marshall W. Baldwin (Philadelphia: University of Pennsylvania Press, 1955), 135–76.

[25] Paul E. Walker, "The Ismaili Da'wa and the Fatimid Caliphate," in *Cambridge History of Egypt*, 141.

Fatimid propaganda and decline 77

achieved through conquest, but also enabled through the da'wa. This network of missionaries consisted of *da'is* or "summoners," calling followers to the Ismaili faith and advancing the claim to the imamate. The development and use of the da'is, combined with the Fatimids' later decline (systemic change), ultimately resulted in system change: change of the composition of the system and its constituents. The da'wa is referred to as being a missionary and propaganda organization, serving those complementary purposes.[26] Da'is have been described as "religio-political agents," reflecting their dual roles as proselytizers and propagandists.[27] Conversion efforts focused on elites with the aim to create a class that could be the basis for future rule.[28] By the end of the ninth century the Ismaili da'wa had established cells throughout the Islamic lands, including modern-day Iraq, Iran, Syria, Bahrain, Yemen, and the Maghreb.[29] They had an especially strong presence in Iraq, Yemen, and North Africa, the latter developing into the Fatimid state.

The Ismaili da'wa gave way to the Fatimid da'wa as the network became based in Cairo and increasingly took on the cause of expanding Fatimid influence. The Fatimid da'wa functioned as a source for expanding political legitimacy and religious authority: the former reinforcing Fatimid political claims and the latter advancing the doctrinal interpretations of the Ismailis. Religious doctrine included adherence to an inner, esoteric meaning of the Quran, known as *batin*, in addition to the outward, exoteric meaning, or *zahir*.[30] The effectiveness and extent of this network are attested by the preoccupation of Seljuk authorities to discredit what they termed *Batiniyya* (Batinis or Batinites).[31] Much of the *Siyasat-Nama*, Nizam al-Mulk's mirror of princes text, is devoted to chronicling this deviation from Sunni and Shia orthodoxy, which was seen as the germ of expanding rebellion against Abbasid and Seljuk

---

[26] Marius Canard, "Da'wa," EIs. See also S.M. Stern, "Cairo as the Centre of the Ismaili Movement," in Stern, *Studies in Early Ismailism* (Jerusalem: Magnes Press, 1983), 234–56. Farouk Mitha, however, downplays the political facet, highlighting the theological and philosophical depths of the message of the da'wa, concluding that it would be "rather reductive, if not downright misleading, to define the Fatimid da'wa as a propaganda organization." Farouk Mitha, *Al-Ghazali and the Ismailis: A Debate on Reason and Authority in Medieval Islam* (London: I.B. Tauris, 2001), 21.

[27] Abbas Hamdani, "Evolution of the Organisational Structure of the Fatimi Da'wah," in *Arabian Studies*, III, ed. Robert B. Serjeant and Robin L. Bidwell (London: C. Hurst & Company, 1976), 86.

[28] Ibid., 97. [29] Walker, "Ismaili Da'wa," 124. [30] Daftary, *The Isma'ilis*, 86.

[31] On the use of Batiniyya and other epithets, see Shakib Saleh, "The Use of Batini, Fida'i, and Hashishi," *Studia Islamica* 82, no. 2 (October 1995): 35–43. For a brief overview of the Seljuk response to the spread of Ismaili influence, see Antonio Jurado Aceituno, "The Seljuk Jihad against Fatimid Shi'ism: An Observation on the Sunni Renewal," *Archiv orientální* 66 (1998): 173–78.

78   The Nizari Ismailis and the Assassin legends

authority.[32] Much of the success in propagating this doctrine, though not ultimately in expanding Fatimid rule, came from the organization and effectiveness of its agents. These individuals were heavily vetted, forced to take strict vows, and had educational credentials that would allow them to spread their faith effectively.[33] Beyond this allegiance, though, the da'is were afforded a great deal of autonomy in how they advanced their political and religious mission.[34]

The Fatimid Empire had its high point in its brief excursion into Baghdad but soon foundered under the weight of external and internal pressures. Externally, the Fatimids struggled with rivals in the Christian world (the Crusades and revived Byzantine power), while suffering losses in Syria to the Seljuks.[35] Internally, according to Lewis, "factional strife led the government ... into a vicious circle of disorder and tyranny, [and] economic upheavals culminated in a series of disastrous famines."[36] Contributing to this cycle was a patronage network that could no longer be supported due to declining Fatimid fortunes. Over time this would give rise to competing patronage networks and a transfer of power from the caliph to military officials.[37] This condition hit its height during the reign of al-Mustansir, whose succession triggered another split in the Ismaili movement. While there was some stabilization, the Fatimids had suffered a severe decline vis-à-vis their Seljuk rivals.[38]

The decline of Fatimid central power contrasted with the success of the da'is' expansion in Persia. One of these da'is, Ibn Attash, was in direct contact with Cairo and controlled their activities in much of Persia, but is best known for discovering Hassan-i Sabbah.[39] Hassan, born in Qomm, at one point considered Ismailism heretical, but was won over and

---

[32] See Hubert Darke, trans., *The Book of Government or Rules for Kings: The Siyasat-nama or Siyar al-Muluk of Nizam Al-Mulk* (London: Routledge, 1960), 213–38.

[33] Farhad Daftary, "The Ismaili *Da'wa* Outside the Fatimid *Dawla*," in *L'Égypt Fatimide: son art et son histoire*, ed. Marianne Barrucand (Paris: Presses de l'Université de Paris-Sorbonne, 1999), 31.

[34] See Daftary, *The Isma'ilis*, 230–31.

[35] Michael Brett, "Abbasids, Fatimids, and Seljuks," in *The New Cambridge Medieval History, Vol. IV, c. 1024–1198, Part I*, ed. David E. Luscombe and John Riley-Smith (Cambridge: Cambridge University Press, 2004), 698–703; and Lewis, "Interpretation of Fatimid History," 293.

[36] Lewis, "Interpretation of Fatimid History," 293. On the factors underlying Fatimid decline, see Paul E. Walker, *Exploring an Islamic Empire: Fatimid History and Its Sources* (London: I.B. Tauris, Institute of Ismaili Studies, 2002), 56–64. For the role of the army in the decline, see Yaacov Lev, "Army, Regime, and Society in Fatimid Egypt, 358–487/968–1094," *International Journal of Middle East Studies* 19, no. 3 (August 1987): 337–65.

[37] Sanders, "Fatimid State," 171–72.

[38] Farhad Daftary, "Hassan-i Sabbah and the Origins of the Nizari Ismaili Movement," in *Medieval Ismaili History and Thought*, ed. Daftary (Cambridge: Cambridge University Press, 1996), 186.

[39] Daftary, *The Isma'ilis*, 336–67.

Alamut and the "new preaching"   79

initiated by the daʻis.[40] Hassan would spend three years in Cairo, though not much is known of his stay there. From there he returned to Persia, traveled extensively there for nine years taking account of the conditions throughout the Seljuk domains. Eventually, Hassan would be appointed the daʻi of Daylam. The bad fortunes of the Fatimids, according the Farhad Daftary, did not go unnoticed by the eastern Ismailis. "Consequently," Daftary writes, "they did not expect to rely on continued central leadership of the daʻwa headquarters in Cairo," though they were not yet ready to assert their independence from the regime.[41] Daftary surmises that Hassan's time in Cairo would have provided him with a clear picture of Fatimid decline.[42]

The ultimate break was triggered by the support of the eastern Ismailis for Nizar as successor over his brother al-Musta'li, who attained rule after the death of their father al-Mustansir in 1094.[43] The claim of Nizar as rightful heir would be held by the eastern, Persian branch, which would become the Nizari Ismailis. While the succession issue completed the fissure, the independence of the movement had been increasing steadily as the Nizaris developed their own bases of support and strategic goals.[44] This group would forward their doctrine, posing a severe challenge to the Sunni orthodoxy and fomenting armed rebellion against Seljuk rule.

Alamut and the "new preaching"

The success of the Ismaili-Fatimid daʻwa in Persia provided a base of support for the newly independent Nizari sect. The Nizari branch, despite the strictness of its doctrines, attracted both domestic and foreign support.[45] The break with the declining Fatimid state coincided with the initiation of an armed revolt against Seljuk rule. While networks of supporters had been established in cities, the revolt would be centered in the mountainous region of Daylam, outside of the Seljuk's direct rule. Hassan and his supporters expanded their influence and infiltrated a Daylami fortress called Alamut.[46] In Lewis's words, Hassan was interested in finding a secure base of operations, "not a clandestine tryst in a city, in constant danger of discovery and disruption, but a remote and inaccessible stronghold, from which he could with impunity direct his war

---

[40] Ibid., 336.   [41] Ibid., 334.   [42] Daftary, "Hassan-i Sabbah," 186–87.

[43] H.A.R. Gibb, "Nizar b. al-Mustansir," EIs.

[44] Marshall G.S. Hodgson, *The Secret Order of Assassins: The Struggle of the Early Nizari Ismaʻilis against the Islamic World* (Philadelphia: University of Pennsylvania Press, 2005; 1955), 62–71.

[45] Ibid., 72.

[46] For a comprehensive examination of Nizari strongholds in Iran and Syria, see Peter Willey, *Eagle's Nest: Ismaili Castles in Iran and Syria* (London: I.B. Tauris, 2005).

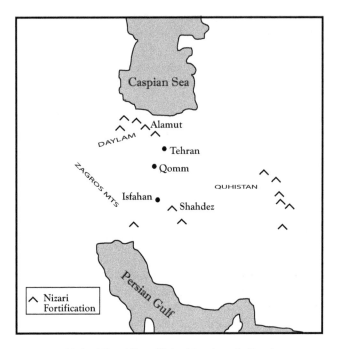

Map 2.3 Major Nizari Ismaili fortifications in Persia
Sources: Peter Willey, *Eagle's Nest: Ismaili Castles in Iran and Syria* (I.B. Tauris, 2005) and Institute of Ismaili Studies (London)

against the Seljuk Empire."[47] Accessible only through a single narrow road, Alamut reportedly had never been taken by force.[48] Through a combination of persistence and guile – including disguise and conversion from within – Alamut was seized in 1090. It would not be destroyed for over one hundred and fifty years, as the Mongols swept through the Islamic lands.

Alamut became the base for open revolt, though one possessing clandestine elements. That base would be followed by a number of other remote fortresses spread throughout the Seljuk realm. These efforts were enhanced due to popular resentment of Turkish rule.[49] The atomized

[47] Lewis, *The Assassins*, 42.
[48] The isolation of Alamut, the "principal reason" it was chosen by Hassan, is discussed in Willey, *Eagle's Nest*, 103.
[49] See W. Montgomery Watt, *Muslim Intellectual: A Study of Al-Ghazali* (Edinburgh: Edinburgh University Press, 1963), 18–19. Daftary points to Iranian nationalism playing a part. Farhad Daftary, "The Isma'ilis and the Crusaders: History and Myth," in *The Crusades and the Military Orders: Expanding the Frontiers of Medieval Latin Christianity*, ed.

Alamut and the "new preaching"

nature of this rule allowed for the defection of some local rulers, and a strategy of piecemeal acquisition of territory and loyalty that proceeded, in Marshall Hodgson's words, "locality by locality, fort by fort."[50] Forbiddingly carved out of pure rock, Alamut would come to provide protection, and later serve as a site for myths associated with Nizari activities. The real activities included a combination of targeted violence and renewed conversion that would provide the means for a newly invigorated Ismaili movement. These efforts aimed at expanding Nizari power and doctrine, the "new preaching," through vigorous missionary work paired with violence against its enemies, each dimension vexing Seljuk authorities and the broader Muslim community.

The goals of the Nizari Ismailis are not clear, and according to Hodgson, "[i]t is easier to tell what they opposed than whether they had any very concrete plans."[51] Maximally, their aims included the rightful claim to the imamate encompassing authority over the Muslim world. With the death of Nizar, and the lack of an heir, there were affirmations of a hidden imam at Alamut. While not claiming to be the imam, Hassan led the Nizari movement as its chief, *hujja*, or supreme central leader and representative of the absent imam.[52] Minimally, according to one observer, their goals were to "realize their dream of a society on the margin of the Muslim world."[53]

Wherever their goals were on that spectrum, from universal rule to mere autonomy and survival, their existence and actions brought them into direct conflict with Seljuk authorities and the Sunni religious establishment. Now without their Fatimid foundation, the Nizaris would face the severe challenge of taking on the militarily far superior Seljuks. In the early phases of the revolt, the presence of the network of da'is allowed for actions in diverse locations. This diffusion of influence would be matched by a similarly diffuse organizational structure. According to Hodgson, "the revolt soon showed a characteristic overall pattern precisely in its coordinated decentralization."[54] With its cells in cities and more secure remote bases, the

---

Zsolt Hunyadi and József Laszlovszky (Budapest: Central European University, 2001), 23–24. Russian anthropologist Vasily Bartold previously diminished the nationalist cast, describing the conflict in socio-economic terms of fortified castles versus more developed towns. Vasily Bartold, *Mussulman Culture*, trans. Shahid Suhrawardy (Philadelphia: Porcupine Press, 1977; 1934), 100–1.

[50] Hodgson, "Isma'ili State," 440.   [51] Ibid., 427.

[52] Hodgson, *Secret Order*, 66–68. Farhad Daftary, *The Assassin Legends: Myths of the Isma'ilis* (London: I.B. Tauris, 1994), 33.

[53] B. Hourcade, "Alamut," EIr, last updated July 29, 2011, www.iranica.com/articles/alamut-valley-alborz-northeast-of-qazvin-.

[54] Hodgson, "Isma'ili State," 439.

82   The Nizari Ismailis and the Assassin legends

movement could both generate armed force and continue to expand its influence. While innovative, this diffuse structure would also leave them vulnerable to Seljuk countermeasures.

From expansion to survival: Seljuk response and Nizari means

The Seljuk response to the Nizari Ismailis would range from halting and ineffective to concentrated and severe. At first their approach was to delegate responsibility to local rulers to control the problem. When that proved ineffective, Malik Shah sent forces to attack the growing threat at the source, in both Quhistan and Alamut.[55] These expeditions were not successful and were interrupted by the deaths of both Malik Shah and Nizam al-Mulk. Nizam al-Mulk's killing was attributed to the Nizaris, though both of these deaths have also been tied to rivals within the court.[56] Regardless, the power vacuum that developed relieved pressure on the nascent Nizari movement. More fortresses mostly in mountainous territories were seized by the Nizaris in scattered areas of the realm, leaving the Sunnis, in Hodgson's words, "baffled and terrified."[57]

During this period the Nizaris vied with local leaders, suffering persecution and massacres, and raided Sunni caravans to supplement their indigenous resource base.[58] The Nizaris employed targeted killings against rival rulers. This is not a method they invented, clearly, but their application would forever associate them with it. Prior to receiving its name, assassination had been a prominent element in the early history of Islam (most notably the killings of the caliphs Uthman and Ali), and it was not at all rare among rival petty rulers throughout the Seljuk domain.[59] The Nizari practice included the employment of *fida'is*, dedicated personnel who would infiltrate (often through disguise and false identity) and kill individuals, most often at the cost of their own lives.[60] The myths associated with these daring, despised acts would propagate the name Assassin and its variants, a label whose true origins and meaning would be lost in later legends. According to Daftary, the Nizaris were neither the first nor the last to use this method, "but they did assign a

---

[55] Hodgson, *Secret Order*, 74.
[56] See Carole Hillenbrand, "1092: A Murderous Year," *Arabist* 15–16 (1995): 281–96; and Hodgson, *Secret Order*, 75.
[57] Hodgson, *Secret Order*, 75.   [58] Ibid., 75–80.   [59] Daftary, *The Isma'ilis*, 352.
[60] Daftary, *Assassin Legends*, 34. Daftary discounts legends concerning the training of fida'is in foreign languages and other subjects in order to enhance their disguise. Hodgson also dispenses with that idea and avers that the term "fida'i" may be anachronistic, referring to a possible later label for a distinct group. Hodgson, *Secret Order*, 82.

Seljuk response and Nizari means

major political role to the policy of assassination, which they utilized rather openly in a spectacular and intimidating fashion."[61]

Targeted killings were not employed against all enemies, and there seems to have been an evolution in its place in Nizari behavior. At first it was used, according to Hodgson, as an "occasional convenience," and an "important auxiliary technique," much like its use by other rulers in the atomized authority structure under the Seljuks.[62] Its use has been attributed to this fractious political condition; there were no big military targets to attack, and the presence of rulers loyal to the Seljuks provided ready targets.[63] But as Seljuk power concentrated, the confrontation with the far more powerful rival made assassination a not only useful but necessary weapon of the weak. Hodgson attributes the use of spectacular killings, those against prominent figures in public places, to their desire to intimidate those who most strongly opposed them.[64] Relying on Hodgson's interpretation, Daftary concludes that while it was a method of convenience early on, "soon with the commencement of their all-out struggle against the much more powerful Seljuks, they began to make relatively systematic and open use of it."[65] Fear and intimidation were amplified by the threat of assassination (sometimes intentionally projected through symbolic warnings) looming for those who worked against the Nizari cause.

While the Nizaris did have limited conventional forces, in the form of loyal villagers and small units, they were, in Hodgson's words, "no ordinary military power."[66] He argues that their ambition was expansive, in contrast to their narrow means. "The Nizari power," Hodgson writes, "aimed to control everyone, everywhere; the scope of its ambition was seen in the variety of its continuing assassinations, not only of amirs but of civilian scholars."[67] While evidentiary spottiness precludes high-confidence judgments, repeated mentions of the atmospheric nature of the danger suggests that the dispersed sources of threat and often sudden, fantastic nature of the violence constituted a threat to ontological security. The extent to which this created an incapacitating state and frustrated an action–identity dynamic cannot be fully known. The reactions to the threat, though, do suggest their impact exceeded those of more conventional actors psychologically in addition to the material threat to existence.

---

[61] Daftary, *Assassin Legends*, 34.
[62] Hodgson, "Isma'ili State," 440; Daftary, *Assassin Legends*, 34.
[63] Hodgson, "Isma'ili State," 440–41; Daftary, *The Isma'ilis*, 352.
[64] Hodgson, "Isma'ili State," 441.   [65] Daftary, *The Isma'ilis*, 352–53.
[66] Hodgson, *Secret Order*, 95.   [67] Ibid.

84   The Nizari Ismailis and the Assassin legends

Decline, dissimilation, and concealment

How could such an unorthodox power emerge within such a materially ominous and ideologically hostile setting? The decline of the Fatimids, and the emergence of the Nizaris, coincided with Seljuk rule that allowed for a measure of regional autonomy. Despite the coincidence of diminished central rule and Fatimid decline, it is fairly clear that the latter was the most significant trigger for the Nizaris to become an autonomous entity. It was not Seljuk fragmentation but rather Fatimid failings that set the course of Nizari ascent. To what extent was the initial association with the Fatimids instrumental in the Nizaris' success? It is evident that the network established while associated with the Fatimids was pivotal, illustrating what is termed here "blowback." Though it is unclear to what extent the Nizaris would then act contrary to Fatimid interests, it was clearly the relationship with the Fatimids that provided the Nizaris the wherewithal to overcome initial collective action challenges. Fatimid support provided the capacity for the Nizaris to establish their following and the resources necessary to maintain themselves under severe duress. Fatimid rule also gave Ismailism a measure of legitimacy (some based on their doctrinal advancement), which was fused with nationalist sentiments, gaining support against Turkish rule. The cultivation of leaders like Hassan-i Sabbah seems to have been a central factor in their success.

Determined Seljuk measures eventually checked the period of Nizari expansion. Sultan Barkyaruq encouraged resentful inhabitants to identify and massacre Ismailis, building on increasing popular fear and rivalry with local amirs.[68] The local rivalries would take a significant toll on the Nizaris, with stories of pyramids of Ismaili skulls attesting to the severity of the threats they faced.[69] The internal difficulties that had weakened the reign of Barkyaruq were followed by a period of cohesion under Sultan Muhammad beginning in 1105. The lack of a rival and the support of the *Nizamiyya* – madrasas established by Nizam al-Mulk – gave Muhammad the capacity to address the Nizari threat in a concerted manner.[70]

Military efforts against the Nizaris previously had limited effects, with attempts to eject them from their strongholds resulting in temporary removal followed by a return to Nizari control.[71] During Muhammad's reign there was greater success. Gains in checking Nizari expansion and removing them from some of their strongholds were trumpeted and

---

[68] Lewis, *The Assassins*, 52.   [69] Ibid., 70.

[70] Carole Hillenbrand, "The Power Struggle between the Saljuqs and the Isma'ilis of Alamut, 487–518/1094–1124: The Saljuq Perspective," in *Medieval Ismaili History*, 209.

[71] On Seljuk concern with Nizari reoccupation, see Farhad Daftary, "Dezkuh," EIr, last updated November 22, 2011, www.iranica.com/articles/dezkuh.

Decline, dissimilation, and concealment

exaggerated as great victories by the Seljuks and the Sunni orthodoxy.[72] The neutralization of the Nizari presence in Isfahan was followed by a siege of Alamut in 1118, still the center of Nizari power. This siege failed and with Muhammad's death the same year, and a succession struggle that followed, pressures on the Nizaris diminished. While this period marked the end of the rapid expansion of Nizari influence and presence, significant areas of control across Iran remained and their dispersed fortresses withstood repeated Seljuk assaults.

Seljuk rule had been robust enough to mount a serious response to Nizari gains, checking their expansion, but ultimately failed to eradicate them. The military system of the Seljuks meant that the conventional forces that the Nizaris did employ were of little use except for local rivalries. Limitations on manpower, weaponry, and territory shaped the Nizaris' factors of protection and opportunity structure. Rather than territorial concentration, a series of mountainous sanctuaries and urban-based networks constituted a "state within a state." Highly skilled and organized leaders made the best of what they had in challenging a conventionally far superior adversary. In this context the practice that would become known as assassination developed from an adjunct technique into a systematic practice. Together these behaviors constituted the range of logics of concealment, particularly hiding and dissimulation, with deception a byproduct at least.

What these developments meant for the Nizaris has been interpreted differently by historians. Lewis saw in their setbacks, and particularly the death of Hassan in 1124, the end of the Nizaris as an effective movement. During the stalemate with the Seljuks, the "passion seemed to go out of Ismailism." While later leaders of the Nizaris would gain further footholds, these were "a meager haul compared with the great days of Hassan-i Sabah." The middle of the first half of the twelfth century was a period of devolution, with the movement's elements increasingly embroiled in local politics. Lewis stresses that the atomized leaders were less concerned with broader Ismaili aims. They had become just like local dynastic polities, which like them practiced political murder from time to time.[73] Carole Hillenbrand accepts this interpretation, labeling the post-Hassan Nizaris as "one group among many, vying for power in localized contexts."[74]

While clearly their expansive and millenarian aims were rendered fanciful, the association of the Nizari Ismailis of this period with local rulers is likely too severe. Evidence suggests that while not like the

---

[72] Hillenbrand, "The Power Struggle," 209.   [73] Above, Lewis, *The Assassins*, 68–70.
[74] Hillenbrand, "The Power Struggle," 216.

86   The Nizari Ismailis and the Assassin legends

cresting of the early phases, Hassan's successors managed to maintain a viable organization that extended beyond the localities in its extent and aims. Hassan's immediate successor Kiya Buzurg-Ummid (r. 1124–1138) seized new strongholds and strengthened others. With the revolutionary headiness lessened by its opponents' brute force, the aims of the group became directed toward survival and independence, which they would maintain until their removal by the Mongols.[75] Hodgson writes that the "pattern of the Nizari revolt eased almost imperceptibly into one of a permanent Nizari state with a fixed, though scattered, territory."[76] For Hodgson the vitality of the Nizaris was exhibited in their very survival. Five parcels of territory, despite limitations on mutual material assistance, maintained their ties while responding to the authority based at Alamut. Together they remained an effective, viable power, though ultimately not the foundation for transforming the entire Islamic world.[77] While not quite as effusive as Hodgson, Daftary sees the Nizaris as having by the end of Buzurg's rule "clearly established an independent state of their own." He characterizes Alamut as the center of authority, though each part by necessity would maintain a measure of independence. Despite this local autonomy, the Nizari state, according to Daftary, "maintained a remarkable cohesion and sense of unity both internally and against the outside world."[78]

Synthesizing both sets of interpretations, one may conclude that while local politics preoccupied Nizari elements, this did not preclude their actions as a broader collectivity. Local issues, a mild way to describe conflict and massacres, had long been a concern. While their efforts did not lead to the overthrow of the Turks, nor accession to the leadership of the Islamic world, they did outlast their Seljuk rivals.[79] These phases of expansion and survival overlapped with the extension of Nizari presence into Syria. There, encounters with the Christian West would do much to frame our impression of the Nizari Ismailis, and spread those images well beyond the craggy heights of Alamut.

---

[75] See Daftary, *The Isma'ilis*, 365; and Hodgson, *Secret Order*, 99.
[76] Hodgson, *Secret Order*, 99.
[77] See Hodgson, "Isma'ili State," 455–57; and Hodgson, *Secret Order*, 115–20. For a list of Nizari influenced territories, see Daftary, *The Isma'ilis*, 381.
[78] Daftary, *The Isma'ilis*, 380–81.
[79] The Seljuk dynasty lasted until 1157, succumbing to invasion and internal revolts (particularly by Oghuz tribesmen in 1153), though elements persisted in Rum (Anatolia) until the early fourteenth century.

Nizari Ismailis in Syria

While the struggle with the Seljuks progressed, Hassan-i Sabbah expanded the movement. Nizari da'is had been sent to Syria at the beginning of the twelfth century when it was under the suzerainty of the declining Fatimids and receding influence of the Seljuks.[80] This region was also host to crusaders who had recently taken Jerusalem. The crusaders would eventually establish themselves in the Frankish or Crusader states, including the Kingdom of Jerusalem, Edessa, Antioch, and Tripoli. These statelets would also host the roving military orders, most notably the Hospitallers and the Templars, who received their funding from donations and landholdings in continental Europe.

So when the da'is arrived in Syria they experienced a plural system of multiple actors, and multiple loyalties, that had yet to congeal. In this swell the Nizaris would imitate the practices of their Persian sponsors, seeking fortress strongholds and at times dispatching their enemies through targeted killings. The Syrian Nizaris, however, found this especially tough going, and in their first several decades struggled to establish secure strongholds.[81] In their perilous condition they entered brief, unreliable alliances with a number of factions: Christian and Muslim, Shia and Sunni. They also fought with these groups, at times employing fida'is, and were subject to massacres.[82] Coming to be based in Aleppo and Damascus, the Syrian wing depended on the protection of local leaders. This vulnerable condition placed a premium on securing a local base of support, a goal that would lead to increasing independence from their Persian originators.

While the early phases of the Syrian Nizari Ismailis were troublesome, they did manage to acquire some mountain redoubts in the last two decades of the first half of the twelfth century.[83] During this period they consolidated their position in the Jabal Bahra region. There, the pattern of temporary alliances, massacres, and targeted killings continued.[84] Raymond II of Tripoli became the first Frankish victim of the fida'is, provoking massacres of Muslims (apparently not sect specific) and leading to the Templars forcing the sect to pay annual tribute.[85] It was only

---

[80] Nasseh Ahmad Mirza, *Syrian Ismailism: The Ever Living Line of the Imamate* (Richmond, Surrey: Curzon Press, 1997), 7.

[81] See Daftary, *Assassin Legends*, 64–65.

[82] On this period, see Mirza, *Syrian Ismailism*, 7–16; and Hodgson, *Secret Order*, 89–94; 104–7.

[83] Daftary, *Assassin Legends*, 67.

[84] See Othman Ali, "The *Fidawiyyah* Assassins in Crusades and Counter-Crusades," *Intellectual Discourse* 4, nos. 1–2 (1996): 46–61.

[85] Daftary, *Assassin Legends*, 67.

88 The Nizari Ismailis and the Assassin legends

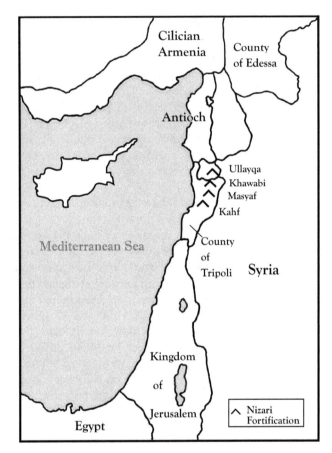

Map 2.4 Major Nizari Ismaili fortifications in Syria
Sources: Jonathan Riley-Smith, ed., *The Atlas of the Crusades* (Times Books/Facts on File, 1991), Peter Willey, *Eagle's Nest: Ismaili Castles in Iran and Syria* (I.B. Tauris, 2005), and Institute of Ismaili Studies (London)

under the leadership of Rashid al-Din Sinan that the Syrian Nizaris managed to consolidate their position. Sinan, who had trained at Alamut and briefly served as chief da'i of Basra, implemented a number of policies that secured their presence. Nizari castles were fortified, internal divisions were soothed, relations with the Frankish states were regularized, and the core of fida'is was reorganized.[86]

[86] Ibid., 67–68; Mirza, *Syrian Ismailism*, 27.

Significance and dissimilarity 89

Among the fortifications that were improved was one near Masyaf and another near Kahf, along with a number of others.[87] These strongholds were strategically located, allowing monitoring of positions held by Muslim and Frankish rivals. Salah al-Din (Saladin) had replaced the ailing Fatimid rulers of Egypt, establishing the Ayyubid dynasty. The Nizaris clashed with Saladin's forces, targeting him for assassination as Masyaf was besieged.[88] Truces and reports of collusion between Saladin and Sinan (which are suspect) reinforce the fluidity and complexity of this subsystem. The consolidation under the leadership of Sinan coincided with a gradual easing of ties with Alamut. Sources suggest that Sinan remained dependent on Alamut, but the nature of the relationship is unclear.[89] According to one source, Alamut restored authority over its western wing following Sinan's death in 1192.[90] These ties remained until the fall of Alamut to the Mongols in 1256 – an outside actor that itself was irregular in structure and behavior – which was followed by the Syrian Nizari submission to the Mamluks in 1273.

A challenging exception: significance and dissimilarity

The discussion of case selection in the book's introduction emphasized the need to establish that the actor was systemically significant and was sufficiently distinct in form from other actors in the system. The criteria offered focus on a combination of duration as an autonomous actor and responses by other actors in the system. For dissimilarity it is important to establish that dominant modes of organization and interaction existed and that the actor deviated significantly from those modes.

It is relatively easy to fix a starting and ending date to the system in question, though there is always some choice. Here the disintegration of the Abbasid Caliphate, which gave rise to the successor states, and the invasion of the Mongols provide fairly reliable start and end points. That would fix the system between roughly 945 and 1256, the same time the Nizaris in the East were neutralized.[91] The Nizaris lasted as an independent power from roughly 1094 to 1273 (or 1256 if you do not

---

[87] Mirza, *Syrian Ismailism*, 28–29. On the Syrian fortifications, see Willey, *Eagle's Nest*, 216–45.

[88] See Bernard Lewis, "Saladin and the Assassins," *Bulletin of the School of Oriental and African Studies* 15, no. 2 (1953): 239–45. See also Mirza, *Syrian Ismailism*, 31–36.

[89] Mirza, *Syrian Ismailism*, 30.   [90] Daftary, *The Isma'ilis*, 419.

[91] While the defeat of the Nizaris by the Mongols is often depicted as decisive, evidence suggests their persistence (in a much weaker state) after the Mongol onslaught. See Shafique N. Virani, "The Eagle Returns: Evidence of Continued Isma'ili Activity at Alamut and in the South Caspian Region Following the Mongol Conquests," *Journal of the American Oriental Society* 123, no. 2 (April–June 2003): 351–70.

90   The Nizari Ismailis and the Assassin legends

include the Syrian wing). Using the shorter time frame, the Nizaris persisted for roughly 160 years, and roughly 180 counting the Syrian wing, meaning the Nizaris played a part in over half the system's duration.

One problem that arises in assessing these types of actors is that their particular articulations and expressions of power may distort interpretation of their significance. If one of the premises of the study is that uncertainty caused by structural and behavioral deviations has discernible effects on norms and identity formation, then it is possible that the actual impact of the actors is distorted in the record. Clifford Bosworth argues that the methods employed by the Nizaris exaggerated their actual power.[92] On the other end of the scale is Hodgson's assessment, which has them as comparable to the Mongols in the length of their reach and extent of their ambitions.[93] This almost certainly overstates their actual impact on the system. Nevertheless, Hodgson sees the Nizaris' relations with numerous and diverse players as a good indicator that the group was taken seriously as an independent political entity. The range of alliances, however contingent, held between the Nizaris and a host of actors (local rulers, Frankish states, Ayyubids, Mamluks, and possibly Mongols) indicates more than a passive or merely irritating presence.[94] The priority placed by the Mongols on their destruction during their conquest of western Asia – which preceded their targeting of the Abbasid Caliphate in Baghdad – provides another clue to their significance.[95]

It is possible to find some mean between Bosworth's dismissal and Hodgson's generous portrayal. Bosworth's contention that the threat perceived was amplified by uncertainty is consistent with an interpretation that a varied articulation of violence may enhance a group's systemic effects, compensating for material weakness. Those perceptions and their effects on the formation of norms and identity, however, ought not be used as an indicator of significance in order to avoid circularity in the

---

[92] Clifford E. Bosworth, *The New Islamic Dynasties: A Chronological and Genealogical Manual* (New York: Columbia University Press, 1996), 203; and Bosworth, "Political and Dynastic History," 71.

[93] Hodgson, *Secret Order*, 255.

[94] See Charles Melville, "'Sometimes by the Sword, Sometimes by the Dagger': The Role of the Ismailis in Mamluk–Mongol Relations in the 8th/14th Century," in *Medieval Ismaili History*, 247–65. On indications of Nizari–Mongol collusion, see Timothy M. May, "A Mongol–Ismaili Alliance? Thoughts on the Mongols and Assassins," *Journal of the Royal Asiatic Society* 14, no. 3 (November 2004): 23–39.

[95] Farhad Daftary has the Mongol ruler Möngke assigning the "first priority to the destruction of the Nizari state in Persia, and of the Abbasid Caliphate." Daftary, *The Isma'ilis*, 419. It is believed that an assassination plot against Möngke was one possible reason for this prioritization. See Christopher Dawson, ed., *Mission to Asia* (Toronto: University of Toronto Press, 1980), 184–85; and May, "A Mongol–Ismaili Alliance?" 235.

Significance and dissimilarity 91

argument – with distorted impressions as both cause and effect. Only if the magnifying effects vastly exceeded the tangible import, to the point where they comprised the primary substance of their challenge, would this present an impediment. With the Nizaris the uncertainty and fear they induced was a byproduct of a real threat, albeit an important one for their success.

Due to the combination of their duration and the quality and quantity of relationships with multiple actors, the Nizari Ismailis should be considered a systemic actor. But were they different from other actors? In the Alamut phase it seems pretty clear that the group was structurally dissimilar. The anarchic system that emerged after the Abbasids consisted of multiple actors that were mostly contiguous and centrally organized. Even if the Seljuk Empire was fragmented at times, centrally directed administration was an ongoing goal. That the local polities at times resembled the individual Nizari dominions is clear. These local polities, though, remained local and lacked the "coordinated decentralization" exhibited by the multiple Nizari elements. The Nizaris' deviation from standard behavior is argued above. Though targeted killing was not uncommon, the Nizaris' systematic employment of it and its condition as a core behavior were.

Complicating matters was the status of the Syrian wing. The subsystem into which it emerged was decidedly plural in character. The Nizaris in this setting were more similar than not in terms of organizational mode. Where this becomes complicating for the central arguments of the study is that the legends about the Nizaris were formed and transmitted primarily due to interaction between the Christian West and the Syrian branch. If structural and associated behavioral differences have important roles in the formulation of norms and identity, then their similarity with the other actors stands out. This concern is tempered when considering that the modes of organization and behavior exhibited in the Levant were transmitted through directives and practices originating from Alamut. These include the use of terrain and citadels for strongholds and the systematic use of targeted killing. While the Syrian Nizaris exhibited a level of autonomy from Alamut, and at times outright independence, the imprint of their eastern origins was clear. It was these modes and behaviors that provided the fodder for Western legends concerning the Assassins, with the plural system of the Levant serving as a conduit.

92   The Nizari Ismailis and the Assassin legends

Responses in the Islamic world

The Nizaris represented not only a physical threat but a threat to the Sunni synthesis that had claimed to overcome various challengers to the orthodoxy.[96] They were threats to both physical and ontological security, as individuals feared sudden death from unknown quarters, and efforts to enforce orthodoxy were challenged by what were seen as peculiar, dangerous deviants. The orthodoxy's self-image had been cultivated through heresiography that sought to create the image of a doctrinally monolithic Islamic community with few detractors.[97] Denounced as *malahida* (deviators or heretics) by both Sunni and Shia authorities, the Nizaris were subject to campaigns to discredit them.[98] While deviation was nothing new in the Islamic world, the Nizaris coupled theirs with a severe political challenge. Righting this disruption would require machinations that addressed both the normative and identity frameworks of Muslim society. Neither alone would be sufficient to address the threat to the physical existence of the orthodoxy and their authority nor lessen the state of ontological insecurity the Nizaris' disposition imposed.

Among those recruited by the Abbasid caliph al-Mustazhir (r. 1094–1118) to undermine the rightfulness of the Nizari rebellion was noted Islamic scholar Abu Hamid al-Ghazali. By tradition, determining the legitimacy of rebellion involved assessing the two pillars of rightful resistance in early Islam: *ta'wil* (a plausible, though considered wrong, interpretation of religious doctrine) and *shawka* (the power of the group determined by the number of followers).[99] Al-Ghazali's extensive refutation emphasized the cleverness and trickery the Nizaris used to spread their doctrines, and sought to diminish them in number as "the little gang of Batinites."[100] By their numbers, at least, the Nizari resistance would have to be considered rightful. Accordingly, the focus would have to be on the plausibility of their doctrines.

Al-Ghazali focused on the Ismaili views on resurrection as the basis for the ruling that their interpretation went beyond tolerable dissent.[101] That

---

[96] Hodgson, "Isma'ili State," 427.

[97] W. Montgomery Watt, "The Great Community and the Sects," in *Theology and Law in Islam*, ed. G.E. von Grunebaum (Wiesbaden: Otto Harrassowitz, 1971), 35.

[98] Daftary, *Assassin Legends*, 36; Lewis, *The Assassins*, 6.

[99] See Khaled Abou El Fadl, *Rebellion and Violence in Islamic Law* (Cambridge: Cambridge University Press, 2001), 184; and Sherman A. Jackson, "Domestic Terrorism in the Islamic Legal Tradition," *The Muslim World* 91, nos. 3–4 (Fall 2001): 293–318.

[100] Abu Hamid al-Ghazali, "The Infamies (Enormities) of the Batinites and Virtues (Merits) of the Mustazhirites," in *Al-Ghazali: Deliverance from Error*, trans. Richard J. McCarthy (Louisville, Ky.: Fons Vitae, 1980), 236.

[101] Mitha, *Al-Ghazali*, 89. Frank Griffel emphasizes the political motivations behind al-Ghazali's interpretation. Frank Griffel, "Toleration and Exclusion: Al-Shafii and Al-

Responses in the Islamic world 93

moved the Nizaris from being merely misguided in their doctrine (ta'wil), amenable to correction and thus subject to some measure of restraint, to the status of common criminals. The threshold for plausible interpretation to that point had been minimal, intended to seek reconciliation among those holding doctrinal disputes as dictated in the Quran.[102] It was the sophistication of the doctrines developed by the da'is that required the defenders of the Sunni orthodoxy to mount their extensive rebuttal.[103] Against the Ismailis al-Ghazali reaches the strongest refutation with the fatwa of *takfir*, declaring their followers as apostates. According to Farouk Mitha, al-Ghazali associated the "Batiniyya" with "archetypes of betrayal and corruption" referred to in the Quran and Sunna.[104] This reference framed the problem in terms of the legal management of apostasy, entailing the "most direct form of exclusion."[105]

Recognition of, in Hillenbrand's words, the "deeply disturbed nature of his own time ... a time overflowing with afflictions and strife," drove al-Ghazali and his sponsors to disavow and delegitimize a major source of that condition.[106] Al-Ghazali, Mitha writes, "had to put forward a defense of the Sunni order built on the vocabulary of ideals and not merely on realpolitik considerations."[107] He went about this by casting the Ismailis as an organized conspiracy bent only on power and domination.[108] The da'wa was portrayed as an organization whose primary aim was to dupe, deceive, and promote doubt, preying on popular disaffection.[109] Their trickery in dissimulation was emphasized, though this is only explicitly tied to their unarmed missionary activity.[110] "In the case of the Nizaris," Hodgson writes, "the Sunnis had to face directly the problem of drawing the outer limits of the Muslim community's catholicity."[111] At the same time, the orthodoxy or "normative center" had to be

---

Ghazali on the Treatment of Apostates," *Bulletin of the School of Oriental and African Studies* 64, no. 3 (2001): 353. Another al-Ghazali scholar argues that the incompatibility of Ismaili doctrines with the majority of the Persian population made the interpretation less a political contrivance than an expression of the will of the majority. F.R.C. Bagley, trans. and ed., *Ghazali's Book of Counsel for Kings (Nasihat Al-Muluk)* (London: Oxford University Press, 1964), xxx.

[102] Khaled Abou El Fadl, "Political Crime in Islamic Jurisprudence and Western Legal History," *U.C. Davis Journal of International Law and Policy* 4, no. 1 (Winter 1998): 16.

[103] The role of the da'is, many of whom were "outstanding thinkers and scholars" in their own right, is described in Daftary, *The Isma'ilis*, 231–33.

[104] Mitha, *Al-Ghazali*, 70.   [105] Ibid.

[106] Carole Hillenbrand, "Islamic Orthodoxy or Realpolitik? Al-Ghazali's Views on Government," *Iran: Journal of the British Institute of Persian Studies* 26 (1988): 84.

[107] Mitha, *Al-Ghazali*, 26.   [108] Ibid., 37.   [109] Ibid., 39.

[110] Henry Corbin, "The Ismaili Response to the Polemic of Ghazali," in *Ismaili Contributions to Islamic Culture*, trans. James Morris, ed. Seyyed Hossein Nasr, (Tehran: Imperial Iranian Academy of Philosophy, 1977), 72.

[111] Hodgson, *Secret Order*, 126.

94   The Nizari Ismailis and the Assassin legends

reinforced, identifying in al-Ghazali's term the "people of the prophetic tradition and of the community/consensus."[112] Mitha characterizes al-Ghazali's portrayal as a "crude, fictional caricature" that gives the Ismailis a face, "albeit one that effectively demonizes them."[113] A "black legend" had been associated with the Ismailis from the tenth century.[114] But it was only in response to the Nizari threat (physical and doctrinal) that this transformed from general denunciations to more specific legal rulings of apostasy.[115]

The discussion here has focused on reactions to Ismaili doctrines that had effects on common identity, but another question arises. Does a norm against assassination exist or emerge around this time in Islamic jurisprudence in response to their actions? The answer is "yes," but only indirectly. It is important to recall both the urge to achieve unity in the *Umma* (community of believers) and the fractious nature of early Islamic history. Those that possessed both shawka and ta'wil were considered *bughat*, rebels who while erring did not act as bandits and did not follow doctrines that amounted to apostasy.[116] This approach to rebellion allowed for treating such rebels with a measure of restraint, including determining such matters as their responsibility for damaged property and burial rites. *Ahkam-al-Bughat*, the line of jurisprudence dealing with rebellion, according to Khaled Abou El Fadl, had a "rather technical and absolute character, with normative value assigned."[117] Historical precedent was more important than doctrinal sources. The killer of Ali (661) was deemed to have acted without shawka (numbers) and therefore was considered to have committed the act outside of any general rebellion.[118]

Indirectly, then, a norm against assassination existed, one that was tied to the nature of the offending group and whether it met the standards for bughat. The ruling that the Nizaris did not would begin to address the needs of security by resorting to negative identification by

---

[112] Mitha, *Al-Ghazali*, 88.   [113] Ibid., 39.   [114] See Daftary, *Assassin Legends*, 26–27.

[115] Discussions concerning the status of the Nizaris had practical implications, as when they seized fortifications at Shahdez (Dezkuh). The retaking of Shahdez was delayed after the Nizari leader there appealed to the Sunni ulama of Isfahan that the Nizaris were true Muslims. While the appeal was ultimately denied, the debate that ensued may have delayed retaking the fort for almost a year. Daftary, "Dezkuh," 354.

[116] El Fadl, "Political Crime." See also Khaled Abou El Fadl, "*Ahkam al-Bughat*: Irregular Warfare and the Law of Rebellion in Islam," in *Cross, Crescent, and Sword: The Justification and Limitation of War in Western and Islamic Tradition*, ed. James T. Johnson and John Kelsay (New York: Greenwood Press, 1990); John Kelsay, *Islam and War: A Study in Comparative Ethics* (Louisville, Ky.: Westminster/John Knox Press, 1993), 81–93; and Joel L. Kraemer, "Apostates, Rebels, and Brigands," *Israel Oriental Studies* 10 (1980): 34–73.

[117] El Fadl, "*Ahkam al-Bughat*," 152.   [118] Ibid., 162.

Responses in the Islamic world 95

means of a ruling of apostasy. This addressed concerns posed by both physical and ontological security – *how* we are, *who* we are, and how we relate to others, now rendered "others" – particularly in reference to the enemy who would then be rendered a stranger apart from "us" in terms of identity though not yet in space. When considered with standing proclamations against treachery (the first of the "ten commands" of the first caliph Abu Bakr), the indirect nature of a norm against assassination is reinforced.[119] It was the establishment of the Nizaris' doctrinal deviation, though, that placed the group beyond the pale of rightful rebellion, highlighting the interdependence between categorization and discrimination in the determination of normative deviation and the formation of identities.

That the system was characterized by pervasive uncertainty and that the Nizaris were a major contributor to this is demonstrated in the historical record, but was this instrumental in terms of the development and transmission of norms? By the time of the Seljuk counteroffensive, the Nizari threat to defeat the Seljuks outright, if it ever existed, was gone. What remained was a persistent and often intense menace of unexpected death from unidentified sources affecting the Seljuk leadership and its supporters. Did this lead to the establishment of norms and rules intended to mitigate this uncertainty, as posited in the relief thesis? No, not directly or in a manner that can be interpreted as wholly instrumental. It is difficult, however, to detach the identity formation that occurred from the norms and rules that were reinforced. The lack of a clear, explicit norm against assassination required a resort to existing norms concerning rebellion. The requirement that any group conducting a rebellion have sufficient numbers effectively barred tactics like targeted killing by small groups. The challenge of the authorities, both clerical and secular, was to fit the Nizaris into an existing set of norms, a particular status where their actions were not considered acceptable acts of rebellion. This categorization left the Nizaris unprotected from restraints in countering rebellion, consistent with the enforcement thesis and its emphasis on categorization and the exceeding of established norms for punishment. While a new norm was not formed in this setting, the systemic exigency forced processes of categorization and discrimination that facilitated the application and amplification of existing norms. The outcomes of those processes *did* carry over and influence norm formation elsewhere, in particular following the encounters, real and imagined, between these actors and

[119] Sohail H. Hashmi, "Interpreting the Islamic Ethics of War and Peace," in *Islamic Political Ethics: Civil Society, Pluralism, and Conflict*, ed. Hashmi (Princeton: Princeton University Press, 2002), 211.

96   The Nizari Ismailis and the Assassin legends

Europeans. This, however, as explained in the subsequent sections, did not occur in a straightforward manner, by the creation of new norms and direct transmittal to new contexts.

The role of systemic uncertainty in sparking collective and corporate identity formation within the Muslim world is strongly suggested. While these determinations were founded on an assessment of common historical experience and shared values among Muslims (based on the tenuous Sunni synthesis), they were sparked by the Nizaris' odd and dangerous modes of organization and interaction. In this respect, it is difficult to give primacy to either homogeneity or common cultural bonds as factors shaping collective identity formation, as both were in play. The corporate identity formation that occurred was striking and severe. These were not only rebels but apostates, "as vile as dogs ... accursed ... [with] evil machinations and unclean beliefs."[120] The potency of the denunciations presented Islamic and later Western observers with a clear caricature that they could feed into any number of narratives, a process that persisted over centuries. The plurality of the system of the Syrian branch actually enhanced the transmission of these identities, with the combination of an increased measure of interaction with other constituents (compared to the Persian Nizaris) and a lack of cultural bonds between them and the Western actors.

The origins and diffusion of the Assassin legends

The advent of the Crusades provided the setting for an encounter between the "black legend" of the Ismailis and Westerners whose territorial rapaciousness matched their voraciousness in consuming fantastic stories from the Latin East. Existing hostility toward the Nizaris combined with what Daftary terms the crusaders' "imaginative ignorance" resulting in remarkably potent and persistent misrepresentations.[121] This ignorance and gullibility combined with a preexisting view of Islam that was shallow and largely unaware of the divisions and sects that had so characterized its history.[122] Western interpretations of the Nizaris that continue to this day were forged during this time, including distortions of their rituals, leadership, and very name. "Hashishin" was likely a general term of reprobation referring to Islamic prohibitions concerning

---

[120] Thirteenth-century Persian historian 'Ata-Malik Juvayni quoted in Virani, "Eagle Returns," 354.

[121] Daftary, "The Isma'ilis and the Crusaders," 35.

[122] Daftary, *Assassin Legends*, 62. See also Bernard Hamilton, "Knowing the Enemy: Western Understanding of Islam at the Time of the Crusades," *Journal of the Royal Asiatic Society, Series 3*, 7, no. 3 (November 1997): 373–87.

The origins and diffusion of the Assassin legends   97

intoxicants.[123] The word's corruption, "Assassin," became a focal point for interpreting the group's purported exotic rituals, committed killers, and devious dealings.

Much of what dazzled and disturbed the crusaders about this odd sect concerned their means and rituals, as well as their claimed hyper-obedience.[124] Stories of Assassin followers jumping to their deaths at the order of their leaders demonstrated the depths of their zealousness (another historically eponymous term).[125] Among the most potent myths concerned the indoctrination of the fida'is. Depicted as doped up and unsuspecting dupes introduced into a garden filled with doe-eyed virgins, the myth follows that they were rudely awakened and charged with the task of murder in exchange for a permanent stay in paradise.[126] Medieval chroniclers such as William of Tyre, Arnold of Lubeck, and Marco Polo helped transmit these outright fabrications and exaggerations to credulous Western audiences.[127] Marco Polo's version became the standard European account, with its vivid portrayal of the "Old Man of the Mountain."[128] That moniker was a perversion of the honorific *shaykh*, meaning leader or elder, an error compounded by its application to both Hassan-i Sabbah and Rashid al-Din Sinan.

The theory offered posits that the emergence of dissimilar actors (in both form and behavior) has effects on the formulation of norms and identity formation. In this case it is important to determine to what extent the Nizaris (Assassins) were part of a broader process of identity formation associated with the West's encounter with Islam generally, rather than this particular actor. While depictions of the "Saracens" by European sources did provide the West with distinctions as a source of corporate identity formation, the Assassins were highlighted in order to magnify the Saracen threat.[129] Bruce Lincoln points to Marco Polo's treatment of

---

[123] Daftary, *Assassin Legends*, 34–35. Shakib Saleh presents the possibility that the term had to do with a similar word that refers to a form of dress. See Saleh, "Use of Batini," 42.

[124] Daftary, *Assassin Legends*, 69.

[125] For examples, see Bernard Lewis, *A Middle East Mosaic: Fragments of Life, Letters, and History* (New York: Modern Library, 2001), 276–79.

[126] The credibility of this account is even more dubious when you consider that not only determination but also a great deal of sophistication – necessary for taking on complex missions including assuming false identities – must have been required for some of the more daring fida'i missions.

[127] Daftary, *Assassin Legends*, 73.

[128] Henry Yule, trans. and ed., *The Book of Ser Marco Polo, The Venetian, Concerning the Kingdoms and Marvels of the East, Vol. I* (London: John Murray, 1926), 139–48. On the cultural transmission of these myths, see Frank M. Chambers, "The Troubadours and the Assassins," *Modern Language Notes* 64, no. 4 (April 1949): 245–51; and Wolfgang Fleischhauer, "The 'Ackerman Aus Böhmen' and the Old Man of the Mountain," *Monatshefte* 45 (1953): 196–97.

[129] On the general antipathy toward, and view of, the "Saracens," see John V. Tolan, *Saracens: Islam in the Medieval European Imagination* (New York: Columbia University

98   The Nizari Ismailis and the Assassin legends

"the Old Man and his minions as an emblematic part of the Saracen world," and its abuse by Europeans to highlight the view of a dangerous and threatening Islam.[130] Other chroniclers make a clear distinction between the Assassins and the broader grouping of Saracens, labeling them a "certain race of Saracens ... [who] live without law."[131] Revised versions of Marco Polo's account make clear the heretical status of the Assassins.[132] We can also compare these depictions with the crusaders' view of Saladin, leader of a more conventional Islamic power. While invective labeled Saladin a "pimp, whose kingdom was located in brothels," what emerged was a deep respect for his "knightly qualities" and even a widespread myth of his actual knighthood.[133] Collective identification based on homogeneity, adherence to "knightly" behaviors in this case, is suggested but not strongly supported due to the varying treatments of Saladin and the Saracens, but the enduring nature of the corporate, negative identification of the Nizaris is clear.

The idealization of Saladin is in stark contrast to the exaggerated and diabolical depictions of the Assassins rooted in the crusaders' fascination with the practice of targeted killing.[134] It was the systematic application of assassination, their "habit of killing ... in an astonishing way" in the words of one envoy, that transfixed the crusaders and European chroniclers.[135] The fact that the myths concerning rituals and indoctrination still developed and persisted to the extent they did, despite sustained systemic interactions and alliances, demonstrates the pervasive cultural misunderstanding that conditioned their formation and diffusion. Indeed, the limited base of knowledge seems to have enhanced these processes of identity formation, though cultural distinctions were not in and of themselves an independent cause.

Fear of disorder and generalized assassination

Tales of the Assassins did not remain mere reflections of far off curiosities. The figures of the Old Man of the Mountain and his devotees were appropriated by rivalrous Europeans to represent more proximate menaces. The story of the Old Man, Wolfgang Fleischhauer observed, "grew and thrived in the climate of European power politics in the late

---

Press, 2002); and Debra H. Strickland, *Saracens, Demons, and Jews: Making Monsters in Medieval Art* (Princeton: Princeton University Press, 2003), 165–92.

[130] Bruce Lincoln, "An Early Moment in the Discourse of 'Terrorism:' Reflections on a Tale from Marco Polo," *Comparative Studies in Society and History* 48, no. 2 (April 2006): 248.

[131] Lewis, *The Assassins*, 2.   [132] Lincoln, "Early Moment," 251, n. 28; 257.

[133] Hamilton, "Knowing the Enemy," 382–84.

[134] Daftary, "Isma'ilis and the Crusaders," 35.   [135] Lewis, *The Assassins*, 3.

Fear of disorder and generalized assassination   99

12th and 13th centuries."[136] The murder in 1192 of Conrad of Montferrat – a key figure in the Third Crusade and slated successor to the Kingdom of Jerusalem – became a *cause célèbre* throughout Europe, and the Assassins gained "universal notoriety."[137] The widespread use of the Assassin legends for propaganda purposes persisted as spurious associations between the group and European leaders were used to defame. The rivalry between Philip Augustus of France and Richard the Lionheart saw accusations that Richard commissioned the killing of Conrad, and planned a similar demise for Philip himself.[138] The charges against Richard depicted him as an English version of the Old Man, indoctrinating young boys to do his evil dealings to support false doctrines.[139] Others were presented as potential victims of lurking Assassins (the term still capitalized), and such images infused the rivalry between the papacy and the Holy Roman Empire.

Pope Gregory IX denounced the tendency of military orders to align with the Nizaris, decrying connections with "the Assassins, the enemies of God and of the Christian name, who formerly dared to slay treacherously Raymond ... and many other magnates and Catholic princes."[140] The decree of the First Council of Lyon (1245) contained the Papal bull excommunicating Frederick II (Holy Roman Emperor), including the charge of "[u]sing the deadly and hateful service of other unbelievers against the faithful." The reference to "other unbelievers" associates Frederick II with a defined and maligned out-group, at the same time it reinforces a norm against assassination. It also contained a general prohibition "On homicide," which noted that "there are people who with a terrible inhumanity and loathsome cruelty thirst for the death of others and cause them to be killed by assassins." In justifying the prohibition on such killings, both functional and identity-based drivers are fused: "We do so especially since some persons of high standing, fearing to be killed in such a way, are forced to beg for their own safety from the master of these assassins, and thus so to speak to redeem their life in a way that is an insult to Christian dignity."[141]

The prominent place of the Assassins in the political discourse, where charges were "hurled about freely by European monarchs," contributed to

---

[136] Wolfgang Fleischhauer, "The Old Man of the Mountain: The Growth of a Legend," *Symposium* 9, no. 1 (1955): 85; Fleischhauer, "'Ackerman Aus Böhmen,'" 190–95.

[137] Fleischhauer, "Growth of a Legend," 85. On the murder of Conrad, see Mirza, *Syrian Ismailism*, 36–37; and Lewis, *The Assassins*, 117–18.

[138] Fleischhauer, "Growth of a Legend," 85. Saladin was also accused of involvement.

[139] Ibid., 86.   [140] Daftary, *Assassin Legends*, 76.

[141] "The Bull of Deposition of the Emperor Frederick II," and "On Homicide," First Council of Lyon, 1245, in *Decrees of the Ecumenical Councils, Vol. 1, Nicaea I to Lateran V*, ed. Norman P. Tanner (London: Sheed & Ward, 1990), 282; 290.

100   The Nizari Ismailis and the Assassin legends

widespread awareness of the legends.[142] It also resulted in the eventual incorporation of "assassin" and "assassination" as general appellations, increasingly disassociated from historical caricatures. The stories of the Assassins and their propagandistic usage waned, though the legends were not forgotten. The earliest generic usage of "assassin," according to Daftary, occurs in Dante's *Divine Comedy*, where the "treacherous assassin" appears detached from any colorful mythology.[143] This seeping into the languages of Europe represents the impact that this group had on politics and culture, while also making it more difficult to distinguish between the use of the terms to represent the historical group or political killing in general. The increasingly generic nature of "assassin" and "assassination" also makes it more challenging to trace the longer-term effects of the historical actors on the diffusion of associated norms and identities.

Norms against assassination have been capably surveyed elsewhere.[144] Ward Thomas notes that the norms that existed did little to contain the practice, which became widespread in early modern Europe. Thomas argues that it was the upheaval caused by certain killings, particularly the assassination of the French King Henry IV, that added another element to the evolving norm. A general fear of disorder, and the specific severe turmoil of the Thirty Years' War, fed an increasing need to reinforce reason and reduce uncertainty in politics.[145] In response to the Rye House Plot of 1683 (a purported planned assassination against Charles II and his brother), Oxford University issued a decree against "barbarous assassination" that proclaimed the "utmost detestation and abhorrence of that execrable villainy, hateful to God and man."[146]

In the formation of norms concerning assassination in early modern Europe, the role of the historical Assassins was present but not instrumental. The prominence of the Assassins as a symbol in the discourse on assassination waned. The "horrid practice of murdering kings," absent explicit historical association, was a sufficiently potent source of disdain.[147]

---

[142] Charles E. Nowell, "The Old Man of the Mountain," *Speculum: A Journal of Mediaeval Studies* 22, no. 4 (October 1947): 510.

[143] Daftary, *Assassin Legends*, 121; Dante Alighieri, *The Divine Comedy: Part I, The Inferno*, trans. Mark Musa (New York: Penguin Classics, 2003), 242.

[144] For treatments of political murder and norms associated with assassination, see Franklin L. Ford, *Political Murder: From Tyrannicide to Terrorism* (Cambridge: Harvard University Press, 1985); and Ward Thomas, "Norms and Security: The Case of International Assassination," *International Security* 25, no. 1 (Summer 2000): 105–33.

[145] Thomas, "Norms and Security," 116.

[146] "The Judgment and Decree of the University of Oxford, Passed in Their Convocation, July 21, 1683...," in *Divine Right and Democracy: An Anthology of Political Writing in Stuart England*, ed. David Wootton (Indianapolis: Hackett Publishing, 2003), 120.

[147] "The Catholick Cause; Or, The Horrid Practice of Murdering Kings...," in *The Harleian Miscellany, Vol. II* (London, 1809), 130.

Enlightenment and revolution: fanaticism and secrecy 101

While the Old Man and the Assassins did make an appearance now and then, this was more like the cameo of a faded movie star.[148] In Francis Bacon's denunciation of the Anabaptists, he draws direct parallels with the Assassins. Bacon compares the two groups based on a claimed blind obedience to their rulers and a lack of adherence to law in favor of secret doctrine. This made the Assassins, Bacon argued, "an engine built against human society," and worthy to be cut "off from the face of the earth."[149] These themes of obedience and secret doctrines would be revived – as would the historical Assassins – in the discourse of the Enlightenment and the counterrevolutionary writings that followed, serving the symbolic order that would delineate civilized and uncivilized behaviors.

Enlightenment and revolution: fanaticism and secrecy

"For six hundred years," Voltaire wrote of the Assassins, "the story has been told over and over again."[150] He combined his *Philosophical Dictionary* entry to include the Assassins and the practice of assassination, the crime next to poisoning "most cowardly and deserving in punishment." Voltaire dismissed the Assassins as "wretched little people of mountaineers" and little more than "banditti." They serve later, though, as a representative for Voltaire's *bête noire*, fanaticism, and religion more generally. "Fanaticism is to superstition what delirium is to fever," it festers in men's minds, an incurable canker and "pest of the soul."[151] Philosophy served as the only remedy. Fanatics, he stated, are usually guided "by rascals, who put the dagger into their hands. They resemble that old man of the mountain who, it is said, made imbeciles taste the joys of paradise."[152]

Edward Gibbon's brief account of the Assassins took place in the context of his examination and comparison of "civilized" and

---

[148] One example is Lord Bolingbroke's claim that the Pope's authority made him "as terrible as the old man of the mountain." Lord Bolingbroke, *The Philosophical Works of the Late Right Honorable Henry St. John, Lord Viscount Bolingbroke, Vol. III* (London: Elibron Classics, 2005; 1776), 264–65. Bolingbroke elsewhere stated that the Pope's authority was like that of the "king of assassins," and that it had "proved fatal to Henry the Third, and Henry the Fourth of France." Lord Bolingbroke, *The Works of Lord Bolingbroke, Vol. I* (Carey and Hart, 1841), 367.

[149] Francis Bacon, "An Advertisement Touching a Holy War," in *The Works of Francis Bacon, Vol. 3* (London, 1825), 488.

[150] Voltaire, "Assassin–Assassination," in *The Philosophical Dictionary, The Works of Voltaire, Vol. VI* (Akron, Oh.: Werner Company, 1904), 88–92.

[151] Voltaire, "Fanatisme: Fanaticism," in *Philosophical Dictionary*, trans. and ed. Theodore Besterman (London and New York: Penguin Books, 1972), 205.

[152] Ibid., 203. The Old Man and his followers also served Helvétius as a despotic caricature. Jean François Saint-Lambert Helvétius, *Oeuvres Complètes d'Helvétius, Vol. 3, De L'Homme* (Paris, 1818), 410.

102   The Nizari Ismailis and the Assassin legends

"barbarous" peoples. Jeremy Black argues that the crucial relationship between the two categories was based on force, "the means by which each put pressure on the other." A competitive system of civilized polities "was necessary to progress."[153] Europe's division into contesting rivals was essential to their quality of governance. In Gibbon's words "in peace, the progress of knowledge and industry is accelerated by the emulation of so many active rivals."[154] Progress through competitive emulation and cultural transmission led to increased homogeneity. While progress was clearly associated with civilized states, barbarians were appreciated for both their virtues and, occasionally, their acts. Black emphasizes that Gibbon was clearly influenced by the Enlightenment's reevaluation of "primitive peoples."[155] The Assassins, though, escaped this favorable assessment. They were fanatics who exhibited blind obedience to their "vicar," placing them in a class apart from barbarians:

Among the hills to the south of the Caspian, these odious sectaries had reigned with impunity above a hundred and sixty years; and their prince, or Imam, established his lieutenant to lead and govern the colony of Mount Libanus, so famous and formidable in the history of the crusades. ... The daggers of his missionaries were felt both in the East and West: the Christians and the Moslems enumerate, and persons multiply, the illustrious victims that were sacrificed to the zeal, avarice, or resentment of *the old man* (as he was corruptly styled) *of the mountain*. But these daggers, his only arms, were broken by the sword of Holagou, and not a vestige is left of the enemies of mankind, except the word *assassin*, which, in the most odious sense, has been adopted in the languages of Europe.[156]

Black notes that Gibbon misjudged the contemporary threat to order, one that originated from within rather than outside of Europe.[157] Edmund Burke's polemics against the French Revolution are rife with allusions to assassins, with Condorcet set as a member of a "sect of philosophic robbers and assassins."[158] Revolutionary France was the "Republick of Assassins," and elsewhere he refers to the "infamous, cruel, and cowardly practice of assassination."[159] Burke's excoriation would further set France apart from the sociability necessary to participate

---

[153] Jeremy Black, "Gibbon and International Relations," in *Edward Gibbon and Empire*, ed. Rosamond McKitterick and Roland Quinault (New York: Cambridge University Press, 2002), 224.

[154] Quoted in Ibid.   [155] Ibid., 220.

[156] Edward Gibbon, *The History of the Decline and Fall of the Roman Empire: Vol. III*, ed. David Womersley (London: Penguin, 1994; 1788), 800–1. [Emphasis in original.]

[157] Black, "Gibbon and International Relations," 236.

[158] Emma Rothschild, "Condorcet and the Conflict of Values," *The Historical Journal* 39, no. 3 (September 1996): 679.

[159] Edmund Burke, *Empire and Community: Edmund Burke's Writings and Speeches on International Relations*, ed. David P. Fidler and Jennifer M. Welsh (Boulder, Colo.: Westview Press, 1999), 293; and Edmund Burke, "A Letter to a Member of the

Enlightenment and revolution: fanaticism and secrecy 103

in his "diplomatic republic of Europe." The association of assassination and the revolution as contrary to civilization is repeatedly reinforced, again conflating functional and identity formation requirements:

> [I]f ever a foreign prince enters into France, he must enter it as into a country of assassins. The mode of civilized war will not be practised: nor are the French who act on the present system entitled to expect it. . . . The new school of murder and barbarism, set up in Paris, having destroyed (so far as in it lies) all the other manners and principles which have hitherto civilized Europe, will destroy also the mode of civilized war, which, more than any thing else, has distinguished the Christian world.[160]

In his *Further Reflections on the Revolution*, Burke uses a variant of the term "assassin" twenty-one times. What is missing in Burke's usage, though, is a clear, direct reference to the historical Assassins.[161] While specific associations may be sparing, the French Revolution did advance further study of the Nizari Ismailis. This attention was spurred, according to Lewis, by an increased public interest in conspiracy and murder following the revolution.[162] Silvestre de Sacy's study of the Assassins and Austrian Orientalist Joseph von Hammer-Purgstall's *History of the Assassins* were both published in 1818.[163] These works perpetuated the Assassin legends, endorsing them and giving them a measure of scholarly legitimacy.[164] Von Hammer-Purgstall's account also had a polemical intent, offering a clear association of the Assassins with the revolution. His primary purpose in writing it, he wrote, was "to present a lively picture of the pernicious influence of secret societies in weak governments, and of the dreadful prostitution of religion to the horrors of unbridled ambition."[165] Fanaticism and secrecy, then, were further embedded as contrary to society and civilization, and so too was the "lively," inaccurate picture of the Assassins.

National Assembly," in *Reflections on the Revolution in France*, ed. Leslie G. Mitchell (Oxford: Oxford University Press, 1999), 276.

[160] Burke, "A Letter," 276.

[161] We can be fairly sure a man as learned as Burke was aware of the group. But a clear connection cannot be established without a thorough scouring of his library and private letters. The historical account of Camille Falconet was available in French, Camille Falconet, "Dissertation sur les Assassins, peuple d'Asie," *Mémoires de Littérature, tires de l'Académie Royale des Inscriptions et Belles Lettres* 17 (1751): 127–70; and we can have some confidence that Burke was aware of Voltaire's *Philosophical Dictionary*. The reference to the "infamous practice" suggests some historical resonance, but a firmer association has not been established.

[162] Lewis, *The Assassins*, 11.

[163] Silvestre de Sacy, "Memoir on the Dynasty of the Assassins, and on the Etymology of their Name (1818)," trans. Azizeh Azodi, in *Assassin Legends*, 136–88; Joseph von Hammer-Purgstall, *The History of the Assassins*, trans. O.C. Wood (London: 1835; 1818).

[164] Daftary, *Assassin Legends*, 122–23.

[165] von Hammer-Purgstall, *History of the Assassins*, 218.

104   The Nizari Ismailis and the Assassin legends

Civilization and savagery: juridical and political discourse on assassination

Having lost its association with the historical Assassins in international legal discourse, assassination became almost exclusively associated with early modern European and classical referents. Hugo Grotius relied on the latter in deriving the permissibility of assassination in public (i.e., lawful) war, and was likely focused on much more recent events such as the killing of Henry IV.[166] Alberico Gentili mentioned just about every historical actor *but* the Assassins in gainsaying dissimulation in killing leadership.[167] Emerich de Vattel broke this trend, seeing in assassination a threat to the functioning of the sovereign state system due to the uncertainty and vulnerability it presented to its leaders:

Had Titus lived in the time of the *old man of the mountain*, –; though the happiness of mankind centered in him, – though punctual in the observance of peace and equity, he was respected and adored by all potentates, – yet, the very first time that the prince of Assassins might have thought proper to quarrel with him, that universal affection would have proved insufficient to save him; and mankind would have lost their "darling." Let it not here be replied, that it is only in favour of the cause of justice that such extraordinary measures are allowable: for all parties, in their wars, maintain that they have justice on their side. Whoever, by setting the example, contributes to the introduction of so destructive a practice, declares himself the enemy of mankind, and deserves the execration of all ages.[168]

Vattel highlighted the diplomatic procedures and restraints on war that comported with the emerging state system.[169] At the same time, while emphasizing the functional requirements of an international society that allowed both peace and conflict, he established assassination as contrary not only to state practice but also to mankind itself. From then on, the personage of the Old Man and the Assassins fade from the legal discourse, though the negative association of assassination and civilization remained.

In the New World the civilizational discourse concerning assassination continued, rising to the more bound understanding of a "standard of civilization." Thomas Jefferson mentioned "[a]ssassination, poison,

---

[166] Hugo Grotius, "Selections from *The Law of War and Peace* (1625)," in *The Law of War: A Documentary History, Vol. 1*, ed. Leon Friedman (New York: Random House, 1972), 38–41.

[167] Alberico Gentili, *De Iure Belli Libri Tres, Vol. Two*, trans. John C. Rolfe, Classics of International Law (reprint Buffalo: William S. Hein & Co., 1995; 1612), 63–72. See also Thomas, "Norms and Security," 108.

[168] Emerich de Vattel, *Law of Nations; or Principles of the Law of Nature Applied to the Conduct and Affairs of Nations and Sovereigns*, ed. Joseph Chitty (Philadelphia: T. & J.W. Johnson & Co., 1863; 1758), 359.

[169] April Carter, *The Political Theory of Global Citizenship* (London: Routledge, 2001), 33.

Juridical and political discourse on assassination 105

perjury" as acts associated with the dark ages, and disparaged Haitians as cannibals and assassins.[170] The Lieber Code, named after jurist Francis Lieber, provided instructions for the Union Army and later the US Army in the field. "Civilized nations," it read, "look with horror upon offers or rewards for the assassination of enemies as relapses into barbarism."[171] Later, during the Philippine–American War, acts of violence associated with Filipino guerrilla warfare were used to justify colonialism and the brutal suppression of the insurgency, excluding the insurgents from the protections of the laws of civilized warfare.[172] A scorched earth policy was deemed necessary to counter the "savage hordes of naked bolomen" who "sneaked upon them in unguarded moments."[173]

A most evocative depiction of the historical actors as outside of civilization comes from a curious source. In the interim between the Haiti and Philippines episodes, another threat to civilization was seen, this one from within. Charles Sumner's May 1856 Senate speech "Crime against Kansas" decries the pro-slavery attacks during the Bleeding Kansas episode: "Hirelings, picked from the drunken spew and vomit of an uneasy civilization . . . leashed together by secret signs and lodges, have renewed the incredible atrocities of the Assassins and Thugs." The theme of the danger of secret societies and blind obedience is personified by the Assassins (armed with bowie knives instead of daggers), while heartlessness is exemplified by the Thugs (armed with revolvers rather than nooses).[174]

In the previous chapter I noted that the various theses associated with the development of norms would serve as guideposts, with observations in the cases serving to develop and refine rather than provide an up-or-down test of their applicability. Notably, the particular modes posited by the transmission thesis and the idea of norms of partiality – the diffusion of norms across space and time becoming generalized, institutionalized,

---

[170] Jefferson quoted in Thomas, "Norms and Security," 112; "cannibals and assassins" in Conor Cruise O'Brien, *The Long Affair: Thomas Jefferson and the French Revolution, 1785–1800* (Chicago: University of Chicago Press, 1996), 293.

[171] See Thomas, "Norms and Security," 113.

[172] See Paul A. Kramer, "The Pragmatic Empire: U.S. Anthropology and Colonial Politics in the Occupied Philippines, 1898–1916," PhD dissertation, Princeton University, 1998, 106–11.

[173] Quoted in Ibid., 109. Harsh measures by US forces also provoked revulsion and resulted in a further demarcation of civilized and savage warfare. See Guénaël Mettraux, "U.S. Courts-Martial and the Armed Conflict in the Philippines (1899–1902): Their Contribution to National Case Law on War Crimes," *Journal of International Criminal Justice* 1, no. 1 (April 2003): 135–50.

[174] Charles Sumner, "The Crime against Kansas: The Apologies for the Crime. The True Remedy," Speech in the Senate of the United States, May 19–20, 1856 (Boston: John P. Jewett, 1856), 31. The speech led to Sumner's caning at the hands of Preston Brooks.

106   The Nizari Ismailis and the Assassin legends

and hierarchical – were apparently not operative in this case. The development of the norms among European powers, however, was influenced in a less direct way, by transmitting potent symbols of alien perfidy, allowing long-used modes of killing to be cast as the extension of foreign villainy. The use of such tactics would eventually be associated with the legitimacy of the actors who resorted to them, and the symbol of the Assassins for a time proved useful and evocative for those charting the bounds of civilized behavior.

Legitimacy entails rightful membership and conduct, and in this case those two aspects are inextricable. For the Sunni orthodoxy, as well as more orthodox Shia, the determination of rightful conduct was settled by the judgment of rightful membership. Over time, as assassination became more closely associated with generic activity, and the Assassin legends faded, rightful conduct began to determine rightful membership. The judgment of assassination as beyond the pale of civilization was clearly established. The Enlightenment firmed the suspicion of fanaticism and blind obedience, while the French Revolution realized these aberrancies according to its critics. One should not overstate any primary causal significance of the imagery of the Old Man of the Mountain and his fanatic followers. They did, however, provide a reference point for determining where civilization would be without the progress and restraint of reasoned society. Vattel's emphasis on the safety of princes reflected his concern for the maintenance of the sovereign state system, with its constant but relatively predictable conflict. This illustrated the overlapping needs of physical and ontological security, recalling Bill McSweeney's characterization of being "safely in cognitive control of the interaction context."[175] The fickleness and callousness of the Old Man provided a refracted image of what the state system would be like without the common constraints of international society. In some measure informed by those depictions, a standard of civilization arose that saw assassination as an indication of savagery, a standard reinforced by a long-standing suspicion of fanaticism and secrecy and their combined effects.

[175] Bill McSweeney, *Security, Identity, and Interests: A Sociology of International Relations* (Cambridge: Cambridge University Press, 1999), 157.

3 *"A furore Tartarorum libera nos"*
The Mongol eruption and aftermath

They differed from Comanche and Apache in that capacity for military organization which gave them such terrible efficiency; but otherwise they were not much more advanced, and the civilized peoples who fell under their sway experienced a fate as dreadful as would be the case if nowadays a civilized people were suddenly conquered by a great horde of Apaches. . . . The scourge of the Mongol conquests was terrible beyond belief, so that even where a land was flooded but for a moment, the memory long remained. It was not long since in certain churches in Eastern Europe the litany still contained the prayer, "From the fury of the Mongols, good Lord deliver us."

—Theodore Roosevelt, in Jeremiah Curtin, *The Mongols: A History*

Introduction

"Kicked to a pulp and then put to the sword. . . . So was the world cleansed which had been polluted by their evil."[1] Such was the judgment of an early historian concerning the eradication of the Nizari Ismailis by the Mongols. Edward Gibbon later labeled the destruction of the Assassin strongholds "a service to mankind."[2] Favorable accounts of the Mongols, however, would not ultimately typify their representation, due in part to their unique impact and in part to their essential nature. While anthropologists have long seen nomads and pastoralists as favored subjects, according to Rudi Lindner, "[h]istorians dislike nomads." He attributes this antipathy to the dissonance resulting from their mode of life, which keeps "us from a full comprehension of people whose prosperity depended so much on continual movement and opportunistic raiding."[3]

---

[1] 'Ata-Malik Juvayni, *Genghis Khan: The History of the World Conqueror*, trans. John A. Boyle (Manchester: Manchester University Press, 1997; 1958), 725.

[2] Edward Gibbon, *The History of the Decline and Fall of the Roman Empire, Vol. III*, ed. David Womersley (London: Penguin, 1994; 1788), 800–1.

[3] Rudi Paul Lindner, "What Was a Nomadic Tribe?" *Comparative Studies in Society and History* 24, no. 4 (October 1982): 689. On the treatment of Inner Asian political formations in world history, see Nicola Di Cosmo, "State Formation and Periodization in Inner

108   The Mongol eruption and aftermath

For this study the case of the Mongols is valuable not only for the insights it provides but for the variation it presents as a deviant case. The rest of the cases examine persistent survivors, with the further persistence of Al Qaeda to be determined. Though the other actors posed serious challenges to the powers in their respective systems, they never came close to the level or extent of Mongol dominance. Yet the Mongols are quite like the other cases presented in that they did not emulate the structures or behaviors of the dominant actors in the system. An account of the Mongols' success and its impact in international systemic and societal terms thus should help firm up the assessment of the mechanisms and processes behind their uncommon achievements.

In outlining a structural-systemic account of the expansion of the Mongols, it is not intended to offer a deterministic model. Elements of individual leadership play a key role in explaining an unlikely series of events. These events were unlikely not solely because of their rarity, with an irregularly structured actor not only surviving but thriving and dominating the system. They were unlikely because they required not only uncommon leadership but an uncommon set of structural circumstances. It is a story prefaced by an anarchic subsystem of steppe tribes, a weak and marginalized future leader, and a set of materially enriched but internally decaying sedentary powers. The story ends with the name Genghis Khan (the familiar version of the preferred Chinggis Khan) as synonymous with naked aggression and wanton killing.

This chapter covers that progression, first identifying the conditions from which the Mongol polity emerged in order to account for its unification from the disparate tribes that had composed a distinct subsystem. The actors associated with the Mongol ascendance are introduced, including the dominant sedentary powers and the steppe tribes that would become the inchoate Mongol state under Chinggis's leadership. While the system examined entails the united Mongol polity and its competition with the sedentary states that surrounded it, delving into the history and dynamics of the precursor steppe system helps

---

Asian History," *Journal of World History* 10, no. 1 (Spring 1999): 1–40. See also Denis Sinor, "Reflections on the History and Historiography of the Nomad Empires of Central Eurasia," *Acta Orientalia Academiae Scientiarum Hungaricae* 58, no. 1 (April 2005): 3–14. Concerning the historiography of the Mongols, see Peter Jackson, "The State of Research: The Mongol Empire, 1986–1999," *Journal of Medieval History* 26, no. 2 (2000): 189–210; and Bat-Ochir Bold, *Mongolian Nomadic Society: A Reconstruction of the "Medieval" History of Mongolia* (Richmond, Surrey: Curzon: 2001), 1–24. For the challenges presented to indigenous Mongolian historiography, including the role of Mongolia's powerful neighbors in suppressing it, see Thomas N. Haining, "The Vicissitudes of Mongolian Historiography in the Twentieth Century," in *The Mongol Empire and Its Legacy*, ed. Reuven Amitai-Preiss (Leiden: Brill, 1999), 332–46.

Prologue: sedentary states and steppe tribal confederations   109

provide a fuller picture of the Mongols' unlikely emergence and ascendance to empire. This is accomplished by an account of Chinggis's improbable rise, including the role of his relationship with his future adversary the Jin dynasty, and the circumstances of the declining powers that would become the first targets of conquest. That story prefaces discussion of the Mongol Empire's expansion (1206–1260 CE) and its distinctiveness from contemporary rivals. Following this description of the changing composition of the system, the Mongols' impact on the norms and identities of those not directly enveloped, and their longer-term effects on international society, are elaborated.

The variation of the level of success the Mongols obtained compared to the other cases helps isolate the effects of some of the posited mechanisms. Those circumstances, however, complicate the assessment of the posited effects on international society due to conditions of domination imposing rather than merely shaping the development of norms. Their menace bounded and loomed, across Central and Western Europe, respectively. Swift movement and odd comportment terrified and befuddled Christian populations who struggled to situate this strange enemy in their cosmic order with the hopes of preserving their physical security while restoring ontological security. By looking at the impact of the Mongol invasions on those on the edge of the conquests and those who had a near-miss (Western Europe), we see pronounced effects of their deviating behavior on the formation of identities. Over time these effects diffused as the once modest steppe tribe became a recurring symbol of the potentially explosive peril seen in those who act contrary to the tenets of civilization. A lack of fixity would become correlated with aggression even as sedentary societies began to perfect their capacity for violent expansion, and they would later be evoked to highlight modern powers' excesses in destruction.

Prologue: sedentary states and steppe tribal confederations

The geographic setting for the tribal consolidation under the Mongols has been given a number of labels, including Central Eurasia and Inner Asia. Central Eurasia encompasses a belt that extends from western Manchuria to the Danube.[4] The eastern portion of this region is also defined in terms of China and its Inner Asian frontier, or Northern Zone. This distinctly Chinese perspective describes the ecological and cultural frontier

---

[4] Nicola Di Cosmo, *Ancient China and Its Enemies: The Rise of Nomadic Power in East Asian History* (Cambridge: Cambridge University Press, 2002), 13–14.

110   The Mongol eruption and aftermath

between China and the pastoral, nomadic peoples on its northern periphery.[5] During the two centuries prior to the Mongol eruption, the grouping of states that constituted China interacted as a system within a broader East Asian international system. The states of tenth-century China treated each other as foreign lands, conducting diplomacy and sending envoys as they did with non-Chinese states.[6]

The northern Chinese states were referred to as the Five Dynasties, while the south was referred to as the Ten Kingdoms. Foreign powers took advantage of their disunion, and the north faced the interference and a direct threat from the Khitan, who occupied Manchuria in the form of the Liao dynasty. Edmund Worthy notes that while this period was "Byzantine" in its complexity and intrigues, it is best understood as a period of shifting balances among Chinese states and their neighbors, each of which had claims of legitimacy and sought unification.[7] This balance was disrupted by the eventual success of the Song (or Sung) in consolidating control over most of inner China in the latter half of the tenth century. This period is referred to as the Northern Song and lasts until 1127 when the Jurchen Jin dynasty ejected the Song from northern China.

The Jurchen occupied the forests and steppes of Manchuria and were one of three "barbarian" (i.e., non-Chinese) powers in the north, the others being the Hsi Hsia (Xi Xia)[8] and Khitan Liao.[9] Thomas Barfield examined the structural dynamic between China and these steppe peoples, and characterized the occasional unifications of the steppe as "shadow empires."[10] Dependent on exploitation of sedentary societies (through pillage, tribute, and trade) the steppe empires that arose relied on the unification and prosperity of China. This process of consolidation and unification led to symbiotic relationships between Chinese and steppe empires, with steppe empires occasionally aiding the sedentary powers when they faced internal or external threats.[11]

---

[5] Ibid.

[6] Edmund H. Worthy, Jr., "Diplomacy for Survival: Domestic and Foreign Relations of Wu Yüeh, 907–978," in *China among Equals: The Middle Kingdom and its Neighbors*, ed. Morris Rossabi (Berkeley and Los Angeles: University of California Press, 1983), 19.

[7] Ibid., 37.

[8] For an overview of the Hsi Hsia, see Ruth Dunnel, "The Hsi Hsia," in *The Cambridge History of China, Vol. 6, Alien Regimes and Border States, 907–1368*, ed. Herbert Franke and Dennis Twitchett (Cambridge: Cambridge University Press, 1994), 154–215.

[9] For background on the Khitan Liao, see Dennis Twitchett and Klaus-Peter Tietze, "The Liao," in *Cambridge History of China*, 43–153.

[10] Thomas J. Barfield, "The Shadow Empires: Imperial State Formation along the Chinese–Nomad Frontier," in *Empires: Perspectives from Archaeology and History*, ed. Susan E. Alcock, et al. (Cambridge: Cambridge University Press, 2001), 10.

[11] Ibid., 22–23.

Prologue: sedentary states and steppe tribal confederations   111

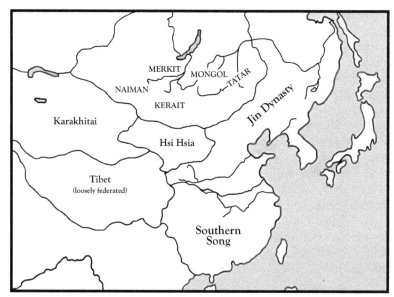

Map 3.1 Sedentary states and steppe tribes
Sources: Frederick Mote, *Imperial China 900–1800* (Harvard University Press, 1999) and Herbert Franke, "The Chin Dynasty," in *Cambridge History of China*, Vol. 6, ed. Herbert Franke and Dennis Twitchett (Cambridge University Press, 1994)

What resulted from this mix was a multi-state system that extended from Manchuria to Central Asia, populated by largely centralized, sedentary states. One subservient branch of the Jurchens, who inhabited a large portion of eastern Manchuria, had been reliable when divided. Once united they settled their grievances with the Liao dynasty in a series of invasions in the second decade of the twelfth century. The Jin (meaning "gold") dynasty was declared in 1121, and expanded into the territories of the Northern Song, capturing their capital in 1127.[12] The defeated Khitan, meanwhile, migrated westward to establish the Karakhitai (Qara Khitai) or Western Liao dynasty in 1141.[13]

---

[12] David Sneath, "Beyond the Willow Palisade: Manchuria and the History of China's Inner Asian Frontier," *Asian Affairs* (London) 34, no. 1 (March 2003): 6–7. For an overview of the Jin dynasty, see Herbert Franke, "The Chin Dynasty," in *Cambridge History of China*, 215–320.

[13] Detailed studies of the Karakhitai can be found in Michal Biran, *The Empire of the Qara Khitai in Eurasian History: Between China and the Islamic World* (Cambridge: Cambridge University Press, 2005); Michal Biran, "Like a Mighty Wall: The Armies of the Qara Khitai," *Jerusalem Studies in Arabic and Islam* 25 (2001): 44–91; and Denis Sinor, "The

112   The Mongol eruption and aftermath

The Jurchen Jin accomplished a more extensive conquest of northern China than their former Khitan overlords. They inherited the administrative structures of the Liao dynasty (which were adopted from Chinese patterns), establishing a central capital in Beijing. The Jurchen combined cavalry (reflecting their semi-nomadic origins) with Chinese weapons and infantry to force the Song into southern China. This initiated the period identified as the Southern Song, leaving those two powers in control of the central and eastern portions of China.[14] The Hsi Hsia in the northwest and the loosely federated Kingdom of Tibet to the west, meanwhile, were both too weak to pose a major threat.[15]

The competition between the Jurchen and the Song would be characterized by both conflict and accommodation. A cycle of war, trade, treaties, broken treaties, and revanchism followed, continuing into the early years of the thirteenth century.[16] Over that time the Jurchen struggled to adapt from conquest to sedentary modes of rule.[17] Adopting Khitan Liao and Chinese institutions the Jurchen struggled throughout their rule to maintain their own "Jurchenness."[18] Their imitation was fostered both by their lack of institutional solidity, and, in Herbert Franke's words, a desire "to emulate the power and splendor" of more developed states.[19] The difficulties of administration and internal dissension would contribute to their weakness preceding the Mongol invasion. Further to the west, the rival powers of the Karakhitai and Khorezmshah played minor roles in the dynamics of the Chinese system, though they would later be sites of Mongol conquest.[20]

Kitan and the Kara Khitay," in *History of Civilizations of Central Asia, Vol. IV, Part 1*, ed. Muhammad S. Asimov and Clifford E. Bosworth (Paris: UNESCO, 1998), 227–42.

[14] Thomas J. Barfield, *The Perilous Frontier: Nomadic Empires and China, 221 BC to AD 1757* (Cambridge, Mass.: Blackwell, 1989), 179.

[15] The Jin had mostly stabilized their relationship with the Hsi Hsia, which was established as an "outer vassal." Franke, "Chin Dynasty," 226–29.

[16] These events are covered in Hok-lam Chan, "Commerce and Trade in Divided China: The Case of Jurchen–Jin Versus the Northern and Southern Song," *Journal of Asian History* 36 (2002): 135–38; and Franke, "Chin Dynasty," 226–50. These relations as they affected the Song are covered in Frederick W. Mote, *Imperial China 900–1800* (Cambridge: Harvard University Press, 1999), 289–322.

[17] Barfield, *Perilous Frontier*, 180; 141.

[18] The phases of Jin political development are covered in Mote, *Imperial China*, 222–43; and Franke, "Chin Dynasty," 239–40. See also Jing-shen Tao, *The Jurchen in Twelfth-Century China: A Study of Sinicization* (Seattle: University of Washington Press, 1976).

[19] Franke, "Chin Dynasty," 217.

[20] For background on the Khorezmshah (referring to the ruler and the land of the Khorezm), see David Christian, *A History of Russia, Central Asia, and Mongolia, Vol. I, Inner Eurasia from Prehistory to the Mongol Empire* (Oxford: Blackwell, 1998), 377–78. See also Ali Sevim and Clifford E. Bosworth, "The Seljuqs and Khwarazm Shahs," in *History of Civilizations of Central Asia*, 161–75.

Prologue: sedentary states and steppe tribal confederations   113

While the sedentary states vied for dominance, a fluid subsystem of nomadic tribes existed in their shadow. Tribal federations contested for control over the steppe, an area roughly the size of Alaska, often with the active interference of sedentary states. The tumultuous and amorphous nature of this subsystem was vulnerable to outside influence and resistant to unification. During the twelfth century the steppe tribes consisted of a number of loose tribal federations (also referred to as *ulus*) that competed for predominance and survival. The names of these groups, David Christian explains, "describe fragile and unstable alliance systems headed by local aristocratic or royal clans and include many heterogeneous elements."[21] Divisions within the units were based on a number of factors including tribe and lineage. Thomas Allsen describes these political formations as "arbitrary and temporary constructions, [which] were by nature dynamic, flexible, and unstable."[22]

The major tribal federations that comprised the subsystem included the Tatar, Mongol, Kerait, Merkit, and Naiman (as they were roughly situated from east to west).[23] While most of these groups were pastoral, they were varied in their ecological and commercial practices, reflecting the diversity of their environments from the forests of the eastern portions to the trade routes to the west.[24] Traditionally, the Tatars were the most powerful tribe in eastern Mongolia, supported by the Jin, and were a longtime enemy of the Mongol tribes. As the twelfth century proceeded, and Tatar power grew, Jin support would shift to other steppe tribes.

The derivation of the name "Mongol" is uncertain, though it may have come from the Onon river (Onon gol) where the Mongols' predecessors had migrated beginning in the tenth century.[25] In 1161, with the support of the Jin, the Tatars defeated the Mongol tribes under Qabul Khan (the grandfather of Temüjin, later Chinggis Khan).[26] The Kerait, who were

---

[21] Christian, *History of Russia*, 388.

[22] Thomas T. Allsen, "The Rise of the Mongolian Empire and Mongolian Rule in North China," in *Cambridge History of China*, 325.

[23] Peter Golden also includes the Oirat and Önggüt peoples as significant power blocs during this period. Peter Golden, "Inner Asia c. 1200," in *The Cambridge History of Inner Asia, Vol. 1, The Chinggisid Age*, ed. Nicola Di Cosmo, Allen J. Frank, and Peter B. Golden (Cambridge: Cambridge University Press, 2009), 18–25. The Önggüt, who lived in forest areas abutting the Jin Dynasty, would play a significant role by providing military support to Chinggis to attack the Jin. See Peter Jackson, "The Mongol Age in Eastern Inner Asia," in *Cambridge History of Inner Asia*, 33.

[24] Christian, *History of Russia*, 388.

[25] Ibid. Questions concerning the origins of the Mongol tribes are detailed in Zhao Zhan, "On the Origins of the Mongols," *Journal of the Anglo-Mongolian Society* 9, nos. 1–2, (December 1984): 43–47; and Tamura Jitsuzô, "The Legend of the Origin of the Mongols and Problems Concerning Their Migration," *Acta Asiatica* 24 (1973): 1–19.

[26] Shagdaryn Bira, "The Mongols and Their State in the Twelfth to the Thirteenth Century," in *History of Civilizations of Central Asia*, 244.

114   The Mongol eruption and aftermath

Nestorian Christians, would rival Tatar power in the latter half of the twelfth century.[27] The Merkit suffered from internal divisions but remained a substantial force.[28] More advanced due to their interaction with sedentary neighbors, the Naiman maintained a greater level of continuity and unity than the other tribes.[29]

Sedentary powers exploited rivalries, seeking to ensure that no one group would ascend and become a threat. Using their knowledge of tribal and pastoral nomadic politics, the Jin rulers exercised a divide-and-rule strategy, cultivating the leaders of weaker tribes to check the power of stronger ones.[30] This support shifted as the power relations did. While effective, Barfield notes, this strategy entailed risks by supporting minor powers and potentially cultivating new leaders who could also exploit tribal rifts.[31] Indeed, this strategy would help give rise to a new leader, and result in a devastating blowback against Jin interests. What these circumstances highlight is how the relative gains calculus derived from great power interaction loses explanatory power in contexts with multiple competitors with differential resources. Supporting potential future rivals as a near-term exigency was followed even with the knowledge of potential future peril, though it is unlikely the Jin saw the Mongols as an extraordinary risk due to their extremely modest position. How Chinggis Khan could overcome his tribe's, and his own, marginal position is directly tied to relationships with the Jin, and to the internal condition of that dynasty and others as the twelfth century closed.

Mongol consolidation and sedentary decline

Temüjin was born around 1162. He was a descendant of two of the original Mongol khans and part of the ruling Borjigid lineage. Despite his noble birth, Temüjin came of age in a period when the Mongol tribes had been defeated by the Tatars, who poisoned his father, and weakened by both outside threats and internal divisions. Stories of Temüjin's youth emphasize the hardships he faced and the leadership qualities and bravery he demonstrated under harsh conditions.[32] The semi-mythical character

---

[27] See Isenbike Togan, *Flexibility and Limitation in Steppe Formations* (Leiden: Brill, 1998), 65–71.

[28] Paul Ratchnevsky, *Genghis Khan: His Life and Legacy*, trans. Thomas N. Haining (Malden, Mass.: Blackwell, 1991; 1983), 5.

[29] Allsen, "Rise of the Mongolian Empire," 323.   [30] Barfield, *Perilous Frontier*, 182–84.

[31] Ibid., 184.

[32] These events are summarized in Allsen, "Rise of the Mongolian Empire," 334–35; and Ratchnevsky, *Genghis Khan*, 19–31. One primary source for early Mongol history is *The Secret History of the Mongols*. The most recent and comprehensive translation is Igor de

Mongol consolidation and sedentary decline

of these stories ought not diminish the reality of the weakened and marginal position that he occupied.[33] How Temüjin forged alliances and attracted followers, and became Chinggis Khan, attests to his acumen, endurance, and dexterity in navigating the politics of the steppe and sedentary powers. While much of the period of his rise and the unification of the steppe is uncertain in terms of its chronology, key relationships and events mark his ascent to power.

Crafting vital alliances, Temüjin around 1182 convinced To'oril Khan, a friend of his father and powerful chief of the Keraits, to act as his patron as he cemented ties with childhood friend Jamuqa. With these early relationships Temüjin could build on his ruling lineage and begin to overcome his weakened position. The patronage of To'oril provided protection as Temüjin's standing rose.[34] Around 1184 the daring rescue of his kidnapped wife, with the assistance of To'oril and Jamuqa, heightened his reputation.[35] His prowess and leadership capacity attracted more and more followers. As Temüjin ascended, his alliance and friendship with Jamuqa frayed, leading to a clash between them for leadership of the Mongols, which Temüjin lost.

Temüjin disappears from the record in the late 1180s, only to reappear as an ally of the Jin around 1196. The Tatars were the latest steppe group to alarm the Jin. As the Jin allied with To'oril, Temüjin assisted them in defeating the new threat. This relationship formalized with the conference of a title to To'oril, who became known as Ong Khan ("prince khan"). Temüjin received the Jin title of *zhaotaoshi*, "bandit suppression commissioner," or "pacification commissioner."[36] But according to some sources he received a lesser title that just acknowledged him as an allied chieftain.[37] Another observer interprets his cooperation with the Jin as "accepting a position in the Chin [Jin] world order," and his title as "a

---

Rachewiltz, trans. and ed., *The Secret History of the Mongols: A Mongolian Epic Chronicle of the Thirteenth Century* (Leiden and Boston: Brill, 2004).

[33] Thomas Barfield, "Inner Asia Cycles of Power in China's Imperial History," in *Rulers from the Steppe: State Formation on the Eurasian Periphery, Vol. II*, ed. Gary Seaman and Daniel Marks (Los Angeles: Ethnographics Press, 1991), 48–49.

[34] Ratchnevsky, *Genghis Khan*, 33. Up to that time, Temüjin had been, "no more than one among several Mongol chieftains who were fiercely ambitious to acquire status and power." Mote, *Imperial China*, 419.

[35] Barfield, *Perilous Frontier*, 189; Christian, *History of Russia*, 390–91.

[36] On this title, see Charles O. Hucker, *A Dictionary of Official Titles in Imperial China* (Stanford: Stanford University Press, 1985), 117; and Christopher P. Atwood, *Encyclopedia of Mongolia and the Mongolian Empire* (New York: Facts on File, 2004), 98; 275.

[37] Paul D. Buell, "The Role of the Sino–Mongolian Frontier Zone in the Rise of Cinggis-Qan," *Studies on Mongolia: Proceedings of the First North American Conference on Mongolian Studies* (1979): 65.

116   The Mongol eruption and aftermath

chief in the service of the Chin who exerts control over different tribes."[38] Historians have addressed the significance of Temüjin's absence from the record, and the nature of his relationship with the Jin. Some suggest that after his defeat by Jamuqa, Temüjin was held captive by the Jin; and that this is not reflected in the Mongol accounts due to the ignominy of such an episode and the suggestion of potential cooptation.[39] Earlier Mongol rulers had similarly close ties with the Jin, including vassal status and titles, and this was also not reflected in the primary Mongol histories.[40]

Paul Buell argues that Temüjin's relationship with the Jin has to be understood in the context of the complex frontier system devised to control tribes along their border.[41] "Temüjin's association with Chin frontier organization," Buell contends, "in particular his formal recognition as a chieftain by the court, could not have failed to give form and definition to what must have been a rather amorphous following."[42] Elsewhere, he tempers this assertion by saying that it "may have helped consolidate" his following.[43] Even without Temüjin's formal association with the Jin, he was essentially a vassal to a Jin vassal in the more powerful To'oril, whose association with the Jin was clear-cut.[44] Early military successes within this arrangement solidified his position and were crucial in building his following.

To appreciate how these relationships helped Temüjin ascend, it is important to understand how stratification along clan, lineage, and tribal lines led to a system where success was a primary currency for political legitimacy. In the harsh political climate of the steppe, associations were fluid, and "common political interest was typically translated into the

[38] Togan, *Flexibility and Limitation*, 86. See also Togan's graphical illustration of the relationships between Temüjin, the Kerait, and the Jin (Figure 6, page 162).

[39] Elizabeth Endicott, "The Mongols and China: Cultural Contacts and the Changing Nature of Pastoral Nomadism (Twelfth to Early Twentieth Centuries)," in *Mongols, Turks, and Others: Eurasian Nomads and the Sedentary World*, ed. Reuven Amitai and Michal Biran (Leiden: Brill, 2005), 465.

[40] Franke, "Chin Dynasty," 238.

[41] Buell, "Frontier Zone," 64–65. This manner of attempting to manage the frontier, "to control barbarians by using other barbarians," was a common Chinese strategy. See Chusei Suzuki, "Chinese Relations with Inner Asia: The Hsiung-Nu, Tibet," in *The Chinese World Order: Traditional China's Foreign Relations*, ed. John King Fairbank (Cambridge: Harvard University Press, 1968), 191.

[42] Buell, "Frontier Zone," 65.

[43] Paul D. Buell, *The A to Z of the Mongol World Empire* (Lanham, Md.: Scarecrow Press, 2010), 11.

[44] Paul Buell describes To'oril as "Temüjin's principal supporter and the primary ally of the Jin in the deep steppe" (Ibid.). Highlighting the importance of his association with To'oril, Isenbike Togan makes the claim that "it is doubtful whether there would be a Chinggis Khan as we know him without the Kerait experience." Togan, *Flexibility and Limitation*, 121.

Mongol consolidation and sedentary decline 117

idiom of kinship."[45] In such a system, a talented person, particularly one with a royal lineage, could demonstrate his prowess, cultivate his following, and eliminate his rivals.[46] While talent and lineage surely played a role in the rise of Temüjin to Chinggis Khan, so too did key relationships with near and far forces. This includes those with the Jin that, at the very least indirectly, allowed him to bound and rebound into steppe politics, fostering his ascent to power from what Barfield characterizes as an "extremely marginal position."[47]

With the Tatars defeated, the Kerait and Naiman were left the most powerful groups in northern Mongolia.[48] Temüjin appears to have been content to remain a junior partner to the Kerait, while Ong Khan exploited the rivalry between Temüjin and Jamuqa to assure this subordination.[49] Eventually, after a series of intrigues and attacks against rival tribes, Temüjin managed to neutralize his competitors within the Mongols and defeat Ong Khan, securing control over the Kerait. Controlling the strategic Orkhon river valley, Temüjin and his expanding forces defeated a challenge from an alliance led by the Naiman, and then attacked the remaining Merkit.[50] Temüjin had removed any remaining rivals and was proclaimed Chinggis Khan, "oceanic" or "universal" ruler. The *quriltai* or assembly of 1206, where Chinggis was acclaimed, also set up the institutions of the united Mongol polity providing the foundation for expansion and empire.

While the steppe was becoming more unified and institutionally solidified, its sedentary neighbor, the Jin dynasty, was moving in the opposite direction. By the last decades of the twelfth century, the Jin dynasty had passed its prime in its military supremacy and economic prosperity, suffering from a litany of internal and external problems. These woes included, according to Hok-lam Chan, "rising government expenses, depletion of state reserves, sporadic inflation, and the flooding of the Yellow River in the 1170s and 1180s."[51] The problems were

---

[45] Allsen, "Rise of the Mongolian Empire," 325. See also Thomas J. Barfield, "Tribe and State Relations: The Inner Asian Perspective," in *Tribes and State Formation in the Middle East*, ed. Philip S. Khoury and Joseph Kostiner (Berkeley and Los Angeles: University of California Press, 1990), 165.

[46] On this common steppe phenomenon, see Di Cosmo, "State Formation," 18–19.

[47] Barfield, "Inner Asia Cycles," 49. Owen Lattimore writes that the relatively minor title given to Temüjin suggests that the Jurchen underestimated him, thinking that he was "just another border freebooter." Owen Lattimore, "The Geography of Chingis Khan," *The Geographical Journal* 129, no. 1 (March 1963): 6.

[48] Barfield, *Perilous Frontier*, 190.   [49] Ibid.

[50] See Barfield, *Perilous Frontier*, 190–91; and Allsen, "Rise of the Mongolian Empire," 338–42.

[51] Hok-lam Chan, "From Tribal Chieftain to Sinitic Emperor: Leadership Contests and Succession Crises in the Jurchen–Jin State, 1115–1234," *Journal of Asian History* 33, no. 2 (1999): 125.

118   The Mongol eruption and aftermath

compounded by political challenges including deteriorating relations with the Song, depredations by steppe tribes, uprisings by its Khitan and Chinese subjects, and decline within the Jurchen elite.[52] War with the Song lasted from 1204 to 1208, followed quickly by a succession crisis.[53] Devolution to local rulers and deterioration of central control, combined with rife corruption, reflected and added to these ills.[54] Buell points to Jin preoccupation with internal difficulties in explaining the weakening of its influence on the steppe.[55] In 1207 there was an uprising of *Jüyin*, a category of steppe peoples that served as a reserve of military labor, leading to the loss of control over several key groups on the frontier who had provided an important part of the Jin frontier defense.[56] Their defection gave the tribes united under the Mongols greater control over the frontier zone, bolstering Mongol power. More generally, the decline of the Jin and their other sedentary rivals would help trigger Mongol expansion from a steppe contender to a world power.

Eruption and expansion

The reorganization and consolidation of Mongol power provided the basis for unprecedented conquest and expansion.[57] The first steps in this expansion were campaigns to mop up remaining resistance from peripheral steppe tribes and establish the submission of the Uighurs and Hsi Hsia, resulting in valuable revenue and troop levies. The first major attack of the Mongol expansion involved their former Jin overlords, which began in 1211 but would only lead to the eradication of the dynasty in 1234.[58] While those events unfolded, the Mongols expanded westward, conquering Central Asia: defeating a former Naiman rival leading to the submission of the Karakhitai (1218), besieging Bukhara (1220), vanquishing the Khorezmshah (1221), and destroying several cities that resisted their efforts.[59] Prior to the death of Chinggis in 1227 (who was

---

[52] Ibid.   [53] The conflict is detailed in Franke, "Chin Dynasty," 245–50.

[54] Tao, *The Jurchen*, 87–88.   [55] Buell, "Frontier Zone," 65–66.

[56] Ibid., 67. On the use of Jüyin auxiliaries, see Rachewiltz, *Secret History of the Mongols*, vol. 1, 300–1; vol. 2, 893, 972; and Paul D. Buell, "Tribe, Qan, and Ulus in Early Mongol China: Some Prolegomena to Yüan History," PhD dissertation, University of Washington, 1977.

[57] Thomas Barfield details the organization of the Mongols under Chinggis in *Perilous Frontier*, 193–97.

[58] The early stages of the war with the Jin are portrayed as back-and-forth efforts to coerce and extract loot from a weakening Jin court. See Ibid., 199–201.

[59] Christian, *History of Russia*, 401; Sinor, "The Kitan," 241. These campaigns to consolidate hold of the steppe and secure its periphery are detailed in Paul D. Buell, "Early Mongol Expansion in Western Siberia and Turkestan (1207–1219): A Reconstruction," *Central Asiatic Journal* 36 (1992): 1–36. Dates of these conquests vary among sources.

Eruption and expansion 119

replaced by Ögedei in 1229), Mongol forces made probing attacks into the Caucasus region and Russia (1222–1223), and began the ultimate destruction the Hsi Hsia (1227).[60]

Historians have explained Mongol expansion in a variety of ways. Revenge against previous domination and humiliation (by the Jin), ideology (that conferred Chinggis a divine right to universal rule), historical accident (the inability of the Jin to satisfy Mongol tribute demands), and faulty decision-making (the killing of a Mongol trade delegation by agents of the Khorezmshah) have all been cited as causes for the expansion.[61] Explanations encompass a mixture of drivers that, together, paint a curious picture of a leader entitled to world domination, but deeply reluctant to realize that mandate. "Neither hatred nor a frenzied demand for revenge," one observer writes, "nor even a fierce desire to conquer and rule motivated them."[62] The expansion itself, purportedly unwillingly engaged, generated its own momentum, with campaigns increasing demands from followers for rewards – a dynamic originating in the steppe subsystem.[63] This framing of the Mongol expansion may explain some of the dynamics, particularly in the early phases, though the reluctance for conquest and rule seems belied by the increasing bent toward domination. While accounting for the overdetermined causation for Mongol expansion (the roles of ideology, individual motivations, contingency, and agency), it is essential to focus on the triggers that began the Mongol expansion beyond the steppe, and beyond the scale of any previous steppe empire.[64]

What set the Mongol conquests in motion? Arnold Toynbee forwarded an explanation of nomadic expansion focusing on twin forces: the "push" of climatic conditions on the steppe (increased aridity), and the "pull" of sedentary societies that offered opportunities for plunder (particularly

---

[60] On the attacks on the Russians and their Kipchak allies, see John Fennell, *The Crisis of Medieval Russia, 1204–1304* (London: Longman, 1983), 63–68. These attacks, while damaging to those who suffered through them, were more of a preface to the concerted assault that would come fourteen years later.

[61] See Christian, *History of Russia*, 402. The ideological foundations of Mongol expansion are highlighted in Igor de Rachewiltz, "Some Remarks on the Ideological Foundations of Chingis Khan's Empire," *Papers on Far Eastern History* 7 (March 1973): 21–36.

[62] Mote, *Imperial China*, 243. See also Bira, "Mongols and Their State," 253; and Lattimore, "Geography of Chingis Khan," 7. The theme of revenge, though, is prominent in the *Secret History of the Mongols*. See Larry V. Clark, "The Theme of Revenge in the *Secret History of the Mongols*," in *Aspects of Altaic Civilization II*, ed. Larry V. Clark and Paul A. Draghi (Bloomington: Indiana University, 1978), 37–57.

[63] Christian, *History of Russia*, 399.

[64] See Gareth Jenkins, "A Note on Climatic Cycles and the Rise of Chinggis Khan," *Central Asiatic Journal* 18 (1974): 217–18. Jenkins comments on the acceptance of founding myths and the proliferation of explanations for the Mongol expansion.

120   The Mongol eruption and aftermath

during their decline).[65] Nomadic societies, according to the "push" thesis, were the "perpetual prisoners" of their environmental conditions.[66] Diminishing the role of climate, Owen Lattimore referred to the "mechanical agency" of this explanation, one that also served to explain the "backwardness" of nomadic civilizations, perpetually engaged in survival rather than striving for more advanced modes of life.[67]

The ecological setting and its constraints were critical conditioning factors in the nature of their society, their relationships with their neighbors, and, it will be argued, in how the Mongol polity evolved.[68] The trigger for the Mongol "eruption," however, was more closely associated with the decline of dominant powers in the system. According to William Atwell, "virtually everywhere the Mongols attacked during this brief period [1220s to early 1230s] recently had experienced, or was just then experiencing, significant economic problems caused, at least in part, by 'anomalous' climatic conditions."[69] These circumstances give more credence to the "pull" side of Toynbee's formula, though for an explanation best associated with decline more generally than one founded on climatic variations. The beginning of the Mongol conquest coincided with a Jin court that was "in a state of chaos," brought on by droughts, famine, and indigenous internal rebellion.[70] Some emphasize the breakdown of stable trade relations, including tribute, as a trigger in the switch from external extractive strategies to conquest.[71] But this deterioration should be placed in a broader context of Jin decline that had internal sources, which broke their hold on the steppe and left them vulnerable to Mongol advances. The Jüyin uprising and further rebellion by Jin subjects around 1207 allowed the Mongols to assert their influence on the frontier zone.[72] This provided a

---

[65] This is discussed in Owen Lattimore, "The Geographical Factor in Mongol History," *The Geographical Journal* 91, no. 1 (January 1938): 1–3. See also Arnold J. Toynbee, *A Study of History, Vol. III* (London: Oxford University Press, 1934), 15.

[66] Cited in Lattimore, "Geographical Factor," 2.   [67] Ibid., 2–3.

[68] See Joseph Fletcher, "The Mongols: Ecological and Social Perspectives," *Harvard Journal of Asiatic Studies* 46, no. 1 (June 1986): 12–16; and Anatoly Khazonov, "Ecological Limitations of Nomadism in the Eurasian Steppes and Their Social and Cultural Implications," *Asian and African Studies: Journal of the Israel Oriental Society* 23 (1990): 1–15.

[69] See William S. Atwell, "Volcanism and Short-Term Climatic Change in East Asian and World History," *Journal of World History* 12, no. 1 (2001): 45.

[70] Franke, "Chin Dynasty," 253–57.

[71] Sechin Jagchid and Van Jay Symons, *Peace, War, and Trade along the Great Wall: Nomadic–Chinese Interaction through Two Millennia* (Bloomington: Indiana University Press, 1989), 19–20.

[72] Buell, "Frontier Zone," 68. On the importance of the disintegration of the Jin frontier zone defense system, and its exploitation by the Mongols, see Allsen, "Rise of the Mongolian Empire," 348–50. According to Igor de Rachewiltz, the Jüyin troops were

Eruption and expansion

platform first for raiding and then, by about 1214, the beginning of a piecemeal conquest.[73]

The submission of the Karakhitai also came at a time when that state was undergoing substantial political changes. According to Buell, the Mongol advance was "in many ways, a direct response to the weakening and gradual breakup of the powerful [Karakhitai] empire."[74] Further west, the attack on the Khorezmshah (Muhammad) has been tied to the baffling decision by one of his governors to kill traveling merchants (likely spies) and Mongol envoys. While conquest may have been inevitable, the timing was most likely due to the decline within the Khorezmshah's realm beset by "internal discord and feuds."[75] The weakness was such that, despite having a large army, they mounted no effective resistance. The Khorezmshah "could not trust his troops" and had split them into garrisons.[76] The conquest of the Jin and the destruction of the Khorezmshah extended the Mongols beyond the range of previous tribal confederations. The weakness of the Mongols' main sedentary rivals, those with the greatest means to check their advance, also deviates from previous patterns where steppe empires developed in response to the *strengths* of their sedentary neighbors in order to check their advances.[77]

While the delay of the fall of the Jin dynasty says more about the distracted attentions of the Mongols (campaigning in Central Asia) than about Jin resilience, it also speaks to some initial limitations in Mongol

---

among the most capable of the Jin forces, which suggests that their defection was doubly damaging. Rachewiltz, *Secret History of the Mongols*, vol. 2, 893.

[73] Buell, "Frontier Zone," 68–69.

[74] Paul D. Buell, "Sino-Khitan Administration in Mongol Bukhara," *Journal of Asian History* 13, no. 2 (1979): 126–27. The decline of the Karakhitai is summarized in Biran, *Empire of the Qara Khitai*, 84–86.

[75] Bira, "Mongols and Their State," 252. The weaknesses afflicting the Khorezmshah are discussed in Vasilii V. Barthold, *Turkestan Down to the Mongol Invasion* (London : E.J.W. Gibb Memorial Trust, 1977), xxxi; 373–80.

[76] David O. Morgan, *The Mongols* (Oxford: Blackwell, 1986), 68–69. Timothy May argues that the Khorezmshah had increased in power since an earlier run-in with the Mongols in 1209, mentioning expansion into Iran and Iraq while noting its tenuous consolidation of its new holdings. Timothy M. May, "The Mechanics of Conquest and Governance: The Rise and Expansion of the Mongol Empire, 1185–1265," PhD dissertation, University of Wisconsin-Madison, 2004, 245–46. Expansion, though, is not necessarily inconsistent with decline. As May notes, there was dissension in the ranks of the Khorezmshah's domain, and the Mongols exploited that weakness. The expansion itself badly weakened them. Edward G. Browne, *A Literary History of Persia, Vol. II* (Richmond, Surrey: Curzon Press, 1999; 1906), 435. Paul Ratchnevsky makes it clear that Chinggis was well aware of those dissensions and sought to exploit them. Ratchnevsky, *Genghis Khan*, 173.

[77] A good example of this trend is the Hsiung-Nu (or Xiongnu), which emerged as a power around 209 BCE and lasted until around 155 CE. See Di Cosmo, *Ancient China*, 161–205.

122   The Mongol eruption and aftermath

capabilities.[78] The means that were available on the steppe, horses and space mostly, were in stark contrast to those available to sedentary societies. These deficiencies were addressed through the exploitation of local administrative and military technologies and talents. While the organization and effectiveness of the Mongol armies were evident, their ultimate ability to expand and consolidate their gains depended in large part on their capacity to adapt and integrate means and methods from their conquered territories.[79] What may be seen as an unwillingness to hold territory in the early phases may have had less to do with nomadic atavism than strict limitations on the means available to steppe-based empires.

The severe constraints faced by the Mongols as they confronted their materially more powerful adversaries required their ingenuity combined with the exploitation of their rivals' resources. This compensation for limited means, conceptualized in this study in terms of its opportunity structure, was achieved in a number of ways. Shortages of manpower were addressed through levies in conquered territories, often incorporating other nomadic peoples who could readily adopt their war-making style.[80] This selective incorporation also applied to military technology, including technicians from China and Persia, who contributed to the development of sophisticated siege engines and later artillery.[81] Human capital in the form of individuals with bureaucratic skills and local knowledge was also absorbed into the growing Mongol administrative apparatus.[82] What may be considered a *bounding* opportunity structure emerged, suggesting its motion and dynamism, and a *binding* one as

[78] Owen Lattimore attributes the delay to an effort to consolidate the steppe and avoid the mistakes of earlier tribal confederations that moved too quickly to extract and rule their rich neighbors. Lattimore, "Geography of Chingis Khan," 6–7. David Morgan finds this explanation appealing but notes a lack of any evidence that this was Chinggis's intent rather than just an outcome. Morgan, *The Mongols*, 73.

[79] On the organization and structure of the Mongol military, see H. Desmond Martin, "The Mongol Army," *Journal of the Royal Asiatic Society* 75, nos. 1–2 (January 1943): 46–85; and Ch'i-ch'ing Hsiao, *The Military Establishment of the Yuan Dynasty* (Cambridge: Harvard University, 1978), 9–12.

[80] Mote, *Imperial China*, 243. The Jin dynasty was estimated to have a population of around 40 million and was being attacked by a united Mongol nation of around a million. The numbers are provided by Frederick Mote, but no methodology is presented (Ibid.). Others have the number of Mongols at around 700,000. Christian, *History of Russia*, 400.

[81] The role of the Mongols in transferring military technology throughout their empire, including the transmission of gunpowder, is examined in Thomas T. Allsen, "The Circulation of Military Technology in the Mongolian Empire," in *Warfare in Inner Asian History (500–1800)*, ed. Nicola Di Cosmo (Leiden: Brill, 2002), 265–93. See also Kate Raphael, "Mongol Siege Warfare on the Banks of the Euphrates and the Question of Gunpowder," *Journal of the Royal Asiatic Society*, Series 3, 19, no. 3 (July 2009): 355–70.

[82] Morgan, *The Mongols*, 49. See also David O. Morgan, "Who Ran the Mongol Empire?" *Journal of the Royal Asiatic Society* (1982): 133.

Eruption and expansion 123

well, with the melding of successful sedentary practices. The skillful incorporation of unfamiliar technologies and nonnative resources allowed the Mongols, for a time at least, to construct an empire that maintained the fundamental characteristics of steppe society, but expanded well beyond its previously sustainable scale.

An analysis of this length would be fortunate to capture a fraction of the factors relevant to the expansion of the Mongol Empire. For this study the structural-systemic forces and their effects on the events and processes have been emphasized, which for the Mongols entailed the decline of the dominant powers in the system and their reaction to a strained opportunity structure. The one yawning gap that such a focus reveals is the role of individual leadership; first evident in the case of Hassan-i Sabbah and maybe even more prominent here. The role of Chinggis Khan in forging a new people out of a fractious many and his ability to expand from severely constrained circumstances are conspicuous.[83] But it is only in the structural-systemic context of these events that these accomplishments can be fully appreciated, and their sequence understood. Examining these events in a way that emphasizes power and resources provides a picture of unnatural abilities and context-transforming agency, set against harsh constraints and daunting but ultimately surmountable odds.

"Chinggis Khan recognized opportunities," writes Timothy May, and he skillfully perceived and exploited critical weaknesses among dominant powers.[84] In this case there was a veritable cascade of decline affecting *three* major powers that allowed the Mongol Empire in its early stages to expand and, critically, gain access to human and material resources to consolidate and continue its conquest. Does that variation account for the variation in the success of the Mongols when compared to the other cases? Not only were the Mongols able to survive, they were able to expand and, eventually, dominate the system. That outcome seems highly unlikely absent the weakening of rivals that preceded their ascent. Severe resource constraints made the Mongols unlikely future hegemons. Though vested with environmentally specific means (horses and space), their poverty in the pillars of sedentary empires (technology and manpower) presented an impediment to expansion. "Chinggis Khan was forced to seek out new structural solutions," according to Barfield, "because he rose to power

---

[83] Joseph Fletcher writes, "Chinggis Khan must have been a leader of extraordinary talent, capable of iron discipline and the ability to inspire loyalty, and superior in these respects to other steppe leaders of the time." Fletcher, "The Mongols," 34.

[84] May, "Mechanics of Conquest," 242. Timothy May does differ in his interpretation of the relative power and decline of surrounding sedentary powers.

124   The Mongol eruption and aftermath

from a marginal position."[85] This condition was as true concerning the nascent Mongol state as it was with Temüjin's early status on the steppe. The resourcefulness of the Mongols in adopting and adapting technology allowed them to exploit their bounding and binding opportunity structure. As conquests mounted so too did their access to resources that further enhanced their ability to expand and consolidate their gains.

Consolidation and devolution

Despite occasional setbacks, after Chinggis Khan's death Mongol advances went largely unchecked. Following the defeat of the Jin in 1234, the Mongols would go on to attack Russia in earnest (1237), ravage Poland and Hungary (1241), menace Western Europe, and destroy the remnants of the Abbasid Caliphate (1258).[86] Their only major defeat would come later at the hands of the Mamluks (1260), who maintained a long rivalry (a "Cold War") with the Ilkhanid state, one of the successor states of the Mongol Empire.[87] Lattimore characterizes Chinggis Khan's conception of empire as one that was almost wholly derived from the steppe, while arguing that his successors departed from steppe principles.[88] As it expanded, its rulers established the systems of taxation, census taking, and other bureaucratic mechanisms necessary to maintain the empire.[89] Möngke, who was elected khan in 1251, succeeded in completing the conquests of his predecessors (Chinggis, Ögedei, and Güyük), and brought the empire to its apex.[90]

---

[85] Thomas J. Barfield, "Something New Under the Sun: The Mongol Empire's Innovations in Steppe Political Organization and Military Strategy," Paper presented at the 8th International Congress of Mongolists, Ulaan Baatar, August 5–12, 2002.

[86] For the attacks on Russia and its neighbors, which resumed in earnest in 1237 after probing attacks in 1223, see Fennell, *Crisis of Medieval Russia*, 76–90. The campaigns against Eastern Europe are discussed in Nora Berend, *At the Gate of Christendom: Jews, Muslims, and "Pagans" in Medieval Hungary* (Cambridge: Cambridge University Press, 2001), 34–36. Mongol penetration into the central Islamic lands is covered in John A. Boyle, "Dynastic and Political History of the Il-Khans," in *The Cambridge History of Iran, Vol. 5, The Saljuq and Mongol Periods*, ed. Boyle (Cambridge: Cambridge University Press, 1968), 345–52.

[87] The Mongol–Mamluk rivalry is detailed in Reuven Amitai-Preiss, *Mongols and Mamluks: The Mamluk–Ilkhanid War, 1260–1281* (Cambridge: Cambridge University Press, 1995). See also Reuven Amitai-Preiss, "In the Aftermath of Ayn-Jalut: The Beginnings of the Mamluk–Ilkhanid Cold War," *Al-Masaq* 3 (1990): 1–21.

[88] Lattimore, "Geography of Chingis Khan," 7.

[89] Morgan, "Who Ran the Mongol Empire?" 133. The census was used for taxation as well as to levy military manpower and identify skilled craftsmen and technicians. Allsen, "Rise of the Mongolian Empire," 403. See also John Masson Smith, Jr., "Mongol and Nomadic Taxation," *Harvard Journal of Asiatic Studies* 30 (1970): 46–85.

[90] Allsen, "Rise of the Mongolian Empire," 411.

Consolidation and devolution 125

Reversion to steppe principles, rather than departure from them, has been cited in the dissolution of the empire. These were the very patterns that had mired the steppe in strife and disunion, but now on an imperial scale. The empire had been organized along supra-tribal lines from its earliest stages, and the increasing conquests were assigned to loyal and trusted followers. Over time, in the words of one observer, "a fairly effective condominium" under the authority of the great khan had been achieved.[91] Kinship ties had ruled the steppe even longer, though, and even as Chinggis sought to replace them with loyalty-based bonds, these would not survive expansion and succession. His successors would acquire "semi-hereditary power over regions, so that within a few generations, traditional forms of chieftainship re-appeared."[92] Maintaining a scaled-up version of the steppe practice of assigning conquered territories to members of the Mongol ruling class (as well as a tradition of hereditary succession) was necessary to preserve the legitimacy of the *qaghan*, or great khan, despite its fissiparous tendencies.[93] Up until the death of Möngke in 1259, the empire maintained effective centralization, with the qaghan determining foreign policy and exerting extensive influence over the internal affairs of the regional khanates.[94] Long-standing rivalries among Chinggis's descendants, distributed among the khanates, would become full-blown civil wars after Möngke's death. These wars marked the emergence of the khanates as independent successor states divided among the descendants.[95]

The empire devolved into roughly structurally similar centralized states. This might seem to redeem neorealist arguments concerning emulation and unit isomorphism, but this would be incorrect. The

[91] Barfield, *Perilous Frontier*, 197; Morgan, "Who Ran the Mongol Empire?" 125.
[92] Christian, *History of Russia*, 398. See also David Christian, "Inner Asia as a Unit of World History," *Journal of World History* 5, no. 3 (Fall 1994): 205.
[93] See Thomas T. Allsen, *Mongol Imperialism: The Policies of the Grand Qan Möngke in China, Russia, and the Islamic Lands, 1251–1259* (Berkeley: University of California Press, 1987), 222–23.
[94] Ibid., 45–46.
[95] The successor states were the Yuan dynasty (established in China), Chagatai khanate (Central Asia), Ilkhanate (Persia and Near East), and the Golden Horde (Russia). Their power struggles are detailed in Barfield, *Perilous Frontier*, 210–18; and Peter Jackson, "The Dissolution of the Mongol Empire," *Central Asiatic Journal* (1978): 186–244. See also John W. Dardess, "From Mongol Empire to Yüan Dynasty: Changing Forms of Imperial Rule in Mongolia and Central Asia," *Monumenta Seria* 3 (1972–1975): 117–65. Peter Jackson's dating of the dissolution of the Mongol Empire at 1260 is corroborated by David Morgan. Dissolution entails, in Morgan's characterization "the end of the Mongol Empire as any kind of unitary state ruled from a central capital by a paramount emperor and his governmental machine." David O. Morgan, "The Decline and Fall of the Mongol Empire," *Journal of the Royal Asiatic Society*, Series 3, 19 (October 2009): 429. See also Peter Jackson, "From *Ulus* to Khanate: The Making of Mongol States, c.1220–c.1290," in Amitai-Preiss, *Mongol Empire and Its Legacy*, 28–32.

126   The Mongol eruption and aftermath

power of the Mongols had been largely unchecked by external sources, and their weakness was not the result of more successful rivals but of succession crises and internal divisions. Peter Jackson observes that the "disintegration of their empire into a number of rival khanates seriously impaired the Mongols' capacity to prosecute expansionist campaigns on any front, whether in China, in Eastern Europe, in Syria or in India."[96] According to Jackson, in order to see why the Mongol expansion ebbed we must look "at circumstances within the empire [rather] than at local military factors such as reverses in Syria."[97] Those reverses came at the hands of the Mamluks, but happened as the empire dissolved and the Ilkhanid independent successor state was established. While the increased administrative capacity at the level of the regional khanate made devolution a possibility, it was the character of Mongol rule and its failure to persist as its scale magnified that resulted in its transformation.

Empire on horseback: dissimilarity and deviation

The Mongols would distinguish themselves from both their contemporaries and previous steppe empires. Earlier steppe empires had united and competed with Chinese dynasties, but none constituted what Joseph Fletcher termed a "fully nomadic steppe-based empire," one that is capable of conquest without its own full absorption and sedentarization.[98] Barfield notes that steppe empires have risen and fallen in tandem with sedentary neighbors. When there was anarchy on both the steppe and in China, "Manchurian candidates," like the Khitan or Jurchen, would exploit this weakness and establish sedentary dynasties. When the Chinese dynasties were strong, steppe empires or confederacies would form (as "shadow empires") in order to resist Chinese pressure, exploiting their resources through raiding and tribute.[99] The Mongol Empire, Barfield notes, was an exception to this pattern, a "unique hybrid" that combined "nomadic mobility, striking power, and strategic thought with the ability to capture walled cities [that] produced a combination stronger than any other force previously known in Eurasia."[100] This represented a qualitative as much as a quantitative change in steppe-based power.[101]

---

[96] Peter Jackson, *The Delhi Sultanate: A Political and Military History* (Cambridge: Cambridge University Press, 1999), 110.

[97] Jackson, "Dissolution," 188.   [98] Fletcher, "The Mongols," 16.

[99] See Barfield, "Shadow Empires," 10–41.   [100] Barfield, *Perilous Frontier*, 298.

[101] See Michal Biran, "The Mongol Transformation: From the Steppe to Eurasian Empire," *Medieval Encounters* 10, nos. 1–3 (2004): 345.

Dissimilarity and deviation 127

There is evidence that historical learning may have played a role in the decision not to emulate either sedentary rivals or previous steppe-based invaders. The fear of losing their nomadic identities, and the risk of softening like their Sinicized predecessors, led to a conscious effort to avoid that fate. This cultural explanation may be necessary but is not sufficient. Constraints on resources shaped behavior by limiting options and fostering innovation. Their expansion at times necessitated local imitation of administrative structures and military practices. Overall, though, the Mongols maintained a form that extended the nomadic pastoral structure over a transcontinental span. It was their skill in selective military emulation, copying only those traits that fit their overall organizational template, that enabled dissimilar administrative practices to be realized on a wide scale.

Mongol rulers maintained nomadic principles while expanding to encompass sedentary states and towns. "Neither the qaghan nor the [Mongol] princes, however," John Dardess writes, "lived permanently in these towns. They did not closely associate themselves with sedentary urban cultures, nor did they personally involve themselves in the continuous supervision of bureaucratic operations."[102] This reluctance, at least in part, was rooted in cultural codes, though ones that had practical consequences. "They despised city-dwellers," J.J. Saunders observed, "and held aloof from them, fearing that the virile and martial qualities of their people would be lost in the enervating luxury of wealthy towns."[103] Dardess describes the Mongol Empire prior to 1260 as a three-tiered structure of loosely integrated parts. Conquered sedentary areas were ruled from the "steppe interstices" between areas of dense settlement, with Mongol court towns located in the steppe or along its margins.[104] This interstitial presence allowed for the maintenance of the mobility that shaped nomadic society. The establishment of Karakorum as a capital was in response to increasing awareness that, as a Khitan counselor advised, though the empire was created on horseback it could not be governed on horseback.[105] Karakorum, however, remained only "in a limited sense" a capital, "a 'city' by courtesy" whose lack of

---

[102] Dardess, "Mongol Empire," 120.

[103] J.J. Saunders, "The Nomad as Empire-Builder: A Comparison of the Arab and Mongol Conquests," in *Muslims and Mongols: Essays on Medieval Asia by J.J. Saunders*, ed. G.W. Rice (Christchurch: University of Canterbury, 1977), 49.

[104] Dardess, "Mongol Empire," 121.

[105] Saunders, "Nomad as Empire-Builder," 47–48. The Chinese termed important nomadic states *ma-shang hsing-kuo*, or "states on horseback." This, according to Sechin Jagchid and Van Jay Symons, indicated "their great mobility and the different relationship nomadic people had with their land." Jagchid and Symons, *Peace, War, and Trade*, 193, n. 6.

128   The Mongol eruption and aftermath

refinement shocked emissaries from sedentary states, and, according to Jackson, "in no sense was a fixed capital, but one of a number of halting-places in the annual imperial itinerary."[106] Indeed, the Khitan's advice would only be followed somewhat, and up until its dissolution it remained to a significant degree an empire on horseback.[107]

William of Rubruck, one of a number of emissaries who tried to figure out the Mongols and their mysterious ways, found Möngke encamped in a grassland outside of Karakorum, with guards posted in the city to protect imperial buildings and storehouses.[108] What Chinese historians wrote about Möngke could be applied to the Mongol Empire as a whole: "He would not succumb to or imitate what other nations did."[109] As part of this compound structure "mobile secretariats," in the Chinese translation, were "constantly on the move," according to Allsen, overseeing imperial administration in Möngke's reign.[110] These mobile secretariats would act in concert with local imperial agents to assure submission and enable extraction from the empire's dependent territories.

In this form the Mongols would eventually succumb due to the constraints on the expansion of such a hybrid entity. The Mongols ruled over their sedentary subjects laterally, but this arrangement had limits of scale. The empire, Dardess explains, could only extend so far, and expansion

---

[106] Dardess, "Mongol Empire," 122. Peter Jackson notes that Karakorum established its first permanent buildings around 1235. Jackson, "Mongol Age in Eastern Inner Asia," 35. On the principle of mobility at the core of the Mongol Empire, see Mark A. Whaley, "An Account of 13th Century Qubchir of the Mongol 'Great Courts,'" *Acta Orientalia Academiae Scientiarum Hungaricae* 54, no. 1 (June 2001): 7. Morris Rossabi refers to Karakorum as an "artificially created capital," established only at the behest of the qaghan's sedentary advisers. Morris Rossabi, *Khubilai Khan: His Life and Times* (Berkeley: University of California Press, 1988), 11. The movements of the Mongol qaghans are tracked in John A. Boyle, "The Seasonal Residences of the Great Khan Ögedei," in *The Mongol World Empire* (London: Variorum, 1977), VI, 145–51.

[107] Sedentary modes of governance did increasingly become necessary as the Mongols expanded. This, according to Nicola Di Cosmo, occurred gradually, from the original trade-tribute model that persisted under Chinggis, all the way to a direct taxation model that took root after the death of Möngke. See Di Cosmo, "State Formation," 33–34.

[108] Dardess, "Mongol Empire," 120.   [109] Ibid., 121.

[110] Thomas T. Allsen, "Guard and Government in the Reign of the Grand Qan Möngke, 1251–59," *Harvard Journal of Asiatic Studies* 46, no. 2 (December 1986): 502. Among the most important administrative agents of the empire was the *tanma* or *tamma*, according to Paul Buell, a special military force to secure control over conquered areas "along the borders of the nomadic and sedentary spheres." Buell sees the word coming from the Tibetan meaning "the end, rim, border, or frontier," and concludes the basic meaning to be "that group constituting the border, the frontier" or "nomadic garrison force on the frontier." Paul D. Buell, "Kalmyk Tanggaci People: Thoughts on the Mechanics and Impact of Mongol Expansion," *Mongolian Studies* 6 (1980): 45; 55, n. 40. This interpretation would be consistent with the mobile secretariats mentioned above. See also Donald Ostrowski, "The *Tamma* and the Dual-Administrative Structure of the Mongol Empire," *Bulletin of the School of Oriental and African Studies* 61, no. 2 (1998): 262–77.

Dissimilarity and deviation 129

"tended to attenuate and jeopardize its structural order." Dardess estimates that beyond a 900 mile range outside of the putative capital maintaining control over subordinate areas of the empire proved difficult.[111] "The factor of distance alone," he explains, "ensured the real or potential political and economic independence of the princes appanaged outside the perimeter of [Karakorum's] immediate production areas."[112] While loyalty to the qaghan was maintained throughout (temporary episodes of querulous khans notwithstanding), the combination of the extension of the empire and increasing localized administrative capacity made it increasingly vulnerable to internal upheavals, even as it continued its competitive successes vis-à-vis outside powers.

What impresses about the rise of the Mongol Empire is not how fragile it became but just how long it persisted and how far it was able to expand. Given their material disadvantages, the Mongols' ability to forage – both in the narrow sense of feeding their soldiers and mounts and the broader sense of feeding the machine of empire – is central to explaining their success. Mastery of free-floating resources allowed for a dynamic that runs contrary to the expectations of emulation, resulting in highly effective competition absent broad organizational imitation. The Mongols emulated locally while they dissimilated globally. They were able to selectively extract and imitate local military and administrative practices, and diffuse these throughout their empire, while maintaining a distinct organizational form that affected the quality of their interactions with subjects and neighboring states alike.

The constraints the Mongols faced, however, resulted not only in creative innovation but also in structures and behaviors that were at times tenuous and aberrant. These behaviors manifested at the macro- and micro-levels, both with macro-level consequences. At the macro-level the peculiar and fragile mode of governance was highly dependent on continuity in the office of the qaghan and was vulnerable to hiccups during succession transitions. This reliance affected their expansion and operations, which would occasionally grind to a halt as quriltais were held to determine the next qaghan.

---

[111] Dardess, "Mongol Empire," 122.

[112] Ibid., 126. The role of Karakorum as an imperial capital reflected the hybridity of the Mongol polity, with the steppe elite using their capitals "as tethering points for mobile courts. . . . reflect[ing] an approach to centralized space that exploits the fluid and mobile setting in which steppe politics were conducted while maintaining an imperial city that was indeed the center of the medieval world." William Honeychurch and Chunag Amartuvshin, "States on Horseback: The Rise of Inner Asian Confederations and Empires," in *Asian Archaeology*, ed. Miriam T. Stark (Cambridge: Blackwell, 2006), 271.

130   The Mongol eruption and aftermath

At the micro-level, despite efforts to rescue them from their blood-thirsty image, there is no ignoring the ruthlessness with which the Mongols coerced and dispatched their victims.[113] These were unkind times, and slaughter and rapine were not uncommon in the Middle Ages. The systematic nature of the Mongol actions, and potential systemic influences behind them, nevertheless distinguish them. Alternative explanations for the bloodshed include a deeply rooted hatred of sedentary societies,[114] ingrained cultural coding that scaled up the harsh winner-take-all logic of the steppe, as well as its intentional employment for psychological coercion against potential future adversaries, a kind of "steppe-extortion."[115] Cultural explanations, however, fall short in explaining Mongol behavior. Steppe warfare, at least as Chinggis unified the steppe, involved not slaughtering defeated adversaries, but incorporating them into a polity with a supranational identity. During the expansion the incorporation of non-Mongols was utilitarian in nature. While their application was, to say the least, indelicate (e.g., using sedentary levies as "arrow fodder" after plucking the skilled from the rest of the population), their cruel practicality suggests a hardened mindset rather than a culturally wired one.[116]

John Masson Smith argues that severe disparities in population between the Mongols and their sedentary rivals were instrumental in shaping their destructive behavior. He writes that the "Mongols' fear of cities was anything but blind and unreasoning," and that "the enormous disparity in population must have been known to the Mongols and

---

[113] Typical of the apologists is Bernard Lewis, who qualifies the massacres as "trivial by modern standards," yet also describes them as "terrible and overwhelming." Bernard Lewis, *Islam in History: Ideas, People, and Events in the Middle East* (Chicago: Open Court, 1993), 192. Michal Biran adds to his mention of "calculated and accidental devastation" the efforts by Mongol rulers to limit damage and restore productivity to conquered lands. Biran, "Mongol Transformation," 353–54. For a critique of such interpretations, see David O. Morgan, "The Mongols in Iran: A Reappraisal," *Iran: Journal of the British Institute of Persian Studies* 42 (2004): 131–36. Thomas Barfield concludes that, despite efforts at rehabilitation, "Chinggis Khan was indeed guilty as charged." Thomas J. Barfield, "The Devil's Horsemen: Steppe Nomadic Warfare in Historical Perspective," in *Studying War: Anthropological Perspectives, Vol. 2, War and Society*, ed. Stephen P. Reyna and R.E. Downs (Langhorne, Penn.: Gordon and Breach, 1994), 177.

[114] See Saunders, "Nomad as Empire-Builder," 48–49.

[115] See Fletcher, "The Mongols," 42.

[116] On these practices, see John Masson Smith, Jr., "Demographic Considerations in Mongol Siege Warfare," *Archivum Ottomanicum* 13 (1993–1994): 332. Accounts of selective killing, sparing skilled craftsmen and slaves while making sure to kill nobles, are found in the likely credible chronicle of missionary Friar Giovanni DiPlano Carpini, *The Story of the Mongols Whom We Call the Tartars*, trans. Erik Hildinger (Boston: Branden Publishing, 1996), 78.

European reactions and Mongol interactions 131

considered in their strategic thinking."[117] While this understanding should not soften our judgment of these actions, it can help us fix them less in innate depravity than in material constraints – depravity being an effect rather than a root cause. Practices such as "thinning" population areas for pasturage, given the nature and configuration of the Mongol polity, have a certain (albeit cruel and awful) logic to them.[118] With our tolerance for indecency strained further, the practice of punishing the populations of resisting cities also contained a brutal and effective calculus, cowing future resisters into submission.[119] The "annihilation, transfer, and downgrading" of Eurasian elites rounded out this terrible, and for a time terribly efficient, set of practices.[120]

Toward the latter phases of the Mongol Empire there was recognition that certain destructive practices had become counterproductive. As the Mongols became more powerful, flush with spoils and levies from sedentary subjects, one truism became apparent: corpses cannot pay taxes.[121] Möngke enacted reforms intended to minimize destruction and curtail disruption of taxation.[122] Baghdad was excepted from this restraint. The caliph had refused to submit to advancing Mongol forces and an example was set for potential future conquests. Regardless, according to Allsen, "it is generally conceded that, despite the outrage at Baghdad, Mongol methods of warfare were less destructive in Möngke's time than in that of Chinggis Qan."[123] Without diminishing or excusing the damage that occurred in either era, it is clear that the utilitarian functions of the violence waned as the empire increased in manpower and resources. While certain practices were maintained (for instance slaughter for strategic signaling), it appears others were curtailed, and the decreasing material constraints over time provide a more convincing explanation for this shift than those that emphasize cultural coding.

Sine capite: European reactions and Mongol interactions

The astounding success of the Mongols and their ability to dominate and impose their own institutions makes a nuanced assessment of the effects of their deviating interactions problematic. Their cruel and terrifying efficiency complicates accurate gauging of their effects on norms and

---

[117] Smith, "Demographic Considerations," 332; 330. See also Barfield, *Perilous Frontier*, 203.
[118] Dardess, "Mongol Empire," 122, n. 19; and Allsen, *Mongol Imperialism*, 89. The qaghan's acceptance of this policy, it seems, was dependent on its continuing ability to generate revenue. See Allsen, "Rise of the Mongolian Empire," 375–81.
[119] Allsen, *Mongol Imperialism*, 83–84.   [120] Biran, "Mongol Transformation," 346.
[121] See Ibid., 347–48.   [122] Allsen, *Mongol Imperialism*, 83.   [123] Ibid., 88.

132   The Mongol eruption and aftermath

identities. While the Mongols' relative power and widespread conquest limited their *contemporary* influence on the development of norms, the case provides opportunities to examine the effects of encounters with the Mongols on common identity formation, both collective ("we-feeling") and corporate ("others"). Determining the roots of collective identity formation in common cultural bonds or homogeneity also benefits from the empirical investigation. The areas most immediately affected by the Mongol onslaught were China, Central Asia, the Middle East, and Russia. In the case of China there was long-standing familiarity with "barbarian" steppe armies by the Jin dynasty (outsiders themselves) and the Song. The amplification of the threat from the steppe was understood in terms of well-established cultural categories.[124] Though the scale of the threat was much greater in a quantitative sense, there was little qualitative deviation from earlier episodes. The proximity of the steppe, moreover, led to a substantial measure of mutual emulation, within the broader framework of local imitation and global dissimilation. Accordingly, there is little reason to expect much change based on the qualitative elements of Chinese interaction with the Mongols. A somewhat different issue complicates appreciation of the effects of the Mongols on the Middle East, east of the Levant, where the devastation was especially severe and vast. The destruction of Baghdad was, and in some corners still is, considered an unparalleled calamity. The most extensive observers from inside this region were either largely co-opted by the Mongols or forced to flee.[125] In this case of outright domination and widespread destruction the negative identity formation evident is not the least bit surprising or extraordinary.[126]

[124] On Chinese attitudes toward the steppe, and their "greedy and cruel" inhabitants, see Denis Sinor, "The Greed of the Northern Barbarian," in *Aspects of Altaic Civilization*, 171–72. For a discussion of the reaction to the Mongols by the Song, see Charles A. Peterson, "First Sung Reactions to the Mongol Invasion of the North, 1211–17," in *Crisis and Prosperity in Sung China*, ed. John Winthrop Haeger (Tucson: University of Arizona Press, 1975), 215–52. The northern barbarians were compared to wolves due to the impression of their insatiability (231).

[125] The key contemporary observers and chroniclers of the Mongols in the Middle East were 'Ata-Malik Juvayni, Minhaj Siraj Juzjani, and Ibn al-Athir. Juvayni's constraints as a Mongol court historian are charitably described by Edward G. Browne: his circumstances "compelled him to speak with civility of the barbarians whom it was his misfortune to serve." Others were less charitable describing his "servile" and "nauseating" flattery. See (including Browne quotation) David O. Morgan, "Introduction to the 1997 Edition," in *Genghis Khan: The History of the World Conqueror*, xxi–xxii. Ibn al-Athir's account of the Mongol invasion can be found in Browne, *A Literary History of Persia*, 427–31.

[126] See David O. Morgan, "Persian Historians and the Mongols," in *Medieval Historical Writing in the Christian and Islamic Worlds*, ed. Morgan (London: University of London, 1982), 109–24.

European reactions and Mongol interactions 133

The closer the Mongols came to Europe, though, the more discernible their distinctive effects become. As the Mongols approached Russia and Eastern Europe, they began to interact with polities that had longtime experience with nomads, but little understanding of the sources and nature of the Mongol threat.[127] The first forays leading to the Battle of Kalka in 1223, when the Mongols "appeared out of nowhere," shocked the Russians and their Polovtsian allies, themselves pastoral Kipchaks (Cumans) of the Pontic steppe.[128] The Mongols became known as "Tartars," a corruption of the tribal name Tatar and its conflation with Tartarus, mythological hell. Elsewhere, the Mongols would be equated with Prester John, the mythical Christian monarch of the East. This association was not embraced by the Russians, according to Charles Halperin, as "they were too familiar with Asian nomads to confuse the Mongols with the saviors of Christendom."[129] As the "Tartar Yoke" descended on Russia, religious scholars tried to deny that the Mongols, in Halperin's words, "had changed the rules of the game" by referring to them in the same terms they had used to describe other nomadic peoples.[130] But the Mongols *had* changed the rules, and this soon became undeniable.

The weak states of Central and Eastern Europe were also familiar with nomads but ill-prepared to cope with the Mongols, in either the sense of defense or cognition, to restore either physical or ontological security. The fall of Kiev in 1240 marked the completion of the conquest of Russia and was followed by the invasions of Poland and Hungary. Panic spread across Europe. Appeals for help by King Béla of Hungary, casting his land as an imperiled "gate of Christendom," went unheeded by a Europe severely divided between Frederick II and the papacy.[131] The nomadic Cumans had long interacted with the Hungarians and were at first afforded protection from the advancing armies, but were soon subject to vilification and attacks as they became associated with the Mongols.[132]

---

[127] Leo de Hartog, *Russia and the Mongol Yoke: The History of the Russian Principalities and the Golden Horde, 1221–1502* (London: I.B. Tauris, 1996), 51. For Russian views of the nomads and the "northeastern realm of evil," see Leonid S. Chekin, "The Godless Ishmaelites: The Image of the Steppe in Eleventh–Thirteenth Century Rus," *Russian History* 19, nos. 1–4 (1992): 9–28.

[128] Charles J. Halperin, *Russia and the Golden Horde* (Bloomington: Indiana University Press, 1985), 64. The sweep of the Mongol period of Russian history is covered in George Vernadsky, *The Mongols and Russia: A History of Russia, Vol. III* (New Haven: Yale University Press, 1953).

[129] Halperin, *Russia and the Golden Horde*, 64.   [130] Ibid., 20.

[131] Fennell, *Crisis of Medieval Russia*, 83.

[132] See James Ross Sweeney, "'Spurred on by the Fear of Death': Refugees and Displaced Populations during the Mongol Invasion of Hungary," in *Nomadic Diplomacy, Destruction, and Religion from the Pacific to the Adriatic*, Toronto Studies in Central and

134 The Mongol eruption and aftermath

The Mongol invasion, according to Nora Berend, "conformed to previous raids to some extent: a nomad tribal alliance broke into the kingdom, killed and pillaged, then withdrew."[133] But as Berend notes, this was not just another raid.

The overall effects of the invasion were captured in the Hungarian term, *tatárjárás*, which attaches the same suffix used to describe hordes of locusts, and according to Berend has a "connotation of directionless, protracted movement."[134] Locusts seem to come from nowhere, and their actions are furious and seemingly indiscriminate, providing what seemed an apt comparison.[135] The effects of the Mongol attacks on Hungary have been the subject of debate, with some estimating a 15–20 percent loss of population.[136] Some scholars, according to Berend, argue that the damage was exaggerated, and that the accounts were "generated not by the weight of devastation but by the appearance of a little known and even less understood, therefore mythified enemy."[137]

To the west, European reaction to the Mongols varied over time: from hopeful anticipation, to fear and confusion based on complete ignorance, to dread and curiosity based on a little knowledge fostered by increased diplomatic contacts. Throughout these stages the nature of the interactions of the Mongols around the edges of Europe combined with cultural unawareness to confound observers, compounding uncertainty, fear, and wonder. When the Mongols first began their expansion the known menace of the Saracens was foremost on the minds of European powers, along with their own severe internal divisions. The Mongol attacks on Muslim powers, along with the presence of Nestorian Christians, fed the impression that the Tartars were the forces of Prester John, or King David.[138] As the Mongols expanded, expectations of deliverance gave way to fears expressed in imagery and prophesy and to far less sanguine forecasts of their intentions. Prester John was replaced by

---

Inner Asia, no. 1, ed. Michael Gervers and Wayne Schlepp (Toronto: Joint Centre for Asia Pacific Studies, 1994), 39.

[133] Berend, *Gate of Christendom*, 34.   [134] Ibid.

[135] Locusts are evoked in a letter attributed by Matthew Paris to Frederick II: "Some time since a people of a barbarous race and mode of life called (from what place or origin I know not) Tartars, has lately emerged from the regions of the south, where it had long lain hid, burnt up by the sun of the torrid zone, and, thence marching toward the northern parts ... and remaining for a time, multiplied like locusts." John A. Giles, trans., *Matthew Paris's English History, From the Year 1235 to 1273, Vol. I* (London: George Bell & Sons, 1889), 341. Russian chroniclers also mentioned locusts when referring to the "countless numbers" of Tartars. Pentti Aalto, "Swells of the Mongol-Storm around the Baltic," *Acta Orientalia Academiae Scientiarum Hungaricae* 36, nos. 1–3 (1982): 11.

[136] Berend, *Gate of Christendom*, 37.   [137] Ibid.

[138] Peter Jackson, *The Mongols and the West, 1221–1410* (Harlow: Pearson, 2005), 138.

European reactions and Mongol interactions 135

Gog and Magog, the ferocious tribes that served as a biblical reference and gave the Mongols an eschatological significance matching their increasing reputation for destruction.[139]

The near-complete lack of understanding, with reports filtered and distorted through Eastern Europe and the Holy Land, helped lead to that mythologized framing. Given this lack of interaction, according to C.W. Connell, "it is little wonder that the West tended to shape its views of the unknown world of the Mongols in the likeness of the world it did know, and to seek clues to the origins of unknown peoples in the Bible."[140] The efforts to understand the Mongols in familiar terms did little to calm observers. "Men of letters tried in vain to find out the origins of these invaders," Jean Richard writes, "all the more terrifying that they remained mysterious."[141] Richard writes of a "climate of fear" that pervaded the West and Latin East around 1241, as illusions of amity faded and the Mongols penetrated into Armenia and Georgia.

It was not merely a lack of familiarity and the perilous encroachment that shaped that condition. How the Mongols interacted with their conquests and the unconquered West amplified the uneasiness and contributed a strong element of uncertainty to that climate. Ögedei died in 1241, requiring the Mongol aristocracy to return to elect a new qaghan. It also halted the Mongol advance and likely saved Western Europe from invasion. At the same time it injected a level of doubt and uncertainty that would hang over Europe for decades. "The Mongols retreated," Antti Ruotsala writes, "as mysteriously and rapidly as they had appeared."[142]

[139] William R. Jones, "The Image of the Barbarian in Medieval Europe," *Comparative Studies in Society and History* 13, no. 4 (October 1971): 399. For an extensive discussion of this mythology, see Andrew R. Anderson, *Alexander's Gate, Gog and Magog, and the Inclosed Nations* (Cambridge, Mass.: Medieval Academy of America, 1932). On the varying eschatological interpretations of the Mongols, see Felicitas Schmieder, "Christians, Jews, Muslims – and Mongols: Fitting Foreign People into the Western Christian Apocalyptic Scenario," *Medieval Encounters* 12, no. 2 (2006): 274–95; Debra Higgs Strickland, *Saracens, Demons, and Jews: Making Monsters in Medieval Art* (Princeton: Princeton University Press, 2003), 228–39; and Bernard McGinn, *Visions of the End: Apocalyptic Traditions in the Middle Ages* (New York: Columbia University Press, 1979), 149–57.

[140] Charles W. Connell, "Western Views of the Origins of the 'Tartars': An Example of the Influence of Myth in the Second Half of the Thirteenth Century," *Journal of Medieval and Renaissance Studies* 3 (1973): 121.

[141] Jean Richard, "The Mongols and the Franks," *Journal of Asian History* 3 (1969): 45.

[142] Antti Ruotsala, *Europeans and Mongols in the Middle of the Thirteenth Century: Encountering the Other* (Helsinki: Finnish Academy of Science and Letters, 2001), 34. George Lane writes of Möngke's death in 1259: "Möngke died of dysentery while on campaign in China, and once again the worldwide campaigns of the Mongols came to a sudden halt." George Lane, *Daily Life in the Mongol Empire* (Westport, Conn.: Greenwood Press, 2006), 9.

136   The Mongol eruption and aftermath

English chronicler Matthew Paris relates one contemporary observer's account of the Mongols' mercurial exchanges: "In a moment all that execrable race vanished, all those riders returned into wretched Hungary. As suddenly as they had come, so suddenly did they disappear; *a circumstance which creates the greater fear in the minds of those who witnessed it.*"[143] The halted Mongol advance did not alleviate concerns, and, in Richard's words, "the fright caused by the Mongol invasion continued to give rise to worrisome rumors."[144]

The back-and-forth nature of the Mongol intrusions at the operational level, accounts of which permeated Western images and assessments, compounded that macro-level interactive uncertainty.[145] Mongol behaviors, in Denis Sinor's phrase their "curious comportment in war," were very much in line with those practices that had led to their stunning successes over more materially powerful adversaries.[146] Contemporaries viewed Mongol actions with puzzlement. The very rapidity of the Mongol operations, "[t]he speed and daring with which the aggressors accomplished their purpose and then disappeared," helped reinforce images of the attackers as inscrutable and otherworldly.[147] In one prophesy the Mongols are referred to as wanderers, people "without a head" (*sine capite*), leading Robert Lerner to conclude that they "were probably deemed 'headless' because their swift armies appeared to terrified Westerners to be without a leader."[148] Depicted as rootless and

---

[143] [Emphasis added.] Giles, *Matthew Paris's English History*, 470. For more on the internal crisis that precipitated the withdrawal, and a similar episode around 1260, see Stephen G. Haw, "The Deaths of Two Khagans: A Comparison of Events in 1242 and 1260," *Bulletin of the School of Oriental and African Studies* 76, no. 3 (October 2013): 361–71.

[144] Richard, "Mongols and the Franks," 46. While Western Europe had been spared, this did little to diminish "an acute awareness of peril" and "feeling of impending doom." See Igor de Rachewiltz, *Papal Envoys to the Great Khans* (Stanford: Stanford University Press, 1971), 83. "Timor Tartarorum," Bronislaw Geremek writes, "seems to have been a universal feeling" and was evident in the "terror that had seized European opinion." Bronislaw Geremek, *The Common Roots of Europe*, trans. Jan Aleksandrowicz, et al. (Cambridge: Polity Press, 1996), 91.

[145] Observations made in one area where the Mongols encroached describe a "terror-stricken" population "paralyzed by fear," and note the habits of the Mongols in appearing, "disappearing as suddenly as they came," and reappearing, enhancing their debilitating effects. Schelomo Dov Goitein, "Glimpses from the Cairo Geniza on Naval Warfare in the Mediterranean and on the Mongol Invasion," in *Studi Orientalistici in onore di Giorgio Levi Della Vida, Vol. 1* (Rome, 1956): 400–1.

[146] Denis Sinor, "On Mongol Strategy," reprinted in *Inner Asia and its Contacts with Medieval Europe* (London: Variorum Reprints, 1977) XVI, 245. According to Sinor, ironically, this loathed irregularity often had to do with their strict adherence to timetables.

[147] Connell, "Western Views," 120.

[148] Robert E. Lerner, *The Powers of Prophecy: The Cedar of Lebanon Vision from the Mongol Onslaught to the Dawn of the Enlightenment* (Berkeley: University of California Press, 1983), 22.

European reactions and Mongol interactions 137

dangerous wanderers, perceived Mongol behavior fit well with their projected image as vehicles of God's punishment.[149] These behaviors were also accompanied by occasional intentional efforts at deception and dissimulation. Mongol forces were reported to have employed diplomatic subterfuge at times, and are said to have carried crosses to gain safe passage, taking advantage of the Christian West's anticipation of King David.[150] But the deception and dissimulation were not either distinctive or widespread enough to be considered significant deviations. Deception on the battlefield and in diplomacy was not aberrant, the Mongols just did it better than their adversaries, and the evidence of dissimulation is not good enough to establish it as a general behavior. Deception and dissimulation were not essential behaviors for their survival in order to counteract conditions of vulnerability, as posited for actors in this study, though deception did maximize their effectiveness in conquest. The Mongols were, in fact, a force behind establishing and reinforcing norms that protected embassies.[151] Indeed, most of Mongol diplomacy was quite open and direct, to put it mildly, clearly communicating the message "submit or suffer a terrible fate."

As the Mongols' capabilities grew those practices associated with the logics of concealment were not as necessary as they might have been for a lesser power. While the steppe provides some topographic insulation, this was not employed for defensive position. The Mongols were skillful in deception, but this was the result of capable military leadership and superior tactics and only indirectly the result of material constraints. The evidence of intentional dissimulation is fragmentary and does not suggest a recurring pattern of behavior. So what explains this deviation from deviation? As the Mongols gained predominant power they were able to inflict terror of the top-down kind. Indeed, clear communication of strategic intentions became a Mongol hallmark, frightening potential adversaries into submission. On the other hand, some unintended outcomes of behaviors resulted from their atypical structure and modes of interaction. Both on the strategic (with wholesale withdrawals due to succession crises) and operational-tactical levels (with rapid advances and withdrawals) there were increased levels of

---

[149] Giles, *Matthew Paris's English History*, 469.

[150] Jackson, *Mongols and the West*, 48–49. The Mongol practice of "feigning friendship towards Christians" cited by Pope Alexander IV in 1260, was by then "a well-established practice that seemingly went back to the time of Chinggis Khan himself." See Peter Jackson, "The Mongols and the Faith of the Conquered," in *Mongols, Turks, and Others*, 252.

[151] See Denis Sinor, "Diplomatic Practices in Medieval Inner Asia," in *The Islamic World: From Classical to Modern Times*, ed. C.E. Bosworth, et al. (Princeton: Darwin Press, 1989), 337–55.

138   The Mongol eruption and aftermath

uncertainty among their actual and potential adversaries. This underscores, and adds to our understanding of these types of actors, that the intentional behaviors characterized here as logics of concealment do not exhaust the range of uncertainty-inducing effects they may have on international systems.

Some of the same considerations of the Mongols' relative power, the ascendance to systemic dominance rather than survival and persistence, affect the potential for norms to serve a functional role for dominant actors. The contemporaneous or near-contemporaneous advancement of behavioral norms that negate advantages for irregular actors is not evident in the Mongol case. Norms did not serve to check an emerging weak power because the emergence was rapid and the weakness brief. Any potential development and transmission of a norm against massacres, for instance, would do little to halt this behavior or marginalize its practitioners as they increased in power. Self-preservation in the form of fleeing or submission was preferable. There was little left to do but to decry the practice, which enunciated but did little to establish a norm. Indeed, the Mongols were not really violating a norm against wholesale slaughter as much as they were perfecting a not-uncommon practice. The horrors of modern warfare would be necessary to begin to drive norms concerning violence against civilians. Though the Mongols would play a role in distinguishing civilized from uncivilized practices in warfare, this would come well after their empire faded into history.

Upon earth there is not his like: fear, uncertainty, and identity

While the effects of the Mongols on the contemporary articulation and establishment of norms were weak, argued here as a result of their relative power, their effects on the formation of identities in the near-term were quite strong. Compensation for debts in physical security would be found in firming ontological security through overlapping strands of culturally infused common identity. Was the reaction to the Mongols a function of their numbers, swelled with levied troops from conquered territories, or the qualitative aspects of their behavior? Some combination of the quantitative and qualitative aspects of Mongol power, witnessed through the cultural dissonance in their relations with Europe, seems most convincing. Contemporary observers of the Mongols often cited their seemingly limitless numbers.[152] This

---

[152] Timothy May refers to the debate concerning the reasons for Mongol success, including the "weight of numbers" school that holds that Mongol conquests were due to

Fear, uncertainty, and identity 139

characterization matched biblical allusions to Gog and Magog, who in *Revelation* are numbered "as the sand of the sea."[153] Comparisons based on their numbers were accompanied by associations of the Mongols (*gens tartarorum*) with the Devil, as described in the Bible: "Upon earth there is not his like."[154]

On the operational and tactical levels it is evident that their manner of fighting amplified interpretations of their innumerableness. Even as constraints lessened by way of expansion the tactics remained highly effective. The Mongol employment of fear and intimidation also enhanced the sense, according to one historian, that "blind fury was felt to be unleashed by God for the chastisement and purification of Christendom."[155] Continued bafflement over the nature and origins of the Tartars spurred numerous missions to understand this unfamiliar threat, combining intelligence gathering and conversion as goals.[156] William of Rubruck declared that the Mongols seemed to belong to "some other world."[157] Growing knowledge of the Mongols, however, would lead to increased humanization, away from being biblical monsters toward being part of mankind and God's order.[158] This tempered perception allowed for continued hopes for conversion and alliance against the Saracens.[159]

Since the first panicked accounts seeping out from Russia and Eastern Europe, the Mongol presence had affected the religious consciousness of

---

overwhelming numbers recruited from conquered territories. May pokes holes in this argument, emphasizing the need for highly trained horsemen over raw conscripts. May, "Mechanics of Conquest," 12. The size of the invading Mongol forces was certainly exaggerated in contemporary accounts. While some claimed the army that invaded Hungary numbered near half a million, "at a very conservative estimate one can set the strength of the Mongol invading forces between 105,000 and 150,000 men." Denis Sinor, "The Mongols in the West," *Journal of Asian History* 33, no. 1 (1999): 19.

[153] Anderson, *Alexander's Gate*, 5.   [154] Ruotsala, *Europeans and Mongols*, 63.

[155] Devin DeWeese, "The Influence of the Mongols on the Religious Consciousness of Thirteenth Century Europe," *Mongolian Studies* 5 (1978): 50. The atrocities of the Mongols, according to Peter Jackson, caused them to be identified with Satan, evoking biblical prophecy. Peter Jackson, "Christians, Barbarians, and Monsters: The European Discovery of the World beyond Islam," in *The Medieval World*, ed. Peter Linehan and Janet Nelson (London: Routledge, 2001), 99.

[156] Jackson, *Mongols and the West*, 89–92. These missions did little, however, to divine intentions beyond the desire for domination, and revealed some of the less savory aspects of Mongol power. See Richard, "Mongols and the Franks," 52.

[157] Quoted in Jackson, *Mongols and the West*, 139.

[158] Ruotsala, *Europeans and Mongols*, 135. See also DeWeese, "Influence of the Mongols," 55. The representations of Tartars as fantastic beings, cannibals, and other demonic manifestations are discussed in Strickland, *Saracens, Demons, and Jews*, 192–208.

[159] On the interaction of the Christian powers (European and Crusader states), the Mongols, and the Muslim powers, see Timothy M. May, "The Mongol Presence and Impact in the Lands of the Eastern Mediterranean," in *Crusaders, Condottieri, and Cannon: Medieval Warfare in Societies around the Mediterranean*, ed. Donald J. Kagay and L.J. Andrew Villanon (Leiden: Brill, 2003), 133–56.

140   The Mongol eruption and aftermath

Europe. Pope Innocent IV was a force behind the efforts both to resist the threat and to mold the Mongols into his papal vision of world order. In a letter to Güyük he admonished the qaghan for not submitting to the hierarchy established by God, and declared that he had broken "the bond of natural ties that united humankind."[160] Innocent sought to unite European efforts against the Tartars, building on a common Christian identity. The First Council of Lyon had the threat posed by the Tartars high on its agenda.[161] Due to the numerous political and religious divisions, however, the raising of religious consciousness had little lasting effect on the unification of the Christian community of Europe.[162] By the time the Mongols conquered Baghdad and threatened Syria around 1259–1260, hopes of accommodation had dissolved, and both the unity of Christendom and the susceptibility of the Mongols to submission proved chimerical.

Resistant to incorporation and submission, depictions that tended toward exclusion and emphasized their bent toward domination would come to pervade European framing of the Mongols. According to Daniel Baraz, the Mongols represented a higher form of "otherness" than long-time rivals the Saracens. This was due not only to their status as pagans, unlike the Muslims, but also to the lack of "reciprocity of violence" in their relations with the West.[163] The Mongols as victimizers, as unequal in their doling out of violence, is matched by the lack of symmetry in violence as a form of interaction or "social" exchange. It was as much that asymmetry, the content rather than the volume of violence, that contributed to distorted comprehensions and representations. These interpretations of the Mongols would endure, and images of indiscriminate barbarity and cruelty, rather than ingenuity and resourcefulness, would predominate and come to define them.

---

[160] Güyük, not surprisingly, was unmoved. Robert A. Williams, *The American Indian in Western Legal Thought: The Discourses of Conquest* (New York: Oxford University Press, 1990), 49.

[161] See the section on the Tartar threat, "On the Tartars," First Council of Lyon, 1245, in *Decrees of the Ecumenical Councils, Vol. 1, Nicaea I to Lateran V*, ed. Norman P. Tanner (London: Sheed & Ward, 1990), 297.

[162] Geremek, *Common Roots of Europe*, 92. For the fractures in European politics, see Rachewiltz, *Papal Envoys*, 58–64; and Jackson, *Mongols and the West*, 22–23. On Pope Gregory's earlier effort to declare a crusade against the Mongols, which foundered due to these fissures, see Peter Jackson, "The Crusade against the Mongols (1241)," *Journal of Ecclesiastical History* 42, no. 1 (January 1991): 1–18. The ultimately fruitless efforts of popes Gregory IX and later Innocent IV to forge unity between the Roman and Eastern Orthodox churches in the face of the Mongol threat are examined in James J. Zatko, "The Union of Suzdal, 1222–1252," *Journal of Ecclesiastical History* 8 (1957): 33–52.

[163] Daniel Baraz, *Medieval Cruelty: Changing Perceptions, Antiquity to the Early Modern Period* (Ithaca: Cornell University Press, 2003), 76.

Enlightenment and mobility 141

There is evidence of collective identity formation based on common modes of organization and interaction (homogeneity), as well as on common cultural bonds. Another complication emerges, though, considering the relative power of the Mongols. This study emphasized the distinction between fear, based on estimation of imminent peril, and uncertainty, the result of inestimable risk and potential peril. Western Europe experienced both fear and uncertainty during this time. The fear was firmly based on the advances of the Mongols and a relatively clear understanding of what the Mongol presence boded. The uncertainty was rooted in the irregular and unpredictable behavior they evinced. Clearly, both conditions were evident, affecting both physical and ontological security. How the conditions of pervasive estimable fear and uncertainty interacted, and which was dominant in the formation of identities, is difficult to determine.

Identity formation in conditions of fear and uncertainty involved both theological and political motivations. This demonstrates the collusion of common culture and functional drivers in orienting responses to uncertainty, including corporate and collective identity formation. Biblical-based identity formation provided an initial equilibrium, one that would give way to a more practical understanding of the Mongols as proto-Christian, potential allies who could be brought under the order of God. The collective identity formation did not yield much in the way of collective action or longer-term effects as it did not transcend the deep divisions of Christian Europe. Cultural codes framed the types of identity formation. The myth of Prester John provided a collective frame, while Gog and Magog provided a ready-made category for corporate identity formation, a progression that would come to associate the Mongols with hell itself. Later interactions with the Mongols humanized them somewhat but still emphasized their brutal nature and backward practices.

Cruel hands of the Tartars: Enlightenment and mobility

"The Tartars have no abiding city," William of Rubruck wrote, "nor do they know of one that is to come."[164] Later images of the Mongols as aimless, rootless, and savage, the antitheses of society, would serve to help delimit civilization. The threat from the Mongols would mostly abate as the empire dissolved, though Temür (Tamerlane) would attempt to reprise Chinggis Khan's accomplishments, evoking the conqueror's memory.[165] The travels

---

[164] Christopher Dawson, ed., *Mission to Asia* (Toronto: University of Toronto Press, 1980), 93.
[165] Jackson, *Mongols and the West*, 358–60.

142   The Mongol eruption and aftermath

of Marco Polo, and the desire for a reopening of the trade routes that had
flourished under the "Pax Mongolica," made some treatments more favorable. But by the time of the Enlightenment, and the contrasting of the West
with Asia, the Mongols would, according to Jack Weatherford, become "the
symbol of everything evil or defective in that massive continent."[166]

In a mocking account of the princely propensity for war, Voltaire cited
the occupation of "a small country with more murderous mercenaries
than Genghis-Khan, Tamburlaine, and Bajazet ever brought along with
them." Voltaire deemed Roman warfare quainter, though it was clearly as
voracious and ultimately more dependent on mercenary arms.[167] The
philosophe extended his treatment of Chinggis Khan – or "Genghis," one
of a number of European versions – well beyond passing references. His
play, *The Orphan of China*, casts Genghis as a key character, which
Voltaire himself played onstage. The play sought to "demonstrate the
existence of natural morality in the world beyond Christian influence."[168]
The Mongol and Chinese races are contrasted as the Tartar chief's
instincts to kill a young female member of the royal family are overcome
by the civilizing forces of Chinese society.[169] The play, according to Ros
Ballaster, "is a hymn to the force of civilization as a counterweight to
political might."[170]

Montesquieu repeatedly evoked the Tartars, "Asia's natural conquerors," to contrast European practices with the pathologies of Asia.[171] The
Tartars, he wrote, govern "by the lash. The spirit of Europe has always
been contrary to these mores."[172] The presence of large standing armies
in Europe was "a new disease" that drained resources, brought permanent taxation, and threatened property. With more and more soldiers,
Montesquieu wrote, "we shall have nothing but soldiers and we shall be
like the Tartars."[173] Allusion to landlessness is made in Montesquieu's
backhanded praise of the Mongols' religious tolerance: "As the Tartars
did not live in houses, they did not know of temples."[174] Elevation of
permanent attachment to land would be a prominent focus in the early
modern period. The Mongols, according to Voltaire, were "wild sons of

---

[166] Jack Weatherford, *Genghis Khan and the Making of the Modern World* (New York: Three
Rivers, 2004), 254.

[167] Voltaire, *Political Writings*, trans. and ed. David Williams (Cambridge: Cambridge
University Press, 1994), 8.

[168] Marvin A. Carlson, *Voltaire and the Theatre of the Eighteenth Century* (Westport, Conn.:
Greenwood Press, 1998), 99.

[169] Ibid., 99–100.

[170] Ros Ballaster, *Fabulous Orients: Fictions of the East in England, 1662–1785* (Oxford:
Oxford University Press, 2005), 213.

[171] Charles de Secondat, Baron de Montesquieu, *The Spirit of Laws*, trans. and ed. Anne M.
Cohler, et al. (Cambridge: Cambridge University Press, 1989; 1748), 282.

[172] Ibid., 290–91; 282.   [173] Ibid., 224–25.   [174] Ibid., 481.

Enlightenment and mobility 143

rapine, who live in tents, in chariots, and in fields."[175] The association of mobility and savagery would become equally enduring in the delineation and establishment of standards of civilization.

Gibbon emphasized the clash between barbarian and civilized states, Jeremy Black notes, and the "constant pressure on settled peoples of migrant, mobile, fluid forces."[176] Gibbon's sympathies were not invariably with the civilized states, which had their disreputable features, nor was he without admiration for certain "barbarian" qualities. Nevertheless, his depictions of barbarians provide a clear distinction between them and the forces of civilization. Gibbon's discussions of various nomadic and pastoral peoples cover a range of historical groups, and he often treats them collectively. Invading nomads are seen as indistinguishable in sociological terms, giving the impression, characterized by J.G.A. Pocock: "When you have seen one pastoral nomad you have seen them all."[177]

In the section of *The Decline and Fall*, "Manners of the Pastoral Nations," Gibbon referred to Scythians and Tartars (a collective label), who were "renowned for their invincible, and rapid conquests." The emergence of this ageless presence "has spread terror and devastation over the most fertile and warlike countries of Europe." Pastoral manners, he wrote, should not be associated with the "fairest attributes of peace and innocence," but rather "are much better adapted to the fierce and cruel habits of military life." The modes of living of pastoral nomads are highlighted, as their "indolence refuses to cultivate the earth," and "their restless spirit disdains the confinement of sedentary life." The different characters of the "civilized of the globe" (Europe and China) may be attributed to the "use, and the abuse, of reason," while the Scythians or Tartars operate on instinct: "the savage tribes of mankind, as they approach nearer to the condition of animals." Later, Gibbon referred more specifically to a "Tartar sovereign" whose subjects, like him, are accustomed to "blood and rapine" and might excuse acts of tyranny "as would excite the horror of a civilized people."[178]

---

[175] Quoted in Weatherford, *Genghis Khan*, 255.
[176] Jeremy Black, "Gibbon and International Relations," in *Edward Gibbon and Empire*, ed. Rosamond McKitterick and Roland Quinault (New York: Cambridge University Press, 1997), 220.
[177] J.G.A. Pocock, "Gibbon and the Shepherds: The Stages of Society in the *Decline and Fall*," *History of European Ideas* 2, no. 3 (1981): 198–99. See also David O. Morgan, "Edward Gibbon and the East," *Iran: Journal of the British Institute of Persian Studies* 33 (1995): 86–88.
[178] Paragraph, Edward Gibbon, *The History of the Decline and Fall of the Roman Empire, Vol. I*, ed. David Womersley (London: Penguin Press, 1994; 1781), 1025; 1032.

144   The Mongol eruption and aftermath

The racial characteristics of the Tartars are mentioned by Gibbon, with the "hardships of savage life" leading to an "ugly, and even deformed race."[179] Comte de Buffon also cited severe climatic conditions and associated modes when explaining the "swarthy" appearance of the Tartars. He refers to their exposure to the elements; to "their having no cities or fixed habitations; to their sleeping constantly on the ground; and to their rough and savage manner of living."[180] This persistent association of manners, customs, and appearance with modes of living is no accident. Gibbon distinguished a pastoral stage, which is savage, and an agricultural stage, where specialization allows for the development of civilization.[181] Antoine-Yves Goguet, a lawyer and counselor to the Parlement of Paris and said to be an influence on Gibbon's writings, established "a basic correlation between mobility and savagery."[182] In establishing this relationship he emphasized the ease of movement of the "Savages, Tartars, and Arabians" who "might in very little time spread themselves over the different climates of our hemisphere."[183] Civility is threatened by the constant movement of peoples, Pocock summarizes Goguet, which "risked the loss of their humanity."[184] The association of mobility and savagery was not limited to Western observers. Ibn Khaldun had earlier observed Bedouins as a threat to sedentary society and civilization itself: "The very nature of their existence is the negation of building, which is the basis of civilization. ... Their sustenance lies wherever the shadow of their lances falls."[185]

Adam Smith praised Voltaire's play, and particularly its depiction of a child saved from the "cruel hands of the Tartars."[186] Smith also placed the Tartars in an earlier stage of society, one marked by a lack of agriculture, but with the possession of some property. This "age of shepherds" marks a greater level of development than the "age of hunters," which is characterized by the highest level of mobility. The amount of property and the level of fixity determined the stage of society. High levels of mobility, which corresponded to low amounts or no amount of property

---

[179] Gibbon, *History of the Decline and Fall of the Roman Empire, Vol. I*, 1037.

[180] George-Louis Leclerc, Comte de Buffon, "The Geographical and Cultural Distribution of Mankind," in *Race and Enlightenment: A Reader*, ed. Emmanuel Chukwudi Eze (Malden, Mass.: Blackwell, 1997), 26.

[181] Pocock, "Gibbon and the Shepherds," 198.

[182] J.G.A. Pocock, *Barbarism and Religion, Vol. 4, Barbarians, Savages, and Empires* (Cambridge: Cambridge University Press, 2005), 45.

[183] Ibid., 45.   [184] Ibid., 58.

[185] Ibn Khaldun, *The Muqaddimah: An Introduction to History*, abridged edition, trans. Franz Rosenthal (Princeton: Princeton University Press, 1969), 118.

[186] Adam Smith, *The Theory of Moral Sentiments*, ed. David D. Raphael and Alec L. Macfie (Indianapolis: Liberty Classics, 1982; 1759), 227.

Enlightenment and mobility 145

or agriculture, were negatively associated with societal advancement.[187] Adam Ferguson extolled the virtues of property, demeaning living "like a Tartar ... seized with the folly of breeding and attending his cattle."[188] In solid and settled civilized society, warfare is "grafted on" and "brought to perfection" rather than being an essential quality. The Tartars again serve as exemplars of "warlike barbarians" who, in contrast to the aspiration toward civil society, have war and expansion at the core of theirs, and have "the aspect of banditti and robbers."[189]

For those observers the Mongols (as "Tartars") served as a surrogate to emphasize the warlike nature of the nomadic pastoralist.[190] This nature is tied to a manner of living, one that predisposes to aggression and provides the skills and hardiness to prosecute wars swiftly and severely. Nomadic societies were considered not just backward but menacing, and the Mongols and Genghis Khan were employed to highlight this association. Genghis and the Mongols were often paired with other historical figures, populating these lists as a common component. Clear distinctions were made, in Smith's words, between the violence of the "splendid" Caesar and Alexander and the "savage" violence "of an Attila, a Gengis."[191] Their bellicosity and cruelty were natural phenomena, which could only be transformed by a manmade one, the encroachment of civilization in the form of fixity, cultivation, and reason.

Emphasizing a positive correlation between rootlessness and aggression was a first step in marginalizing peoples in order to justify dominating them. Here the intertwined nature of identity formation (in this case corporate identity and the delineation of "others") and efforts consistent with the enforcement thesis (to justify exceeding regular norms of enforcement) is demonstrated. Alien peoples needed to be reinforced as such to justify domination and at times elimination. This association of

---

[187] Adam Smith, "The Four Stages of Society," in *The Scottish Enlightenment: An Anthology*, ed. Alexander Broadie (Edinburgh: Canongate Books, 1997), 476–79.

[188] Adam Ferguson, *An Essay on the History of Civil Society*, ed. Fania Oz-Salzberger (Cambridge: Cambridge University Press, 1995; 1767), 95. For discussion of Ferguson's consideration of the "rude state" of pastoral peoples, see Ronald L. Meek, *Social Science and the Ignoble Savage* (Cambridge: Cambridge University Press, 1976), 150–57.

[189] Ferguson, *An Essay on the History of Civil Society*, 148–49. The bellicose nature of people of "Mongol extraction" was tied by Immanuel Kant to their horsemanship, which gave them a propensity to "warlike pursuits." Immanuel Kant, "Perpetual Peace: A Philosophical Sketch," in *Political Writings*, ed. H.S. Reiss (Cambridge: Cambridge University Press, 1991; 1795), 111.

[190] Whether the label "Tartars" refers to the Tatars, the pastoral people of Eurasia, or is used as an epithet for the historical Mongols is not always clear. Indeed, this conflation of the two serves the purpose of valuating either party.

[191] Smith, *Theory of Moral Sentiments*, 253.

146   The Mongol eruption and aftermath

mobility, savagery, and inhumanity found a place in international jurisprudence. Emerich de Vattel discussed the lawfulness of war:

Nations that are always ready to take up arms on any prospect of advantage, are
lawless robbers: but those who seem to delight in the ravages of war, who spread it
on all sides, without reasons or pretexts, and even without any other motive than
their own ferocity, are monsters, unworthy the name of men. . . . All nations have a
right to join in a confederacy for the purpose of punishing and even exterminating
those savage nations. Such were several German tribes mentioned by Tacitus –
such those barbarians who destroyed the Roman empire. . . . Such have been the
Turks and other Tartars – Genghis Khan, Timur Bec or Tamerlane, who, like
Attila, were scourges employed by the wrath of Heaven, and who made war only
for the pleasure of making it. Such are, in polished ages and among the most
civilized nations, those supposed heroes, whose supreme delight is a battle, and
who make war from inclination purely, and not from love to their country.[192]

Vattel went further when labeling the cultivation of the soil as a natural
obligation. Nations that disdain cultivation such as "some modern
Tartars" who "choose to live by plunder ... deserve to be extirpated as
savage and pernicious beasts."[193] This justification for expansion against
peoples deemed barbaric or savage was the subject of debate, with Hugo
Grotius supporting violence against them.[194] Samuel Pufendorf had a
more restrictive view concerning colonial expansion and warfare. He
made an exception, however, for those who deserved no "esteem,"
including those who "are not content to acquiesce in the Enjoyment of
their own *Rights* at *home*, but invade and ravage the rest of the world."[195]
Richard Tuck concludes that Pufendorf was referring to the Mongols or
Turks and their early incursions into Christendom.[196]

The association of the modes of life of the Tartars with "backward"
peoples occurred with some frequency. English observers of the Irish
stressed the latter's lack of civilization by highlighting their modes of
existence, as in the "idyle following of heards as the Tartarians,
Arabians, and Irishe men doo."[197] English common law that rested on

[192] Emerich de Vattel, *Law of Nations; or Principles of the Law of Nature Applied to the Conduct
and Affairs of Nations and Sovereigns*, ed. Joseph Chitty (Philadelphia: T. & J.W. Johnson
& Co., 1863; 1758), 304–5.

[193] Ibid., 35–36.

[194] Paul Keal, *European Conquest and the Rights of Indigenous Peoples: The Moral
Backwardness of International Society* (Cambridge: Cambridge University Press,
2003), 94.

[195] Quoted in Richard Tuck, *The Rights of War and Peace: Political Thought and the
International Order from Grotius to Kant* (Oxford: Oxford University Press, 1999),
161–62.

[196] Ibid., 162.

[197] William W. Bassett, "The Myth of the Nomad in Property Law," *Journal of Law and
Religion* 4, no. 1 (1986): 140. On English attitudes toward Irish pastoralists, see Michael

Enlightenment and mobility

property rights fed into the image of the nomad, in one scholar's characterization, as "rootless, transient, unreliable, and unstable" and helped provide justification for colonial expansion.[198] Jurist Henry Wheaton would deny the right of sovereignty to nomadic peoples, investing allusions of nomadic menace in distinguishing a state "from an unsettled horde of wandering savages not yet formed into a civil society," requiring a "fixed abode, and definite territory."[199] The explicit reference to the Mongols and Genghis was absent but the essential association of menace and rootlessness remained, even as applied to much weaker societies that posed no meaningful threat to rapidly expanding colonial powers.

The question of nomadism and the origins of Native Americans provides another example of the association of the Tartars with menace and incivility. Some observers believed the Native Americans were descendants of the lost tribes of Israel. In one account the Israelites had migrated through Asia, spending time in Tartary only to be corrupted by its backward ways. This was used to explain what some saw as cultural similarities of the Amerindians and the Tartars, and allowed for a return to a civilized state through Christianity from "some other kinde of being and condition."[200] Expressing his disdain for crude efforts to compare Native Americans with other peoples, John Adams mocked the thinking that associated the "seven hundred thousand soldiers of Zingis," and the "infernal scream" of their battle cry with the Native American war cry. Further venting his frustrations to Thomas Jefferson, Adams wrote, "I am weary of contemplating nations from lowest and most beastly degradations of human life to the highest refinement of civilization."[201]

The Mongols and Genghis Khan continued through the nineteenth century as symbols of rootless and reasonless belligerence. Benjamin Constant labeled Napoleon "another Attila, another Genghis Khan, but more terrible and more hateful because he has at his disposal the resources of civilization."[202] Hegel tied the behavior of the then present-day Mongolians to topography and climate. They wandered without

---

Adas, *Dominance by Design: Technological Imperatives and America's Civilizing Mission* (Cambridge, Mass.: Belknap Press, 2006), 48–49.

[198] Bassett, "Myth of the Nomad," 150.

[199] Henry Wheaton, *Elements of International Law*, 8th ed. (London: Samson Low, 1866), 30. For an in-depth discussion of the denial of sovereignty rights to indigenous peoples, see Keal, *European Conquest*, 102–7.

[200] Above, see Richard W. Cogley, "'Some Other Kinde of Being and Condition': The Controversy in Mid-Seventeenth-Century England over the Peopling of Ancient America," *Journal of the History of Ideas* 68, no. 1 (January 2007): 45; 53.

[201] "John Adams to Thomas Jefferson, June 28, 1813," in *The Writings of Thomas Jefferson, Vol. XIII* (Washington, D.C.: Thomas Jefferson Memorial Association, 1904), 287–88.

[202] Stephen Coote, *Napoleon and the Hundred Days* (Cambridge, Mass.: Da Capo Press, 2005), 160. After issuing that statement, Constant went into Napoleon's service.

148   The Mongol eruption and aftermath

property, and were subject to "agitation" as that of Genghis and Tamerlane who "destroyed all before them; then vanished again ... possessing no inherent principle of vitality."[203] The partition of Poland was explained by Carl von Clausewitz as a result of Poland being a "Tartar state," and "their turbulent political condition, and their unbounded levity went hand in hand, and so they tumbled into the abyss."[204]

Mongol aggression and civilization

Later discussions would come to focus less on their unsettled state and more on the Mongols and Genghis Khan as exemplars of brutality and aggression.[205] No explanation was needed when "Genghis" was evoked; it was clear they were not referring to his lawmaking or religious tolerance. British critics of Union actions in the American Civil War cited the "wanton barbarity" of the Federal troops, "as though they sought to emulate the ravages of Attila and Genghis-Khan."[206] General Sherman was labeled a man "more evil than Ivan the Terrible or Genghis Khan."[207] In *The Great Illusion* Norman Angell cited an analysis of the Turk as "kind to children and animals," that is until "the fighting spirit comes on him, [and] he becomes like the terrible warriors of the Huns or Genghis Khan, and slays, burns, and ravages without any mercy or discrimination."[208]

Nazi propaganda struck the theme that Bolshevik "world revolutionary fanatics" represented a "second Genghis Khan."[209] (Arthur de Gobineau had earlier tied the behavior of the Mongols to "ethnical characteristics" resulting from an "erratic life" that was a racially distinct trait.)[210] After the war, the enormity of the crimes committed by the Nazi regime

---

[203] G.W.F. Hegel, *The Philosophy of History*, trans. J. Sibree (New York: Colonial Press, 1900), 88–89.

[204] Carl von Clausewitz, *On War*, trans. J.J. Graham (New York: Barnes & Noble, 2004), 381.

[205] A more subtle incorporation is the phrase "to catch a Tartar," which means "to get hold of one who can neither be controlled nor got quit of; to tackle one who unexpectedly proves to be too formidable." *Oxford English Dictionary Online*, s.v. "Tartar, Tatar."

[206] James G. Blaine, *Twenty Years of Congress from Lincoln to Garfield, Volume II* (Norwich, Conn.: Henry Bill, 1886), 481.

[207] Mark Grimsley, *The Hard Hand of War: Union Military Policy toward Southern Civilians, 1861–1865* (Cambridge: Cambridge University Press, 1995), 1.

[208] Norman Angell, *The Great Illusion: A Study of the Relation of Military Power to National Advantage*, 4th ed. (New York: G.P. Putnam's Sons, 1910), 392.

[209] Jeffrey Herf, *The Jewish Enemy: Nazi Propaganda during World War II and the Holocaust* (Cambridge: Harvard University Press, 2006), 142.

[210] Arthur de Gobineau, *The Moral and Intellectual Diversity of Races* (Philadelphia: J.B. Lippincott, 1856), 233.

Mongol aggression and civilization   149

required a clear benchmark for savagery. This was emplaced to have been exceeded by the Nazis cementing their depravity as far beyond any concept of civilized warfare, that is, *even worse* than Genghis Khan. Winston Churchill would refer to Nazi crimes as surpassing "the rough-and-ready butcheries of Genghis Khan, and in scale reduces them to pigmy proportions."[211] In deriving the new term "genocide" historical referents were needed. While atrocities associated with the destruction of Carthage, the siege of Jerusalem in the First Crusade, and European religious wars were cited, those of Genghis and Tamerlane were termed "special wholesale massacres."[212] The names of Genghis Khan and Tamerlane, Leo Kuper writes, "have become synonyms for the genocides of a later period."[213]

As the twentieth century unfolded and closed, these images were repeatedly conjured. While other leaders were evoked, it was Genghis that served as the go-to khan for symbolism of savagery and unrestrained aggression. For the United States it would be the firebombing of Dresden and the atomic bombings.[214] More recently, Middle Eastern critics of the Iraq War revived the sacking of Baghdad, labeling the war an act of the "New Mongols."[215] In the 2004 US presidential campaign, tapes of a young John Kerry were dug up, where he characterized the actions of US soldiers in Vietnam as having "razed villages in a fashion reminiscent of Genghis Khan." Critics blanched at the comparison to such a ruthless and rapacious conqueror, the antithesis of civilized warfare.[216]

The negative characterization of the Mongols survived as they became closely associated with cruel practices, massacres, and general naked aggression. This impression, like most good caricatures, is based on a distortion of an existing trait, and does have some historical merit. It was

---

[211] Winston Churchill, *Memoirs of the Second World War* (Boston: Houghton Mifflin, 1959), 12. In a ruling one Nuremberg judge commented on Rudolf Hoess, commander of Auschwitz: "In comparison to Hoess, Genghis Khan was a Sunday school boy, Torquemada an entertaining Micawber, and Ivan The Terrible, an innocuous, benevolent, old man." *Trials of war criminals before the Nuremberg Military Tribunals under Control Council law no. 10, Nuremberg, October 1946–April 1949, Volume 5* (U.S. Government Printing Office, 1950), 1131.

[212] Raphaël Lemkin, *Axis Rule in Occupied Europe* (Washington, D.C.: Carnegie Endowment, 1944), 80.

[213] Leo Kuper, *Genocide: Its Political Use in the Twentieth Century* (New Haven: Yale University Press, 1982), 11–12.

[214] See Michael Janeway, *The Fall of the House of Roosevelt: Brokers of Ideas and Power from FDR to LBJ* (New York: Columbia University Press, 2004), 237, n. 16; and Peter H. Maguire, *Law and War: An American Story* (New York: Columbia University Press, 2001), 101.

[215] See Sam Hamod, "The New Mongols," *Al-Jazeera*, November 19, 2004; and Loretta Napoleoni, *Insurgent Iraq: Al Zarqawi and the New Generation* (New York: Seven Stories Press, 2005), 147–56.

[216] One example is Ernest W. Lefever, "America Is Not Genghis Khan," *Washington Times*, May 2, 2004.

150 The Mongol eruption and aftermath

applied, though, in a manner that distinguished this violence from that perpetrated during the same and subsequent periods by other actors. Mongol warfare indicated a type of hyper-violence devoid of purpose and not rooted in the advancement of civilization. Perversely, this would serve to elevate certain types of warfare as less horrific and more justifiable.

Judgments of rightful membership and conduct consistent with the conference of legitimacy eluded the Mongols because of a lack of cultural understanding, aberrant modes of organization, and the severity of their behavior, which was in part due to the stringency of their circumstances. Mobility and savagery would become causally associated, and, in turn, the Mongols were disassociated from society and civilization. That the Mongols possessed a civilization of their own is not acknowledged in this discourse, as they became archetypes of the unreasoned violence of the steppe. The prevalence of extreme violence against noncombatants in warfare deemed more just, as the siege of Jerusalem, was easily elided through ready reference to Mongol butchery. As modern-day conquerors arose, rather than Raymonds or Godfreys they became Attilas and Tamerlanes, and nearly always Genghis Khans.

To be a Genghis Khan is not only to be violent but to be violent to no end, either in extent or purpose. This association with unrestrained and aimless violence complemented representations of nomadic and pastoral peoples that depicted them as not only backward but potentially danger-ous. The ability of Genghis to scale up nomadic pastoralism to a trans-continental empire invested these peoples with looming menace. Mobility and rootlessness were not evidence of quaint practices but of a vagabond and threatening character. They were too close to nature, too far from society, and their subjugation and dispossession would be seen as removing or taming a dangerous element, providing a valuable service to mankind. To the treachery and fanaticism of the Assassins was added a separate dimension of incivility. This both condemned and excused violence, by and against the rootless, respectively, seeking to control both the quantitative and qualitative aspects of violence to benefit and validate sedentary civilization. The standards in part derived from one of history's greatest powers would seek to counter the mobility and transi-tory conditions that threatened sedentary societies, and give excesses against weaker manifestations of nomadic modes a noble veneer. These standards of civilization would then be used to seek to check the levels of destruction that sedentary societies had achieved and, for a time, monopolized.

4 Out of the shadow of God
Power and piracy along the Barbary Coast

O'ER the glad waters of the dark blue sea,
Our thoughts as boundless, and our souls as free,
Far as the breeze can bear, the billows foam,
Survey our empire, and behold our home!
. . . .
Corsair! thy doom is named – but I have power
To soothe the Pacha in his weaker hour. . . .
—Lord Byron, "The Corsair"

Introduction

"The steppes are like the sea," historian François Hartog wrote, referring to the burial of a nomadic Scythian.[1] In Arnold Toynbee's characterization both are "highly uncongenial" elements, but in their vastness they are open to possibilities for those who can manage their expanses.[2] Just as the Mongols stretched the possibilities of political organization so too did another group of polities. The Barbary powers tested their limitations by extending far into the sea and well beyond the limits their resources would suggest. The Mediterranean had long known piracy, but the Barbary powers exceeded the traditional economics of sea-raiding.[3] For Algiers, Tunis, and Tripoli it became "an intrinsic part of public finance and commerce" and each established what were essentially city-states, maintaining their presence and significance as that mode of organization was being left behind in favor of more dominant centralized territorial states.[4]

---

[1] François Hartog, *The Mirror of Herodotus: The Representation of the Other in the Writing of History*, trans. Janet Lloyd (Berkeley and Los Angeles: University of California Press, 1988), 132.

[2] John Sellars, "Nomadic Wisdom: Herodotus and the Scythians," in *PLI: Warwick Journal of Philosophy* 7 (1998): 92, n. 68.

[3] See Peregrine Horden and Nicholas Purcell, *The Corrupting Sea: A Study of Mediterranean History* (Oxford: Blackwell, 2000).

[4] John L. Anderson, "Piracy and World History: An Economic Perspective on Maritime Predation," in *Bandits at Sea: A Pirates Reader*, ed. C.R. Pennell (New York: New York University Press, 2001), 90.

152   Power and piracy along the Barbary Coast

While piracy was not exceptional in the Mediterranean, the Barbary powers would be. One nineteenth-century observer referring to the Barbary powers wrote, "*De telles Monstruosités sociales ne peuvent pas durer*" ("Such social monstrosities cannot last").[5] Yet they had lasted, and fairly effectively for much of the seventeenth century and beyond, compelling great powers to tolerate and collude with their depredations.

Those depredations according to one estimate included enslaving over a million Europeans over two and a half centuries, menacing coasts from Iceland to England to southern Spain and Sicily.[6] To this day the saying "*(no) hay Moros en la costa*" survives in Spanish to indicate that a danger exists or has passed, and remnants of towers, intended to provide early warning to protect fisherman or coastal dwellers, still dot southern European coastlines. In Sicily, the saying "*pigliato dai turchi*" (taken by the Turks, referring to corsairs) still indicates being surprised or caught off guard.[7] The historical meaning of those phrases has been lost in language, much like the generic term "assassin." But the Barbary powers' persistence and their discursive and legal trails further refine our understanding of how the system's dominant actors' grappling with unfamiliarity and adapting to atypicality contributed to the development of international society.

How the Barbary powers achieved their impact on the system and maintained it, despite strong pressures from their more centralized and powerful European antagonists, is one focus of this chapter. The effects of that antagonism on the development of norms and identities, and consequently international society, is the other. The chapter will proceed in the manner of the previous two. First, there will be a description of the international systemic context into which the Barbary powers emerged and its most important actors. Next, the relationship between the corsairs and the Ottoman Empire and how that was affected by an episode of Ottoman decline are examined. The limitations on the Barbary powers' ability to establish sovereignty beyond their city walls, and how this affected their political development, are then covered. Following this, the assertion of the Barbary powers as independent entities, and how this affected their relationships with the major powers of Europe, are outlined. The case study then moves to questions concerning how encounters with these odd powers shaped norms and identities. This includes examination of their position in international law, how Enlightenment figures characterized them, and their effects on identities in both Britain and

---

[5] Eugène Cauchy, *Le Droit Maritime International, Considéré Dans Ses Origines et Dans Ses Rapports Avec Les Progrès de la Civilisation, Vol. I* (Paris: Guillaumin, 1862), 155.

[6] The numerical estimate, discussed in greater depth below, is taken from Robert C. Davis, "Counting European Slaves on the Barbary Coast," *Past and Present* 172 (2001): 89; 118.

[7] See Robert C. Davis, *Holy War and Human Bondage: Tales of Christian–Muslim Slavery in the Early-Modern Mediterranean* (Santa Barbara, Calif.: Praeger, 2009), 27.

Maghrebian anarchy and great power rivalry 153

the newly independent United States. The chapter concludes with a discussion of their unique contribution to the considerations of piracy and slavery as contrary to emerging standards of civilization.

Since the Barbary powers emerged at a time of conflict between major powers with strong confessional identities, their development has often been couched in terms of a clash between Islamic and Christian civilizations. This interpretation has persisted through many generations of scholarship.[8] After September 11, the abnormal violence and a putative collision of civilizations led a number of observers to see "echoes of Barbary" in present circumstances.[9] This chapter does not dismiss these confessional elements entirely but looks deeper at factors lying at the level of the international system. In so doing, it is hoped, we can see to what extent those echoes reflect the actual substance revealed about these actors and events.

Maghrebian anarchy and great power rivalry

The system that preceded the establishment of the Barbary powers arose from three main forces: the rise of the Ottomans, the anarchic condition of the Maghreb, and the expansion of Spanish power on the Iberian peninsula and beyond. Under Mehmed II (r. 1444–1446; 1451–1481) the Ottomans established their influence around the Black Sea and set the Danube as a northern frontier.[10] After fighting a series of wars against

[8] Examples of this wave of scholarship include Robert L. Playfair, *The Scourge of Christendom: Annals of British Relations with Algiers Prior to the French Conquest* (Freeport, N.Y.: Books for Libraries Press, 1972; 1884); Stanley Lane-Poole, *The Story of the Barbary Corsairs* (New York: G.P. Putnam's Sons, 1890); and Edward H. Currey, *Sea-wolves of the Mediterranean: The Grand Period of the Moslem Corsairs* (New York: Dutton, 1910). Aiming to correct many of the misconceptions surrounding the Barbary corsairs, Godfrey Fisher wrote what has been widely concluded to be an overly generous and sanguine portrayal. Godfrey Fisher, *Barbary Legend: War, Trade, and Piracy in North Africa, 1415–1830* (Oxford: Clarendon Press, 1957). General treatments of piracy have tended toward popular rather than scholarly audiences, though some attained high quality. See Philip Gosse, *The History of Piracy* (Glorieta, N.M.: Rio Grande Press, 1995; 1932). Other scholarly treatments include collected volumes by Pennell, *Bandits at Sea*; and Claire Jowitt, ed., *Pirates? The Politics of Plunder, 1550–1650* (Basingstoke: Palgrave Macmillan, 2007).

[9] See Rand Fishbein, "Echoes from the Barbary Coast," *The National Interest* 66 (Winter 2000/2001): 50–51; and Richard Brookhiser, "Echoes of Barbary," *Wall Street Journal*, May 30, 2006. Paul Silverstein notes that "the Barbary Analogy has been a potent arm in the ideological battle that has paralleled the post-September 11th war on terror." Paul A. Silverstein, "The New Barbarians: Piracy and Terrorism on the North African Frontier," *CR: The New Centennial Review* 5, no. 1 (Spring 2005): 183. Robert Turner wrote that "Jefferson led America in its first battles with state-sponsored international terrorism." Robert F. Turner, "State Responsibility and the War on Terror: The Legacy of Thomas Jefferson and the Barbary Pirates," *Chicago Journal of International Law* 4, no. 1 (Spring 2003): 121.

[10] Halil Inalcik, *The Ottoman Empire: The Classical Age, 1300–1600*, trans. Norman Itzkowitz and Colin Imber (New Rochelle, N.Y.: Orpheus Publishing, 1973), 29.

154   Power and piracy along the Barbary Coast

numerous rivals, and consolidating control over Anatolia and Rumelia, the Ottomans attacked Genoese and Venetian positions that had dominated trade routes and left Ottoman shores vulnerable.[11] Early in the sixteenth century, the Ottomans would confront other major Muslim powers, including Safavid Persia and the Mamluks. The rivalry with the Shia Safavids to the east would continue until the early seventeenth century, while the defeat of the Mamluks (1517) would lead to Ottoman control of Egypt, its first foothold in North Africa.[12] This expansion led to their establishment as a major land and emerging sea power, increasing their influence around the Mediterranean. Mehmed's claim as founder of this burgeoning empire was trumpeted in his title, "Sovereign of the Two Lands and of the Two Seas" – the Black Sea and the Mediterranean.[13] One of his successors, Suleyman (r. 1520–1566), would attempt to consolidate control over the Mediterranean, using that title, as well as announcing his claim as ruler of the Islamic world, the "Shadow of God on Earth."[14]

To the west of Egypt, in the Maghreb (or the "West") the circumstances were unstable. The former Roman province of Africa (Arabised as *Ifrikya*) consisted of Tripolitania, modern Tunisia, and eastern Algeria. The Far West (*al-Maghreb al-Aqsa*) consisted of modern western Algeria, Morocco, and Mauritania.[15] Since the expansion of Islam these areas had seen a number of Berber dynasties, including the Almoravids, Almohads, Marinids, Hafsids, and Zayyanids.[16] Conditions degenerated in this region, which would be given its moniker "Barbary" after its Berber inhabitants.[17] Based in Tunis, the Hafsid dynasty, which had broken off

---

[11] Andrew C. Hess, "The Evolution of the Ottoman Seaborne Empire in the Age of Oceanic Discoveries, 1453–1525," *American Historical Review* 75, no. 7 (December 1970): 1903.

[12] Andrew C. Hess, "The Ottoman Conquest of Egypt (1517) and the Beginning of the Sixteenth-Century World War," *International Journal of Middle East Studies* 4, no. 1 (January 1973): 55–76.

[13] Antony Black, *The History of Islamic Political Thought: From the Prophet to the Present* (New York: Routledge, 2001), 205.

[14] The name he is best known as is Suleyman the Magnificent. See Hess, "Ottoman Seaborne Empire," 1919. The "Shadow of God on Earth" is likely of Persian origin, prior to the Islamic period, and was later adopted as a caliphal title. Black, *History of Islamic Political Thought*, 109; 126; 205. See also Halil Inalcik, "State and Ideology under Sultan Suleyman I," in *The Middle East and the Balkans under the Ottoman Empire*, ed. Inalcik (Bloomington: Indiana University, 1993), 78.

[15] Roland Oliver and Anthony Atmore, *Medieval Africa, 1250–1800* (Cambridge: Cambridge University Press, 2001), 32.

[16] For an overview of these dynasties, see Jamil M. Abun-Nasr, *A History of the Maghrib in the Islamic Period* (Cambridge: Cambridge University Press, 1987), 76–143.

[17] The term "Berber" is believed to be derived from the Greek *barbaroi*, Latin *barbarus*, but has also been given a more indigenous derivation. See Michael Brett and Elizabeth Fentress, *The Berbers* (Oxford: Blackwell, 1996), 283, n. 5.

Maghrebian anarchy and great power rivalry

from the Almohads in the thirteenth century, had fallen on hard times due to plague, economic decline, and political fractiousness.[18] The Zayyanids were based in Tlemcen in western Algeria and vied with the Marinid dynasty based in Morocco.[19] The Maghreb as a whole was severely weakened, with economic and social dislocation and chronic political instability.[20]

The political weakness in the Maghreb provided an opportunity for European powers, particularly Spain. Under Ferdinand (II) and Isabella, the united Castille and Aragon captured Granada in 1492, removing Islamic rule from the Iberian Peninsula. Habsburg rule would split into the Spanish and Austrian branches, and each would confront an element of Ottoman power, at sea and on land, respectively. The Reconquest also resulted in forced conversion, destruction of Islamic institutions, and the expulsion of Spanish Muslims (Moriscos), a process that would stretch across the sixteenth and into the early seventeenth century.[21] Those remaining in Spain, many under at least a pretense of conversion, appealed to the emerging Ottoman power as a new protector of Islamic peoples, while others migrated to the Maghreb.[22] While communal identities and motivations did drive both Habsburg Spain and the Ottomans, the clash of these two powers is best understood as rising great powers seeking control and influence over a key strategic territory. Within the shadow of that broader struggle lesser powers would begin to build the foundations for their own emergence. The rivalry between the Ottomans and Spain in the Mediterranean would come to involve the major Christian powers of Europe and peripheral actors that inhabited what would become known as the Barbary Coast.

Expansion to the coast of North Africa was a natural objective of Habsburg Spain, now abutting the former "Islamic lake" of the Mediterranean. Having gained momentum with the Reconquest, religious zeal would suggest the continuation of a holy war and the permanent occupation of the central Maghreb.[23] But, as Robert Mantran notes, while "the initial pretext for the Spanish Crusade was the struggle of

---

[18] Oliver and Atmore, *Medieval Africa*, 37.

[19] See Weston F. Cook, Jr., "Warfare and Firearms in Fifteenth Century Morocco, 1400–1492," *War & Society* 11, no. 2 (October 1993): 25–40.

[20] M.H. Cherif, "Algeria, Tunisia, and Libya: The Ottomans and Their Heirs," in *General History of Africa, Vol. 5, Africa from the Sixteenth to the Eighteenth Century*, ed. Bethwell A. Ogot (Paris: UNESCO, 1992), 234.

[21] See Andrew C. Hess, *The Forgotten Frontier: A History of the Sixteenth-Century Ibero–African Frontier* (Chicago: University of Chicago Press, 1978), 127–55; and Leonard P. Harvey, *Muslims in Spain, 1500–1614* (Chicago: University of Chicago Press, 2005).

[22] Hess, *Forgotten Frontier*, 136–37.

[23] Abun-Nasr, *History of the Maghrib in the Islamic Period*, 147.

156   Power and piracy along the Barbary Coast

Christianity against Islam … this soon became subordinate to the political and material considerations aroused by the breaking up of the Maghrib."[24] Beginning in the end of the fifteenth century those goals would be sacrificed in favor of concentrating on Italy, where Spain and France would struggle for control over the next several decades. Spanish attention to the Maghreb would come in the form of outposts, *presidios*, placed in areas of strategic importance in the first decades of the sixteenth century, leaving the interior to native inhabitants. Established between 1509 and 1512 in Oran, Algiers, Tripoli, and Tunis, among others, these garrisons had the added benefits of helping to control the increasing incidence of piracy, protecting and taxing commerce, and supporting Spain's ambitions in Italy.[25] This policy, begun under Ferdinand II, would continue under Charles V, who as Holy Roman Emperor competed with rivals on several fronts, including France and the Ottomans.

Formidable on land, the relative weakness of the Ottoman navy limited their effectiveness at sea. A concerted effort to address this deficiency had begun in the last decades of the fifteenth century, and naval conflict with Venice as the century ended demonstrated increased Ottoman capabilities.[26] Improved naval power aided the defeat of the Mamluks and the conquest of Egypt, and additional naval building would facilitate further expansion.[27] The expansion occurred on land and at sea, with Belgrade falling in 1521 and Rhodes in 1523, greatly alarming the powers of Europe. Like Spain, though, the emphasis would tilt toward land campaigns, and in 1526 Suleyman would redirect Ottoman attention toward Europe. This led to the siege of Vienna in 1529, which would mark the end of Ottoman expansion into central Europe.[28] Following the checking of their land power, Ottoman attention again went seaward. Clashes with Spain and the combined powers of various Holy Leagues would lead the Ottomans to decisive naval victories, including the battles of Preveza (1538) and Djerba (1560). Ultimately, this power too would be checked,

---

[24] Robert Mantran, "North Africa in the Sixteenth and Seventeenth Centuries," in *Cambridge History of Islam, Vol. 2, The Further Islamic Lands*, ed. Peter M. Holt, et al. (Cambridge: Cambridge University Press, 1970), 249. Nevill Barbour concurs with this assessment, noting that among the populations it was considered a holy war but the rulers considered it an issue of national expansion. Nevill Barbour, "North West Africa from the 15th to the 19th Centuries," in *The Last Great Muslim Empires: The Muslim World, A Historical Survey, Part III*, ed. Hans J. Kissling, et al. (Leiden: E.J. Brill, 1969), 113.

[25] Abun-Nasr, *History of the Maghrib in the Islamic Period*, 147; Aurelio Espinosa, "The Grand Strategy of Charles V (1500–1558): Castille, War, and Dynastic Priority in the Mediterranean," *Journal of Early Modern History* 9, nos. 3–4 (2005): 243–44.

[26] Daniel Goffman, *The Ottoman Empire and Early Modern Europe* (Cambridge: Cambridge University Press, 2002), 145.

[27] See Hess, "Ottoman Seaborne Empire," 1907–11.   [28] Ibid., 1914.

The rise of the Barbarossa brothers 157

indicated by defeats at Malta (1565) and Lepanto (1571). Under this arc of Ottoman power the intricate and symbiotic relationships with the incipient power centers along the North African coast were established, providing the context for their development into autonomous forces.

The Sultan's admiral: the rise of the Barbarossa brothers

Piracy was nothing new to the Maghreb: its coastal topography and active sea lanes made raiding a natural vocation. During this period significant numbers would seek that calling: displaced Muslims (including some from the large influx of Moriscos), European adventurers (mostly English and Dutch who would either genuinely or opportunistically convert to Islam, becoming "renegades"), and natives of the Maghreb (seeking fortune or mere survival). The Ottomans recognized the value of these sea *ghazis*, the naval equivalent of land ghazis (or warriors), particularly in light of the empire's naval deficiencies. The experience and expertise of these seamen led to their recruitment into the Ottoman service.[29]

Among those seaborne adventurers and opportunists was Arudj. He was born on the island of Midilli (Mytilene, ancient Lesbos) to a Turkish soldier (or a Greek convert to Islam) and a Greek mother. It is not certain when Arudj arrived in North Africa, with most sources saying it was in the first few years of the sixteenth century.[30] Arudj set up bases on the Tunisian coast, first at Goletta and shortly thereafter on the island of Djerba, exchanging a share of his booty with the Hafsid ruler to maintain access.[31] These bases were used for raids in the western Mediterranean and Spanish coast, yielding some notable prizes and attracting followers. One of his brothers, Khizr, would also operate in the area but was in the shadow of his highly successful brother. Arudj soon ran afoul of the Hafsids due to his perceived political ambitions and took refuge in Djidjelli. With Turkish assistance he later seized control of Algiers, which had been menaced by a Spanish fortress on the island of Peñon. Entrusting rule over Algiers to his brother, Arudj advanced toward Tlemcen. He seized the town but this left his contingent isolated and endangered by Spanish and local forces, which killed him in the fall of

[29] See Ibid., 1905; and Palmira J. Brummett, *Ottoman Seapower and Levantine Diplomacy in the Age of Discovery* (Albany: State University of New York Press, 1994), 105–6.
[30] See Svat Soucek, "The Rise of the Barbarossas in North Africa," *Archivum Ottomanicum* 2 (1971): 238–50; and Svat Soucek, "Remarks on Some Western and Turkish Sources Dealing with the Barbarossa Brothers," *Güney-Dogu Avrupa Arastirmalari Dergisi* 1 (1972): 63–76.
[31] Roger Le Tourneau, "Arudj," *Encyclopaedia of Islam Online*, ed. P. Bearman, et al., Brill Online, 2006 (hereafter EIs); and Abun-Nasr, *History of the Maghrib in the Islamic Period*, 148.

158   Power and piracy along the Barbary Coast

1518. Inaction and miscalculation by Spanish and Italian forces in this highly vulnerable period likely saved the inchoate Algerine polity from being completely vanquished.[32]

Khizr would rule Algiers and later take the name Khayr al-Din, but would be known to Europeans as Barbarossa, a name drawn from either his red beard or as an honor to his late brother Baba (Father) Arudj. Khizr had realized that his forces were insufficient to repel the Spanish and indigenous powers, and pledged submission to Sultan Selim I (r. 1512–1520) in exchange for military support for the vulnerable, embryonic polity.[33] This assistance would come in a number of forms, including the provision of troops, the first of which included 6,000 janissaries.[34] A mix of forces, primarily corsair captains and janissaries, would come to dominate the politics of Algiers. Khayr al-Din would have the Ottoman title of *pasha* and serve as the governor general of the Ottoman North African holdings.

Shortly after Khayr al-Din's accession, his forces were ejected from Algiers by restive tribesmen allied with the Hafsids. Algiers was reconquered in 1525, followed by the presidio at Peñon in 1529 and Tlemcen in 1532. Khayr al-Din's naval forces helped wrest control of the Spanish holdings, and would essentially serve as the Ottoman navy of the western Mediterranean. This role was formalized in 1533 when Khayr al-Din was appointed *Kapudan Pasha*, commander of the Turkish fleet. He would also serve a diplomatic role in advancing a budding alliance between the Ottoman Porte and France under Francis I. Initial successes in attacking Tunis in 1534 were reversed by Spanish forces the next year, leading some Ottoman critics to doubt Khayr al-Din's judgment and intentions.[35] The mutually beneficial nature of the relationship, however, was soon reinforced. The navy defeated the combined Christian fleet under Andrea Doria (the Genoese captain and, most of the time, ally of Spain) at Preveza in 1538, and in 1541 an attack on Algiers was repulsed, causing significant damage to the Spanish fleet.[36]

---

[32] John B. Wolf, *The Barbary Coast: Algeria under the Turks, 1500–1830* (New York and London: W.W. Norton, 1979), 10.

[33] Abun-Nasr, *History of the Maghrib in the Islamic Period*, 150.

[34] Tal Shuval, "The Ottoman Algerian Elite and Its Ideology," *International Journal of Middle East Studies* 32, no. 3 (August 2000): 325. The number of janissaries would grow to 12,000 by the beginning of the eighteenth century. Soldiers that served during this period of Ottoman suzerainty and after are commonly called "janissaries," though not all or even most would match a stricter definition.

[35] Rhoads Murphey, "Seyyid Muradi's Prose Biography of Hizir Ibn Yakub, Alias Hayreddin Barbarossa," *Acta Orientalia Academiae Scientarium Hungaricae* 54, no. 4 (2001): 520.

[36] Aldo Galotta, "Khayr al-Din (Khidir) Pasha, Barbarossa," EIs; and Oliver and Atmore, *Medieval Africa*, 40.

The rise of the Barbarossa brothers 159

The secular core of the Ottoman–Habsburg conflict has been emphasized, a judgment reinforced by the collaboration of the Ottomans with the French against their common enemies. This subordination of religious motivations to economic and political realities seems also to apply to the corsairs and their budding polities.[37] While the Ottomans had rejected the requests of Andalusian Muslims to rescue them from Spanish persecution, Khayr al-Din became a folk hero for his Iberian forays.[38] Following heresy trials in Valencia in 1531, Khayr al-Din organized convoys to rescue refugees and transport them to North Africa.[39] While the humanitarian motivations of these convoys (said by one probably overenthusiastic chronicler to have saved 70,000 Muslims) can be accepted at face value, they also came at a time of severe manpower shortages that hindered larger naval operations.[40] Andalusian Muslims were particularly valuable to Khayr al-Din as they had no connections to restive indigenous tribes.[41] While swelling the population of Algiers, they also proved eager to engage the Spanish at sea.[42] The seamen among them had the added advantages of knowing the Spanish coastlines and being able to pass themselves off as Spaniards.[43] Revenge against their former oppressors and religious zeal, though, are not nearly sufficient to explain the scale and organization of the corsair raids, which served broader interests in the struggle against Spanish power.

Ottoman naval weakness led to rebuilding efforts following defeats to the Knights of Malta and the Spanish in 1531–1532.[44] The Ottoman Empire was flush with almost all of the makings of a good navy, including timber, shipyards, soldiers, and gunnery technology.[45] Extending their

[37] The ambivalence of religious identity and motivations among corsairs in the sixteenth century, including the Barbary and Maltese corsairs, is discussed in Molly Greene, "Beyond the Northern Invasion: The Mediterranean in the Seventeenth Century," *Past & Present* 174, no. 1 (February 2002): 58–63.

[38] See Harvey, *Muslims in Spain*, 339.

[39] Murphey, "Seyyid Muradi's Prose Biography," 530–31.

[40] Ibid., 528. Manpower issues were an ongoing concern for the Barbary powers. See John F. Guilmartin, Jr., *Gunpowder and Galleys: Changing Technology and Mediterranean Warfare at Sea in the Sixteenth Century* (London: Cambridge University Press, 1974), 118–19.

[41] Andrew C. Hess, "Firearms and the Decline of Ibn Khaldun's Military Elite," *Archivum Ottomanicum* 4 (1978): 186.

[42] See J.D. Latham, "Towns and Cities of Barbary: The Andalusian Influence," *Islamic Quarterly* 16 (1973): 201.

[43] Ellen G. Friedman, "North African Piracy on the Coasts of Spain in the Seventeenth Century," *The International History Review* 1, no. 1 (January 1979): 4.

[44] Rhoads Murphey, "Süleyman I and the Conquest of Hungary: Ottoman Manifest Destiny or a Delayed Reaction to Charles V's Universalist Vision?" *Journal of Early Modern History* 5, no. 3 (August 2001): 207.

[45] Subhi Labib, "The Era of Suleyman the Magnificent: Crisis of Orientation," *International Journal of Middle East Studies* 10, no. 4 (November 1979): 444; and Brummett, *Ottoman*

160 Power and piracy along the Barbary Coast

naval influence in the western Mediterranean would require skilled seamen. Many of the corsairs of European descent carried with them knowledge of advanced naval technologies.[46] The Ottomans also needed a capable high command for their naval forces, replicating the role played by Andrea Doria.[47] Khayr al-Din and the corsairs provided that leadership, while benefiting from the material sustenance that could not be obtained in the Maghreb. This support helped expand the power of the North African polities well beyond what would have otherwise been sustainable. Once sea-raiders seeking opportunity in lawless domains, the corsairs benefited from legitimation by association with the Ottoman Empire.[48] In 1545 Khayr al-Din retired in Istanbul and died a year later, one of the few voluntary retirements of the leaders of the Barbary powers.[49] This period would also represent a high water mark in the collaboration between the nascent polities of North Africa and the Ottoman Empire.

The Barbary powers and Ottoman decline

The mid-sixteenth century would see a heightening of the Ottoman–Habsburg struggle over North Africa.[50] This would result in the Ottoman capture of Tripoli in 1551, where the Knights of Malta had established a base, and of Tunis from the Spanish in 1574.[51] Under the corsair captain Turgut (Dragut to the Europeans) Tripoli developed into a rival center of power and sea-raiding.[52] With Tunis extracted from Hafsid rule, three major centers of power under Ottoman suzerainty emerged. The Ottoman colonies would be ruled during most of the sixteenth century by officials appointed by Istanbul. The *beylerbey*, a military governor, was the primary office from about 1519 to 1587,

---

Seapower, 96. On Ottoman naval material abundance and requirements, see Stanford J. Shaw, "Selim III and the Ottoman Navy," *Turcica* 1 (1996): 212.

[46] Colin H. Imber, *The Ottoman Empire, 1300–1650: The Structure of Power* (Basingstoke: Palgrave Macmillan, 2002), 291.

[47] Labib, "Era of Suleyman," 444. The fruits of a more centrally organized navy and ambitious shipbuilding efforts were seen fairly quickly in the victory at Preveza. See Murphey, "Süleyman I," 207–8.

[48] Hess, *Forgotten Frontier*, 65; Wolf, *Barbary Coast*, 12.

[49] Between 1516 and 1596, Algiers had thirty-one rulers, most with very short reigns. Jacques Heers, *The Barbary Corsairs: Warfare in the Mediterranean, 1480–1580*, trans. Jonathan North (London: Greenhill Books, 2003), 160–61.

[50] See Andrew C. Hess, "The Moriscos: An Ottoman Fifth Column in Sixteenth-Century Spain," *American Historical Review* 74, no. 1 (October 1968): 10–12.

[51] See Daniel Panzac, *Barbary Corsairs: The End of a Legend, 1800–1820*, trans. Victoria Hobson (Leiden: Brill, 2005), 10–11; and Oliver and Atmore, *Medieval Africa*, 40–41.

[52] Oliver and Atmore, *Medieval Africa*, 40.

The Barbary powers and Ottoman decline   161

when the three provinces were officially established.[53] The "period of the triennial pashas" (provincial governors who served three-year terms) followed, lasting until 1659, though the pashas were not the primary centers of power.

The provinces of Algiers, Tunis, and Tripoli would become known in Europe as "regencies." Algiers would rise to become the most powerful and distinctive of these. As such, it will be the primary focus of this investigation, while important differences among the regencies and their development will be highlighted. In Algiers, two centers would come to dominate politics. The first was the *ujaq*, the association of janissaries that established their own base of power. The pashas were initially assisted by the *divan*, a council of high-ranking Turkish officers.[54] As the Ottoman Empire weakened, though, the ujaq would assert its authority and its independence from Istanbul through that institution.[55]

The other locus of power was the *ta'ifat al-ra'is* or community (guild) of sea captains. In Algiers these captains had been the center of power in the period of the beylerbeys. The sea captains had less influence in Tunis due to its more fertile hinterland and lesser dependence on sea-raiding for revenue.[56] Unlike in Tunis, piracy would become a state monopoly in Algiers, rather than an adjunct means of subsistence.[57] Tripoli was the weakest of the three, and as such its dependence on piracy was even greater than that of Algiers.[58] Accordingly, the influence of its sea captains was similar, though Tripoli's overall power paled in comparison.[59] There was mutual dependence as well as rivalry between the ujaq and the ta'ifat al-ra'is in Algiers. The captains recognized the military power of the janissaries, while the ujaq relied on the revenue and prestige of the corsairs. Violence was commonplace within and between these power centers.[60] The balance of power between these two groups depended largely on their ability to generate revenue in a region with limited resources.

The question of the nature of Istanbul's authority over the Barbary powers is entangled in broader considerations of the nature of Ottoman

---

[53] Tal Shuval, "Cezayir-i Garp: Bringing Algeria Back into Ottoman History," *New Perspectives on Turkey* 22 (Spring 2000): 88.

[54] Cherif, "Algeria, Tunisia, and Libya," 239.   [55] Wolf, *Barbary Coast*, 77–78.

[56] Philip Curtin, "Africa North of the Forest (1500–1880)," in *African History: From Earliest Times to Independence*, 2nd ed., ed. Curtin, et al. (New York: Longman, 1995), 162; Mantran, "North Africa," 260.

[57] Abun-Nasr, *History of the Maghrib in the Islamic Period*, 159.

[58] See Keith S. McLachlan, "Tripoli and Tripolitania: Conflict and Cohesion during the Period of the Barbary Corsairs (1551–1850)," *Transactions of the Institute of British Geographers* 3, no. 3 (1978): 290.

[59] Curtin, "Africa North of the Forest," 161.   [60] See Shuval, "Cezayir-i Garp," 90.

162   Power and piracy along the Barbary Coast

decline. Corrections to Western and Orientalist depictions of Ottoman decline have recast it more as an adjustment to changing realities than a lengthy deterioration due to despotism and decadence.[61] These discussions do much to revise the image of Ottoman decline, but do little to distract from the fact of decline itself. The beginnings of the decline of the Ottoman Empire can be traced to the latter part of the sixteenth century, though the empire would rebound from this episode. The factors contributing to the decline were numerous. Military pressures and expenditures would check what had been a dramatic expansion of Ottoman land power.[62] At sea, an allied fleet of Christian powers, including Spain, Venice, and the papacy, would defeat the Ottomans in the Battle of Lepanto in 1571, destroying two-thirds of the fleet.[63] Lepanto is often seen as the beginning of the waning of Ottoman sea power and influence in the Mediterranean. "After 1571 the very nature of warfare on the Mediterranean changed," writes Daniel Goffman, "along with the composition of the participants." From this point, he announces, it was the era of the corsair, and the end of "large and treasury-depleting armadas."[64]

The chief causes of Ottoman decline were internal, including inflation, population pressures, and corruption, though many of the troubles were tied to changing external circumstances.[65] It is clear that the depiction of chronic Ottoman decline required correction, but this does not diminish the existence and effects of an acute crisis that took hold during this period. This decline resulted in imperial retrenchment. "Rather than speaking of decline," Albert Hourani writes, "it might be more correct to say that what had occurred was an adjustment of Ottoman methods of

[61] Examples include Shuval, "Cezayir-i Garp," which provides a measured refutation of the decline thesis, and Caroline Finkel, who is more adamant arguing that "[v]iews of the Ottoman Empire widely held today have been shaped less by knowledge of Ottoman history than by how Europeans wished to project themselves and their society in relation to the Empire." Caroline Finkel, "'The Treacherous Cleverness of Hindsight': Myths of Ottoman Decay," in *Re-Orienting the Renaissance: Cultural Exchanges with the East*, ed. Gerald MacLean (Basingstoke: Palgrave Macmillan, 2005), 170. Finkel seems to overstate her case, though, particularly considering that one of the foremost advocates of this period of decline is Halil Inalcik, a Turkish historian based in Turkey, who cites contemporary Ottoman observers of the decline. See Inalcik, *Ottoman Empire*, 47.
[62] Between 1578 and 1606 the Ottomans would enter into exhausting land wars against Persia and the Habsburgs; the conquest of Cyprus (1570–1571) represented "the last great Ottoman military success." See Inalcik, *Ottoman Empire*, 41–42.
[63] Hess, *Forgotten Frontier*, 90–91.   [64] Goffman, *Ottoman Empire*, 161.
[65] Inalcik, *Ottoman Empire*, 45–47. Sources of Ottoman decline are discussed in Stanford J. Shaw, *History of the Ottoman Empire and Modern Turkey, Vol. I, Empire of the Gazis, The Rise and Decline of the Ottoman Empire, 1280–1808* (Cambridge: Cambridge University Press, 1976), 169–94; and Bernard Lewis, "Ottoman Observers of Ottoman Decline," in Lewis, *Islam in History: Ideas, People, and Events in the Middle East*, 2nd ed. (Chicago: Open Court, 1993), 211–12.

The Barbary powers and Ottoman decline   163

rule and the balance of power within the empire to changing circumstances."[66] Emphasizing a distinction between decline and retrenchment
misses the fact that these phenomena are far from inconsistent, and
decline has often served as a trigger for retrenchment for other major
powers.[67] Whether this was a forward-thinking strategy of a declining
hegemon, or what Timothy Garton Ash described as "Ottomanization,"
an "unplanned, piecemeal, and discontinuous emancipation ... of the
constituent states from an imperial center," both the cause (decline) and
the results (regional autonomy) were the same.[68]

As power in the North African provinces increased, Ottoman interest
in its increasingly costly naval ambitions diminished, along with the
raison d'être for their collaboration.[69] Initial assertions of Barbary autonomy preceded the circumstances of Ottoman decline and retrenchment.
Even in the period of the beylerbeys the janissaries had been troublesome,
particularly when they were not paid, but these revolts had been put
down. The corsair captains were not always cooperative, either, participating in naval engagements as they suited their interests. Yet, in the
period of the beylerbeys, the Ottomans could and often did remove their
appointed officials, including Khayr al-Din's son Hasan. At least
one captain was executed for his freelancing attacks against French shipping.[70] Into the seventeenth century corsair captains would cooperate
with the Porte on naval missions, but decreasing compensation for
corsair losses made such expeditions less appealing.[71]

While some observers emphasize continued Ottoman influence,[72]
according to Jamil Abun-Nasr, by the beginning of the seventeenth

---

[66] Albert Hourani, *A History of the Arab Peoples* (Cambridge: Belknap Press, 1991), 250. See
also Karen Barkey, *Bandits and Bureaucrats: The Ottoman Route to State Centralization*
(Ithaca: Cornell University Press, 1994).

[67] See Steven E. Lobell, "The Grand Strategy of Hegemonic Decline: Dilemmas of Strategy
and Finance," *Security Studies* 10, no. 1 (Autumn 2000): 86–111.

[68] Timothy Garton Ash, "The Empire in Decay," *New York Review of Books*, September 29,
1988, 88.

[69] Realizing that the contest for North Africa had played out, and with each power having
pressing matters elsewhere, the Ottomans and Spain completed a truce in 1580, though
hostilities and more limited Ottoman naval designs would later rekindle. See Rhoads
Murphey, "The Ottoman Resurgence in the Seventeenth-Century Mediterranean: The
Gamble and its Results," *Mediterranean Historical Review* 8 (1993): 186–200.

[70] Wolf, *Barbary Coast*, 64.   [71] Shuval, "Cezayir-i Garp," 101.

[72] For an example of this interpretation, see Andrew C. Hess, "The Forgotten Frontier: The
Ottoman North African Provinces during the Eighteenth Century," in *Studies in
Eighteenth Century Islamic History*, ed. Thomas Naff and Roger Owen (Carbondale:
Southern Illinois University Press, 1977), 85–86. Others characterize the regencies as
"semi-autonomous" and as "vassal principalities." See Bruce Masters, "Semi-
Autonomous Forces in the Arab Provinces," in *The Cambridge History of Turkey, Vol. 3,
The Later Ottoman Empire, 1603–1839*, ed. Suraiya N. Faroqhi (Cambridge: Cambridge

164   Power and piracy along the Barbary Coast

century in each of the three regencies the captains were "acting independently" of the Ottoman Kapudan Pasha. Moreover, in Algiers "the captain of the sea came to have full control over the affairs of the marines, whereas internally the *diwan* of the Janissaries exercised real authority, with the pasha remaining as the nominal head of the administration."[73] From the 1580s onward, another observer notes, Ottoman control was "largely nominal and the corsair cities in this area made their independent wars."[74] Philip Curtin writes that by 1610, leaders of the Barbary powers "began to act like independent monarchs, though recognizing the theoretical authority of Istanbul."[75] The Barbary powers still benefited from Ottoman legitimation and material assistance, including some military recruits.[76] The Ottoman Empire, though, did not control the foreign affairs of the Barbary powers, and during the seventeenth and eighteenth centuries they often refused to honor agreements they had not negotiated themselves.[77] By the eighteenth century all that Istanbul could do was threaten sanctions and military aid cuts when the Barbary powers contravened their interests.[78]

The autonomy of the Barbary powers was a result of mutual calculation by the regencies and the empire in the face of the latter's decline.[79] Early in their development, due to a lack of resources and severe vulnerability, the Barbary powers were dependent on aid and assistance from the Ottomans. They would not have survived, let alone established autonomous rule, without the extensive integration that took place. While the corsairs did not turn against their former sponsors, blowback in lesser but still vexing forms was evident. Once they rid themselves of the "shadow of Turkish rule," they continued some level of collaboration, but

University Press, 2006), 202–6; and Suraiya N. Faroqhi, *The Ottoman Empire and the World around It* (London: I.B. Tauris, 2004), 83–84.

[73] Jamil M. Abun-Nasr, *A History of the Maghrib*, 2nd ed. (Cambridge: Cambridge University Press, 1975), 174.

[74] Jan Glete, *Warfare at Sea, 1500–1650: Maritime Conflict and the Transformation of Europe* (London: Routledge, 2000), 107.

[75] Curtin, "Africa North of the Forest," 160.

[76] Faroqhi, *Ottoman Empire and the World*, 83.

[77] Alain Blondy, "The Barbary Regencies and Corsair Activity in the Mediterranean from the Sixteenth to the Nineteenth Century," *Journal of Mediterranean Studies* 12, no. 2 (2002): 243–44; Faroqhi, *Ottoman Empire and the World*, 83.

[78] Hess, "Ottoman North African Provinces," 80.

[79] Other groups of "Christian" pirates, such as the Knights of Malta and Uskoks of Senj, did not break away from their sponsors and as a result were constrained. On the Knights of Malta, see Jonathan Riley-Smith, *Hospitallers: The History of the Order of St. John* (London: Hambledon Press, 1999). On the Uskoks of Senj, see Catherine W. Bracewell, *The Uskoks of Senj: Piracy, Banditry, and Holy War in the Sixteenth-Century Adriatic* (Ithaca: Cornell University Press, 1992); and Gunther E. Rothenberg, *The Austrian Military Border in Croatia, 1522–1747* (Urbana: University of Illinois Press, 1960).

Consolidation and deviation of Barbary power 165

increasingly flouted the Porte's dictates and acted contrary to Ottoman interests.[80] "From the middle of the sixteenth century [Lepanto] onwards," Alain Blondy writes, "the inhabitants of Barbary set about organizing their world according to their own rules."[81] Barbary autonomy was not sudden and was primarily the result of, in Fernand Braudel's words, the "growing lassitude of the major states." These were the Habsburgs and Ottomans, he recounts, "the greatest states, the political monsters who had found it so difficult to retain their respective halves of the sea."[82] Just as the Nizari Ismailis before them, the Barbary powers would see their fortunes as misaligned with an ailing great power. They would instead base their futures on their increasing exploitation of the sea lanes and the coasts of Europe, and internally through their efforts to consolidate the hinterland, twin efforts that met with mixed results.

Consolidation and deviation of Barbary power

"[T]he calamitous end of Islam in Spain," Andrew Hess writes, "and the expansion of Christian activities in the Maghrib brought North Africa into the era of firearms and highly centralized states."[83] How did the regencies fare? The answer is, not very well, but well enough to survive, albeit in dissimilar forms. The decline of the Ottomans and the autonomy of the regencies would accompany processes consistent with the logic of dissimilation. This entailed mostly failed efforts at territorial consolidation resulting in unit structures dissimilar from the dominant forms that were taking hold among their European competitors. Each adapted in similar but distinct ways to their varying but always limited resources, their opportunity structures channeling their energies toward the sea while struggling to control populations that saw the leaders as a foreign presence. Just how much control they would exert beyond their capitals is a critical consideration. Over time the regencies would be given a number of labels, including "states," "city-states," "kingdoms," "military republics," "warlike cities,"[84] and "piratical states."[85] How state-like would they become, and how did they differ from the dominant states of Europe that would be their chief competition?

---

[80] Curtin, "Africa North of the Forest," 170.   [81] Blondy, "Barbary Regencies," 243.

[82] Fernand Braudel, *The Mediterranean and the Mediterranean World in the Age of Philip II*, Vol. *II*, trans. Siân Reynolds (Berkeley and Los Angeles: University of California Press, 1995), 884; 1165.

[83] Hess, "Firearms," 195.

[84] Oded Löwenheim, *Predators and Parasites: Persistent Agents of Transnational Harm and Great Power Authority* (Ann Arbor: University of Michigan Press, 2007), 88.

[85] Thomas Jefferson, *The Writings of Thomas Jefferson*, Vol. *XVII* (Washington, D.C.: Thomas Jefferson Memorial Association, 1907), 145.

166   Power and piracy along the Barbary Coast

From the seventeenth century, when corsairing was at its peak, well into the eighteenth century, these polities could best be described as city-states that sought to exploit revenue sources both inward and seaward. Their seaward exploitation came in the form of sea-raiding, which would be extensive and profitable particularly in the early seventeenth century. The external relations of the regencies, however, were tied in large measure to their varying degrees of success in obtaining and maintaining sources of revenue internally. The question of the extent of their centralization, like Ottoman decline, is accompanied by charges of Western distortion.[86] Depictions of the regencies were certainly refracted through Western lenses, as much of the second half of this chapter will attest. As with the case of Ottoman decline, however, the corrections go too far in depicting the political development of the Barbary powers as on par with Europe. To the "fiction of Ottoman suzerainty," in Mantran's words, we can add the fiction of Barbary sovereignty, that is, effective control over territory beyond coastal cities.[87] Limitations on resources and indigenous resistance within the regencies would make centralization problematic in differing degrees.

In Algiers the period of the beylerbeys was followed by the ascendance of the divan, in which both the ujaq and the ta'ifat al-ra'is had representation.[88] Power shifted toward the janissaries in 1659 when the *agha* (commander of the janissaries) seized control.[89] A disastrous defeat of Algerine ships in 1671 by the British occasioned the assassination of the agha and the reassertion of power by the captains, who emplaced a leader with the title of *dey*.[90] The ujaq would eventually reassert control, and by 1689 the dey would be selected by the janissaries. The corsair captains would remain as part of the government, but there was a decisive shift toward the militias, in part reflecting the decline of corsairing that occurred over the course of the seventeenth century. Prior to the shift away from the ta'ifat al-ra'is, according to Mantran, the rulers of Algiers "did not much concern themselves with Algeria itself," instead focusing on the spoils available due to the weakness of European navies.[91] Inroads into the hinterland would give the land-based forces a source of revenue just as the returns from corsairing were diminishing. In Algiers administrative structures would result in the rule of *beys* who would

---

[86] See Shuval, "Cezayir-i Garp," 87.   [87] Mantran, "North Africa," 265.

[88] Faroqhi, *Ottoman Empire and the World*, 83.

[89] Abun-Nasr, *History of the Maghrib in the Islamic Period*, 159.

[90] "Dey" had been used as a title in Tunisia since the end of the sixteenth century. Ibid., 160. See also Roger Le Tourneau, "Dayi," EIs.

[91] Mantran, "North Africa," 256. The name "Algeria" was not formally applied until 1838.

Consolidation and deviation of Barbary power 167

function as governors in the three provinces of Constantine, Tittari, and later Oran, acting with substantial autonomy as long as taxes were remitted to Algiers.[92]

The tilting toward the janissaries would occur much earlier in Tunis when they asserted control in 1591, though corsairing would remain a profitable and important source of revenue.[93] There, an unstable division between the city-based deys and the beys who operated in the countryside would prevail through much of the seventeenth century.[94] In the beginning of the eighteenth century, hereditary regimes would be founded in both Tunis and Tripoli, under the Husayni and Karamanli dynasties, respectively.[95] Struggles among the regencies for their share of the naval spoils would grow to include competition and armed conflict, particularly between Algiers and Tunis. Though piracy remained profitable, revenue demands from the janissary corps compelled increased movement into the interior where Arab shaykhs and tribal elements would make such efforts difficult.

Tunis was gifted with a fertile hinterland and achieved routine local interactions with central authority, providing a stable revenue base. The main vehicle for revenue collection was the *mahalla* (meaning military column, or camp), which consisted of twice yearly military expeditions to collect revenue from the interior tribes.[96] This institution "was founded on the permanent mobility of the prince and the state apparatus, [which] constituted a necessary response to mobile and aggressive tribalism."[97] The beys became ascendant, focusing their attention on the countryside, leaving the dey with little more than policing duties in the capital. A mutually profitable arrangement between the beys and local officials called *qa'ids*, who served as tax collectors, enriched both groups.[98] Nevertheless, apart from these more pliable tribes there were others whose recalcitrance required continued used of armed coercion, with

---

[92] Abun-Nasr, *A History of the Maghrib*, 176.

[93] Abun-Nasr, *History of the Maghrib in the Islamic Period*, 170.   [94] Ibid., 172.

[95] Algiers would not enjoy such relative stability. Of the over thirty deys that ruled between 1671 and 1818, fourteen were violently overthrown. Curtin, "Africa North of the Forest," 170.

[96] See Dalenda Larguèche, "The *Mahalla*: The Origins of Beylical Sovereignty in Ottoman Tunisia during the Early Modern Period," *Journal of North African Studies* 6, no. 1 (Spring 2001): 105–16; Charles Pellat, "Mahalla," EIs; and L. Carl Brown, *The Tunisia of Ahmad Bey, 1837–1855* (Princeton: Princeton University Press, 1974), 127–33.

[97] Larguèche, "The *Mahalla*," 109. Daniel Panzac argues that in Tunisia, at least, these "visits" from the mahalla were not "fiscal raids" nor "pillaging expeditions." By the latter half of the eighteenth century there were few if any uprisings, suggesting a degree of authority. Panzac, *Barbary Corsairs*, 16.

[98] Abun-Nasr, *History of the Maghrib in the Islamic Period*, 175.

168   Power and piracy along the Barbary Coast

centralization only consolidated in the late eighteenth century.[99] Between the mahallas, which were a main source of revenue,[100] and its relationship with the qa'ids, Tunis was not nearly as dependent on corsairing as the other regencies. Their focus was more on trade, and, while piracy was tolerated and its benefits shared, its prominence was comparatively minor.[101]

Tripoli was blessed, or cursed, with a good defensible harbor that had attracted corsairs from the Knights of Malta and later Turkish vassals.[102] While trade links, particularly with Saharan and sub-Saharan partners, would prove an important source of revenue, according to C.R. Pennell, "receipts from corsairing, vulnerable though they were, were much more reliable than those from the interior."[103] Tripoli's straitened circumstances included a severe lack of arable land and rainfall and led to "economic marginalization and the consequent reliance on the precarious fruits of corsairing."[104] Under the Karamanli government Tripoli was beset by crises, and has been described as a "nest of corsairs."[105] This label reflects Western bias as to the menace they posed, but it is also a fairly accurate reflection of the nested physical setting of a city-state in unsteady conditions that did not bode well for its long-term survival.[106]

Somewhere along the middle of this spectrum, between Tripoli's impoverishment and isolation and Tunis's routinized but fractious internal exchange, was Algiers. Flush with the spoils of sea-raiding – gold, slaves, and ships – Algiers was by far the most powerful of the regencies. (Compare the roughly seventy-five ships of the Algerine fleet in the early seventeenth century to the seventeen ships and several brigantines

---

[99] Ibid., 177. See Asma Moalla, *The Regency of Tunis and the Ottoman Porte, 1777–1814* (London: Routledge Curzon, 2004), 137. The use of the mahalla as a tool of centralization in the late eighteenth century is described in Larguèche, "The *Mahalla*," 110–12. Larguèche contrasts the situation in Algiers with the "irreversible trend toward city hegemony in Tunisia."

[100] Moalla, *Regency of Tunis*, 19.

[101] See Abun-Nasr, *History of the Maghrib in the Islamic Period*, 175–77.

[102] At one point the city had been sold by one Genoese conqueror, much as an asset, "rather as if the city was an entity totally separate from the area surrounding it." See McLachlan, "Tripoli and Tripolitania," 286.

[103] C.R. Pennell, "Tripoli in the Late Seventeenth Century: The Economics of Corsairing in a 'Sterill Country,'" *Libyan Studies* 16 (1985): 110. Due to the restiveness of the Arab and Berber tribes, these periods of stable trade with the interior "rarely amounted to more than short respites between unsettled conditions." McLachlan, "Tripoli and Tripolitania," 289–90.

[104] Pennell, "Tripoli in the Late Seventeenth Century," 102.

[105] McLachlan, "Tripoli and Tripolitania," 290; and Seton Dearden, *A Nest of Corsairs: The Fighting Karamanlis of Tripoli* (London: John Murray, 1976), 2.

[106] "How did they live," Seton Dearden writes, "this large mixed community, perched on the north African coast, surrounded by deserts, and with few natural resources?" Dearden, *Nest of Corsairs*, 14.

Consolidation and deviation of Barbary power 169

of Tunis.)[107] The deys, based in Algiers, would be the primary governing power, while the beys would eventually carve out their own fiefdoms exploiting the countryside for their personal enrichment.[108] Toward the middle of the eighteenth century this process of extortion was enhanced, with taxation widened and increased due to the suffering corsair economy and increasing European military pressures. The dey's political authority suffered, and the beys cemented ties with local shaykhs and marabouts (holy men), becoming increasingly independent.[109] Even as inroads were made into the hinterland, this came at the cost of centralized political authority.[110]

Legitimate commerce from internal and external trade was modest.[111] Tribute and the spoils of corsairing, combined with the unproductive extraction from the interior, would result in an economy that was based primarily on exploitation with little reciprocal development. The regime in Algiers remained in many respects, despite some more charitable interpretations, an army of occupation.[112] Its authority was mostly limited to its immediate surroundings, and its tottering economy was unable to adjust as the ill-begotten bounties of sea-raiding dried up. The decline in Algerine land power in the latter half of the eighteenth century would leave the regency doubly burdened, and even more beholden to corsairing.[113]

The very name of Algiers comes from the Arabic for "the islands," from the islets off of its coast.[114] Indeed, throughout the seventeenth and into the eighteenth century Algiers remained very much an island, one surrounded by the Sahara and the sea. It was able to establish little more than

---

[107] Abun-Nasr, *History of the Maghrib in the Islamic Period*, 165–70. Another clear indicator of Algiers' relative power was the inability of the rulers of Tunis in the 1680s to stop attacks being made by the Algerine corsairs operating near their ports. Jamil M. Abun-Nasr, "The Beylicate in Seventeenth-Century Tunisia," *International Journal of Middle East Studies* 6, no. 1 (January 1975): 89.

[108] Curtin, "Africa North of the Forest," 161.

[109] Abdallah Laroui, *The History of the Maghrib: An Interpretive Essay*, trans. Ralph Manheim (Princeton: Princeton University Press, 1977), 266–67.

[110] If the leaders of Algiers "were firmly in control of the levers of power in the coastal region, society in the hinterland remained wild and refractory, especially as the tribal warlords learned how to manufacture and effectively use muskets." Oliver and Atmore, *Medieval Africa*, 42.

[111] William Spencer, *Algiers in the Age of the Corsairs* (Norman: University of Oklahoma Press, 1976), 101–6.

[112] Wolf, *Barbary Coast*, 111.

[113] Nehemia Levtzion, "North-West Africa: From the Maghrib to the Fringes of the Forests," in *The Cambridge History of Africa, Volume 4, From c.1600 to c.1790*, ed. Richard Gray (Cambridge: Cambridge University Press, 1975), 146.

[114] Roger le Tourneau, "al-Djazāir," EIs.

170   Power and piracy along the Barbary Coast

contingent coercive relationships in each direction.[115] The resource constraints on the Barbary powers were severe. The difficulties establishing sovereignty, particularly for Algiers and Tripoli, resulted in a circumstance where they exploited both their interiors (unproductively) and the sea space around and beyond them. Especially for Algiers and Tripoli, the incorporation of sea-raiding would be the only viable alternative to other survival strategies. While the decline of the Ottomans created an opportunity for greater autonomy, the result of these constraints on their opportunity structures was a departure from the trend toward centralization that would characterize European political development during this period. By the criteria defining the development of the state in Europe, each of the regencies would fall well short, with Tunis coming closest.[116] Over the long term these failures would leave them vulnerable to domination by their more powerful European contemporaries, but not until well after other sea-extracting city-states of Europe had expanded landward or been absorbed.[117] Adapting to straitened circumstances without adopting prevailing modes of organization, however, provided more than a mere respite. Dependence on predatory means of gaining revenue would be viable when European navies were relatively weak. That relative power would eventually and decisively shift, and the regencies, in Blondy's words, "proved unable to adapt to these new ways and thus ensured

---

[115] Algiers and, to a lesser extent, Tunis were limited in their expansion as cities by their natural surroundings. See André Raymond, *The Great Arab Cities in the 16th–18th Centuries: An Introduction* (New York: New York University Press, 1984), 33; and L. Carl Brown, "Maghrib Historiography: The Unit of Analysis Problem," in *The Maghrib in Question: Essays in History and Historiography*, ed. Michel Le Gall and Kenneth Perkins (Austin: University of Texas Press, 1997), 8.

[116] Those criteria include a controlled, defined, continuous territory; centralization; differentiation; and a monopoly on physical coercion. See Charles Tilly, "Reflections on the History of European State-Making," in *The Formation of National States in Western Europe*, ed. Tilly (Princeton: Princeton University Press, 1975), 27.

[117] It is difficult to determine whether the regencies would have fared any better in the system had their state-making efforts been more successful. The fate of the sea-based economies of the city-states of Venice and Genoa do not suggest the result would have been much different. Each of these formerly powerful trading maritime city-states saw their dominance over trade routes disrupted by piracy and competition from the emerging territorially based empires in Europe. For each, their adaptations would buy some time (landward expansion for Venice and gaining protection from Spain for Genoa), but they would eventually follow the route of other city-states and be absorbed by their larger neighbors. See Glete, *Warfare at Sea*, 95–98. On Venice's inward expansion, see Stephan R. Epstein, "The Rise and Fall of Italian City-States," in *A Comparative Study of Thirty City-State Cultures: An Investigation*, ed. Mogens H. Hansen (Copenhagen: Kgl. Danske Videnskabernes Selskab, 2000), 293, n. 46. On Genoa's attempts to adapt to its systemic constraints in the seventeenth century, see Thomas A. Kirk, *Genoa and the Sea: Policy and Power in an Early Maritime Republic, 1559–1684* (Baltimore and London: Johns Hopkins University Press, 2005), 176–202.

Barbary piracy and the major powers 171

their demise."[118] It would take until the early nineteenth century, though, after nearly two centuries of interaction, for the European states and the newborn independent United States to finally subdue them.

Unruly fellows: Barbary piracy and the major powers

An English Parliament notice in 1625 read, "The boldness and insolence of those pirates was beyond all comparison, no former times having been exampled with the like. Their adventure formerly on those seas was rare, almost unheard of, which made their coming more strange."[119] This and other records reflected the threat posed to the English coastline and to merchants at sea where "the Turks were grown very infestuous."[120] Beginning in the early seventeenth century, according to Tal Shuval, "their strength and range of activity" rendered the corsairs "almost invincible in the eyes of contemporary European powers."[121] Piracy was clearly nothing new, and indeed the crackdown on English and other European originated piracy was one reason skilled seamen had sought new bases to apply their skills. What was new was its intensity, scale, scope, and persistence, in addition to its source. What is often referred to as the "Golden Age of Piracy" lasted roughly from 1650 to 1730 and featured "distinct generations of pirates."[122] These included the Caribbean-based buccaneers who were most active between 1650 and 1680, and the Atlantic raiders who numbered around 4,000 and disrupted trade for an intense ten year period in the second and third decades of the eighteenth century.[123] Unlike these upsurges, the Barbary corsairs would operate for over two centuries and at their peak had an impact well beyond those episodes. How the Barbary powers fared in these pursuits, and, ultimately, how they fared as independent polities, was a result of both the quantitative indices of power versus the major powers, and the qualitative aspects of their power as it extended to the far reaches of Europe.

With the weakness of European navies, piracy or privateering (a distinction raised below) allowed the precariously situated quasi-states to develop well beyond their means, providing gold, commodities, and

---

[118] Blondy, "Barbary Regencies," 246.

[119] Todd Gray, "Turkish Piracy and Early Stuart Devon," *Reports of the Transactions of the Devonshire Association for the Advancement of Science* 121 (1989): 163; and Maija Jansson and William B. Bidwell, eds., *Proceedings in Parliament, 1625* (New Haven: Yale University Press, 1987), 527.

[120] Jansson and Bidwell, *Proceedings*, 527. [121] Shuval, "Cezayir-i Garp," 97.

[122] Marcus Rediker, *Villains of All Nations: Atlantic Pirates in the Golden Age* (Boston: Beacon Press, 2004), 8–9.

[123] Ibid.

172   Power and piracy along the Barbary Coast

slaves.[124] "The days of North African fanaticism were long past," by the early seventeenth century, according to Henry Barnby, "and the North African sea rover was just as anxious to keep a whole skin as his counterpart from Palermo, Leghorn, Nice, or Alicante."[125] From Cádiz to Reykjavik, their absconding with the whole skins of others was an ever-present source of anxiety, one that led to increasing pressures on governments to protect coastal populations. Accounts of raids along the Mediterranean coasts of Italy, France, and Spain, according to Barnby, "had long made the flesh of Northern Europeans creep; and now strange warships" were being reported off of their own coasts.[126] Local records reflect an ongoing preoccupation with these raiders along the southwest English coastline. Spanish and French privateers harassed local shipping, but, according to Todd Gray, these attacks were "sporadic, that is confined to periods of official war. For the southwest the greatest continuous threat came from North Africa."[127]

These developments did not escape the attention of the admiralty, which received notice from an agent in Spain that "the strength and boldness of the pirates (or rather of the Turks) had grown to unknown heights."[128] Long a problem in the Mediterranean, attacks became more frequent on Atlantic shipping lanes and coasts.[129] Along Spanish coasts, "¡Moros en la costa!" ("the Moors have come ashore!") was not as it is now a turn of phrase divorced from its menacing roots, but rather was "a dreaded cry" as expelled Muslims had their opportunity for revenge.[130] But it was less revenge than opportunity that drove most of the men and missions, considering that Iceland is hardly a place that could have done much to offend.[131]

---

[124] Mantran, "North Africa," 256.

[125] Henry Barnby, "The Sack of Baltimore," *Journal of the Cork Historical and Archaeological Society, Part II*, 74, no. 220 (July–December 1969), 112.

[126] Ibid., 111.   [127] Gray, "Turkish Piracy," 159–60.

[128] David D. Hebb, *Piracy and the English Government, 1616–1642* (Aldershot: Scolar Press, 1994), 19.

[129] Hess, *Forgotten Frontier*, 125. Hess is referring to both North African and "Christian" piracy of the Maltese corsairs and others.

[130] Harvey, *Muslims in Spain*, 337. See Alexander H. de Groot, "The Ottoman Threat to Europe, 1571–1830," in *Hospitaller Malta, 1530–1798: Studies on Early Modern Malta and the Order of St. John of Jerusalem*, ed. Victor Mallia-Milanes (Msida, Malta: Minerva Publications, 1993), 203.

[131] On the raids on Iceland, see Bernard Lewis, "Corsairs in Iceland," in *Islam in History*, 239–46. Indicating the presence of the raids in collective historical memory, prior to a 1995 soccer match between Iceland and Turkey a newspaper ad read: "Don't let the Turks ravish us again!" Borsteinn Helgason, "Historical Narrative as Collective Therapy: The Case of the Turkish Raid in Iceland," *Scandinavian Journal of History* 22 (1997): 276.

Barbary piracy and the major powers 173

What was all the more vexing was that these "Turks" were often not Turks at all, but European renegades, many of whom were able seamen who knew the tides, coasts, and coves of their previous haunts. "[T]hese wicked people ... [look] ... exactly like other people," one Icelandic captive recounted of the Europeans among his captors. While the "real" Turks "in their behavior were just like other nations," the former Christians among them killed, cursed, beat, "and did all that is evil."[132] The fear of being enslaved, as galley rowers or concubines, would pervade European coastal communities. Economic losses in shipping were accompanied by the existential threat of captivity by Muslims and apostate Christians, threatening both body and soul. Threats to physical security were compounded by threats to ontological security due to the twin uncertainties of the enemy's origins and their potential threats to their victims' identities.

Where *did* these pirates come from? Confusion as to the physical origins of the Barbary corsairs attended increased attacks along Atlantic coastlines. They were often referred to as Turks and Moors of Sally, or variations on Salé on the Atlantic coast of Morocco. The "Sallee Rovers" operated from Rabat, twin city of Salé, which due to a confluence of circumstances became an outpost for piracy in the Atlantic. Local conditions in Rabat-Salé provided manpower (Moriscos from the Hornachos region of Spain) and a safe haven (due to variations in the degree of central government control). It was external stimuli, though, in the form of the naval commanders and expertise primarily from Algiers that turned Rabat-Salé into an entrepôt and a forward operating base extending their range to exploit Atlantic naval traffic.[133] Though it operated as an independent "pirate republic," its activities and organization were deeply interpenetrated with Algiers.[134] Many Algerine corsairs used Rabat-Salé to subvert agreements made by the regency with European powers or to avoid heavy taxes levied by the government of Algiers.[135]

---

[132] Lewis, "Corsairs in Iceland," 242.

[133] Jerome B. Bookin-Weiner emphasizes the internal political circumstances and the role of sea captains from Algiers in Rabat-Salé's development. Jerome B. Bookin-Weiner, "The 'Sallee Rovers': Morocco and Its Corsairs in the Seventeenth Century," in *The Middle East and North Africa: Essays in Honor of J.C. Hurewitz*, ed. Reeva S. Simon and J.C. Hurewitz (New York: Columbia University Press, 1990), 308.

[134] See Ellen G. Friedman, *Spanish Captives in North Africa in the Early Modern Age* (Madison: University of Wisconsin Press, 1983), 27–28; and Kenneth Brown, "An Urban View of Moroccan History, Salé, 1000–1800," *Hespéris Tamuda* 12 (1971): 52. One attack widely attributed to the "Sallee Rovers," the sack of Baltimore commanded by Murad Reis (the Younger), resulted in a reported 120 captives, at least eighty-nine of whom ended up in Algiers. Nabil Matar, *Britain and Barbary, 1589–1689* (Gainesville: University of Florida Press, 2005), 54.

[135] Hebb, *Piracy and the English*, 194; and Friedman, *Spanish Captives*, 27. On tax evasion as motivation, see Barnby, "Sack of Baltimore," 115–16.

174   Power and piracy along the Barbary Coast

Adding to the confusion over their origins was the practice of flying false flags. This dissimulation allowed for both stealth and a lack of accountability when violating protection agreements. One pamphlet written in 1634 noted that it was impossible to identify their ships either by their build or the flag they flew.[136]

In the first two decades of the seventeenth century there were calls for the English government to deal with the increase in piracy emanating from the Barbary Coast. Petitions to the Ottomans proved futile: "these were unruly fellows not subject to his domain," one official brushed off a complaint.[137] Due to limitations on financing and shipbuilding, no naval action would take place until 1620, when a joint Anglo–Spanish expedition sailed against Algiers. Spain had suffered increased attacks and had begun efforts to revitalize its navy to meet the threat, a development that caused great concern among its neighbors.[138] The expedition was a complete failure. The defenses of Algiers were formidable, its population and manpower were sufficient, and it was able to obtain matériel from opportunistic merchants, including gunpowder from Dutch traders who sold it at double its value.[139]

Recognizing the inability of the Ottomans to control them, while not wanting to negotiate directly with this "wicked crew," English efforts to stem the attacks floundered.[140] Eventually, an accommodation with, in a Venetian observer's words, "the ever formidable pirates of Algiers" was reached.[141] A consulate would be established to oversee trade, complaints concerning attacks on shipping, and the release of captives.[142] These agreements were recognized to be extremely tenuous due to the lack of influence of the Porte, and the regencies' reliance on piracy. As an

[136] Hebb, *Piracy and the English*, 149. On the use of surprise and deception as general pirate tactics, see Benerson Little, *The Sea Rover's Practice: Pirate Tactics and Techniques, 1630–1730* (Washington, D.C.: Potomac Books, 2005).

[137] Daniel Goffman, *Izmir and the Levantine World, 1550–1650* (Seattle: University of Washington Press, 1990), 134.

[138] Friedman, *Spanish Captives*, 17–19; Hebb, *Piracy and the English*, 65; 68. The threat of the Barbary corsairs was certainly not the only or even the main driver of Spanish naval development, yet the threat of piracy cannot be discounted in their calculations. See David Goodman, *Spanish Naval Power, 1589–1665: Reconstruction and Defeat* (Cambridge: Cambridge University Press, 1997), 16–17; 24.

[139] Hebb, *Piracy and the English*, 46; 117. Estimates of the population of Algiers at this time are as high as 100,000, though this number has been questioned based on the city's size and potential population density. See Federico Cresti "Algiers in the Ottoman Period: The City and Its Population," in *The City in the Islamic World, Volume 1*, ed. Salma K. Jayyusi, et al. (Leiden: Brill, 2008), 417–19.

[140] Hebb, *Piracy and the English*, 176–78; 190.

[141] "Alvise Valaresso, Venetian Ambassador to England, to the Doge and Senate," in *Calendar of State Papers, Venice, Vol. XVIII, 1623–1625* (London, 1912), 95.

[142] Hebb, *Piracy and the English*, 186.

Barbary piracy and the major powers 175

English consul observed, "the bashaws of these two ports have their great profit by their shares of prizes, and that hath made them backward to obey, and make peace to their loss."[143] Similar arrangements were reached with Tunis, and other European states made precarious peace with the regencies.[144] While the English had essentially shelved the problem of Algiers, the agreement did not extend to Rabat-Salé, whose activity subsequently crested and became the main threat to English shipping and souls.[145] The English government faced severe political pressure, eventually raising a fleet in 1638 that successfully attacked the port.[146] Numerous factors can account for the differential success of the Algiers and Rabat-Salé missions, including better organization and planning, but the gross disparity in power between Algiers and Rabat-Salé was foremost.[147] While celebrated, the Rabat-Salé mission's effects were marginal, reflecting the transitory nature of the Moroccan bases.[148]

The dependence on corsairing and the ransoms of European captives was so great – in Algiers according to one estimate 25 percent of the population was economically engaged in piracy – that treaties were not sufficient to end the practice.[149] Both the English and French would renew attacks against Algiers and the other regencies from the 1660s to 1680s.[150] The quantitative and qualitative advances in European navies had leveled a relationship based on nearly equal measures of mutual coercion, diplomacy, and trade. Agreements with the regencies would be made, monitored by consuls, and broken. There was an expectation of transgression, confirmed by the role of the consuls in negotiating the release of captives and protesting violations.[151] "Treaties continued to be violated," F. Robert Hunter writes, "in order to obtain desperately needed funds and supplies, or when the moment seemed opportune."[152] Ransom and bombardment coincided with increased

---

[143] Ibid., 192.

[144] For an overview of phases of European relations with the Barbary powers, see Panzac, *Barbary Corsairs*, 25–41.

[145] Barnby, "Sack of Baltimore," 125–26.

[146] See Hebb, *Piracy and the English*, 237; and Matar, *Britain and Barbary*, 51–59.

[147] Hebb, *Piracy and the English*, 260–63.

[148] See N.A.M. Rodger, *The Safeguard of the Sea: A Naval History of Britain, 660–1649* (New York: W.W. Norton, 1998), 385.

[149] Jerome Bookin-Weiner, "Corsairing in the Economy and Politics of North Africa," in *North Africa: Nation, State, and Region*, ed. George Joffe (London and New York: Routledge, 1993), 26.

[150] F. Robert Hunter, "Rethinking Europe's Conquest of North Africa and the Middle East: The Opening of the Maghreb, 1660–1814," *The Journal of North African Studies* 4, no. 4 (Winter 1999): 5.

[151] Ibid., 6.   [152] Ibid., 15.

176   Power and piracy along the Barbary Coast

commercial ties, the latter adding to the European penetration that would help set the stage for future colonization.

Each of the three logics of concealment (hiding, deception, and dissimulation) is evident in the case of the Barbary powers. The use of defensible ports, including the one at Rabat-Salé, was an effective means of insulation and defense. It was also a way to avoid attribution and to subvert agreements made with outside powers. Deception and dissimulation are part and parcel of piracy. Certainly, those actions that decrease suspicion and increase surprise were utilized by the corsairs as a matter of course. False flags were also employed to enhance cunning and stealth, as well as to avoid taxation. The intentions of the Barbary powers were notoriously inscrutable, even as the European powers gained the upper hand. There was a regularity to the irregularity of these interactions. Although the European powers established relations with the Barbary powers, according to G.N. Clark, "[t]he Christian jurists and diplomatists were still, however, confused and uncertain as to what sort of equilibrium they wanted to establish, what sort of relations they should regard as normal."[153]

The odd mixture of belligerence and commerce persisted over the eighteenth century, but the tolerance of the European powers waned as their relative power grew. As the regencies deteriorated their transgressions would be seen as increasingly onerous, a relic of a time when these city-states sought to compete with the centralized states of Europe. The attacks by the United States against the regencies in the Barbary Wars (1801–1805 and 1815) were seen as triumphs for the young republic.[154] The Barbary powers of the late eighteenth and early nineteenth centuries, though, were shadows of their previous selves.[155] Economic disruption from the Napoleonic wars led to a surge of corsairing activity to make up for trade losses.[156] These violations baited the United States, which

---

[153] G.N. Clark, "The Barbary Corsairs in the Seventeenth Century," *Cambridge Historical Journal* 8, no. 1 (1944): 31.

[154] On the relations between the United States and the regencies, see Roger C. Anderson, *Naval Wars in the Levant, 1559–1853* (Princeton: Princeton University Press, 1952), 393–426; Michael Kitzen, "Money Bags or Cannon Balls: The Origins of the Tripolitan War," *Journal of the Early Republic* 16, no. 4 (Winter 1996): 601–24; Richard B. Parker, *Uncle Sam in Barbary: A Diplomatic History* (Gainesville: University of Florida Press, 2004); and Frederick C. Leiner, *The End of Barbary Terror: America's 1815 War against the Pirates of North Africa* (Oxford: Oxford University Press, 2006).

[155] By the latter half of the eighteenth century, according to Nehemia Levtzion, Algiers was mired in poverty and had lost much of its population. Levtzion, "North-West Africa," 145. The Barbary powers were hit with a staggering, near-Biblical series of natural and other disasters, including plague, earthquakes, locusts, drought, and food shortages. Panzac, *Barbary Corsairs*, 303–9.

[156] Panzac, *Barbary Corsairs*, 73–77.

The Barbary powers in international law 177

eventually tested its nascent navy against a badly weakened opponent. The once formidable, but systemically maladapted, polities would be subdued in due course. Over a century of European domination would follow.

What is a state?: The Barbary powers in international law

The Barbary powers' combination of regularity and uncertainty-enhancing behaviors provides a valuable empirical base to examine and refine propositions concerning how norms may have developed as foundational elements of international society. Relations between the European and Barbary powers evolved into a mixture of coercion and appeasement, a mostly stable equilibrium that uneasily suited each party. The Barbary powers were in a constant state of war with whomever they did not reach some accommodation. At roughly the same time a norm concerning piracy was firming, one that would distinguish certain types of sea-raiding as illegitimate. Borrowing from Roman law, pirates would become *hostis humani generis*, "common enemies of humankind."[157]

The problem was in distinguishing piracy, as common seaborne brigandage, from the widespread practice of state-sponsored privateering. The determining factor would become how much like a state the sponsors of such violence were. Without a state there is no state-sponsorship, no basis for regulation, no legitimate authority with which to discuss and remedy injuries. The anomalous condition of the Barbary powers would help to establish this norm distinguishing privateering from piracy. According to Alfred Rubin, "the degree of political organization and economic importance of the Barbary states made it advisable to withhold the word ['piracy'] (and thus its legal results) from those politically stable and functioning communities."[158] The stability and functioning of the Barbary powers, though, were hardly enviable. The generosity expressed as to the "stateness" of the Barbary powers often varied with European state interests.

Acting on behalf of Spanish interests in England in the latter half of the seventeenth century, Alberico Gentili wrote of the legality of the purchases made by English merchants from the Barbary powers under the supervision of their treasury.[159] Gentili had previously argued that war

---

[157] Alfred P. Rubin, *The Law of Piracy*, 2nd ed. (Irvington, N.Y.: Transnational Publishers, 1998), 92. See also Christopher Harding, "'*Hostis Humani Generis*' – The Pirate as Outlaw in the Early Modern Law of the Sea," in *Pirates? The Politics of Plunder*, 20–38.
[158] Rubin, *Law of Piracy*, 93. [159] Ibid., 33.

178 Power and piracy along the Barbary Coast

against pirates was just, as piracy "is contrary to the law of nations and league of human society."[160] He proclaimed in this case that "to Pirates and wild beasts no territory offers safety," and put the activities of the Barbary powers into that category.[161] The implications of judging these circumstances otherwise were made clear. If the official involvement of the Barbary power legitimized such transactions, "the pirates will have indicated to them a very convenient place, which is quite close to the Spanish lines of trade and occupied by English merchants."[162] In another case, however, which concerned seized Venetian property, exceptions were made and Gentili disavowed the labeling of the Barbary powers as piratical.[163] Rubin sums up this juridical dexterity explaining that "legal labels [were] attached not on the basis of facts, but on the basis of their legal and political results by a policy choice."[164] The principles under-lying the recognition or derecognition of pirates could be applied in ways "that could justify the most extreme action against non-European poli-tical societies," and against forces resisting state centralization among expanding European powers.[165]

Hugo Grotius forwarded a more consistent and favorable interpreta-tion of the legal status of the Barbary powers. In his judgment the legal appellation of "pirate" would not apply, according to Rubin, to "the Barbary states or other complete communities, whose primary purpose of association is lawful, i.e., defense, raising families, making war."[166] Grotius argued that the features of states included "a senate, a treasury, the agreement and concord of the citizens, and the power, if the course of events leads thereto, to conclude peace and an alliance."[167] These essen-tial characteristics established whether the entity was a state and, along with its purpose, determined its legitimacy. Grotius recognized the simi-larities between the founding of states and the actions of some criminal bands. He noted that petty chiefs and brigands may transform into lawful rulers, quoting Augustine: "If by accessions of desperate men this evil grows to such proportions that it holds lands, establishes fixed

---

[160] Theodor Meron, "Common Rights of Mankind in Gentili, Grotius, and Suarez," *The American Journal of International Law* 85, no. 1 (January 1991): 114.

[161] Rubin, *Law of Piracy*, 33.

[162] Alberico Gentili, *Hispanicae Advocationis Libri Duo, Vol. 2, The Translation of the Edition of 1612*, trans. Frank F. Abbott (New York: Oxford University Press, 1921; 1661), 71. On the background and context of Gentili's advocacy for Spain, see Frank F. Abbott, "Alberico Gentili and His Advocatio Hispanica," *The American Journal of International Law* 10, no. 4 (October 1916): 737–48.

[163] Rubin, *Law of Piracy*, 34.   [164] Ibid.   [165] Ibid., 36.   [166] Ibid., 39.

[167] Hugo Grotius, *De Jure Belli Ac Pacis Libri Tres, Vol. Two, The Translation, Book I*, trans. Francis W. Kelsey (Oxford: Clarendon Press, 1933; 1625), 630; See also Rubin, *Law of Piracy*, 39.

The Barbary powers in international law 179

settlements, seizes upon states and subjugates peoples, it assumes the name of a kingdom."[168] Grotius focused on the purpose of such associations: "pirates and brigands are banded together for wrongdoing, [while] the members of a state, even if at times they are not free from crime, nevertheless have united for the enjoyment of rights, and they do render justice to foreigners."[169] These judgments, perhaps not coincidentally, were consistent with Dutch interests, being a rebellious province whose increased exertion of sea power was finding its legal footing.[170] It was also consistent with Dutch agreements with the Barbary powers, as by that time they had established a fairly stable *modus vivendi*.[171]

Recognition of the Barbary powers was based in part on the status of the relations between them and European powers. If a European state had diplomatic relations with a Barbary power then that polity had the rights to exist and enter into lawful agreement. Cornelius Van Bynkershoek captured the gist of this legal convenience in 1737: "The peoples of Algiers, Tripoli, Tunis, and Sallee are not pirates, but rather organized states, which have fixed territory in which there is an established government, and with which, as with other nations, we are now at peace, now at war." He continues, closing the circle of his legal reasoning, "[h]ence they seem to be entitled to the rights of independent states. The States-General [of the Netherlands], as well as other nations, have frequently made treaties with them."[172]

Toward the middle of the eighteenth century, as the power of the Barbary "states" ebbed, so too did the international legal forbearance. Emerich de Vattel was not nearly as charitable concerning their transgressions. For him they fell under a scenario in which the nation "is guilty of the crimes of its members. ... when by its manners, and by the maxims of its government, it accustoms and authorizes its citizens indiscriminately to plunder and maltreat foreigners, to make inroads into the neighboring

---

[168] Quoted in Rubin, *Law of Piracy*, 38.   [169] Grotius, *De Jure Belli*, 631.

[170] An argument for the influence of political aspirations on his international legal writings is presented in C.G. Roelofsen, "Grotius and the International Politics of the Seventeenth Century," in *Hugo Grotius and International Relations*, ed. Hedley Bull, et al. (Oxford: Clarendon Press, 1990), 95–132. Grotius was at the forefront of establishing the sovereignty and legitimacy of Holland after the Dutch Revolt. In so doing, he offered arguments that could be utilized for establishing the Barbary powers as states, including "marks of sovereignty" like the right to raise taxes. See Peter Borschberg, trans. and ed., *Hugo Grotius "Commentarius in Theses XI": An Early Treatise on Sovereignty, the Just War, and the Legitimacy of the Dutch Revolt* (Berne: Peter Lang, 1994), 269.

[171] See Panzac, *Barbary Corsairs*, 28–37.

[172] Cornelius Van Bynkershoek, *Quaestionum Juris Publici Libri Duo*, Vol. Two, *The Translation*, trans. Tenney Frank (Oxford: The Clarendon Press, 1930; 1737), 99. See also Rubin, *Law of Piracy*, 73.

180 Power and piracy along the Barbary Coast

countries, etc."[173] Though a sovereign approved their actions, they were undertaken "without any apparent cause, and from no other motive than the lust of plunder."[174] Vattel argued that "[t]he Christian nations would be no less justifiable in forming a confederacy against the states of Barbary, in order to destroy the haunts of pirates, with whom the love of plunder, or the fear of just punishment, is the only rule of peace and war."[175] The constitution of the Barbary powers as states, always a fragile designation, no longer excused their criminal behavior. Their behavior, indeed, would affect the interpretation of their constitution and legitimacy as states.

This shift is evident in French interactions with the regencies as a relationship of mutual antagonism and accommodation gave way to delegitimation and eventual domination. French relations with Tunis, for instance, were complicated by the inability of the bey of Tunis in the latter part of the eighteenth century to control corsair activity.[176] Even though Tunis had the greatest amount of control over its corsairing economy, this relied not on edict but on internal power balances and negotiation, and European powers had become resigned to these complexities.[177] By the end of the eighteenth century, however, this understanding had waned. According to Christian Windler, the continued violations of treaties and doubts over the bey's ability to enforce them led to an assessment: "Did the Bey of Tunis possess the attribute of 'sufficient power' that, in the European law of nations, was an elementary condition of the validity" of their treaties?[178] The principle of the "sufficient power in contracting parties" had come to assume a central place, and the tolerance of the "heterogeneity of the European and Maghrebi laws" was no longer a viable basis for coexistence.[179] Unable to keep up with the state centralization that had occurred across Europe, according to Jörg M. Mossner, "their acts were illegal and not justified by the fact they formed a grouping similar to a State."[180] While the Congress of Vienna (1814–1815) and the Treaty of Aix-la-Chapelle (1818) began the legal suppression of the regencies, it was only after their political

---

[173] Emerich de Vattel, *Law of Nations; or Principles of the Law of Nature Applied to the Conduct and Affairs of Nations and Sovereigns*, ed. Joseph Chitty (Philadelphia: T. & J.W. Johnson & Co., 1883; 1758), 163.

[174] Ibid., 320.   [175] Ibid.

[176] Christian Windler, "Representing a State in a Segmentary Society: French Consuls in Tunis from the Ancien Régime to the Restoration," *The Journal of Modern History* 73, no. 2 (June 2001): 233–74.

[177] Ibid., 269.   [178] Ibid., 236.   [179] Ibid., 239; 274.

[180] Jörg M. Mossner, "The Barbary Powers in International Law (Doctrinal and Practical Aspects)," in *Studies in the History of the Law of Nations*, ed. Charles H. Alexandrowicz (The Hague: Martinus Nijhoff, 1972), 202.

The Barbary powers in international law 181

domination and the decline in its usefulness that privateering itself was abolished – in the Declaration of Paris of 1856.[181]

The application of a judgment of sufficient power recalls a similar criterion (shawka) applied by the Sunni orthodoxy against the Nizari Ismailis, in this case not based on overall numbers but on a polity's unitary nature as an indicator of stateness. This act of categorization was used to exclude the Barbary powers on the basis of their lack of effective sovereignty, helping to make way for French colonial intervention. The Barbary powers, according to a US consul, were "full of barbarous arrogance and ignorance … [but] by a strange ill luck [were] admitted as members of the political system of Europe."[182] This admission had favored the great naval powers of England and France, at the expense of lesser powers that were more vulnerable to corsairs, including the United States. While these machinations favored greater powers, they demonstrate little concerning the role of the Barbary powers in shaping norms associated with piracy. These norms were not generated by interactions with the Barbary powers, as smaller bands of sea-based "robbers" and "brigands" engendered sufficient contempt and efforts to quell piracy. Indeed, most of the great powers were engaged in some form of state-sponsored sea-raiding, which they legitimized as privateering. But even in times outside of major power conflict, when there was lesser value in privateering than in safe commercial passage, the categorization and legal valuations of the Barbary powers tended to be favorable. This came even at the cost of heightened uncertainty and continued depredations against shipping. What can explain this deviation from this study's posited mechanisms concerning the development of norms?

Karl-Dieter Opp, who outlined the relief thesis and its emphasis on norms for the amelioration of uncertainty, explains that norms may not develop in certain circumstances of insecurity. Opp writes that "a necessary condition for the development of norms in situations of insecurity is that insecurity causes costs and that the statement of norms diminishes these costs." The cost of stating and enforcing norms may be so high as to prevent the emergence of norms in cases when that cost exceeds the cost of insecurity.[183] Early on in the seventeenth century, enforcing norms

---

[181] The Congress of Vienna and its treatment of piracy is discussed briefly in Wilhelm G. Grewe, *The Epochs of International Law*, trans. Michael Byers (Berlin: Walter de Gruyter, 2000), 552–53. The Declaration of Paris was attached to the Treaty of Paris, and is discussed in Janice E. Thomson, *Mercenaries, Pirates, and Sovereigns* (Princeton: Princeton University Press), 69–75.

[182] Grewe, *Epochs of International Law*, 552.

[183] Karl-Dieter Opp, "The Emergence and Effects of Social Norms: A Confrontation of Some Hypotheses of Sociology and Economics," *KYKLOS: International Review for Social Sciences* 32 (1979): 794.

182   Power and piracy along the Barbary Coast

against the Barbary powers was prohibitively costly. Even as the great powers' effectiveness against the regencies grew, their usefulness in creating insecurity for lesser powers decreased the incentives in formulating and enforcing norms. In this case that entailed categorizing Barbary sea-raiding as the actions of a state, or quasi-state, thus falling under the category of privateering.

"Often insecurity is not at all costly," Opp argues, "but even rewarding."[184] Despite the level of insecurity and uncertainty generated by the regencies in the seventeenth century, the application of existing norms against the Barbary powers was a lesser concern. More direct means of coercion made these conditions manageable for the major powers, as they benefited from the burden placed on less powerful naval competitors. Partiality, at least initially, was achieved through the *exclusion* of the Barbary powers from the normative framework. Later, as these equations changed, the application of existing norms against piracy were realized. This shifted their categorization to include the regencies as piratical – a process facilitated by complementary processes of negative identity formation – and would expand those norms to other domains like slavery.

As in the cases of the Nizari Ismailis and the Mongols, the explanations offered by the relief, transmission, and enforcement theses – the cumulation of new norms that transmit to other contexts and allow for exceeding normal enforcement – have limited power when examined in a purely functional context as a reaction to systemic uncertainty. Relief was found in normative categorical contortions or through other means, including diplomacy and force, measures that themselves over time reduce uncertainty due to increased interaction. The transmission and enforcement effects, however, would occur eventually, mediated through processes of identity formation, legitimation, and the delineation of standards of civilization. Their misconduct would only partially and fitfully exclude the Barbary powers from the diplomatic order, but it would make them a prime example in fusing that order with a symbolic order that would buttress an emerging conception of civilization.[185]

Turning Turk: captivity and identity

By the end of the sixteenth century, the view of the titanic struggle between Christianity and the encroaching rulers of Islam had been mostly discarded. France had long since established ties with the Ottomans, and

---

[184] Ibid.
[185] See Christian Windler, "Tributes and Presents in Franco–Tunisian Diplomacy," *Journal of Early Modern History* 4, no. 2 (2000): 173.

Turning Turk: captivity and identity

the English would do the same. Through these accommodations, considered traitorous to Christianity by some, material interests prevailed. "Neither partner looked upon the other as friend," according to Lee Eysturlid, "but rather as a necessary evil."[186] While the Ottoman threat to Europe had been contained and reframed, the threat of the "Turk" did not similarly recede and took on a new dimension. As the Barbary powers continued their depredations, they would become a necessary evil of a different sort. The Turks had been the successors of the Tartars as the great menace to Christian civilization, cast as "savage beasts" and "barbarians."[187] Comparisons to the barbarous and warlike Turks served the broader purpose of "defining modern notions of Europe and the West – concepts created in dialectical opposition to Asia and the East."[188] Regularized relations with the Ottoman Empire were in contrast with the intensification of irregular interactions with the Barbary powers beginning in the last half of the sixteenth century, just as they began to assert their autonomy. The importance of the Turks in European minds would take on a new and different element, one that added to the physical threat a distinct threat to identity.

Contemporary estimates of the numbers of captives taken by or to the Barbary powers are of questionable reliability and tend toward exaggeration. Even with this caveat, a sense of the scale can be discerned. In one eight-month period, between May 1639 and January 1640, more than sixty-eight English ships and 1200 captives were taken.[189] Robert Davis notes the potential for misrepresentation: "Certainly the resulting 'corsair hysteria' that gripped much of Europe during these centuries was fuelled in good part by fear and fantasy, but there were also some hard figures to back it up." Acknowledging the fuzziness of the figures, he comes up with the staggering conclusion "that between 1530 and 1780 there were almost certainly a million and quite possibly as many as a million and a quarter white, European Christians enslaved by the Muslims of the Barbary Coast."[190] The reliability of this estimate has been reaffirmed

---

[186] See Lee W. Eysturlid, "'Where Everything Is Weighed in the Scales of Material Interest': Anglo–Turkish Trade, Piracy, and Diplomacy in the Mediterranean during the Jacobean Period," *Journal of European Economic History* 22, no. 3 (1993): 623.

[187] See Nancy Bisaha, *Creating East and West: Renaissance Humanists and the Ottoman Turks* (Philadelphia: University of Pennsylvania Press, 2004), 75; and Daniel Baraz, *Medieval Cruelty: Changing Perceptions, Late Antiquity to the Early Modern Period* (Ithaca: Cornell University Press, 2003), 159–60.

[188] Bisaha, *Creating East and West*, 87.   [189] Hebb, *Piracy and the English*, 140–41.

[190] Davis, "Counting European Slaves," 89; 118. Only 5 percent of those captives escaped or were released due to ransom, and Algiers accounted for about 625,000 captives. See William G. Clarence-Smith and David Eltis, "White Servitude," in *The Cambridge World History of Slavery, Vol. 3*, ed. David Eltis and Stanley L. Engerman (Cambridge: Cambridge University Press, 2011), 153.

184   Power and piracy along the Barbary Coast

by other historians of slavery.[191] This pales in comparison to the estimated 10 million black Africans enslaved, but even if the true numbers for Barbary captives are half of their estimated amount, it shows that the effects on Europe were sustained and far from trivial.

The captives, it was reported, were subjected to all sorts of punishments and indignities. The captors developed "a fearsome reputation in Christian Europe for savagery and lechery towards women and boys."[192] In the English parliament "buggery" was repeatedly evoked to ensure that the vividness of their fate was expressed.[193] How poorly the captives were actually treated has been disputed by some, part of a broader effort to rehabilitate the image of the regencies, though conditions were likely quite harsh for most.[194] Regardless, lurid tales made their way into the European consciousness by way of numerous captivity narratives.[195] These first- or second-hand accounts of the conditions informed the social and political discourses of the European powers, particularly England, and made their way into the arts and literature of the time.

Christopher Marlowe's *Tamburlaine* mentions "the cruel pirates of Argier, That damned train, the scum of Africa, Inhabited with straggling runagates."[196] "Runagate," a variation on renegade, meant both deserter and vagabond, and in certain contexts apostate.[197] The fugitive nature of the pirates of the Barbary Coast had been a theme since before their extension into the northern Atlantic. Samuel Purchas, an English traveler and chronicler, described Algiers as "the Whirlepoole of these Seas, the throne of Pyracie, the Sinke of Trade, and the Stinke of Slavery." He goes on, "the Cage of uncleane Birds of Prey, the Habitation of Sea-Devils, the Receptacle of Renegadoes of God."[198] This last passage reveals the overriding concern that would only increase with the corsairs' reach: that

---

[191] Clarence-Smith and Eltis, "White Servitude," 153.

[192] Barnby, "Sack of Baltimore," 120.

[193] See Maija Jansson, ed., *Proceedings in Parliament, 1614 (House of Commons)* (Philadelphia: American Philosophical Society, 1988), 200; 210; and Nabil Matar, *Turks, Moors, and Englishmen in the Age of Discovery* (New York: Columbia University Press, 1999), 109–28.

[194] See Clarence-Smith and Eltis, "White Servitude," 155; and Robert C. Davis, *Christian Slaves, Muslim Masters: White Slavery in the Mediterranean, the Barbary Coast, and Italy, 1500–1800* (Basingstoke: Palgrave MacMillan, 2003), xxvi.

[195] See Daniel J. Vitkus, ed., *Piracy, Slavery, and Redemption: Barbary Captivity Narratives from Early Modern England* (New York: Columbia University, 2001); and Nabil Matar, "English Accounts of Captivity in North Africa and the Middle East, 1577–1625," *Renaissance Quarterly* 54, no. 2 (Summer 2001): 553–72.

[196] Quoted in Samuel C. Chew, *The Crescent and the Rose: Islam and England during the Renaissance* (New York: Oxford University Press, 1937), 345.

[197] *Oxford English Dictionary Online*, s.v. "runagate."

[198] Quoted in Chew, *Crescent and the Rose*, 344.

Turning Turk: captivity and identity 185

these raids were a threat not only to the bodies but also to the souls of those who fell into their grasp. Defectors became acclaimed and reviled, as had Captain John Ward, who left his role as an English privateer and sailed as Yusuf Reis, first out of Rabat-Salé and then Tunis. The increasing power of Ward and others, "to infest the subjects of all Christian princes and estates," triggered a proclamation by King James I against the "enormious" (abnormally wicked) pirates.[199]

The reported forcible conversion the captives would face became a predominant concern.[200] "The panic" that occurred during the raids on the English coast, Gray writes, "was partly the result of difference in religion."[201] The practice of securing the release of slaves (through payment or, at times, coercion) came to be known as redemption, which could be understood in both of its senses, as a transaction and as the saving of souls. The process of corrupting the Christian world from within would take the label of "turning Turk."[202] Replacing the threat of world-dominating Ottoman designs were threats of apostasy due to coercion or premeditation. To turn Turk meant more than conversion but rather "a metamorphosis from goodness into evil."[203] The threat of enslavement, according to Davis, was central "to the European self-conception of the time " and these concerns "served as a basis for addressing and examining such basic human values as community, liberty, the social contract, and the search for salvation."[204] The Barbary powers themselves would serve as symbols and mirrors for European thinkers to address many of the same issues, minus the preoccupation with salvation.

[199] Daniel J. Vitkus, ed., *Three Turk Plays from Early Modern England: Selimus, Emperor of Turks; A Christian Turned Turk; and The Renegado* (New York: Columbia University Press, 2000), 353–56.

[200] Conversions did take place, some voluntary, others coerced. See Nabil Matar, *Islam in Britain, 1558–1685* (Cambridge: Cambridge University Press, 1998), 48–49. Observers note that coercion was not very profitable to captors, who would be obligated to release converted captives. See Franco Cardini, *Europe and Islam*, trans. Caroline Beamish (Oxford: Blackwell, 1999), 167.

[201] Gray, "Turkish Piracy," 161.   [202] See Matar, *Islam in Britain*, 21–49.

[203] Daniel Goffman and Christopher Stroop, "Empire as Composite: The Ottoman Polity and the Typology of Dominion," in *Imperialisms: Historical and Literary Investigations, 1500–1900*, ed. Elizabeth Sauer, et al. (Basingstoke: Palgrave MacMillan, 2004), 142. See also Nabil Matar, "The Renegade in English Seventeenth-Century Imagination," *Studies in English Literature* 33 (1993): 501; and Barbary Fuchs, "Faithless Empires: Pirates, Renegadoes, and the English Nation," *English Literary History* 67, no. 1 (Spring 2000): 49–52.

[204] Davis, *Christian Slaves*, 190. Davis covers the reactions in Italy (139–93), which were similar to those in England. For the French reaction, which also resembles that exhibited elsewhere, see Gillian Weiss, "Barbary Captivity and the French Idea of Freedom," *French Historical Studies* 28, no. 2 (Spring 2005): 231–64.

186 Power and piracy along the Barbary Coast

Mode of Barbary: the Barbary powers and the Enlightenment

Enlightenment thinkers saw in the Barbary powers odd, distorted reflections of what was both ideal and deformed in society and government. These comparisons served an important function. The view of Europe as more than a geographic designation, distanced from the common association of Christendom, required non-denominational distinctions. In Malcolm Yapp's words, "the old religious marker had lost its power to put men into categories, [and] new secular markers were needed to establish cultural and political identity."[205] The Barbary powers would provide one such marker, and their prominence in this discourse would grow out of consideration of their former Ottoman sponsors.

The overriding image of the Ottoman Empire transformed from powerful and menacing to sick and depraved. According to Ann Thomson, the image of the Ottomans had changed along with the diminishing peril it posed, from that of a "warlike and threatening civilization," to "that of ignorant, fanatical and cruel barbarians under whose despotic rule the peoples of their empire had sunk into misery and stupidity."[206] The focus became their internal constitution, their society and governance, helping to form the emerging discourse on Oriental despotism. The Ottoman Empire, according to one observer, would serve as an exemplar of despotism, "of Oriental wickedness and corruption," rooted in a decline that was founded on "fixed and essential qualities of the Turkish way of political and social life."[207] The Barbary powers, according to Thomson, while demeaned roundly, "were not [considered] obvious examples of Oriental despotisms."[208]

Though maintaining a clear delineation between Europe as a distinct entity from "the Turks and Tartary," Voltaire emphasized that the Ottoman government "was no more arbitrary than those of many European states." According to Yapp, "he indeed preferred to describe the Ottoman state as democratic."[209] Voltaire's suspicion of democracy, suited only to "a very small country; and even that fortunately situated," makes this less of a compliment.[210] The Turks, then, were at times

---

[205] Malcolm E. Yapp, "Europe in the Turkish Mirror," *Past and Present* 137, no. 1 (November 1992): 153.

[206] Ann Thomson, *Barbary and Enlightenment: European Attitudes towards the Maghreb in the 18th Century* (Leiden: E.J. Brill, 1987), 17.

[207] Asli Cirakman, *From "Terror of the World" to the "Sick Man of Europe": European Images of Ottoman Empire and Society from the Sixteenth Century to the Nineteenth* (New York: Peter Lang, 2002), 54.

[208] Thomson, *Barbary and Enlightenment*, 55.

[209] Yapp, "Europe in the Turkish Mirror," 152.

[210] Voltaire, *A Philosophical Dictionary, Vol. I* (London: W. Dugdale, 1843), 382.

The Barbary powers and the Enlightenment 187

a "military democracy, which is still worse than arbitrary powers,"[211] and a "republic of Janissaries, who have frequently strangled their sultan, when their sultan did not decimate them."[212] Despite their size and situation, republics, he argued, may also be savage by nature: "The North American savages were entirely republican; but they were republics of bears."[213]

Broadening the class of democracies widely (intent on sullying the lot), in addition to "the Hottentots, the Caffres, and many communities of negroes. . . . [and] the many hordes of Tartars," the Barbary powers are also included. Their composition as "republics of soldiers and pirates" gives a clear indication of their valuation and that of republics and democracies by extension.[214] While their relatively compact size, arguably, may have made a republic possible, their situation (physical location and resources), and certainly their nature, made a republic of this sort less than an exemplar of the form. That the Barbary powers had acquired a reputation for aggression is apparent in Voltaire's correspondence with Frederick the Great, who responded to the philosophe's concern with Austrian designs on Silesia: "*On les recevra, Biribi, A la façon de Barbari, Mon ami.*" ("We will receive them, Twiddledee, in the mode of Barbary.")[215]

What the "mode of Barbary" was in terms of governance was the subject of some dispute. Montesquieu compared Algiers to a phase in the declining Roman empire, considering it an aristocracy, "where the army, which has sovereign power, makes and unmakes a magistrate called the dey."[216] Adam Ferguson disagreed with the description as an aristocracy, considering Algiers a corrupted democracy guided by self-interest instead of virtue. Because its military could remove the sovereign, it was more a republic than a monarchy.[217] Algiers, Ferguson argued, was an example (along with Constantinople) where the principle of popular government did not precede its form, "and where the first is entirely extinguished, the other may be fraught with evil."[218] Also seeing sovereignty resting with the militia, Edward Gibbon accepted Montesquieu's

---

[211] Voltaire, *The Works of Voltaire, A Contemporary Version, Volume XXIX*, trans. William F. Fleming (Akron, Ohio: Werner Company, 1904), 97.

[212] Voltaire, *Philosophical Dictionary*, 383.   [213] Ibid., 382.   [214] Ibid., 383.

[215] Thomas Carlyle, *History of Friedrich II of Prussia, Called Frederick the Great, Volume VI* (Leipzig: Bernhard Tauchnitz, 1862), 324.

[216] Thomson, *Barbary and Enlightenment*, 114. Charles de Secondat, Baron de Montesquieu, *Considerations on the Causes of the Greatness of the Romans and Their Decline* (Indianapolis: Hackett Publishing, 1999), 152.

[217] Thomson, *Barbary and Enlightenment*, 114.

[218] Adam Ferguson, *An Essay on the History of Civil Society*, ed. Fania Oz-Salzberger (Cambridge: Cambridge University Press, 1995), 67.

188   Power and piracy along the Barbary Coast

comparison of Algiers to an "irregular republic" like those of the late Roman empire, but also questioned its labeling as an aristocracy. "Every military government," he wrote, "floats between the extremes of absolute monarchy and wild democracy."[219] Gibbon preferred Montesquieu to use the Mamluks of Egypt as an example of a military republic, "a juster and more noble parallel."[220]

That Barbary was the site of backwardness where democratic forms were bound to lead to unhappiness is an assessment that did not soon, if ever, fade. David Hume criticized British trade policy toward the Netherlands, a state, like the Barbary powers, which had little land and few native commodities. "Were our narrow and malignant politics to meet with success, we should reduce all our neighboring nations to the same state of sloth and ignorance that prevails in Morocco and the coast of Barbary." The consequences of this would be a "want of emulation, example, and instruction: And we ourselves should soon fall into the same abject condition."[221]

The Barbary powers would serve as a touchstone to determine what republics or democracies were, what they were worth, and the requirements for them to function properly. They showed just how a democracy could go wrong if not based on the proper principles and pursuits. There was something in the nature of the Barbary powers, though, that made them irredeemable. An international system, properly constituted, should seek to contain their malign influence and effects. Firm in his role as the cleaner of the Enlightenment's messes, Edmund Burke resorted to his usual vituperations concerning revolutionary France:

For the composition, too, I admit, the Algerine community resembles that of France; being formed out of the very scum, scandal, disgrace, and pest of the Turkish Asia.... But notwithstanding this resemblance, which I allow, I never shall so far injure the Janissarian Republick of Algiers, as to put it in comparison for every sort of crime, turpitude, and oppression with the Jacobin Republick of Paris.... Algiers is not near; Algiers is not powerful; Algiers is not our neighbour; Algiers is not infectious. Algiers, whatever it may be, is an old creation; and we have good data to calculate all the mischief to be apprehended from it.[222]

---

[219] Thomson, *Barbary and Enlightenment*, 114. Edward Gibbon, *The History of the Decline and Fall of the Roman Empire (Abridged Version)*, ed. David Womersley (London: Penguin Books, 2000), 113, n. 53.

[220] Gibbon, *History of the Decline and Fall*, 113, n. 54.

[221] David Hume, "Of the Jealousy of Trade," in *The Philosophical Works of David Hume, Vol. III* (Boston: Little, Brown, and Company, 1854), 363.

[222] Edmund Burke, "First Letter on a Regicide Peace, 1796," in *The Writings and Speeches of Edmund Burke, Vol. IX*, ed. R.B. McDowell (Oxford: Oxford University Press, 1991), 258.

The Barbary powers and the Enlightenment 189

Burke saw in revolutionary France the gravest threat to Europe, and brushed off suggestions that its distortions would ensure a short life: "What can be conceived so monstrous as the republic of Algiers? and that no less strange republic of the Mamelukes in Egypt? They are of the worst form imaginable, and exercised in the worst manner, yet they have existed as a nuisance on the earth for several hundred years."[223]

Familiarity accompanied a long-standing contempt, one that took root during the ascendance of the regencies and would persist as long as they did. Their innate nature and modes of organization and behavior made them a potent surrogate "other," to enhance and in some respects supplant the fading image of the Turk. Considering the effects of the Barbary powers on identity formation, though, there is little evidence to suggest that collective identity formation based on common structural properties was operative. The complex status of the Barbary powers was the result of not only instrumental concerns but also the oddity of the polities themselves. Accordingly, observers saw what they wanted to see in the regencies. Much of the observation was based not on their configurational properties as systemic actors – dissimilar unit structures – but on their mode of internal organization and governance. From there, observers derived a number of interpretations and lessons, from their "democratic" and "republican" structures to their "aristocratic" and "despotic" orientations. Mixed support is apparent for collective identity formation based on common cultural bonds. As the Ottoman Empire became more of a European power, included in the system but not the community of Christian nations, the Barbary powers would stand in and take the mantle of "the scourge of Christendom."[224] The captivity of Christians and collective efforts for redemption did raise levels of national and local community awareness. But there is little evidence that this extended across borders. Deep divisions within the increasingly secularizing "Christian" world, as in the case of the Mongols, made any effects on common cultural identity ephemeral.

Corporate identity formation, distinctions between "us" and "them," was quite evident, however, particularly in English interactions with the "Turk." The processes of negative identity formation proved handy as the behavior of the Barbary powers became increasingly bothersome and anachronistic. The Barbary powers of the seventeenth century enjoyed some tolerance from the great powers, but it would not be accurate to equate this with legitimacy. They operated in a gray area between piracy

---

[223] Edmund Burke, "Thoughts on French Affairs," in *The Works of the Right Honourable Edmund Burke, Vol. III* (London: George Bell, 1891), 375.
[224] Playfair, *Scourge of Christendom*.

190 Power and piracy along the Barbary Coast

and privateering, and their status as not quite states but close enough made their actions just barely sufferable. Their negative standing in terms of corporate identity deprived them of any rightful place in an international society developing increasingly outside of the framework of the Christian world.

Difficulty in fixing the origins of these raiders resulted in a broad categorization that associated them with the Turks, and with the homogenized Muslim "other." In the first half of the seventeenth century, the threat to physical security in the form of coastal raids was accompanied by severe threats to ontological security. Interactions with Muslim raiders, in addition to degrading treatment, could lead to a loss of faith. Turning Turk was a threat not only to the body but also to identity. The renegades that helped constitute that threat were despised even more due to their transgression. The reported forced conversion of captives, itself a dubious contention, served to cast Muslim captors as agents of "Mahomet." Increased interaction exacerbated processes of negative identity formation as captivity narratives provided dramatized accounts of Christian heroism and Muslim cruelty and depravity, images that would transfer to the inheritors of the Enlightenment in the new American republic.

A new Barbary: the early American republic and the Barbary powers

The founders of the United States soon saw themselves at odds with the Barbary powers in word and deed. To the new republic they would serve, according to Timothy Marr, "as a mobile sign symbolizing the dangers faced by nascent liberty when suppressed by the iron hand of despotism."[225] Stripped of its British naval protection, the United States suffered under Barbary–European great power accommodation. The seizure of two American ships in 1785 began a series of clashes. While only two ships were seized in that instance, rumors and conjecture – including fears that the Barbary powers would be sailing for the coasts of the United States and a report that Benjamin Franklin had been taken captive – turned the threat of the Barbary pirates into a *cause célèbre*.[226]

Increased Mediterranean trade was seen as a tonic for a suffering economy, and the rising number of captives would be characterized as

---

[225] Timothy Marr, *The Cultural Roots of American Islamicism* (Cambridge: Cambridge University Press, 2006), 14.
[226] See Lawrence A. Peskin, "The Lessons of Independence: How the Algerian Crisis Shaped Early American Identity," *Diplomatic History* 28, no. 3 (June 2004): 299–300; and Gary E. Wilson, "The First American Hostages in Moslem Nations, 1784–1789," *American Neptune* 41, no. 3 (July 1981): 208–23.

The early American republic and the Barbary powers   191

"victims of independence."[227] Continued captures set up a dilemma between two founding principles: the "sacredness of freedom from tyranny" and the fear of centralized power that would accrue with a concerted federal response.[228] In this circumstance, the United States did what other states had done when their power was insufficient. Signing a treaty in 1796 was a humiliating necessity for an inchoate power with no real navy.[229] Marr observes, "writers actively compensated for this diplomatic disgrace and their lack of global power by projecting fictional representations of national triumph over Algerine despotism."[230] Like the Europeans before them, the Americans grappled with the status of the Barbary powers. Their autonomy from the Ottomans rendered Barbary "a peripheral space that nevertheless embodied the despotic powers associated with Islam."[231] Though there was no firm fix on what they were, Americans were sure they were something that they did not want to be.[232] Disdain for the pirates would serve for a time as a unifying force in a fractious political environment, and Federalists and Republicans would both use the crises to spur naval development.[233]

In the broader domestic context, captivity narratives told heroic stories of Americans surviving unimaginable ordeals.[234] These encounters and the mythology around them reinforced the American self-image as oppressed resisters of despotic rule and spurred a "renewed sense of themselves as a people in chains."[235] Captivity narratives dealing with

---

[227] Peskin, "Lessons of Independence," 298–99.   [228] Marr, *Cultural Roots*, 33.

[229] See James A. Carr, "John Adams and the Barbary Problem: The Myth and the Record," *American Neptune* 41 (1981): 208–23. On this period of accommodation with the Barbary powers, see Martha E. Rojas, "'Insults Unpunished': Barbary Captives, American Slaves, and the Negotiation of Liberty," *Early American Studies* 1, no. 2 (Fall 2003): 159–86.

[230] Marr, *Cultural Roots*, 34.

[231] Ibid., 27. For a discussion of early American views on Islam, see Robert J. Allison, *The Crescent Obscured: The United States and the Muslim World, 1776–1815* (New York: Oxford University Press, 1995).

[232] According to Richard Parker, the Barbary powers were even less familiar with the United States: "The Algerines seem to have had no very clear idea who the Americans were, other than they rebelled against Britain, which had a treaty relationship with Algiers." Parker, *Uncle Sam in Barbary*, 43.

[233] Jared Gardner, *Master Plots: Race and the Founding of an American Literature, 1787–1845* (Baltimore: Johns Hopkins University Press, 1998), 32–33.

[234] On American Barbary captivity narratives, see Paul Baepler, "The Barbary Captivity Narrative in American Culture," *Early American Literature* 39, no. 2 (2004): 217–46; and Elizabeth Maddock Dillon, "Slaves in Algiers: Race, Republican Genealogies, and the Global Stage," *American Literary History* 16, no. 3 (Fall 2004): 407–36. For full texts of these narratives, see Charles H. Adams, ed., *The Narrative of Robert Adams, A Barbary Captive* (Cambridge: Cambridge University Press, 2005); and Paul Baepler, ed., *White Slaves, African Masters: An Anthology of American Barbary Captivity* (Chicago: University of Chicago Press, 1999).

[235] Gardner, *Master Plots*, 33.

192   Power and piracy along the Barbary Coast

Native Americans had, according to Jared Gardner, provided a "model for securing identity in the New World." Tales of Barbary captivity would extend this, providing "a new twist in the old [Native American] captivity tale – now with the young nation in chains in a hostile wilderness of international relations."[236] In addition, the association of the Barbary powers and Britain, due to their unsavory diplomatic relations, helped heighten the Anglophobia that was already prevalent.[237] This would serve to further distance the United States from Britain and its "African emissaries."[238]

France would get similar treatment as a result of the XYZ Affair of 1797, when the seizure of American ships by the French led to a series of loyalty provisions including the Alien and Sedition Acts. It also sparked urgency, according to Gardner, in defining American identity. The French were associated with Algerine corsairs, as shown in the print "Cinque-tetes, or the Paris Monster" of 1798. (See Figure 4.1.) The Algerine corsair is depicted with other "alien" presences, including a devil, a black man, and a Jacobin sympathizer.[239]

The Barbary powers also served as a potent source for negative identity formation among the young republic's elites. Franklin was conscious of the threat from the Barbary powers. The threat, though, was one of emulation. Toward the end of the Revolutionary War, Franklin wrote to English philosopher David Hartley that he did "not wish to see a new Barbary rising in America, and our long extended coast occupied by piratical States." Despite the advantages the United States would have with continued corsairing, Franklin was disturbed by its prevalence during the war. He claimed that his proposal to abolish privateering had "humanity only for its motive," with Barbary serving to presage the potential for a "mankind ... plagued with American corsairs."[240]

Thomas Paine in *Rights of Man* saw Algerine piracy as the result of the self-interest of the despotic and corrupt powers of Europe.[241] In 1803, Paine railed again Federalist policies toward the Barbary powers:

---

[236] Ibid., 35.   [237] Peskin, "Lessons of Independence," 317.

[238] Gardner, *Master Plots*, 33. See also Gary E. Wilson, "American Hostages in Moslem Nations, 1784–1796: The Public Response," *Journal of the Early Republic* 2, no. 2 (Summer 1982): 134.

[239] Gardner, *Master Plots*, 56–58. On anti-French views and their association with Algiers, see Matthew R. Hale, "'Many Who Wandered in Darkness': The Contest over American National Identity, 1795–1798," *Early American Studies* 1, no. 1 (Spring 2003): 173.

[240] Benjamin Franklin, "To David Hartley, 8 May 1783, Desires the Abolition of Privateering," in *The Works of Benjamin Franklin, Vol. IX* (Chicago: Townsend, 1882), 521–22.

[241] Thomson, *Barbary and Enlightenment*, 130.

Figure 4.1 Cinque-tetes, or the Paris Monster (1798)

[T]he federal leaders have been labouring to *barbarize* the United States by adopting the practice of the Barbary States. ... The world would be in continual quarrels and war, and commerce be annihilated, if Algerine policy was the law of nations. And were America, instead of becoming an example to the old world of good and moral government and civil manners, or, if they like it better, of gentlemanly conduct towards other nations, to set up the character of ruffian, that of *word and blow, and the blow first*, and thereby give the example of pulling down the little that civilization has gained upon barbarism, her Independence, instead of being an honour and a blessing, would become a curse upon the world and upon herself.[242]

The United States stood above such behavior, Paine argued: "The conduct of the Barbary powers, though unjust in principle, is suited to their prejudices, situation, and circumstances. ... But this is not the case with the United States. If she sins as a Barbary power, she must answer for it as a Civilized one."[243]

---

[242] Thomas Paine, "Letters to the Citizens of the United States," in *The Political and Miscellaneous Works of Thomas Paine*, Vol. II (London: R. Carlile, 1819), 38.
[243] Ibid.

194   Power and piracy along the Barbary Coast

Thomas Jefferson would echo the theme of their innate belligerence and intransigence. Jefferson was concerned about the future of French-controlled Saint Domingue (soon to be Haiti) and its prospective independence. There was a potential for it to become, in the words of French minister Stéphen Pichon, "another Algiers in the seas of America."[244] The black population of Haiti and their potential independence raised fears of insurrection by American slaves. Jefferson expressed his misgivings to John Adams that "the independent black regime might be converted into a piratical state by European renegades."[245] His most noted comparison to Barbary is often linked to concerns about the degrading effects of the institution of slavery. In his written comments of 1820, Jefferson referred to his fears that Virginia would become "the Barbary of the Union."[246] This characterization, taken out of its proper context, along with Franklin's "new Barbary," would be used by abolitionists, most notably Charles Sumner, to give weight to growing anti-slavery sentiment.[247]

Wall of the barbarian world: piracy, slavery, and civilization

Comparisons between the American republic and the "piratical republics" would take place in a broader context where slavery was increasingly becoming considered contrary to Christian and Western civilization. "North Africa symbolized to Americans a compound of political tyranny and antichristian darkness," Marr writes, "a potent mixture that lent credence to the view that the inhabitants of Barbary were truly barbarians."[248] This view could not be sustained, though, as long as they shared the same practices. Without an unhealthy dose of self-delusion, one could not look at the Barbary powers as opposites. Barbary would increasingly

[244] Tim Matthewson, "Jefferson and Haiti," *The Journal of Southern History* 61, no. 2 (May 1995): 214.

[245] Ibid., 217. See Michael Zuckerman, "The Power of Blackness: Thomas Jefferson and the Revolution in St. Domingue," in Zuckerman, *Almost Chosen People: Oblique Biographies in the American Grain* (Berkeley and Los Angeles: University of California Press, 1993), 175–218.

[246] Thomas Jefferson, "To Joseph C. Cabell, November 28, 1820," in *The Writings of Thomas Jefferson, Vol. XV* (Washington, D.C.: Thomas Jefferson Memorial Association, 1907), 289–90.

[247] See Charles Sumner, "The Barbarism of Slavery, Speech in the Senate, on the Bill for Admission of Kansas as a Free State, June 4, 1860," in *The Works of Charles Sumner, Vol. V* (Boston: Lee and Shepard, 1874), 47–48. Jefferson was referring to the lack of development in the educational system of Virginia, and his comparison was made to the overall backwardness of Barbary, not specifically its practice of slavery.

[248] Marr, *Cultural Roots*, 27.

Piracy, slavery, and civilization   195

serve to highlight the open sore of slavery in America and beyond. Just as sea-raiding and ransom had allowed the regencies to function beyond what their distorted structure would have otherwise allowed, how would the practice of slavery warp the development of *their own* vulnerable, fragile republic?

Shortly before his death, under the pseudonym Historicus, Franklin bitingly mocked pro-slavery arguments that had gained currency.[249] He did so by putting those arguments, as offered by an American senator, in the mouth of an imaginary Algerine divan member. Jamestown had previously been slighted by a Spanish observer as "a New Algiers in America" due to its practice of slavery.[250] The Barbary analogy would become popular among abolitionists, as they seized on the comparison with what Cotton Mather had called "the Fierce Monsters of Africa."[251] Sumner took this comparison to its greatest extent in his speeches and writings. This included his 1847 lecture titled "White Slavery in the Barbary States," where he labeled the slave states the "Barbary States of America."[252] He not only drew parallels with the practice of slavery but also noted that the Barbary powers and the southern states had similar geographic and climatic circumstances, with Algiers situated at the same latitude as the Missouri Compromise.[253]

In a speech all the more bold since an earlier one led to his severe beating on the floor of the Senate, Sumner evoked Purchas's description of Barbary as "the wall of the Barbarian world."[254] Abolitionist writer Edward Coit Rogers used a broad historical sweep to establish the illegality and unconstitutionality of slavery. Absolutism and arbitrary power amounted to robbery and the denial of liberty and justice. While slavery took hold there, "everyone knows that Algiers was not a civil state, but a band of robbers. They opposed the legitimate principles of civil society, for the same reason you oppose them, and for no other."[255] According to Robert Allison, the Barbary powers served as a "disturbing reflection,"

---

[249] Benjamin Franklin, "On the Slave Trade," in *The Works of Benjamin Franklin, Vol. II* (Chicago: Townsend, 1882), 517–21.

[250] Marr, *Cultural Roots*, 140.

[251] Cotton Mather, *Magnalia Christi Americana; or the Ecclesiastical History of New England, Vol. II* (Hartford, Conn.: Silus Andrus & Son, 1853), 671. On the Barbary analogy, see Lofti Ben Rejeb, "America's Captive Freemen in North Africa: The Comparative Method in Abolitionist Persuasion," *Slavery and Abolition* 9, no. 1 (May 1988): 57; Marr, *Cultural Roots*, 134–84; and Baepler, "Barbary Captivity Narrative," 230–32.

[252] Charles Sumner, *White Slavery in the Barbary States* (Boston: John P. Jewett, 1853), 11.

[253] Sumner, "Barbarism of Slavery," 48.   [254] Ibid.

[255] Edward Coit Rogers (O.S. Freeman, pseudonym), *Letters on Slavery, Addressed to the Pro-slavery Men of America; Showing Its Illegality in All Ages and Nations: Its Destructive War Upon Society and Government, Morals and Religion* (Boston: Bela Marsh, 1855), 65.

196   Power and piracy along the Barbary Coast

and reminded Americans, "of how far the United States needed to progress if it was to escape the despotism it abhorred in the North Africans."[256]

While this discourse was unfolding, parallel systemic developments were also establishing piracy and slavery as beyond the pale of civilization. "Caressed and encouraged" by Britain and France, in the words of one critic, the Barbary powers had served to preserve the great powers' naval predominance.[257] The interests of Britain now moved more toward the abolition of slavery, in part to stifle the economy of the newly independent American colonies.[258] The anomaly of Barbary would lead first to half-hearted British efforts to coerce Algiers into abolishing both piracy and slavery.[259] The Congress of Vienna's "Declaration of the Powers, on the Abolition of the Slave Trade" focused on that institution "which has so long desolated Africa, degraded Europe, and afflicted humanity." The great powers committed to abolishing slavery in their countries and to take measures to compel others to do the same.[260] The Vienna Declaration signified the beginning of the movement away from using Christendom "as the communitarian body on which the law of nations rested."[261] Increasingly, the basis for international law would be "the community of civilized nations."[262]

These developments also served to advance the cause of colonialism. For France, Algiers transformed from an uneasy partner to a decadent state beset by slavery, piracy, and anarchy: verdicts that cloaked what were overwhelmingly colonial rather than redemptive designs.[263] "European interventionism in Barbary," Lofti Ben Rejeb observes, "was generally suggested as the necessary dynamic force best suited to soften the collision and reduce the gap between civilization and barbarism."[264] Nineteenth-century international legal writings justified European colonialism in North Africa. In the *Institutes of the Law of Nations* (1883), James Lorimer argued that communities should be deprived of recognition as states based on their degree of "internal freedom" and the

---

[256] Allison, *Crescent Obscured*, 94; Marr, *Cultural Roots*, 141.

[257] Grewe, *Epochs of International Law*, 552.   [258] Ibid., 555.

[259] Ibid., 553; and J.E.G. de Montmorency, "The Barbary States and International Law," *Transactions of the Grotius Society* 4 (1918): 92. See also Oded Löwenheim, "'Do Ourselves Credit and Render a Lasting Service to Mankind': British Moral Prestige, Humanitarian Intervention, and the Barbary Pirates," *International Studies Quarterly* 47, no. 1 (March 2003): 23–48.

[260] Grewe, *Epochs of International Law*, 554.   [261] Ibid., 445–46.   [262] Ibid.

[263] Stefan Goodwin, *Africa's Legacies of Urbanization: Unfolding Saga of a Continent* (Lanham, Md.: Lexington Books, 2006), 132.

[264] Lofti Ben Rejeb, "Barbary's 'Character' in European Letters, 1514–1830: An Ideological Prelude to Colonization," *Dialectical Anthropology* 6, no. 4 (June 1982): 353.

Piracy, slavery, and civilization 197

"presence of a rational will."[265] The conditions that would indicate that unworthiness were nonage (childishness), imbecility, and criminality, with the "Barbary States" serving to illustrate the last of those. Crime being a violation of natural law deprived these communities of the protection of recognition under international law.[266] He notes, incorrectly, that since Grotius denied recognition to "bands of robbers," the Barbary powers were not recognized by European states.[267] As a result, he concludes, France's conquest of Algeria was not contrary to international law. "Had Algeria come to respect the rights of life and property," Lorimer scolded, "its history would not have permanently deprived it of the right of recognition."[268]

The establishment of standards of civilization has been treated thus far in an informal sense. This occurs when the processes of identity formation, norm development, and enforcement intersect, establishing and reinforcing rightful membership and conduct based on logics of appropriateness. In the prior two cases these processes took hold well after the actor in question had faded from the scene. The advancement of a more formal standard of civilization occurred toward the end of the Barbary powers' life span and soon after their effective demise. This standard emphasized the distorting nature of the deprivation of human freedom. The abolitionists made clear comparisons of the abject conditions and fates of both white and black slaves, while the Barbary powers were used to delineate membership in civilization in order to enforce compliance with its standards. Their eventual positioning outside of civilization coincided with their relative weakness, leaving them to the mercy of European states grown ravenous for resources and space, partially validating the enforcement thesis though only after its mediation through processes of identity formation. Those incursions left France in control of Algiers, now Algeria, beginning a lengthy and difficult occupation. Three decades after the French departed, Algeria would again draw the attention of observers who wished to avoid the missteps of its political development, and those of governments throughout the Arab and Muslim worlds, in their own effort to buck the international system.

---

[265] James Lorimer, *The Institutes of the Law of Nations, A Treatise of the Jural Relations of Separate Political Communities, Vol. I* (Edinburgh: William Blackwood and Sons, 1883), 157.

[266] Immanuel Kant had previously identified the actions of the Barbary states as contrary to natural right or law. Unlike Lorimer, though, Kant "rejects conquest or imperial intervention as an equal wrong." See Michael W. Doyle, "Kant, Liberal Legacies, and Foreign Affairs, Part 2," *Philosophy and Public Affairs* 12, no. 4 (Autumn 1983): 325.

[267] Lorimer, *Law of Nations*, 161.   [268] Ibid.

198   Power and piracy along the Barbary Coast

Barbary piracy would also reappear in the symbolic order in a manner similar to the Mongols, though not to the same extent. The use of submarines by the Germans in the First World War was singled out as beyond the pale of civilized warfare, and comparison with Barbary piracy reinforced preexisting standards that derided treachery. In one comparison of the Germans and Barbary powers, the latter were deemed "the most insolent federation for crime in history before these present wars."[269] Like the Mongols, they would be used to establish a scale of depravity that the modern incarnation would match or exceed. The *League of Nations Magazine* declared that "[t]he Barbary Pirates and roving privateers were negligible when compared with the submarines."[270] The sinking of the *Lusitania* was, according to *The Nation*, "a deed for which a Hun would blush, a Turk be ashamed, and a Barbary pirate apologize."[271] For Theodore Roosevelt, it was "piracy, pure and simple," but "none of these old-time pirates [of the Barbary Coast] committed murder on so vast a scale as in the case of the *Lusitania*."[272] As exemplars of the dangers of uncivilized warfare these symbols would not have the potency or staying power of a Genghis Khan. But they would be evoked again, after September 11, when a particular combination of religious identity and systemic irregularity needed a measure of historical depth and leverage in order to begin to comprehend it.

---

[269] De Montmorency, "Barbary States," 93. Elsewhere, J.E.G. de Montmorency makes another comparison, concluding: "In other words, the members of the German Imperial Government were pirates." J.E.G. de Montmorency, "Piracy and the Barbary Corsairs," *Law Quarterly Review* 35 (1919): 133–42.

[270] *League of Nations Magazine* 4 (1918): 712.

[271] Howard Jones, *A History of U.S. Foreign Relations since 1897* (Wilmington, Del.: SR Books, 2001), 73. See also Lee Meriwether, *The War Diary of a Diplomat* (New York: Dodd, Mead, and Company, 1919), 282.

[272] John M. Cooper, *Pivotal Decades: The United States, 1900–1920* (New York: W.W. Norton, 1990), 233; Theodore Roosevelt, "Appendix A: Murder on the High Seas," in Roosevelt, *Fear God and Take Your Own Part* (New York: George H. Doran Company, 1916), 351.

5 In the shadow of the spears
Al Qaeda's clash with civilization

> Praise be to God, who revealed the Book, controls the clouds, defeats factionalism, and says in His Book: "But when the forbidden months are past, then fight and slay the pagans wherever ye find them, seize them, beleaguer them, and lie in wait for them in every stratagem (of war)"; and peace be upon our Prophet, Muhammad Bin-'Abdallah, who said: I have been sent with the sword between my hands to ensure that no one but God is worshipped, God who put my livelihood under the shadow of my spear and who inflicts humiliation and scorn on those who disobey my orders.
>
> —"Declaration of the World Islamic Front Jihad against the Jews and the Crusaders," February 1998

> So when we made war against America we are jackals fighting in the nights.
>
> —Khalid Shaykh Mohammed, March 2007

Introduction

Fanatic and treacherous, mobile and rootless, and holding a doctrinaire disregard for prevailing conceptions of human freedom, the epitome of incivility, Al Qaeda on September 11, 2001 ruptured the veil of security of the world's greatest power. That security was ontological as well as physical, the frontiers of conceivable catastrophe transgressed as fully as actual boundaries. Shock, horror, and uncertainty contributed to that drastic drop in ontological security, our "cognitive control of the interaction context."[1] This condition would in time result in the construction of a potent group of "others" that would inform efforts toward their destruction. Operating on the margins of the international system, Al Qaeda has been categorized as a "non-state" or "sovereignty-free" actor in a "post-international" system.[2] All that these categorical shifts accomplish is to

---

[1] Bill McSweeney, *Security, Identity, and Interests: A Sociology of International Relations* (Cambridge: Cambridge University Press, 1999), 157.

[2] See Richard W. Mansbach, "The Meaning of 11 September and the Emerging Postinternational World," *Geopolitics* 8, no. 3 (October 2003): 22.

200   Al Qaeda's clash with civilization

tell us what Al Qaeda is not, and that the international system has changed. Barry Posen has referred to Al Qaeda as a "transnational anti-system group."[3] This characterization mistakes a temporary exigency – Al Qaeda not conforming to the dominant mode of organization in the system – for its essential status. Although Al Qaeda is very much opposed to the international system, in the sense of the system's current organization and leadership, it is also very much from it, and part of it. The group's leaders aspire to participate in the system in terms of competing with dominant actors, as they seek to replace its normative underpinnings, including the delineation imposed during the establishment of modern nation-states. Al Qaeda is in opposition to the system in the sense of its clash with the dominant actors, norms, rules, and legitimacy that regulate it. But this transformation demands participation in the system in the analytic sense rather than precludes it. An extra-systemic analytic bias has distorted our view of Al Qaeda and its significance in the study of world politics. This has confined it to the world of non-state actors and treated it as a disembodied doppelganger acting on, rather than in, the international system.

Al Qaeda's capacity for adaptation and innovation has been cited to set it apart from others classified as terrorist organizations.[4] It is not just Al Qaeda's high status as a learning organization that distinguishes it, however, but its capacity to realize and apply those lessons on a systemic scale. How did Al Qaeda emerge and survive taking on multiple states including the dominant unipolar power, the United States? This chapter traces Al Qaeda's development from its roots in the struggle against the Soviet occupation of Afghanistan. It goes further by tracing developments in the Muslim world, both the system encompassing the Greater Middle East and the trends in Islamism that preceded that conflict. After describing the systemic setting and the actors that comprised it, some potential systemic explanations for the timing of Al Qaeda's emergence are offered. The decline of the Soviet Union, the ascendance of the United States, and the conditions of globalization are all important factors. It is Soviet decline, however, that best explains the timing of Al Qaeda's emergence as a systemic actor. An account of Al Qaeda's imaginative reactions to its straitened circumstances and its evolution and effects on the international system is then presented. The chapter closes with an assessment of what impact this episode has had so far on the norms and identities that constitute international society, dispelling the notion that these events

---

[3] Barry R. Posen, "The Case for Restraint," *The American Interest* 3, no. 1 (November–December 2007): 13.

[4] See Assaf Moghadam, "How Al Qaeda Innovates," *Security Studies* 22, no. 3 (July 2013): 466–97.

Dominance structures and the Greater Middle East 201

represent a clash of civilizations. They represent, rather, a clash *with* civilization and some of its core standards, shaped in part by interactions with the systemic deviators examined in the previous chapters.

The system: dominance structures and the Greater Middle East

The bipolar nature of the international system during the Cold War was not its only significant structural feature. When looking at the Greater Middle East – the belt from the Maghreb through the Caspian Basin to Pakistan – at least equal emphasis should be placed on what Alexander Wendt and Michael Barnett termed "dominance structures." Wendt and Barnett look to both systemic and unit-level forces in their effort to explain the effects of militarization and relationships with outside powers on developing states.[5] For reasons that lie at both levels, developing states competed militarily on terms that left them dependent on, and necessarily weaker than, their great power sponsors. Wendt and Barnett highlight the adherence of developing states to capital-intensive militarization despite severe disadvantages in capital endowments. The authors point out that those developing states need not have imitated, mentioning that labor-intensive rather than capital-intensive strategies may have held advantages.[6] Systemic forces, distortions of the colonial economy, and internal forces combined to create conditions of dominance and dependence.

With anyone other than their immediate neighbors, who were subject to the same constraints, competition would be on markedly uneven ground. Ian Lustick highlights outside pressures in explaining why no great power emerged in the Middle East.[7] Lustick focuses on the "crucial role of war and coercion in the production of great states" and the infeasibility of large-scale state-building wars as a mechanism for consolidation as the primary reasons why no great powers arose.[8] Britain and the United States undermined certain regimes (including pan-Arab aspirants such as Egypt's Gamal Abdel Nasser) and propped up others (such as the House of Saud), while enforcing norms preventing aggrandizement

[5] Alexander Wendt and Michael Barnett, "Dependent State Formation and Third World Militarization," *Review of International Studies* 19, no. 4 (October 1993): 321–47.
[6] Ibid. See also Roger Owen, "The Cumulative Impact of Middle Eastern Wars," in *Wars, Institutions, and Social Change in the Middle East*, ed. Steven Heydemann (Berkeley: University of California Press, 2000), 332. Reliance on outside military aid resulted in "the influence of suppliers over the size and deployment of the military equipment in question," and also had a "significant impact on the nature of the state."
[7] Ian S. Lustick, "The Absence of Middle Eastern Great Powers: Political Backwardness in Historical Perspective," *International Organization* 51, no. 4 (Autumn 1997): 653–83.
[8] Ibid., 678.

202   Al Qaeda's clash with civilization

by any one power.[9] This precluded the development of a great power that could take advantage of the region's resources and, presumably, pose a challenge to outside influence in the region. In the Middle East they inherited "the structure of the state and the idea of the nation" but were not able or allowed to fuse them.[10]

The United States was preoccupied with preventing Soviet influence, and initially sought to incorporate pan-Arab aspirants like Nasser into the Cold War alliance structure.[11] Like the Baghdad Pact before it, the Eisenhower Doctrine solicited regional states to choose sides, effectively subordinating them. According to John Miglietta, the "U.S. strategy assumed that Arab states would be content with informal Western (American) control, provided that the more overt vestiges of Western colonialism were removed from the region."[12] Egypt opposed this while conservative regimes saw it as a useful check on the internal and external threats posed by the disruptive forces of pan-Arabism. "The implementation of the Eisenhower Doctrine," Ray Takeyh writes, "ushered in the next phase of the administration's involvement in the Middle East. The United States became the guardian of the conservative order."[13] British retrenchment beginning in the late 1950s would leave the superpowers to vie for influence.[14] The United States would increasingly take the role of offshore balancer, resting on a military policy that would emphasize rapid deployment and eschew a sustained presence.

The actors I: superpowers and client states

The Cold War engendered relationships fitting the superpower/subordinate, patron/client molds. However, as Barnett emphasizes, "while

[9] See Martin Kramer, "Don't Absolve the Great Powers," *Middle East Quarterly* 7, no. 4 (December 2000): 25–27. Concerning the effects of norm enforcement by great powers on the nature of conflict, see Stephen L. Spiegel and Jennifer Kibbe, "Emulation in the Middle East," in *The New Great Power Coalition: Toward a World Concert of Nations*, ed. Richard Rosecrance (Lanham, Mass.: Rowman & Littlefield, 2001), 305.

[10] Bruce Maddy-Weitzman, *The Crystallization of the Arab State System, 1945–1954* (Syracuse: Syracuse University Press, 1993), 22. On this result as a general outcome, see Bertrand Badie, *The Imported State: The Westernization of the Political Order*, trans. Claudia Royal (Stanford: Stanford University Press, 2000).

[11] The evolution of early US postwar policy toward Egypt is examined in Peter Hahn, *The United States, Great Britain, and Egypt: Strategy and Diplomacy in the Early Cold War* (Chapel Hill: University of North Carolina Press, 1991).

[12] John P. Miglietta, *American Alliance Policy in the Middle East, 1945–1992* (Lanham, Md.: Lexington Books, 2002), 204.

[13] Ray Takeyh, *The Origins of the Eisenhower Doctrine: The US, Britain and Nasser's Egypt, 1953–57* (Basingstoke: Palgrave Macmillan, 2000), 154.

[14] See Ritchie Ovendale, *Britain, the United States, and the Transfer of Power in the Middle East, 1945–1962* (London: Leicester University Press, 1996).

The actors I: superpowers and client states   203

superpowers might restrict their client's behavior in certain ways, the character of the Cold War enabled clients to act in a surprisingly independent manner in many areas."[15] The level of autonomy of these weaker states, or subsystemic dominance, did not override the overall global systemic dominance held by more advanced states.[16] Both circumstances, subsystemic autonomy and global systemic dominance, would condition behavior throughout the Cold War. Weaker states would fill roles and functions in the bipolar context while attempting to fulfill imperatives driven by regional, local, and domestic interests.

Early Cold War suspicions of India's neutralist stance led the United States to lean toward Pakistan.[17] The beginning of military and economic aid would benefit the Pakistani military, which had begun its serial intrusion into domestic politics.[18] Mohammed Ayub Khan, Pakistan's president and one of its many military rulers, would declare that Pakistan was the United States' "most allied ally in Asia."[19] Despite this claim it became increasingly clear that the benefits were mostly one-sided. Pakistan would take part in regional alliance systems like the Southeast Asia Treaty Organization and the Baghdad Pact. But these efforts fizzled, and the cost of what was overwhelmingly military aid was not yielding the expected US security benefits. By 1957, President Eisenhower called the escalating commitment to Pakistan "a terrible error," but believed reversing it would have troubling repercussions.[20] The security relationship would go through permutations affected by regional conflicts with India, and US Cold War interests. While the United States sought to counter Soviet influence, Pakistan was fixated on the issue of Pashtunistan, a homeland for the Pashtuns that would traverse the Afghanistan–Pakistan border. Meanwhile, the Soviets competed for influence with the United States over Afghanistan as it became dependent on outside powers for aid.[21]

US–Saudi Arabia relations exemplify this condition of subsystemic dominance and global subordination. The importance of oil reserves and the role of the kingdom as an alternative to Nasser-led pan-Arabism

---

[15] Michael N. Barnett, "Review of *Superpowers and Client States in the Middle East: The Imbalance of Influence*," *American Political Science Review* 87, no. 1 (March 1993): 256.

[16] See Philip Windsor, "Superpowers and Client States: Perceptions and Interactions," in *Superpowers and Client States in the Middle East: The Imbalance of Influence*, ed. Moshe Efrat and Jacob Bercovitch (London: Routledge: 1991), 33–54.

[17] Dennis Kux, *The United States and Pakistan, 1947–2000: Disenchanted Allies* (Washington, D.C.: Woodrow Wilson Center Press, 2001), 56.

[18] The effects of US military aid on Pakistani politics are discussed in Robert J. McMahon, *The Cold War on the Periphery: The United States, India, and Pakistan* (New York: Columbia University Press, 1994), 210–11.

[19] Kux, *United States and Pakistan*, 74.   [20] Ibid., 84.

[21] Anthony Hyman, *Afghanistan under Soviet Domination, 1964–91*, 3rd ed. (London: MacMillan, 1992), 28–30; 48.

204   Al Qaeda's clash with civilization

resulted in an increase in economic and military aid.[22] Cheap oil was vital to Western prosperity, the key barrier to Communist encroachment in Europe. In part due to US largesse, all in the name of resources and anti-Communist stability, the Saudis continued their profligate spending and plutocratic tendencies.[23] In order to assert leadership as an alternative to secular pan-Arabism, the Saudis emphasized their role as custodians of the holy places of Mecca and Medina. These efforts included the reconstruction of the Hijaz railroad to carry worshippers to Mecca. There, the renovation of the Great Mosque would occur under the supervision of Yemen-born Saudi industrialist Muhammad bin Laden.[24]

The Saudi cultivation of regional and global influence through the promotion of Islamic causes was consistent with the US emphasis on traditional regimes and religious identity as an alternative to socialism. "The original idea at the outbreak of the cold war," Martin Kramer writes, "was to leverage Islam against international communism; Saudi Arabia provided the lever."[25] Support for the House of Saud, in David Lesch's words, would become "an unofficial corollary to the Eisenhower Doctrine."[26] The OPEC oil embargo would demonstrate the limits of US dominance, but Saudi dependence on the United States would soon return and deepen. The Iranian Revolution would draw the United States and Saudi Arabia even closer.[27] With the later Iraqi aggression, the extent of Saudi dependence would be revealed and, by some, reviled.

The actors II: Islamic awakening and the modern Tartars

With the failure of pan-Arabism as a force for regional unification, Islamic identification increased its prominence in the attempted renewal of

---

[22] Miglietta, *American Alliance Policy*, 204.

[23] Nathan J. Citino, *From Arab Nationalism to OPEC: Eisenhower, King Sa'ud, and the Making of U.S.–Saudi Relations* (Bloomington: Indiana University Press, 2002), 123–24.

[24] Ibid., 126–27.

[25] Kramer, "Don't Absolve the Great Powers," 26. Concerning Islam as a bulwark to Communism, see Nathan J. Citino, "The Pan-Islamic Panacea: Eisenhower, Area Expertise, and the Cold War in the Middle East," Paper presented at the Annual Conference of the Society for Historians of American Foreign Relations, June 23, 2000, 6. For a contemporaneous account of the view of Islam as providing a brake on Communist expansion, see Bernard Lewis, "Communism and Islam," *International Affairs* 30, no. 1 (January 1954): 12.

[26] David W. Lesch, "The 1957 American–Syrian Crisis: Globalist Policy in a Regional Rivalry," in *The Middle East and the United States: A Historical and Political Reassessment*, 2nd ed., ed. Lesch (Boulder, Colo.: Westview Press, 1999), 129.

[27] After 1979, writes Tim Niblock, "[t]he Saudi Government had, in effect, become a partner of the United States in a worldwide campaign against radical and leftist governments." Tim Niblock, *Saudi Arabia: Power, Legitimacy, and Survival* (London: Routledge, 2006), 14.

The actors II: Islamic awakening and the modern Tartars   205

Middle Eastern societies. Anoushiravan Ehteshami identifies perspectives on the rise of Islam as a political force, including the clash of civilizations; the crisis of the nation-state in the Middle East; and Islamism, particularly its most radical forms, as a reaction to modernization.[28] As an explanation for the emergence of Al Qaeda, the crisis of the Middle East state system had far more impact than is generally appreciated, while the overwhelming emphasis on the other two explanations has, on balance, obscured its causes.

The development of grievances and ideological stances into a genuine mass movement gave rise to the Islamic awakening, *al-sahwa al Islamiyya*. The crisis of the nation-state in the Middle East, according to Ehteshami, was rooted in social and economic deprivation and corruption, as well as reliance on the West for defense.[29] Internationally, the defeat by Israel in 1967 was seen as a key indicator of the failure of secular pan-Arab leadership. It was, as Fouad Ajami put it, the "Waterloo of Pan-Arabism," and Arabs suffered "the traumas of being initiated into an international system in which they were not full participants."[30] According to Adeeb Khalid, nationalist regimes failed "partly because of corruption but largely because of global structural problems beyond their control," with the defeat by Israel heightening the scrutiny.[31] Al Qaeda leader Ayman al-Zawahiri adopted this viewpoint in explaining what would develop into the violent manifestation of Islamism: "The 1967 defeat shook the earth under this idol [Nasser and secular pan-Arabism] until it fell on its face, causing a severe shock to its disciples, and frightening its subjects. . . . [returning people] to their original identity: that of members of an Islamic civilization."[32]

In varying degrees it would become apparent to the emerging Islamist opposition that organization and international competition on terms set by the dominant powers in the system would not suffice. Islamist perceptions focus on systemic constraints even while advancing tradition-based prescriptions, drawing attention to Western-imposed division and

---

[28] Anoushiravan Ehteshami, "Islam as a Political Force in International Politics," in *Islam in World Politics*, ed. Nelly Lahoud and Anthony H. Johns (London: Routledge, 2005), 31–32.

[29] Ibid., 31.

[30] Fouad Ajami, "The End of Pan-Arabism," *Foreign Affairs* 57, no. 2 (Winter 1978–79): 357; 369.

[31] Adeeb Khalid, *Islam after Communism: Religion and Politics in Central Asia* (Berkeley and Los Angeles: University of California Press, 2007), 15.

[32] From Ayman al-Zawahiri's *Knights under the Prophet's Banner*, quoted in Montasser al-Zayyat, *The Road to Al-Qaeda: The Story of Bin Laden's Right-Hand Man*, trans. Ahmed Fekry (London: Pluto Press, 2004), 23.

206   Al Qaeda's clash with civilization

exclusion that guarantee conditions of dominance and predation.[33] In other circumstances we might expect regional powers to balance against such outside dominance and interference. That balancing, though, was precluded by conditions at both the domestic and international levels. Islamism should not be singled out as a cause for taking on the nation-state. Inability to take on the form of the nation-state effectively, rather, is one cause of Islamism and its radical manifestations. What has been lacking is appreciation of the material elements, particularly at the international systemic level, that interacted with the ideas that pervaded the Islamist political discourse.

The ideological aspects highlighted as having generated radical Islamism long preceded its violent systemic manifestation. Islamic revivalism is often cited as a formative influence, with thinkers like Sayyid Abu'l-A'la Mawdudi at the forefront, but the roots of the modern violence are identified much earlier.[34] Ibn Taymiyya, the thirteenth- to fourteenth-century Sunni scholar who reacted to the Mongol intrusion into the Islamic lands, is also cited as providing formative ideological influence.[35] His ideas were applied to twentieth-century corrupt rulers in the Muslim world, the "Modern Tartars,"[36] having planted "a seed of revolutionary violence in the heart of Islamic thought," according to Daniel Benjamin and Steven Simon.[37] Another interpretation is that this legacy of ideas matched well with material conditions that obtained at the domestic and international levels 700 years later. Did the seed need certain conditions to grow, or did the conditions suggest a response that required justification found in historical memory that gave depth and meaning to burgeoning revolutionary violence?

What makes radical Islamism so dangerous, according to Ian Buruma and Avishai Margalit, is its "synthesis of religious zealotry and modern ideology, of ancient bigotry and modern technology."[38] Sayyid Qutb – the

---

[33] Yvonne Yazbeck Haddad, "Islamist Perceptions of U.S. Policy in the Middle East," in *The Middle East and the United States*, 436.

[34] See Seyyed Vali Reza Nasr, *Mawdudi and the Making of Islamic Revivalism* (New York: Oxford University Press, 1996).

[35] See Michael S. Doran, "The Pragmatic Fanaticism of Al Qaeda: An Anatomy of Extremism in Middle Eastern Politics," *Political Science Quarterly* 117, no. 2 (Summer 2002): 179; and Emmanuel Sivan, *Radical Islam: Medieval Theology and Modern Politics*, Enlarged Edition (New Haven: Yale University Press, 1990), 99–100.

[36] See Gilles Kepel, *Muslim Extremism in Egypt: The Prophet and the Pharaoh*, trans. Jon Rothschild (Berkeley and Los Angeles: University of California Press, 1985), 194–95.

[37] Daniel Benjamin and Steven Simon, *The Age of Sacred Terror* (New York: Random House, 2002), 50.

[38] Buruma and Margalit see a parallel in the violence of the Khmer Rouge, which fused revolutionary Marxism with Khmer nationalism. Ian Buruma and Avishai Margalit, *Occidentalism: The West in the Eyes of Its Enemies* (New York: Penguin Press, 2004), 144.

The actors II: Islamic awakening and the modern Tartars   207

Muslim Brotherhood member and thinker most often associated with the ideological underpinnings of Al Qaeda – sought to develop an idealized Islamic society adapted to the modern world, selectively adopting aspects of it, particularly its technology.[39] John Gray associates Al Qaeda with modernity, and dismisses the "stupefying" cliché describing Al Qaeda as a "throwback to medieval times." Gray notes that Western observers often equate modernity with likeness, as "societies become more modern, so they become more alike."[40] Islamists, reformist or radical, recognized that the imitation that preceded them led only to subordination. Islamism was fundamentally an adaptive and transformative program, with atavistic elements that provided cohesion and a strong source of identification. Adaptation required removing traits that included values as well as organizational modes at the domestic level. In the eyes of some this program would not go far enough, requiring jettisoning the modes of international interaction that left the Muslim world in such a weakened state.

Observers have managed to place the mutant ideologies of previous revisionist powers into context, including identifying systemic roots for their advent and behaviors, but are less inclined to do so in this case. "One feels a temptation," Michael Doran writes, "to interpret the entire trajectory of Al Qaeda's career as a consequence of its zealotry."[41] Radical Islamism is only by degree more anti-modern than Nazism with its romantic evocation of Teutonic knights and a thousand-year Reich. Nazism was rich with historical allegory and medieval imagery, even dabbling in the occult. Radical Islamism reached back before the time of outside dominance and internal corrosion, when Muslims were on the offensive, Arab knights rather than Teutonic ones.[42] In both modern German and Islamic societies staggering defeats would lead some to ask, "what went wrong?" Fewer would look back prior to the humiliations at a more exalted past in order to model the future.[43] Still fewer would

---

[39] See Adnan A. Musallam, *From Secularism to Jihad: Sayyid Qutb and the Foundations of Radical Islam* (Westport, Conn.: Praeger, 2005). Concerning Qutb's attitude toward technology, see Roxanne L. Euben, *Enemy in the Mirror: Islamic Fundamentalism and the Limits of Modern Rationalism* (Princeton: Princeton University Press, 1999), 68–69.

[40] John Gray, *Al Qaeda and What It Means to Be Modern* (New York: New Press, 2005), 1–2. See also Roxanne L. Euben, "Premodern, Antimodern or Postmodern? Islamic and Western Critiques of Modernity," *The Review of Politics* 59, no. 3 (Summer 1997): 457; 459.

[41] Doran, "Pragmatic Fanaticism," 178.

[42] See Robert Koehl, "Feudal Aspects of National Socialism," *American Political Science Review* 54, no. 4. (December 1960): 921.

[43] See Bernard Lewis, *What Went Wrong? Western Impact and Middle East Response* (Oxford: Oxford University Press, 2002). Concerning evocations of a romantic past in Nazi

208   Al Qaeda's clash with civilization

advocate atrocities to bring this about as especially modern means made
these all too possible.

"Some stirred up Muslims": the mujahedin and the beginnings of Al Qaeda

Afghanistan after the Soviet invasion in December 1979 served as a
"crucible" that brought together Muslims and Islamists from all corners
of the Islamic world.[44] A number of factors drove the intervention,
defensive and offensive, international and domestic, material and ideological.[45] Among those was a fear of the encroachment of Islamic identity-
based resistance in the Soviet Central Asian republics.[46] The intervention
had the opposite effect, however, heightening those identities and fueling
resistance in Soviet-controlled territories.[47]

Pakistan was keenly attuned to the danger of a pro-Soviet regime to its
north, particularly one that had friendly ties with India and could serve
as "anvil to India's hammer."[48] The motives of Pakistan toward the
Afghan resistance extended beyond the immediate conflict. These ran-
ged from establishing a stable and friendly Afghanistan to provide a
buffer to Soviet pressure, to capping Pashtun aspirations and providing
strategic depth in a potential conflict with India.[49] For Saudi Arabia the
Soviet invasion was a boon, providing an opportunity to increase its
prestige as not only the custodian of the Holy Places but also a sponsor
of Islamic causes worldwide.[50] The United States was an increasingly
eager participant, first to bleed the Soviets, to give them their own

Germany, see Koehl, "Feudal Aspects of National Socialism," 923. Understandable
reluctance to make comparisons of Al Qaeda to Nazi Germany may be due to the popular
discourse of "Islamofascism." The comparison here is not so crude and essential. Rather,
it illustrates that each was characterized by modern elements but required atavistic fixes
to make sense of ultimately senseless political programs.

[44] Fawaz A. Gerges, *The Far Enemy: Why Jihad Went Global* (New York: Cambridge
University Press, 2005), 82.

[45] See Henry S. Bradsher, *Afghan Communism and Soviet Intervention* (Oxford: Oxford
University Press, 1999), 85–87.

[46] Odd Arne Westad, "The Road to Kabul: Soviet Policy on Afghanistan, 1978–1979," in
The Fall of Détente: Soviet–American Relations during the Carter Years, ed. Westad (Oslo:
Scandinavian University Press, 1997), 131.

[47] See Alexandre Bennigsen, "Afghanistan and the Muslims of the USSR," in *Afghanistan:
The Great Game Revisited*, ed. Rosanne Klass (New York: Freedom House, 1987),
292–94.

[48] Edward Luttwak, cited in A.Z. Hilali, *U.S.–Pakistan Relationship: Soviet Invasion of
Afghanistan* (Aldershot: Ashgate, 2005), 48.

[49] On Pakistani motivations for intervention, see Robert G. Wirsing, *Pakistan's Security
under Zia, 1977–1988* (New York: St. Martin's Press, 1991), 26–34.

[50] See Thomas Hegghammer, *Jihad in Saudi Arabia: Violence and Pan-Islamism since 1979*
(Cambridge: Cambridge University Press, 2010), 24–30.

The mujahedin and the beginnings of Al Qaeda 209

Vietnam.[51] This revenge motivation, though, was part of a broader geostrategic concern with Soviet encroachment and the surety of Middle East oil supplies. The invasion was a colossal blunder by the Soviets that the United States would not let go unpunished, hoping for an outright Soviet defeat, but short of that aiming to raise the costs of conquest.

From the earliest phases of the joint US–Pakistani–Saudi effort, it was clear the resistance fighters (*mujahedin*) would need help.[52] They were largely unskilled in battlefield tactics, though not lacking in valor. The aid provided everything from assault weapons, to sniper rifles for shooting Soviet officers in Kabul, to training in explosives and sabotage.[53] Saudi Arabia provided matching funds, as well as running intelligence operatives and supporting charities for refugees. The aid organizations also facilitated fighters who wanted to help the broader Islamic cause. Many of these were Islamists released from prisons, others were thrill seekers, and a portion viewed the Afghan war as a call to arms to defend Islam from the incursion of an atheist superpower. These migrant warriors would come to be called the Arab Afghans.[54]

Pakistan served as the "quartermaster," insulating the United States from direct involvement in the distribution of weapons and money.[55] This also left Pakistan in charge of distributing the spoils, including supporting mujahedin factions which held radical Islamist and often anti-American views. Gulbuddin Hekmatyar was a favorite of the Pakistani Inter-Services Intelligence (ISI). Saudi intelligence, along with the United States and ISI, also favored Jalaluddin Haqqani, described by a Western observer as the "Islamic brigade's [Arab Afghans] most

[51] Zbigniew Brzezinski made this intention explicit in an interview in 1998. See Zbigniew Brzezinski, "'Some Stirred-up Muslims': Reflections on Soviet Intervention in Afghanistan (1998)," in *The Middle East and Islamic World Reader*, ed. Marvin Gettleman and Stuart Schaar (New York: Grove Press, 2003), 274.

[52] See Steve Coll, *Ghost Wars: The Secret History of the CIA, Afghanistan, and Bin Laden, from the Soviet Invasion to September 10, 2001* (New York: Penguin Books, 2004), 51.

[53] There were serious misgivings about these programs, and "some on the NSC interagency committee regarded [the urban sabotage campaign] as outright terrorism." Coll, *Ghost Wars*, 137. See also Mahmood Mamdani, *Good Muslim, Bad Muslim: America, the Cold War, and the Roots of Terror* (New York: Doubleday, 2005), 138.

[54] The Arab Afghans, or Afghan Arabs, were not exclusively Arab, but the predominance of Arab financiers and organizers led to this appellation. On the participation of non-Afghan Muslims, see Barnett R. Rubin, "Arab Islamists in Afghanistan," in *Political Islam: Revolution, Radicalism, or Reform?* ed. John L. Esposito (Boulder, Colo.: Lynne Rienner, 1997), 179–202; and Anthony Hyman, "Arab Involvement in the Afghan War," *Beirut Review* 7 (Spring 1994): 73–89.

[55] On the role of Pakistan in supporting the mujahedin, see Rizwan Hussain, *Pakistan and the Emergence of Islamic Militancy in Afghanistan* (Aldershot: Ashgate, 2005), 116–17.

210   Al Qaeda's clash with civilization

celebrated Afghan patron."[56] Abdurrab Rasul Sayyaf was another Pashtun leader, one who held Salafist beliefs, who received significant support.[57]

Each of these leaders would forge a relationship with Osama bin Laden.[58] Bin Laden was making a name for himself supporting construction projects and with his limited, but successfully glorified, participation in battles. The military impact of the Arab Afghans was negligible, a fact often cited by those diminishing the role of outside support in aiding bin Laden's ascent. This argument follows that while the Saudis sought prestige in supporting a popular Islamic cause, and the Pakistanis wanted control and influence, the United States and CIA were concerned primarily with military effectiveness. Bin Laden and his activities were not even a blip in that regard. Assertions that the United States had a meaningful role in the rise of Al Qaeda, another line of defense goes, is "bad history" and "tortured and incorrect logic," since bin Laden and his cohort had their own motives for participating and their arrival predated US support.[59]

These arguments neglect several key considerations. First, military effectiveness was as much a result of the assistance as it was its trigger. In the Afghan political and social milieu, weapons and money enhanced the status of leaders enabling them to fight the Soviets more effectively. "In other words," Antonio Giustozzi writes, "the availability of guns and ammunition was one of the main factors behind the expansion of political influence in the Afghan countryside."[60] Second, military capability as a criterion would have also favored Ahmed Shah Massoud, an effective

---

[56] Anthony Davis, "Foreign Combatants in Afghanistan," *Jane's Intelligence Review* (July 1993): 329. The CIA viewed Haqqani as "perhaps the most impressive Pashtun field commander of the war." Coll, *Ghost Wars*, 202. ISI and CIA supplied an estimated 12,000 pounds of war matériel to the Haqqanis every year during the conflict with the Soviets. Vahid Brown and Don Rasser, *Fountainhead of Jihad: The Haqqani Nexus, 1973–2012* (New York: Oxford University Press, 2013), 5–6.

[57] See Coll, *Ghost Wars*, 118; 131.

[58] Haqqani has been described as "very close to Usama Bin Laden." See "Cracks in the Foundation: Leadership Schisms in Al-Qa'ida, 1989–2006," Combating Terrorism Center, Harmony Project, West Point, N.Y., 2007, 5. Peter Bergen writes that Hekmatyar and bin Laden "worked closely together." Peter Bergen, *Holy War, Inc.: Inside the Secret World of Osama bin Laden* (New York: Simon & Schuster, 2002), 74. For Sayyaf's ties to bin Laden, see Lawrence Wright, *The Looming Tower: Al-Qaeda and the Road to 9/11* (New York: Knopf, 2006), 100; 111–19. According to the 9/11 Commission report, Sayyaf also supported Khalid Shaykh Mohammed while he was in Afghanistan. *The 9/11 Commission Report: Final Report of the National Commission on Terrorist Attacks upon the United States* (New York: W.W. Norton: 2004), 146–49.

[59] Bruce Riedel, *What We Won: America's Secret War in Afghanistan, 1979–1989* (Washington, D.C.: Brookings Institution, 2014), 81.

[60] Antonio Giustozzi, *War, Politics, and Society in Afghanistan* (Washington, D.C.: Georgetown University Press, 2000), 246.

The mujahedin and the beginnings of Al Qaeda 211

military leader and fierce rival of Hekmatyar.[61] Massoud did not have the ties with ISI that Hekmatyar had, and was considered less reliable by some US officials.[62] While military effectiveness was a consideration, a degree of that was self-fulfilling and to a large extent the preferences were predicated on the interests of outside powers. Third, the military effectiveness defense overlooks the *indirect* but essential role assistance played in increasing the Arab Afghans' viability. The role of the Afghan patrons, particularly Sayyaf, Haqqani, and Hekmatyar, was critical in their development.[63] The contention that support for the Afghan patrons was insignificant since the Arab Afghans were self-motivated and began their struggle before the support began is itself historically and logically suspect. An argument that singly vests the group's fortunes and effectiveness in their agency, while overlooking the outside support's effects on their patron-shaped opportunity structure, does not hold up under much scrutiny.[64]

While denying aiding the rise of Al Qaeda, those who executed US policy also profess a level of triumphalism about the US role in defeating the Soviets in Afghanistan. These two positions are incompatible. The United States and its partners (Pakistan and Saudi Arabia) fostered conditions that enabled Al Qaeda to overcome the liability of newness and the especially severe constraints that face new entrants into the modern international system. Accusations of US *direct* contact with bin Laden are based exclusively on innuendo, with no convincing evidence provided.[65] Saudi influence over bin Laden, however, is openly

---

[61] Peter Bergen makes the observation that Massoud was a viable alternative in Bergen, *Holy War, Inc.*, 74.

[62] On US ambivalence toward Massoud, see Coll, *Ghost Wars*, 151. Sayyaf received an estimated 17–18 percent of the weapons distributed to the seven main mujahedin parties based in Pakistan. This is despite the fact that his group, according to Barnett Rubin, was among the smallest and "had too few commanders for them to figure significantly in any of the available data sets on commanders from the mid-1980s." Sayyaf's adherence to Salafist beliefs, and his command of Arabic, were helpful in his ability to attract wealthy Arab donors. See Rubin, "Arab Islamists," 193.

[63] Anthony Davis writes, "[t]he emergence of powerful Afghan patrons financially beholden to Arab [Saudi and Gulf State] financiers encouraged a growth in the numbers of foreigners never before possible." Davis, "Foreign Combatants," 330. Thomas Hegghammer points to the lack of evidence of direct support for the Arab Afghans from outside sponsors but this underestimates the indirect effects of their cultivation by Afghan patrons. Thomas Hegghammer, "The Rise of Muslim Foreign Fighters: Islam and the Globalization of Jihad," *International Security* 35, no. 3 (Winter 2010–11): 62.

[64] While arguing against US culpability, Bruce Riedel acknowledges the huge boost in legitimacy the germinal Al Qaeda received: "Their military contribution to the mujahedin's war was marginal, but the political implications of their actions and the legitimacy that they gained in the eyes of other jihadis was enormous." Riedel, *What We Won*, 86.

[65] Ahmed Rashid has bin Laden building the Khost tunnel complex with the CIA funding the project. Normally very thorough in documenting his reporting, Rashid provides not

212   Al Qaeda's clash with civilization

acknowledged, though whether he was an agent or there was a mere confluence of interests is unclear.[66] These considerations, combined with ample evidence that the United States was well aware of the Arab Afghans and their views, make "see no evil" defenses seem hollow.[67] The United States saw "evil," but was focused on a greater one.[68] Claims that the United States did not know that this aid was reaching groups with avidly anti-American agendas are unsustainable.[69] The United States knew these were dangerous characters with bad intentions, but did not consider it a priority since principals could not imagine this danger affecting US interests in any immediate regard or significant measure.

Cold War monomania, rather than a lack of information, is a more convincing explanation for these oversights: excessive focus rather than obliviousness.[70] Former US National Security Advisor Zbigniew Brzezinski in early 1998 still clung to the notion that the support was an "excellent idea," an unqualified success. "What is most important to the history of the world? The Taliban or the collapse of the Soviet empire? Some stirred-up Muslims or the liberation of Central Europe and the end of the cold war?"[71] It is not difficult to comprehend why the prioritization of national interests favored resistance to Soviet expansion over stemming some undefined threat of Islamist extremism.

one source for this passing observation. Ahmed Rashid, *Taliban: Militant Islam, Oil, and Fundamentalism in Central Asia* (New Haven: Yale University Press, 2001), 132.

[66] Barnett Rubin writes that "[u]ntil at least 1988, and perhaps as late as 1990, bin Laden worked closely with Prince Turki [Al-Faisal]," then Director General of the General Intelligence Directorate of Saudi Arabia. Rubin, "Arab Islamists," 189.

[67] For one example of US awareness and concern, see Digital National Security Archive, "Fifteen Non-Afghan Muslim Volunteers Die in Afghan Jihad," (Declassified) Confidential Cable, July 1, 1987.

[68] Between 1986 and 1990, US aid grew to $600 million a year, up from $30 million a year. These funds were matched by the Saudis. Rubin, "Arab Islamists," 188. Given the substantial investment in cash and matériel, the end user was more than a passing curiosity. Concerns about corruption and siphoning off arms shipments along the pipeline led to "all kinds of extraordinary measures to keep their allies honest. . . . [and] to see where [the arms] ultimately went." George Crile, *Charlie Wilson's War: The Extraordinary Story of the Largest Covert Operation in History* (New York: Atlantic Monthly Press, 2003), 355. See also Mary Anne Weaver, "Arming Afghans: A Tortuous Task," *Christian Science Monitor*, March 18, 1985, 1.

[69] The anti-American stance of these groups was no mystery: the contempt shown by Hekmatyar, who refused to meet President Reagan during a 1985 visit to the United States, was just one of the most glaring indicators.

[70] See Fawaz A. Gerges, *America and Political Islam: Clash of Cultures or Clash of Interests?* (Cambridge: Cambridge University Press, 1999), 71.

[71] Brzezinski, "Some Stirred-up Muslims," 274. Brzezinski later downplayed the significance of Al Qaeda, dismissing it as "a loose confederation of fundamentalist Muslim cells. . . . lacking any of the attributes of modern state power," and unworthy of affecting US calculations in any significant way. Zbigniew Brzezinski, *The Choice: Global Domination Or Global Leadership* (New York: Basic Books, 2004), 45–46.

The mujahedin and the beginnings of Al Qaeda   213

Nevertheless, Reuel Marc Gerecht's understated verdict in the summer of 2001 seems apt: "the CIA's record in Afghanistan and against Islamic radicalism shows few moments of operational foresight."[72] Reducing all US policy to the needs of the broader struggle with the Soviet Union ensured that a policy triumph would nurture the seed of a future policy failure.[73]

Estimates of the numbers of Arab Afghans vary. According to Ahmed Rashid, "[b]etween 1982 and 1992, some 35,000 Muslim radicals from 43 Islamic countries in the Middle East, North and East Africa, Central Asia and the Far East would pass their baptism under fire with the Afghan Mujaheddin."[74] The support of Afghan patrons enabled these groups to form units that by 1989 achieved tactical but not logistical independence from Afghan units.[75] The influx of foreign fighters necessitated record keeping and logistical operations. The most significant was *Maktab al-Khidamat* (MAK), or Office of Services, founded in the early 1980s by Abdullah Azzam, an influential Palestinian cleric, organizer, and recruiter.[76] Bin Laden was the main sponsor of MAK and also founded *Bayt al-Ansar* (House of Supporters) as well as *Ma'sadat al-Ansar* (Lion's Den of Supporters), a training camp outside of Jaji in Afghanistan.[77] There, the Arab Afghans would fight a widely mythologized battle that would help build bin Laden's reputation.

As the Soviets began their withdrawal, these efforts would culminate in the establishment of a new organization. Azzam identified the need for an Islamic vanguard to serve as leaders and protectors of the community of believers. It was in an editorial in *al-Jihad* magazine in April 1988 that Azzam wrote, "Every principle needs a vanguard to carry it forward that is willing, while integrating into society, to undertake difficult tasks and make tremendous sacrifices. . . . It is *al-qaeda al-sulbah* [the solid base]

---

[72] Reuel Marc Gerecht, "The Terrorists' Encyclopedia," *Middle East Quarterly* 8, no. 3 (Summer 2001): 84.

[73] John Prados comes to what seems like a reasonable if somewhat contradictory conclusion on the US role in the rise of Al Qaeda: "There *is* a relationship between these horrors and the CIA war in Afghanistan, not in terms of responsibility but certainly in the empowerment of the perpetrators. One can debate the degree but not the fact." John Prados, *Safe for Democracy: The Secret Wars of the CIA* (Chicago: Ivan R. Dee, 2006), 491.

[74] Rashid, *Taliban*, 130. Lower estimates, between 14,000 and 17,000, are found in Simon Reeve, *The New Jackals: Ramzi Yousef, Osama bin Laden, and the Future of Terrorism* (London: André Deutsch, 1999), 3; and James Bruce, "Arab Veterans of the Afghan War," *Jane's Intelligence Review* (April 1995): 175.

[75] Davis, "Foreign Combatants," 330.

[76] For an overview of MAK and Azzam's and bin Laden's roles, see R. Kim Cragin, "Early History of Al-Qa'ida," *The Historical Journal* 51, no. 4 (December 2008): 1047–52.

[77] Hegghammer, *Jihad in Saudi Arabia*, 42–44; Gerges, *Far Enemy*, 76. Bayt al-Ansar is discussed in Abdel Bari Atwan, *The Secret History of Al Qaeda* (Berkeley and Los Angeles: University of California Press, 2006), 44.

214   Al Qaeda's clash with civilization

that constitutes this vanguard for the hoped-for society."[78] In August 1988, bin Laden and several followers met to set up a new group whose goals would match those laid out by Azzam. Records of that meeting read: "The meeting ended on the evening of Saturday, 8/20. Work of Al Qaeda commenced on 9/10/1988."[79] A little over a year later the Soviets would complete their withdrawal and Azzam would be dead.

The importance of Afghanistan in forging the global jihadist movement in general and Al Qaeda in particular cannot be overstated.[80] "The West," Hilal Khashan argues, "in its desire to harass Soviet troops occupying Afghanistan, tinkered with the ecology of Islamic society and gave, unwittingly, a foundation of considerable strength to Islamic fundamentalism in the 1990s."[81] Zawahiri would emphasize the value of Afghanistan for military training and getting acquainted, as well as for consciousness raising of the need to defend against the enemies of Islam.[82] In addition to these material and motivational advantages, the war gave bin Laden legitimacy and moral authority – based in part on his exaggerated participation in fighting – that would be invaluable as he made strides toward directing the next stage of the struggle. Great and medium power support would not be enough to spur Al Qaeda to become a global organization. It did make it a possibility, though, one that would take a more profound change in the ecology of the international system to be realized.

Persia, Byzantium, and the myth of the superpowers

The decline and collapse of the Soviet Union, rather than the ascent of the United States after the Cold War, is the key structural change in the international system associated with the rise of Al Qaeda. Much of the attention concerning the systemic factors behind Al Qaeda's development and calculations has focused on US hegemony manifested in

---

[78] Philippe Migaux, "Al Qaeda," in *The History of Terrorism: From Antiquity to Al Qaeda*, ed. Gérard Chaliand and Arnaud Blin (Berkeley: University of California Press, 2007), 315.

[79] Peter Bergen, *The Osama bin Laden I Know: An Oral History of Al Qaeda's Leader* (New York: Free Press, 2006), 879–81.

[80] The fighters gained battlefield experience, and they "rubbed shoulders with like-minded militants from around the Muslim world, creating a truly global network." Peter Bergen and Alec Reynolds, "Blowback Revisited," *Foreign Affairs* 84, no. 6 (November–December 2005): 4.

[81] Hilal Khashan, "The New World Order and the Tempo of Militant Islam," *British Journal of Middle Eastern Studies* 24, no. 1 (May 1997): 5.

[82] Ayman al-Zawahiri, "Knights under the Prophet's Banner," in *His Own Words: A Translation of the Writings of Dr. Ayman al Zawahiri*, trans. Laura Mansfield (TLG Publications, 2006), 38.

Middle East military deployments from the 1991 Gulf War. These considerations were crucial, particularly in regard to a shift in Al Qaeda's strategy during the mid-1990s. Those explanations fall short, however, in exhausting the systemic developments and changes that propelled Al Qaeda from an accounting and logistics office to an organization bent on and capable of pursuing global violent jihad.

The invasion of Afghanistan culminated in the withdrawal and, shortly thereafter, collapse of the Soviet Union. Radical Islamists saw the collapse of the Soviet Union as a direct result of their triumph against the invading atheist power. Gilles Kepel observes how the nascent Al Qaeda's leaders and potential followers viewed the momentous changes:

[W]e must appreciate how profoundly the defeat of the Soviet army in Afghanistan in 1989 modified the international context in which Sunni Islamists operated. The jihadists persuaded themselves that they had been the primary cause of this unprecedented victory against a superpower.... This conviction led them to deploy their forces in a new global project guided simultaneously by a mythical reading of Islamic history and a subtle appreciation of the fault lines in America's global hegemony.[83]

This characterization captures both the effects of Soviet decline and collapse on propelling the movement, and the predominance of Islamic imagery and historical memory, distorted to the point of being fantasy, in interpreting structural changes.

The defeat of the Soviets would be central in deriving cues for the transformative opportunities in the international system. The Soviet Union's collapse would open up further possibilities for the expansion of a network of committed and, for the most part, like-minded jihadists, who were seeking new ways to apply their divinely attributed power.[84] Even before the completion of the Soviet withdrawal, but with victory clearly imminent, new purposes for the core of holy warriors were being conceived.[85] Well before the Gulf War, along with his mentor Azzam, "Bin Laden became convinced that the Afghan-Arab mujahideen could play a decisive role in a changing Middle East where the balance of power had shifted dramatically after the defeat of the Soviet forces in Afghanistan."[86] The Soviet Union's decline and collapse would be seen as an opportunity to propel the mujahedin army far afield to places like Bosnia, Somalia, Chechnya, and Central Asia. George Friedman

---

[83] Gilles Kepel, *The War for Muslim Minds: Islam and the West*, trans. Pascale Ghazaleh (Cambridge: Harvard University Press, 2004), 73.

[84] Gerges, *Far Enemy*, 57.   [85] Migaux, "Al Qaeda," 314–16.

[86] J. Millard Burr and Robert O. Collins, *Revolutionary Sudan: Hasan Al-Turabi and the Islamist State, 1989–2000* (Leiden: Brill, 2003), 67.

216   Al Qaeda's clash with civilization

captures both the magnitude and the rarity of the opening presented by Soviet decline:

The rare opportunity was the fall of the Soviet Union. Until then, the Islamic world had been divided between Soviet and American spheres of influence. Indeed, the border of the Soviet Union ran through the Islamic world. The Cold War between the United States and Soviet Union created a tense paralysis in that world, with movement and change being measured in decades and inches. Suddenly, everything that was once certain became uncertain. One half of the power equation was gone, and the other half, the United States, was at a loss as to what it meant. Bin Laden looked at the Soviet withdrawal from Afghanistan and saw a historical opening.[87]

The movement in these early years would achieve the momentum that would later be harnessed by bin Laden to target the West, particularly the sole remaining superpower. Having fighters go back to their home countries and also pursue opportunities for jihad in Central Asia were prominent parts of bin Laden's initial plans, according to Saudi journalist Jamal Khashoggi, who had direct access to him at this time.[88] Even prior to the Soviet withdrawal, the restiveness of the Central Asian republics was clear, inflamed in some measure due to the Afghanistan conflict.[89]

Historical memory often clouds their strategic calculations in Islamic imagery and terminology, but it should not conceal what is at the root of Al Qaeda's development and behavior, a desire for power and influence. "Like almost all Islamist activists," Mamoun Fandy writes, "bin Laden constructs an Islamic tradition and history in which Muslims confronted similar interests and threats and came out as winners." Furthermore, "[w]hile bin Laden's discourse is based on an interpretation of Islamic history, his power is derived from playing on the current social, economic, and political problems of the Muslim world."[90] Bin Laden and other Al Qaeda leaders evoked early Islamic victories over Persia and Byzantium. In this formulation the Soviet Union was Persia, defeated by the advancing Islamic armies, while the United States was Byzantium, a decrepit empire weaker than Persia and on the verge of collapse.[91]

---

[87] George Friedman, "War, Psychology, and Time," Stratfor.com, September 2007.

[88] Bergen, *Osama bin Laden I Know*, 85.   [89] See Coll, *Ghost Wars*, 103–4.

[90] Mamoun Fandy, *Saudi Arabia and the Politics of Dissent* (New York: St. Martin's Press, 1999), 190–91.

[91] One example of this metaphor is found in the 1996 declaration of war, where bin Laden threatens that US Defense Secretary William Perry will meet the same fate as his "grandfather" the Byzantine emperor "Nagfoor [Nikiforos I], the dog of the Romans." Osama bin Laden, "Ladenese Epistle: Declaration of War," in *Al Qaeda Now: Understanding Today's Terrorists*, ed. Karen J. Greenberg (New York: Cambridge University Press, 2005), 183.

Persia, Byzantium, and the myth of the superpowers 217

Afghanistan was Mecca and Medina with each era witnessing the raising of "the banner of Islam."[92]

It was the defeat of the new Persia rather than seeking the downfall of the new Byzantium that would initially propel the movement. The defeat of the Soviet Union, presented as the Arab mujahedin's own doing, was the key development in disabusing the "myth of the superpowers."[93] The ignominious departure of US troops from Somalia would seal this impression, making the United States seem like a "paper tiger."[94] But the prioritization of the United States as the primary adversary had not been clearly established in the early stages of Al Qaeda's development. In significant measure, it was the impression of US *weakness* as a world power rather than its strength that ultimately led to its targeting. Paradoxically, perceptions of the effects of predominant US influence on what they viewed as un-Islamic leaders in the Middle East also led Al Qaeda to make it the top priority.

Pressing the fight in their home countries and against the retreating Soviet Union were the key foci of the Arab Afghan army and the inchoate Al Qaeda. This all changed, according to most accounts, due to the Gulf War. Bin Laden saw Iraq's invasion of Kuwait and the threat to Saudi Arabia as a perfect opportunity to apply this force. Perfectly willing to work *within* the state system at that point, bin Laden pledged his army for the defense of the kingdom.[95] When he proposed sending fighters to deal with Communist South Yemen, his ancestral homeland, he was supported by the Saudis only to the point when his intent to establish an Islamic state became apparent.[96] Prior to this, bin Laden had been a nuisance but not a threat to the Saudi royal family. He advanced a largely reformist agenda along Islamist lines, but one with a partially veiled hint of potential violence.[97] Prior to the Gulf War, his efforts against the United States, which focused on the stand-by Islamist cause of US support for Israel, involved not-so-radical moves like a boycott of US goods.[98] It was his marginalization as much as perceptions of US

---

[92] Osama bin Laden, *Messages to the World: The Statements of Osama Bin Laden*, ed. Bruce Lawrence (London and New York: Verso, 2005), 85.

[93] See Raymond Ibrahim, trans. and ed., *The Al Qaeda Reader* (New York: Broadway Books, 2007), 260–65. Somalia is labeled by bin Laden the "most disgraceful case" as an exhibition of US weakness and irresolution. Bin Laden, "Ladenese Epistle," 179.

[94] Ibrahim, *Al Qaeda Reader*, 260. On bin Laden's interpretations of the weakness of the United States and its implications for international relations theory focusing on reputation, see Vaughn P. Shannon and Michael Dennis, "Militant Islam and the Futile Fight for Reputation," *Security Studies* 16, no. 2 (April–June 2007): 303–10.

[95] Jamal Khashoggi, "Osama Offered to Form Army to Challenge Saddam's Forces: Turki," *Arab News*, November 7, 2001.

[96] Burr and Collins, *Revolutionary Sudan*, 67.   [97] Fandy, *Saudi Arabia*, 181–82.

[98] Burr and Collins, *Revolutionary Sudan*, 67.

218   Al Qaeda's clash with civilization

occupation that aroused bin Laden's ire toward the regime and its key supporter.[99]

Al Qaeda's leaders saw themselves as thrust into the role of defenders of the faith due to US policies. Within the discourse of Al Qaeda's leadership, according to Faisal Devji, "the end of the Cold War is considered to have catapulted the jihad into assuming, inadvertently, the global role of the Soviet Union as the only force willing to resist the absolute dominance of the United States."[100] The Soviet Union's demise did lessen constraints on US power, but it was the power structure that began in the colonial era that was the target of Al Qaeda's wrath. Well into the 1990s, bin Laden still railed against such developments as artificially low oil prices and the mostly useless US weaponry provided to the Saudis. He saw these, with some merit, as artifacts of Western material dominance.[101] In addition to standard Islamist tenets such as divisions within the Islamic world being a source of weakness, bin Laden and other leaders saw the critical importance of material constraints in sustaining conditions of subordination.

As violent jihadist movements began to fail locally in the 1990s, the perceived dominance of the United States was touted as a cause. Bin Laden saw his thwarted efforts in Yemen and Saudi Arabia as a direct result not of his or his movement's failings but of the influence of the United States. As Gregory Gause observes, it was "only with their failure to remake the politics of the region that, in the mid-1990s, bin Laden began to focus his jihad explicitly against the United States."[102] Ejected from the kingdom, bin Laden would see Saudi Arabia as "a branch or agent of the U.S."[103] Zawahiri would highlight French assistance as a source of the failure of the Islamist movement in Algeria and blamed his failures in Egypt on the hidden hand of the United States in the region.[104]

The characterization of Al Qaeda as reacting primarily against a preponderance of US power, balancing really, has limited merit. It is more a case of an emerging revisionist power challenging a status quo power than a case of a defensive response to increased US hegemony.[105] At the same

[99] Bergen, *Osama bin Laden I Know*, 60; 110.
[100] Faisal Devji, *Landscapes of the Jihad: Militancy, Morality, Modernity* (Ithaca: Cornell University Press, 2005), 28.
[101] Fandy, *Saudi Arabia*, 189.
[102] F. Gregory Gause, "Saudi Arabia and the War on Terror," in *A Practical Guide to Winning the War on Terrorism*, ed. Adam Garfinkle (Stanford: Hoover Press, 2004), 92.
[103] Bin Laden quoted in Fandy, *Saudi Arabia*, 189.
[104] Foreign Broadcast Information Service, "Part 11 of New Book by Egyptian Islamic Jihad Leader," *Al-Sharq al-Awsat*, December 12, 2001.
[105] Pascal Vennesson casts Al Qaeda's confrontation with the United States in terms of Robert Gilpin's definition of hegemonic war. Pascal Vennesson, "Globalization and

Persia, Byzantium, and the myth of the superpowers 219

time, dominance structures embedded in the regional and international systems had prevented any serious challenge to Western interests and influence. Al Qaeda resisted hegemony to the extent that the United States perpetuated institutions and norms that prevented aspirants from challenging the regional and global order. But this was a long-standing hegemony, one independent of the new status of the United States as the sole superpower or having troops in the region.

While rooted in the international system, Al Qaeda's ascent was also built on myths. The myth of the superpowers saw the Arab Afghans as key agents of the Soviet Union's demise and depicted the United States as both omnipresent and impotent. Seeing the remaining superpower as weak but its regional influence determinative, bin Laden would press for targeting the "far enemy," the United States, rather than perceived un-Islamic, apostate regimes in the Muslim world, the "near enemy."[106] Bin Laden had studied the collapse of the Soviet Union and, according to former associate Abu Musab al-Suri, "was convinced that with the fall of the United States, all the components of the existing Arab and Islamic regimes would fall as well." The United States was the "head of the snake," which should be targeted rather than "its many tails."[107] Like so many aggressive revisionist powers, he would misread systemic cues, particularly those concerning US power and resolve.

"Rhetoric aside," Fawaz Gerges writes, "jihadis lacked unity and possessed separate local identities and differing goals."[108] In many respects, despite its internationalist pretensions, all jihad was local. This "unconsciously internalized nationalism" was evident in bin Laden as well, though he became the chief advocate for the internationalization of the movement.[109] While harboring deep resentment over the subordination of the Saudis to US power and influence, his local focus on Saudi Arabia and Yemen was not unlike his counterparts' parochial leanings.[110]

Al Qaeda's Challenge to American Unipolarity," in *How 9/11 Changed Our Ways of War*, ed. James Burk (Stanford: Stanford University Press, 2013), 232–60. That interpretation is largely consistent with the one offered here, particularly in the sense that Al Qaeda's response was of a challenger to the United States' perceived predominant influence, rather than a primarily defensive reaction to US presence.

[106] For an overview of the far enemy versus near enemy distinction and debate, see Steven Brooke, "Strategic Fissures: The Near and Far Enemy Debate," in *Self-Inflicted Wounds: Debates and Divisions within Al-Qa'ida and Its Periphery*, ed. Assaf Moghadam and Brian Fishman (West Point: Combating Terrorism Center, 2010), 45–68.

[107] Quoted in Bergen, *Osama bin Laden I Know*, 116.   [108] Gerges, *Far Enemy*, 99.

[109] Ibid., 141.

[110] A remarkable account from a captured document reveals the divergent views concerning the future of the Arab Afghans held by key figures, including Azzam, bin Laden, and probably Zawahiri, each professing their homelands (Palestine, Yemen, and Egypt, respectively) as having primary strategic importance. "Cracks in the Foundation," 9.

220   Al Qaeda's clash with civilization

The Gulf War and the continuing US presence allowed bin Laden to internationalize local struggles and provide an enemy that would help overcome those barely suppressed national identities.[111] In the view of radical Islamists, according to Gerges, the United States had "tipped the balance of power in favor of secular regimes by providing them with decisive political and logistical support."[112] This material focus was not sufficient to stir the hearts of followers. Bin Laden tapped Ibn Taymiyya for justification in attacking the far enemy, just as others had done to justify focusing on the near enemy.[113] The talent for historical allusion gave false temporal depth to a strategy borne of immediate pragmatic necessity. By targeting the United States (and adding the canard of a US–Israel conglomerate) bin Laden fused three of four potential emphases that had been advocated by jihadist leaders – attacking the far enemy, facilitating the overthrow of the near enemy, and defending Muslims seen as under siege worldwide – into one coherent strategy. The fourth goal of liberating Central Asia would wait for the establishment of an Islamic state in the central Islamic lands, part of a general expansion that would placate Zawahiri's continuing fixation on Egypt. Bin Laden's charismatic authority, which was not universally appreciated in jihadist circles, was not the only factor instrumental in his accession. It was also his ability to frame systemic developments and forces, outmaneuver internal rivals, and infuse their goals and actions with radical Islamist symbolism that resulted in his leadership position.[114]

Many within the broader radical Islamist camp thought confrontation with the United States would be suicidal in the strategic sense, but the course had been set. In an interview, Saudi resistance leader Saad al-Faqih characterized this decisive shift:

[111] Michael Doran emphasizes the importance of targeting the United States in overcoming division among radical Islamists in Michael S. Doran, "Somebody Else's Civil War: Ideology, Rage, and the Assault on America," in *How Did This Happen? Terrorism and the New War*, ed. James F. Hoge, Jr. and Gideon Rose (New York: Public Affairs, 2001), 47.

[112] Fawaz A. Gerges, "The Tragedy of Arab-American Relations," *Christian Science Monitor*, September 18, 2001. The 1990–1991 confrontation with Iraq was characterized in the 1998 "Declaration of the World Islamic Front Jihad against the Jews and the Crusaders" as part of a broader US effort "to fragment all the states of the region such as Iraq, Saudi Arabia, Egypt, and Sudan into paper statelets and through their disunion and weakness to guarantee Israel's survival and the continuation of the brutal crusade occupation of the [Arabian] peninsula." Bergen, *Osama bin Laden I Know*, 196.

[113] Bin Laden, "Ladenese Epistle," 168.

[114] These rivals included Zawahiri (chief proponent of the near enemy strategy), Azzam (who had advocated defending Muslims "under siege," including Palestine), and (lesser known in the West) Ibn al-Khattab, whose focus was on liberating former Soviet Central Asia and Chechnya, and who by the latter half of the 1990s "not only competed on equal footing but assembled a more powerful contingent of jihadis than [bin Laden]." Gerges, *Far Enemy*, 58.

Emulation, imagination, and power 221

SF: [I]n late 1997 they [bin Laden and Zawahiri] decided to form a completely new strategy based on global and cosmic confrontation with America....

(Q): What do you mean by 'cosmic'?

SF: Global and full scale confrontation! They decided to conduct their actions relying not on their own resources but by manipulating those of their enemies. In short they decided to convert their enemy into a powerful tool for their own use.[115]

Confrontation with the United States would not be on its own terms, but would be with its own means, adapted and reconfigured for a fierce struggle.

The Manhattan Raid: emulation, imagination, and power

The decline of the Soviet Union and the ascent of the United States are two of the three primary systemic changes that helped bring Al Qaeda about and shape its strategy, respectively. Globalization is another oft-cited systemic cause accounting for Al Qaeda's existence.[116] Peter Bergen associates the end of the Cold War and the acceleration of globalization as allowing for more open borders, enabling Al Qaeda to "flourish."[117] The 9/11 Commission ruefully concluded that Al Qaeda was "more globalized than we were."[118] The end of the bipolar system, Barry Buzan notes, resulted in the expansion of the features of globalization beyond the Western world, including "the spread of communication capacity and access to it, the increasing organization of production, trade and finance on a global scale, and the deterritorialization of many aspects of human activity and identity."[119] Each of these features has had a highly significant impact on the development of Al Qaeda. But when conceiving of the effects of globalization, one should avoid casting it as a root cause. Globalization is better understood as a facilitating condition than as a generative systemic cause, affecting the opportunity structure (the relationship between organizational goals and available means) that was present at the time when systemic structural change (Soviet decline) made expansion a possibility. Globalization did allow certain organizational modes and behaviors to be viable on a much broader scale than

---

[115] Mahan Abedin, "The Essence of Al Qaeda: An Interview with Saad al-Faqih," Jamestown Foundation, *Spotlight on Terror* 2, no. 2, February 5, 2004.

[116] See Vennesson, "Globalization." [117] Bergen, *Holy War, Inc.*, 20.

[118] *9/11 Commission Report*, 340.

[119] Barry Buzan, *The United States and the Great Powers: World Politics in the Twenty-First Century* (Cambridge: Polity Press, 2004), 97.

222   Al Qaeda's clash with civilization

previously possible. This helps to explain how Al Qaeda has succeeded in defying systemic constraints presented by great power challengers despite vast disparities in material capabilities.

The most germane aspect of globalization in understanding Al Qaeda's survival is the increase in interaction capacity.[120] The acceleration of communications, using the term broadly to include transportation, has occurred steadily since the advent of the industrial revolution. State forms of social organization have been able to harness these changes, including in the generation of large-scale violence. They had succeeded in this to the point of having an effective monopoly; other smaller-scale violent actors existed but could not be viable on a global systemic scale. But interaction capacity continued to increase in large part due to the ability of liberal states to expand and maintain global flows, and to the technological competition among great powers. Diffusion of technologies combined with the ability to conceal movements in a system of ever-increasing interactions. This heightened interaction loosened the effective monopoly on violence as different combinatorial possibilities and organizational pathways emerged.

The opportunity structure present at this particular ecological moment affected the organizational potentialities and behaviors of Al Qaeda. Bin Laden perceived that these permissive conditions would enable an assault on US interests, while others feared that such a confrontation was a dangerous folly. He began his peregrinations following his expulsion from Saudi Arabia, first finding refuge in Sudan and later settling in Afghanistan. While there, Al Qaeda's leadership devised and solicited attack plans that would exploit the heightened interaction capacity of the globalized international system. Bucking the system and increasing their prospects for survival, Al Qaeda's leaders recognized they could take advantage of circumstances of both very high interaction capacity (urbanized areas) and very low interaction capacity (lightly governed and less accessible areas).[121] Ensconcing in inaccessible areas constitutes a form

---

[120] On interaction capacity, see Barry Buzan, Charles Jones, and Richard Little, *The Logic of Anarchy: Neorealism to Structural Realism* (New York: Columbia University Press, 1993), 66–80. For the application of the concept to means of violence, or "violence interaction capacity," see Daniel H. Deudney, "Regrounding Realism: Anarchy, Security, and Changing Material Contexts," *Security Studies* 10, no. 1 (Fall 2000): 1–42.

[121] Portions of a purported training manual for Al Qaeda operatives were released to the public shortly after the 9/11 attacks. There is a strong emphasis on concealment. See *Military Studies in the Jihad against the Tyrants: The Al-Qaeda Training Manual*, ed. Jerrold M. Post (Maxwell Air Force Base, Ala.: USAF Counterproliferation Center, 2004), 27; 31–38. On the conditions that allow for safe haven (and hiding) including both the remote, inaccessible "cracks in the system" and cities, such as London, where militants "hide in plain sight," see Michael A. Innes, "Cracks in the System: Sanctuary

Emulation, imagination, and power   223

of hiding, while operating in urban environments necessitates a high level of dissimulation.

The exploitation of the polymorphic possibilities of the late twentieth-century international system made Al Qaeda a dangerous and disruptive presence. The opportunity structure of the system would not allow the group to assume the state form but presented other avenues for organization and competition. Al Qaeda's development at this particular time made it *possible* to avert the state form that had been imposed by the constraints of the contemporary international system. That system had previously made imitation, extinction, or irrelevance the most plausible options for emerging actors.

Al Qaeda's deception is also necessitated by its precarious condition. While its strategic intentions have often been telegraphed, with overt declarations of war, its operational and tactical intentions have remained mostly concealed.[122] This behavior, like hiding and dissimulation, is rooted in the necessity for Al Qaeda to adapt to the prevailing conditions of the international system. Clandestine operatives are the exception among the major powers, reserved for special operations and espionage. Dissimulation as routine was expressed in an interview of key 9/11 figure Ramzi Binalshibh, who explained that "the operation of adopting a security cover is in essence a process aimed at deceiving the security services generally and mystifying the people around [the operative]."[123] Among the final instructions for the 9/11 hijackers was to pray "for victory and strength and perspicuous triumph, and the easing of our task, and concealment."[124]

The behavior of dissimulation is occasionally tied by observers to the Islamic tenet of *taqiyya*, "the process of hiding one's true belief under

---

and Terrorism after 9/11," in *Denial of Sanctuary: Understanding Terrorist Safe Havens*, ed. Innes (Westport, Conn.: Praeger Security International, 2007), 1–20.

[122] Devin Jessee describes how Al Qaeda uses an array of techniques of denial (preventing access to information) and deception (providing false and misleading information) at the operational and tactical levels in order to support its strategic goals. Devin D. Jessee, "Tactical Means, Strategic Ends: Al Qaeda's Use of Denial and Deception," *Terrorism and Political Violence* 18, no. 3 (Fall 2006): 367–88. See also Gaetano J. Ilardi, "The 9/11 Attacks: A Study of Al Qaeda's Use of Intelligence and Counterintelligence," *Studies in Conflict & Terrorism* 32, no. 3 (March 2009): 171–87.

[123] Quoted in Joel Mowbray, "How They Did It. An 'Evil One' Confesses, and Boasts," *National Review* 54, no. 24 (December 2002): 37.

[124] Terry McDermott, *Perfect Soldiers: The Hijackers, Who They Were, Why They Did It* (New York: Harper Collins, 2005), 249. There are some doubts as to the authenticity of the instructions. "Despite all the doubts and uncertainties," Hans Kippenberg writes, "qualified attempts have been made to take the document seriously." Hans G. Kippenberg, "'Consider That It Is a Raid on the Path of God': The Spiritual Manual of the Attackers of 9/11," *Numen* 52, no. 1 (January 2005): 32–34.

224   Al Qaeda's clash with civilization

duress."[125] This attribution of causal significance by mere resemblance is faulty.[126] Dissimulation is no more a manifestation of an Islamic principle than tit-for-tat strategies are an expression of the Golden Rule. Where it is effective and necessary it is employed, not due to its presence in some form somewhere in the history of Islamic thought. The resort to purportedly Islamic tenets to grasp an often inscrutable enemy is understandable, especially given the thicket of religious imagery and rhetoric erected by its members. It also allows observers repulsed by their actions to place them in a normative space – of a "hijacked" Islam – that distances them from the standard awfulness of politically motivated violence, or potentially to malign Islam as a whole. Al Qaeda's employment of religious precepts is shallow, opportunistic, and fraudulent. The group exhibits what Doran astutely labeled a "pragmatic fanaticism," standing "for the principle that Islamic law is the only proper foundation for social and political life," but disregarding that law "with impunity."[127] These contortions are no more evident than in an article by now imprisoned Al Qaeda spokesman Suleiman Abu Geith, called "In the Shadow of the Lances."[128] There, any inkling of meaningful association with Islamic tradition vanishes, as the author justifies the killing of 4 million Americans (of these 2 million children) with chemical or biological weapons, based on a trumped-up interpretation of Islamic law that emphasizes reciprocity.

Coupled with the unimaginable nature of the destruction of the attacks of September 11 was the inconceivability of the attacks themselves. Using advanced industrial society's means against it, Al Qaeda's planners accomplished a convolution and involution of military-technical affairs, which may indeed constitute a revolution. An abundance of imagination on the part of our adversary, more so than constraints on our own imagination, best explains the stunning success and surprise, which upended the ontological security of a society unaccustomed to the

---

[125] Richard H. Shultz and Ruth M. Beitler, "Tactical Deception and Strategic Surprise in Al-Qai'da's Operations," *Middle East Review of International Affairs* 8, no. 2 (June 2004): 58. See also Devji, *Landscapes of the Jihad*, 18.

[126] Taqiyya, according to the *Encyclopaedia of Islam*, is the "'action of covering, dissimulation,' as opposed to *idha'a* 'revealing, spreading information,' [and] denotes dispensing with the ordinances of religion in cases of constraint and when there is a possibility of harm." R. Strothmann-Moktar Djebli, "Takiyya (a.)," *Encyclopaedia of Islam Online*, ed. P. Bearman, et al., Brill Online, 2006. The use of dissimulation across a span of Mediterranean history and traditions casts doubts on the distinct cultural origins of the practice. See Hans G. Kippenberg and Guy G. Strousma, ed., *Secrecy and Concealment: Studies in the History of Mediterranean and Near Eastern Religions* (Leiden: Brill, 1995).

[127] Doran, "Pragmatic Fanaticism," 177.

[128] Excerpts were published as Suleiman Abu Geith, "'Why We Fight America': Al-Qa'ida Spokesman Explains September 11 and Declares Intentions to Kill 4 Million Americans with Weapons of Mass Destruction," *MEMRI Special Dispatch Series*, no. 388, June 12, 2002.

Emulation, imagination, and power 225

intimacy of an unfamiliar violence.[129] Al Qaeda's leaders exploit the interaction capacity in the system to evade and antagonize the system's chief guardians and claimed benefactors. The relative power of imagination may not completely or even nearly compensate for material advantages, but it is in certain circumstances (particularly uncertain ones) an element of overall power. In international politics established powers bolster reputation by displaying capabilities. For Al Qaeda reputation is enhanced mostly by hiding capabilities, with occasional demonstrations, hinting at the possibilities without revealing probabilities. Uncertainty empowers the weak as it bedevils the strong.

The result was an organizational structure and interaction in space that confounded the system. It also confounded observers, who had not seen such levels of violence originate from such a modest-seeming form. In order to compensate for its vulnerability and marginal status, its behaviors have emphasized concealment, including hiding, deception, and dissimulation. These are not just adjunct behaviors, as they are for great powers, but essential attributes shaping their interactions with the rest of the system. Terror is a byproduct of enhanced systemic uncertainty, a condition that Al Qaeda's leaders fully understand and exploit. Beyond this fundamental condition some of their deviant behaviors (including beheadings) were intended to intimidate their enemies and rally followers, acting in a sense as depraved force multipliers, while others (killing "apostate" Muslims and innocents) were justified by some as a purifying necessity.[130] These actions would take on an increasingly ritual and decreasingly instrumental character. As the Mongols did, Al Qaeda's overall leaders began to recognize when excesses did not advance their strategic goals, instructing affiliates to refrain with the aim of gaining popular support.[131]

The difficulties these nefarious acts have brought about was made clear in a communication between Al Qaeda senior leaders and Abu Musab al-Zarqawi, late leader of Al Qaeda in Iraq, which chided the brutality of Zarqawi's tactics including beheadings and the slaughter of

---

[129] The *9/11 Commission Report* (339) cited a failure of imagination along with failures in capabilities, policy, and management. See Daniel L. Byman, "Strategic Surprise and the September 11 Attacks," *Annual Review of Political Science* 8 (2005): 145–70. Indeed, US analysts did fall short in anticipating the potential targets and means, but this ought not obscure the feat of imaginative destruction Al Qaeda leaders and operatives achieved.

[130] On the range of explanations behind jihadist employment of beheadings, see Pete Lentini and Muhammad Bakashmar, "Jihadist Beheading: A Convergence of Technology, Theology, and Teleology?" *Studies in Conflict & Terrorism* 30, no. 4 (April 2007): 303–25.

[131] See Karen DeYoung, "Letter Gives Glimpse of Al-Qaeda's Leadership," *Washington Post*, October 2, 2006.

226   Al Qaeda's clash with civilization

Muslims. While motivation and unity among core followers may have been achieved, these actions have revolted the rest of the world, including portions of the Muslim world they would have to win over to realize their atavistic designs. The use of beheading by this now independent offshoot, the Islamic State of Iraq and Syria (ISIS), has revivified segments of the jihadist movement and amplified attention from Western publics. Its effects on their long-term prospects for local governance based on anything other than intimidation, however, remain likely to be profoundly negative.

Al Qaeda's leaders recognize their distinct advantage in conditions of uncertainty. Indeed, considerable uncertainty exists concerning the nature of the organization and its ability to adapt to increased constraints since 2001. There has been a devolution of initiative and a greater emphasis on the personal authority of Al Qaeda's leadership, as regional affiliates and fellow travelers conduct missions in the name of the organization. Al Qaeda's central leadership, though, retained significant operational influence in a number of attacks, most notably the London transit bombings of July 2005 and the 2006 transatlantic airline plot.[132] The July 2007 US National Intelligence Estimate assessed that Al Qaeda had protected or reconstituted its leadership and safe haven in Pakistan, allowing the organization to plan and train for attacks.[133] Al Qaeda has suffered a slew of losses since that time, and the longevity of its leadership cadre under severe pressure from the United States and its allies remains precarious and increasingly untenable.

Daniel Byman takes notice of these dimming prospects but notes a "silver lining" for Al Qaeda in its regional affiliates, while documenting the complexities and strains in their relationships with the central leadership.[134] It is possible, as in the case of the Syrian wing of the Nizari Ismailis, who first exhibited autonomy but eventually outlived their originators, that Al Qaeda's affiliates will assume the mantle of authority as its central leadership fades. Perhaps like its other predecessor, the Mongols, it will prove inviable in its more centralized form and devolve

---

[132] See Bruce Hoffman, "Radicalization and Subversion: Al Qaeda and the 7 July 2005 Bombings and the 2006 Airline Bombing Plot," *Studies in Conflict & Terrorism* 32, no. 12 (December 2009): 1100–16.

[133] Barbara Sude, "Al-Qaeda Central: An Assessment of the Threat Posed by the Terrorist Group Headquartered on the Afghanistan–Pakistan Border," Counterterrorism Strategy Initiative Policy Paper, New America Foundation, February 2010, 1.

[134] Daniel L. Byman, "Breaking the Bonds between Al-Qa'ida and Its Affiliate Organizations," Saban Center at Brookings Analysis Paper, No. 27, August 2012. See also Byman, "Buddies or Burdens? Understanding the Al Qaeda Relationship with Its Affiliate Organizations," *Security Studies* 23, no. 3 (August 2014): 431–70, in which he concludes that their relationships while beneficial in some ways represent a net loss for Al Qaeda due to organizational problems.

Categorization and concealment   227

into its regional namesakes, presenting a potent but distinct menace. The emergence of ISIS, riding its wave of energized brutality, has raised fears of an even less restrained Al Qaeda competitor or successor. At the same time, individuals motivated by Al Qaeda's or a related ideology present a less potent but nevertheless irksome manifestation of violence.[135] A purely symbolic or motivational role would raise questions about Al Qaeda's "actorhood" in an analytic sense, but we have yet to reach that state. The further fracturing or devolution to affiliates or individuals, indeed, aggravates the conditions of uncertainty as the potential sources of violence increase, while our fixity on the conceptual identity of the actors and their relationships decrease. Gains in physical and ontological security have accrued over time as our understanding of Al Qaeda and the threat it poses expanded, diminishing but not eliminating the uncertainty their presence creates. Ultimately, though, as potential further decline and fragmentation occur, we may end up as, or more, uncertain concerning the waning of the threat from Al Qaeda as we were of its waxing. The rise of ISIS should also give pause not only given that it was previously left for dead by many observers, but also due to the challenges it poses for categorizing the enemy: as a successor, splinter group, or entity unto its own with organizational and ideational characteristics that distinguish it from its forebear.[136]

Permissible stratagems: categorization and concealment

When vilifying its enemies Al Qaeda has consistently mentioned international organizations, seeing them as reflections of the dominant Western powers and their interests. This interpretation is very much in line with a neorealist understanding of the role of norms and rules in the international system. It also comports with some English School theorists who saw in the international reaction after September 11 a reflection of the material power in the system, acting as a brake on the development of international society. Andrew Hurrell writes of the struggle with Al Qaeda and terrorism that "there remains a deep tension between the constitutionalist order represented by international law and institutions and the

---

[135] See Bruce Hoffman, "American Jihad," *The National Interest* 107 (May–June 2010): 17–27.

[136] This typological uncertainty was illustrated by debates over the justification to use force against ISIS by the Obama administration, which cited ISIS leadership's claim to be "the true inheritor of Usama bin Laden's legacy" in order to establish legal continuity between the groups. See Jacob Gershman, "Obama's Fight against ISIS Triggers Debate over War Powers," *Wall Street Journal, Law Blog*, September 11, 2014.

228   Al Qaeda's clash with civilization

power political structures on which patterned political order rests – in this case the unipolar distribution of power."[137] While this observation made shortly after the attacks has held true, there are processes underway that have advanced the development of international society. The predominant power of the United States has been a determining factor in both the institutionalization and erosion of certain norms. Processes of categorization and legitimation have also been underway, reflecting not solely the dominant power of a unipolar system but also the dominant powers in terms of their organization and behavior as states.

Following the attacks, in the United Nations there was a rapid but limited response in the form of Resolution 1373, which "established new legal obligations on states to take specific measures and to cooperate against terrorism."[138] These obligations involved a range of measures to block terrorist activity and enhance information sharing. A previous resolution (1267) against the Taliban regime, made after the 1998 Africa embassy bombings, demanded the extradition of bin Laden,[139] and emplaced mechanisms to enforce sanctions against Al Qaeda, their associates, and the Taliban. These have had mixed success and have been hampered by a lack of cooperation by some member states.[140] Defenders of the UN response have cited its condemnation of the attacks in addition to debates and "eloquent statements."[141]

Much of what limited a more affirmative stance against Al Qaeda was rooted in fundamental issues of categorization. General Assembly resolutions 2621 and 2708 had long declared the right of resistance to colonial rule, including "by all the necessary means."[142] On September 28, 2001, the UN Commission on Human Rights expressed that "they share in the

[137] Andrew Hurrell, "'There Are No Rules' (George W. Bush): International Order after September 11," *International Relations* 16, no. 2 (August 2002): 202.

[138] Ved P. Nanda, "Terrorism, International Law, and International Organizations," in *Law in the War on International Terrorism*, ed. Nanda (Ardsley, N.Y.: Transaction Publishers, 2005), 10–11.

[139] Christopher Greenwood, "International Law and the 'War against Terrorism,'" *International Affairs* 78, no. 2 (April 2002): 303–4. See also Eric Rosand, "The Security Council's Efforts to Monitor the Implementation of Al Qaeda/Taliban Sanctions," *The American Journal of International Law* 98, no. 4 (October 2004): 745–63.

[140] Eric Rosand and Alistair Millar, "Strengthening International Law and Global Implementation," in *Uniting against Terror: Cooperative Nonmilitary Responses to the Global Terrorist Threat*, ed. David Cortright and George A. Lopez (Cambridge: MIT Press, 2007), 57–58. See also Péter Kovács, "The United Nations in the Fight against International Terrorism," in *Law in the War on International Terrorism*, 41–53.

[141] Jayantha Dhanapala, "The United Nations' Response to 9/11," *Terrorism and Political Violence* 17, nos. 1–2 (Winter 2005): 17–23.

[142] Bardo Fassbender, "The UN Security Council and International Terrorism," in *Enforcing International Law Norms against Terrorism*, ed. Andrea Bianchi (Oxford: Hart Publishing, 2004), 97.

Categorization and concealment 229

unequivocal condemnation of terrorism," noting, equivocally, the "dangers inherent in the indiscriminate use of the term 'terrorism,' and the resulting new categories of discrimination."[143] Shortcomings in the UN Security Council counterterrorism efforts have been attributed to "the proliferation of overlapping bodies and mandates," while the council itself acknowledged that its counterterrorism arms "were established in different historical contexts and with different aims."[144] Robert Keohane observed not long after the attacks that "[c]learly, the UN was not to be the director of the anti-terror coalition, but was expected to become a source of *collective legitimation* for American actions."[145]

While the conceptual muddle, organizational shortcomings, and state interests limited the UN response, a focus of the United States was to increase its freedom of action by the inclusion of actors under the rubric of terrorism. The United States had not acknowledged a major role for Al Qaeda in the Chechnya conflict prior to September 11, but did so in part due to Russian cooperation in the military operations in Afghanistan.[146] Similarly, Uighur militants (of the East Turkestan Islamic Movement) and other regionally focused groups (Jaish-e-Mohammed, Lashkar-e-Tayyiba) were added to the US State Department list of foreign terrorist organizations not long after the attacks.[147] Apart from the practical matters associated with enforcing sanctions and other legal mechanisms, this association with Al Qaeda provides a normative anchor that dilutes any claims of the actors' legitimacy. In February 2002, US National Security Advisor Condoleezza Rice emphasized the lack of a normative distinction among terrorist groups: "The United States has made clear to leaders on every continent that there is no such thing as a good terrorist and a bad terrorist. You cannot condemn Al Qaeda and hug Hamas."[148] Threat conflation allowed homogenization of the terrorist threat with Al

---

[143] UN Office of the High Commissioner for Human Rights, "Terrorism and Human Rights," accessed January 8, 2015, www2.ohchr.org/English/issues/terrorism. See also Ben Saul, *Defining Terrorism in International Law* (Oxford: Oxford University Press, 2006), 320.

[144] Rosand and Millar, "Strengthening International Law," 62–63.

[145] Robert O. Keohane, "The Public Delegitimation of Terrorism and Coalitional Politics," in *Worlds in Collision: Terror and the Future of Global Order*, ed. Ken Booth and Tim Dunne (Basingstoke: Palgrave Macmillan, 2002), 144.

[146] James Dao and Patrick E. Tyler, "A Nation Challenged: The Alliance," *New York Times*, September 27, 2001.

[147] See Erik Eckholm, "U.S. Labeling of Group in China as Terrorist Is Criticized," *New York Times*, September 13, 2002; and Sebastian Rotella, "On the Trail of Pakistani Terror Group's Elusive Mastermind behind the Mumbai Siege," *Washington Post*, November 14, 2010.

[148] "Remarks by the National Security Advisor Condoleezza Rice to the Conservative Political Action Conference," The White House, Office of the Press Secretary, February 2, 2002.

230   Al Qaeda's clash with civilization

Qaeda as *primus inter pares*. Existing norms precluded the need for new ones. What was needed was generalization by typification and universalization of application.

The categorization of "unlawful enemy combatants" was intended to legitimize actions against them that would otherwise be contrary to international and domestic law. The shift was to place these new types of enemies into existing categories rather than craft new ones that adequately captured their novelty. Justifying skirting the Geneva Convention Relative to the Treatment of Prisoners of War, President Bush wrote in a memo: "[T]he war against terrorism ushers in a new paradigm, one in which groups with broad, international reach commit horrific acts against innocent civilians, sometimes with the direct support of states. Our Nation recognizes that this new paradigm – ushered in not by us, but by terrorists – requires new thinking in the law of war."[149] A US Department of Defense working group on detainee interrogations in 2003 justified violating the Geneva Convention due to the "unique nature of the war on terrorism in which the enemy covertly attacks innocent civilian populations without warning."[150] The clandestine nature of the enemy, it was argued, required extreme measures (including torture) to obtain information necessary to counteract otherwise unmanageable uncertainty.[151]

Efforts by the United States to try detainees under normative principles derived from experiences with previous enemies have resulted in a clash between domestic legal guidelines and international law concerning armed conflict. At times this has favored international norms over efforts to engineer norms for enforcing the proper conduct of violence. The deliberations of the US military commissions contain strenuous efforts to distinguish Al Qaeda detainees in ways that make them subject to trial for violations of international laws of war. The arguments seek to highlight acts of war considered aberrant in contrast to "permissible stratagems," those lacking treachery and perfidy, and absent measures that

---

[149] Memorandum from the President of the United States, to the Vice President, et al., "Regarding the Humane Treatment of Al Qaeda and Taliban Detainees," February 7, 2002.

[150] "Working Group Report on Detainee Interrogations in the Global War on Terrorism," in *The Torture Papers: The Road to Abu Ghraib*, ed. Karen J. Greenberg and Joshua L. Dratel (Cambridge: Cambridge University Press, 2005), 287.

[151] James Burk sums up what is overlooked in debates over the use of the term "torture" versus its legalistic euphemisms, concluding that "states that torture or otherwise engage in cruel, inhuman, or degrading treatment cause harm to those they hold in captivity and interrogate with coercive techniques, to those who implement or authorize the policy, to the institutions through which the practice of torture is carried out, and ultimately to themselves." James Burk, "Torture, Harm, and the Prospect of Moral Repair," in *How 9/11 Changed Our Ways of War*, 157.

Categorization and concealment 231

conceal identity.[152] This included the legal submission of the "Declaration of the World Islamic Front for Jihad against the Jews and the Crusaders" – imploring followers to "lie in wait for them in every stratagem" – to further establish the essential nature of Al Qaeda as contrary to the just conduct of war.[153]

Citing the Lieber Code, US prosecutors argued that the defendants were guilty of a war crime in their conduct of terrorism, contending that "[m]odern day terrorists, including those that fight for Al Qaeda, can trace their lineage to guerrillas that Lieber ... emphatically condemned."[154] They cite the Lieber Code's association of guerrilla violence and "the idea of intentional destruction for the sake of destruction," and the small size of the groups, "being but slight and the leader utterly dependent on the band, allowing little discipline to be enforced."[155] This depiction is not far from Voltaire's dismissal of the Assassins as "wretched little people of mountaineers" and little more than "banditti." It harkens even further back to the manipulation of norms that distanced Nizari actions from rightful rebellion in Islamic jurisprudence based, in part, on their size, labeling them "the little gang of Batinites."

Treachery and perfidy are the distinguishing factors between acceptable ruses that legitimately "mystify" the enemy and those that constitute violations.[156] Cloaking one's capabilities and intentions is considered legitimate while concealing one's identity and true nature is not. Al Qaeda members were charged with treachery and perfidy in relation to the October 2000 bombing of the USS *Cole* due to the dissimulation of the men on the explosive-laden barge.[157] The feigning of non-combatant status – in arguably one of the acts most closely approximating a conventional "act of war" given its military target – was used to cast the attack as clearly beyond the pale. Charges against Guantánamo detainee and senior Al Qaeda leader Abd al-Hadi al-Iraqi focus, in part, on his "treachery and perfidy" while commanding Al Qaeda forces in Afghanistan.

---

[152] US Military Commission Case against Ali Hamza Ahmad Suliman al Bahlul, "Government's Motion for Appropriate Relief (Request for Judicial Notice of Law) with FM27-10 The Law of Land Warfare (1956)(con'td) Attached [Part 6]," 22.

[153] US Military Commission Case against Ali Hamza Ahmad Suliman al Bahlul, "DFM/ 39–9 Translation of The International Islamic Front for Jihad against the Jews and the Crusaders, A Legal Fatwa," 1.

[154] US Military Commission Case against Ahmed Mohammed Ahmed Haza al Darbi, "Government Response to Defense Motion to Dismiss for Lack of Subject Matter Jurisdiction over Ex Post Facto Charges (D-007) Part 3," 27.

[155] Ibid., 26.

[156] US Military Commission, "Government's Motion for Appropriate Relief," 22.

[157] US Military Commission Case against Abd al-Rahim Hussein Muhammed Abdu Al-Nashiri, "Referred Charges Dated 12/19/2008," 8.

232   Al Qaeda's clash with civilization

Al Qaeda's use of deception and dissimulation are emphasized in the charges:

[Abd al-Hadi al-Iraqi invited] the confidence and belief of at least one person that a vehicle appearing to be a civilian vehicle was entitled to protection under the law of war, and, intending to use and betray that confidence and belief, did, thereafter, make use of that confidence and belief to detonate explosives in said vehicle thereby attacking a bus carrying members of the German military.[158]

The charges mention him dressing "in local attire in order to blend in with the local civilian population in order to commit treacherous and perfidious acts," and presenting "a fraudulent passport with a number of counterfeit entry stamps to conceal his true identity."[159] Given that Al Qaeda could not conceivably be successful without such ruses, it is clear that these norms extend to the actor as much as to its acts. These norms of partiality simulate equality but if abided by would guarantee mortality. The partiality of these norms is underscored in the legal discourse concerning perfidy, which has tended to place the use of civilian clothes by the special forces of state powers under the category of legitimate "ruses of war."[160] This is not to say that this inconsistency is inherently unjust, but that some mediation of identity in the form of defining a "them" is necessary to contrast similar actions undertaken by "us" when gauges of objective standards of behavior are insufficient. Contrasting the good people who disguise themselves from the bad ones is not possible absent the role of common identity formation in firming up normative categories, providing a stable set of expectations – gallantry from the former and treachery from the latter. Identities here are serving as categories telling us who we and others are.[161]

Charges of conspiracy accompanied those of treachery and perfidy as prosecutors sought to try those they saw as members of the group, but could not necessarily tie them to specific acts. These efforts portrayed them as following the "al-Qaeda plan," and as part of a murderous cabal bent on the destruction of innocent lives and unrestrained by

---

[158] "U.S. Military Commission Form 458 (Jan 2007) – Continuation of the Charges and Specifications in the case of United States of America v. Abd al-Hadi al-Iraqi," 10.

[159] Ibid., 3; 6.

[160] See Richard B. Jackson, "Perfidy in Non-International Armed Conflicts," in Kenneth Watkin and Andrew J. Norris ed., *International Law Studies, Vol. 88, Non-International Armed Conflict in the Twenty-first Century* (Newport, R.I.: Naval War College, 2012), 243–44; and W. Hays Parks, "Special Forces' Wear of Non-Standard Uniforms," *International Law Studies, Vol. 80, Issues in International Law and Military Operations* (Newport, R.I.: Naval War College, 2012), 69–119.

[161] See Ted Hopf, "The Promise of Constructivism in International Relations Theory," *International Security* 23, no. 1 (Summer 1998): 174–75.

Uncertainty, restraint, and legitimacy 233

civilized modes of war. The size of the actor again was cited, casting all members as conspirators, with concealment confirming all participants as transgressors:

Unlike an entire political party of a nation the size of Germany, the evidence will show that al Qaida is a fairly discrete number of terrorists, banded together in common purpose to commit attacks that violate the law of war, and that its members, to include the accused [Salim Hamdan], were well aware of its plans toward America.[162]

Conspiracy charges have been a source of controversy in the military tribunals, and the absence of conspiracy as a war crime in international law has complicated efforts to prosecute accused Al Qaeda militants.[163] This example of international norms restraining efforts by the system's most powerful actor to prosecute its enemies is tempered somewhat since the United States did ultimately include conspiracy charges in the case of Abd al-Hadi al-Iraqi, though their constitutionality remains contested.[164] This limited instance of restraint, moreover, was only evident more than a decade after the conflict's inception and pales in comparison to earlier examples where constraints on state power largely disintegrated.

Off the grid: uncertainty, restraint, and legitimacy

Following the September 11 attacks, norms and rules in place to counter what had been largely a domestic-level phenomenon with transnational implications had to counter an international actor with demonstrated global impact. Noah Feldman observes the doubly problematic nature of norm enforcement against American-born enemies: "If the Guantánamo detainees were in a place that was off the grid, [Yaser Esam] Hamdi and [Jose] Padilla were off the legal grid even inside the United States."[165] The process of placing these individuals on a grid consistent with domestic and international norms has been laborious. These exertions have required greater concordance with foreign governments, many holding divergent views as to the nature of the threat, and

---

[162] US Military Commission Case against Salim Ahmed Hamdan, "Government Reply to Motion to Pre-Admit the Documentary Motion Picture (The al Qaida Plan) (P-003)," 3.

[163] See Jess Bravin, "Judges Question Use of Conspiracy Charges for Terror Suspects," *Wall Street Journal*, October 22, 2014; and Charlie Savage, "U.S. Legal Officials Split over How to Prosecute Terrorism Detainees," *New York Times*, January 8, 2013, A14.

[164] On the inclusion of conspiracy in the Abd al-Hadi al-Iraqi charges, see Steve Vladeck, "Military Commissions, Conspiracy, and al-Iraqi," *Lawfare* Blog, February 18, 2014.

[165] Noah Feldman, "Enemy-Criminals: The Law and the War on Terror," in *The Enemy Combatant Papers: American Justice, the Courts, and the War on Terror*, ed. Karen J. Greenberg, et al. (New York: Cambridge University Press, 2008), xviii.

234   Al Qaeda's clash with civilization

have raised concerns about state compliance with existing norms. European parliamentarians in 2007 expressed their apprehension concerning a case dealing with the rights of detainees at Guantánamo. The case, the lawmakers asserted, "boils down to the simple, but crucial question of whether the system of legal norms that purports to restrain the conduct of states vis-à-vis individuals within their power will survive the terrorist threat."[166]

The erosion of restraints from existing international norms and rules following the attacks included those concerning the use of force and the meaning of the right of self-defense.[167] This involved the manipulation of categories to include "state sponsors" of terrorism as culpable in the acts of groups purportedly operating in and from their territories. In his State of the Union Address prior to the invasion of Iraq, President Bush announced: "Some have said we must not act until the threat is imminent. Since when have terrorists and tyrants announced their intentions, politely putting us on notice before they strike?"[168] This was a new kind of system populated by actors – terrorists and tyrants – that did not play by the existing rules, and new rules were characterized as a necessity in response.[169] Marieke de Goede explicitly ties this norm engineering to an interpretation of systemic conditions where "the sheer uncertainty and randomness of terrorist attack renders conventional risk assessment techniques inadequate," and "moves to incorporate this uncertainty into policymaking."[170]

These incidences supporting confirmation of the enforcement thesis – concerning categorization and valuation of actors in order to exceed existing norms on enforcement – have to be weighed against the international reaction these measures evoked. Efforts to subvert long-standing norms associated with armed conflict, facilitated by categorization as terrorists or unlawful enemy combatants, have to some degree reinforced those norms, internationally and domestically.[171] The dominant power in

[166] Linda Greenhouse, "Guantánamo Legal Battle Is Resuming," *New York Times*, September 2, 2007.
[167] See Nico Schrijver, "September 11 and Challenges to International Law," in *Terrorism and the UN: Before and after September 11*, ed. Jane Boulden and Thomas G. Weiss (Bloomington: Indiana University Press, 2004), 63.
[168] Quoted in Fassbender, "UN Security Council," 95.
[169] For an examination of the effects of the political discourse following September 11 on the foreign policy process leading to the Iraq War, see Ronald R. Krebs and Jennifer K. Lobasz, "Fixing the Meaning of 9/11: Hegemony, Coercion, and the Road to War in Iraq," *Security Studies* 16, no. 3 (July 2007): 409–51.
[170] Marieke De Goede, "The Politics of Preemption and the War on Terror in Europe," *European Journal of International Relations* 14, no. 1 (March 2008): 161–85.
[171] Joshua L. Dratel, "Repeating History: Rights and Security in the War on Terror," in *The Enemy Combatant Papers*, xiv.

Uncertainty, restraint, and legitimacy

the international system has sought to thwart or has altered those norms to cope with a transformed security environment, while the response abroad has been both opposition and capitulation. Barak Mendelsohn points to the apparently contradictory roles of the United States as norm enforcer and breaker, but concludes that it is "not completely surprising because in seeking to reform the international society and legitimize new norms, a hegemon is likely to promote policies that necessitate deviating from the accepted rule of 'rightful conduct' and breaking current norms." There is a limit, though, as Mendelsohn notes, where norm transgression may produce diminishing returns in terms of leadership and legitimacy.[172] A decade and a half into the conflict, it is difficult to discern whether these enforcement norms were transformed irrevocably by US actions or reinforced through rejection of their revision.

The generation of norms predicted in the relief thesis, those that aid coping with heightened uncertainty in the system, has also not been clearly confirmed. What has occurred so far is the increased salience of previously existing norms concerning terrorism, serving the relief and enforcement functions. This has required an effort by those best served by those norms to categorize Al Qaeda, as well as other actors, under the rubric of terrorism, and to establish the treacherous nature of their acts. In so doing, the critical role of categorization cannot be overstated. While the norms have been reinforced and enforced in order to lessen the strategic uncertainty in the system, they have also been manipulated in order for the dominant powers to retain their dominance and monopoly on violence. Up to a point, this is clearly a good thing, particularly as it is applied to Al Qaeda and its ilk. But the expansion of norms concerning terrorism to state actors has been widely considered deleterious to world order, and harsh treatment of detainees has been firmly established as contrary to civilized society, international and domestic. Overall, those observers who emphasize state interests overcoming normative constraints will find plenty to support their case, as will those emphasizing the restraining power of international society, reinforcing the futility of settling that sticky debate.

The effort since September 11 in sorting and valuation has placed actors and actions into an unambiguous set of categories that erases any legitimacy for those acting outside of the normal bounds of international conduct and conflict. The provision of even limited legal personality to Al Qaeda, Eric Heinze observes, presents a risk of conferring legitimacy to actors based solely on their ability to produce violence.[173] Keohane

---

[172] Barak Mendelsohn, *Combating Jihadism: American Hegemony and Interstate Cooperation in the War on Terrorism* (Chicago: University of Chicago Press, 2009), 15.

[173] Eric A. Heinze, "The Evolution of International Law in Light of the 'Global War on Terror,'" *Review of International Studies* 37, no. 3 (July 2011): 1092–93.

236   Al Qaeda's clash with civilization

speculates that the delegitimization of non-state violence in the seventeenth and eighteenth centuries associated with piracy was analogous to the post-September 11 system.[174] Then, states eventually found the actions of pirates, including those of the Barbary powers, to be contrary to their interests and had the power to suppress them. Now, Al Qaeda operates from the cracks in the system, its interstices, and its shadows, and this applies to legal and normative frameworks as well as the physical setting. Fixing these conditions requires not only physical force but also rhetorical force, with the latter illustrating the reinforcing interaction of normative shifts and identity formation.

New kind of evil: identity formation and the enemy within

Reformulating norms to fit transgressions of expected behavior coincided with processes of corporate and collective identity formation that facilitated the instigation of severe sanctions. While the evidence to date of the normative underpinning of international society in reaction to Al Qaeda has been equivocal, as in the other cases, indications of common identity formation have not. The most prominent of these have been efforts to cast those associated with Al Qaeda, and terrorism more generally, as uncivilized and reprobate. President Bush's contributions to that discourse consistently cast Al Qaeda and its followers as irredeemably evil. "They are devious and ruthless," and the "depth of their hatred is equaled by the madness of the destruction they design."[175] He highlighted both the amorality and novelty of the threat they posed: "This is a new kind of evil, and we understand, and the American people are beginning to understand, this crusade, this war on terrorism, is going to take a while.... We will rid the world of the evildoers."[176]

This new kind of evil was cast in terms of civilization versus barbarism.[177] After the attacks, President Bush exhorted the nation with a broadcast: "We wage a war to save civilization itself," and later characterized the conflict as a "struggle for civilization."[178] Attorney General John

---

[174] Keohane, "Public Delegitimation," 148–49.
[175] Richard Jackson, *Writing the War on Terrorism: Language, Politics, and Counter-Terrorism* (Manchester: Manchester University Press, 2005), 62–63. On US presidential rhetoric in response to the attacks, see John M. Murphy, "'Our Mission and Our Moment': George W. Bush and September 11th," *Rhetoric & Public Affairs* 6, no. 4 (Winter 2003): 607–32.
[176] Quoted in Laura J. Rediehs, "Evil," in *Collateral Language: A User's Guide to America's New War*, ed. John Collins and Ross Glover (New York: New York University Press, 2002), 64.
[177] See Marina A. Llorente, "Civilization versus Barbarism," in *Collateral Language*, 39–51.
[178] Quoted in Richard Kearney, *Strangers, Gods, and Monsters* (London: Routledge, 2003), 112. See also "Bush Declares a 'Struggle for Civilization,'" CTV News, September 11, 2006.

Identity formation and the enemy within

Ashcroft stated, "the attacks of September 11 drew a bright line of demarcation between the civil and the savage.... On one side of this line are freedom's enemies, murderers of innocents in the name of a barbarous cause."[179] CIA director General Michael Hayden described an "al-Qaeda campaign of almost satanic terror" in Iraq.[180] This language, according to Richard Jackson, served "to establish clear boundary markers between 'them' and 'us' – between citizens and aliens, foreign and domestic, inside and outside."[181] Michael Mazarr observed the tendency to deny "any legitimacy whatsoever" to the enemy, noting that "if the enemy is simply a force of evil, unconnected to any real human hopes or fears or angers, then the only thing left to do is to annihilate them."[182] President Obama has been more restrained in his rhetoric, casting Al Qaeda and its actions as beyond the pale, but in less absolute, theological frames. This shifted somewhat in his September 2014 speech to the UN General Assembly, describing ISIS in stark terms reminiscent of earlier years as being out of the fold of civilization, urging member states to use force against this especially maleficent threat to international society:

No God condones this terror. No grievance justifies these actions. There can be no reasoning – no negotiation – with this brand of evil. The only language understood by killers like this is the language of force. So the United States of America will work with a broad coalition to dismantle this network of death.[183]

Al Qaeda's strong association with wanton destruction provides a focal point for collective identity formation, reinforcing identities among state actors as legitimate purveyors of violence. That collective identification seems rooted in both homogeneity and common cultural bonds, commonly accepted modes of interaction and shared values, respectively. The aberrant nature of Al Qaeda and its actions helps contrast normal violence with the abnormal as it exhibits modes and manners considered both essential and irredeemable. The casting of the conflict with Al Qaeda as one between those who love freedom and those bent on suppressing it has drawn a stark distinction between good and evil. Efforts have been made in official discourse to distinguish between Al Qaeda and the broader Muslim world. But existing biases that associate Islam with violence and

---

[179] Jackson, *Writing the War on Terrorism*, 62.
[180] Dafna Lizner and Walter Pincus, "Taliban, Al-Qaeda Resurge in Afghanistan, CIA Says," *Washington Post*, November 16, 2006.
[181] Jackson, *Writing the War on Terrorism*, 5.
[182] Michael J. Mazarr, *Unmodern Men in the Modern World: Radical Islam, Terrorism and the War on Modernity* (New York: Cambridge University Press, 2007), 3.
[183] "Remarks by President Obama in Address to the United Nations General Assembly," The White House, Office of the Press Secretary, September 24, 2014.

238   Al Qaeda's clash with civilization

the Muslim world with oppression and disorder reinforce at least uncon-scious cultural associations.[184]

The accounting for peril from without is accompanied by concerns about impurity within. Processes of corporate identity formation require establishing an "us" and a "them." These have at times drawn on resources of collective identification rooted in a conception of common cultural bonds, one threatened by the mere presence of Muslim coreligionists and punctuated by isolated and mostly limited applications of extremist violence. The aptitude of Al Qaeda in transgressing the division between an inside and outside of sovereign boundaries has complicated this, leading to suspicions of a propensity to "turn terrorist," just as the specter of "turning Turk" haunted early modern Europe. In Britain the effort to identify threats while avoiding the perils of negative identity formation has been problematic. Following the London transit bombings, London counterterrorism police chief Peter Clarke commented that "what we've seen all too graphically and all too murderously is that we have a threat which is being generated here within the United Kingdom.... [with] the numbers of people who we have to be interested in ... into the thousands."[185] That these people of interest are mostly Muslims is obvious, and Tarique Ghaffur, assistant commissioner in the London Metropolitan police, asserted that anti-terror laws risked criminalizing ethnic minorities.[186] US Senator Conrad Burns' comment that we face enemies who "drive taxi cabs in the daytime and kill at night," may be dismissed as xenophobic ramblings, except that it drew no rebuke from within his party, let alone any public shaming like that which eventually checked US Senator Joseph McCarthy's scaremongering.[187] Significant public sentiment in the United States associates Islam with violence, providing another form of corporate identification that melds with the clash of civilizations framework.[188] Irregular violence by an exceedingly

---

[184] See Bruce Mazlish, *Civilization and Its Contents* (Stanford: Stanford University Press, 2004), 142–43.

[185] Alan Cowell, "British Police Arrest 14 Men in Anti-Terror Raids," *New York Times*, September 2, 2006.

[186] Riazat Butt and Vikram Dodd, "Anti-Terror Laws Alienate Muslims, Says Top Policeman," *The Guardian*, August 7, 2006.

[187] Matt Gouras, "Burns Says Terrorists Drive Taxis by Day," Associated Press, August 31, 2006.

[188] According to a 2009 Pew Research Center poll, 38 percent believed Islam encourages violence more than other faiths. "Muslims Widely Seen as Facing Discrimination," Pew Research Center, September 9, 2009. In another poll, an astounding 38 percent said Muslims should not have the same rights to build houses of worship as people of other faiths, with 25 percent holding that American communities should be able to prohibit the construction of mosques. "Public Remains Conflicted over Islam," Pew Research Center, August 24, 2010.

A clash *with* civilization 239

small proportion of Muslims has been used to reinforce the idea of an irrevocable civilizational divide.

Corporate identification's crudeness allows for seemingly clear designations between an inside and an outside, between good and evil, peace and war. But when the foundations and true actors in the conflict are obscured the result is a violence of a different, inward kind. Existing fears of "Islamic fundamentalism" were exacerbated by the violent intrusion of a group, like the Nizari Ismailis, on the fringe of a fringe of a fringe of the Muslim world. Efforts to correct those misconceptions, though, have been made more challenging due to attacks by "homegrown terrorists" such as Ft. Hood shooter Nidal Hasan and the Tsarnaev brothers behind the Boston Marathon bombings. Such events have been used to reinforce fears of a fifth column of Muslim extremists, whether the Muslims are active or latent in their purported bent toward violence. Efforts to emphasize that civilizational divide as eroding the foundation of Western societies internally has been further fueled by the resurgence of ISIS. A Danish lawmaker cited a claimed propensity for moderate Muslims to become extreme over time, casting arrests in Europe and an attack by a single extremist as evidence of a "clash of civilizations."[189]

The intermingling of norm and identity formation has resulted in processes of threat and actor homogenization. Innate biases and cultural ignorance provide fodder for negative identification by some, portraying a proposed mosque in Manhattan as a symbol of violent triumphalism rather than a site of peaceful worship.[190] While these typifications thankfully have not been universally applied to Muslim populations, crude characterizations of our enemies have been used to firm up normative categories and blur internal inconsistencies in our justifications of the use of force. The magnification of traits and innate natures sets a clear, irrevocable divide between just and unjust violence, enabling excesses in enforcement justified as *in extremis* acts necessary for survival. It was through those processes that a conflict with a materially badly outmatched opponent would be seen by some as a struggle for civilization itself.

A clash *with* civilization

According to Bernard Lewis, "For Osama bin Laden, 2001 marks the resumption of the war for the religious dominance of the world that began in the seventh century. For him and his followers, this is a moment of

---

[189] Anthony Faiola and Souad Mekhennet, "Europe's Muslims Feel under Siege," *New York Times*, November 1, 2014.

[190] Nikola Krastev, "Controversial Islamic Center Near New York's Ground Zero Quietly Advances," Radio Free Europe/Radio Liberty, November 21, 2011.

240   Al Qaeda's clash with civilization

opportunity."[191] Both Western sources and Al Qaeda have cast the conflict in terms of a clash of civilizations.[192] This is unfortunate, and quite possibly self-fulfilling, as stark distinctions and clumsy cultural associations combine with continuing peril and a sustained condition of systemic uncertainty. Al Qaeda makes for a pretty potent "other." Its behavior is abhorrent and its capacity for bad acts seems boundless, even at times shocking its own following.[193] This is true no matter whether these acts are rooted in structural constraints or moral depravity.

Establishing a Manichean division between the freedom loving and the enemies of civilization, however, presents risks to a world order built on a level of restraint and accommodation. Posing a division between the civilized and the savage makes way for a return of the "barbarian option," where aggression against those outside of the fold of civilization is deemed not only rightful but necessary. This is captured in the US *Manual for Military Commissions*, which explains that "[t]reacherous or perfidious conduct in war is forbidden because it destroys the basis for a restoration of peace short of the complete annihilation of one belligerent by the other."[194] Andrew Phillips notes that "political orders crystallize at the intersection of ethical and coercive modes of action."[195] Casting Al Qaeda as evil and essentially subhuman due to their inhumane acts, while at the same time categorizing the threat so broadly, allowed for a political order that made extreme acts a byproduct of efforts to restore physical and ontological security. Violence visited on agents whose own restraints on violence fell short of civilizational standards was intended to prop up a moral order but ultimately contravened precepts of civilized behavior. The dehumanization of Abu Ghraib and CIA prisons is less surprising, but no less disturbing, if we consider the prevailing portrayal of an implacable, ruthless, and baneful enemy. Accounting for these processes is essential to check our own potential for transgressing the bounds of civilization.[196]

---

[191] Bernard Lewis, "The Revolt of Islam," *The New Yorker*, November 19, 2001.

[192] Bin Laden repeatedly embraced the concept. When asked whether a clash of civilizations was inevitable, he replied: "I see no doubt about that." Quoted in James S. Robbins, "Battlefronts in the War of Ideas," in *Countering Terrorism and Insurgency in the 21st Century, Vol. 1, Strategic and Tactical Considerations*, ed. James J.F. Forest (Westport, Conn.: Praeger, 2007), 299.

[193] See Mohammed M. Hafez, "Tactics, Takfir, and Anti-Muslim Violence," in *Self Inflicted Wounds*, 19–44.

[194] *Manual for Military Commissions*, United States (2010 Edition), April 27, 2010.

[195] Andrew Phillips, *War, Religion, and Empire: The Transformation of International Orders* (Cambridge: Cambridge University Press, 2011), 15.

[196] Nicholas Rengger examines the tensions between technologically advanced warfare and the just war tradition, including calls to "take the gloves off" in response to September

A clash *with* civilization 241

Distrust of fanaticism, treachery, rootlessness, and mobility are standards of civilization that developed, in part, due to clashes with historical systemic deviants. The ideas of the necessity of statehood (the antithesis of rootlessness and mobility) as a prerequisite for legitimate violence, revulsion at mass civilian casualties, and the value of free human souls were shaped in part by encounters with those irregular actors. The abnormal development of Al Qaeda, wrought by opportunities and constraints in the system, resulted in a clash with these fundamental tenets of international society. That this society is rooted in European modes of order gone global does not diminish the conclusion that the present conflict is not the result of civilizations clashing, but rather of Al Qaeda clashing with civilization. These modes of order have long been secular in purpose and function. The resistance to them is not primarily the result of sacred rage but due to the impediments this order presents.

Al Qaeda's severe aberration in form and behavior rather than its clear deviation from Islamic tenets best explains its trajectory as a systemic actor. Competition may very well bear out neorealist predictions that such forms have only transitory significance, particularly in systems marked by structural similarities, as the United States has largely been able to check the group's grander ambitions. This was also true of the Seljuk Turks and their Nizari rivals, the latter persisting beyond their more powerful adversary. But this is a completely different technical setting where intense violence can be applied rapidly in the most remote areas. Constraints on ruling from a distance should not be confused with those on destroying from a distance, though the ultimate efficacy of that approach may prove limited. The label "Long War" may be little more accurate than "Cold War," which killed millions. That moniker poses the risk of being self-fulfilling, particularly if it is cast in ambiguous terms against "Islamic extremism" or "terror" rather than Al Qaeda and its offshoots as discrete actors.[197]

Al Qaeda's long-term viability remains in question, and its ability to realize shorter-term goals – striking major Western targets, portraying itself as defeating the United States in Afghanistan, or destabilizing regional governments – will go a long way in determining whether it or its successors maintain a following. Its followers may be zealots but even zealots like a winner, even more so, as evidenced by the surge of support

---

11. Nicholas Rengger, "On the Just War Tradition in the Twenty-First Century," *International Affairs* 78, no. 2 (2002): 353–63.

[197] There is little question that Al Qaeda benefits from prolonging the conflict, and has often portrayed it as a generation or more long struggle, matching well with guerrilla warfare strategy that attempts to wear out a materially stronger adversary. See Craig Whitlock, "On Tape, Bin Laden Warns of Long War," *Washington Post*, April 24, 2006.

ISIS achieved after its seizure of portions of Iraq in the summer of 2014. The conditions that helped bring about this and previous deviating modes exhibit remarkable similarities. Comparison with this historical set of actors may inform us how Al Qaeda ends, complementing studies of how modern terrorist groups met their end.[198] What the historical episodes examined here may tell us about Al Qaeda's future will be considered in the conclusion. The demise of each of these predecessors, ominously, took a great deal of time. The pace of the modern, or late modern, international system is much quicker, though, making generations-length forecasts seem overly pessimistic. Our policies will foreshorten this process if they are founded on a sober understanding of Al Qaeda's origins and functions and the roots of our own actions. Judgments and actions based on shallow foundations, contesting with a civilization rather than an outgrowth of international systemic and societal deviation, are most likely to extend it.

[198] See Audrey Kurth Cronin, *How Terrorism Ends: Understanding the Decline and Demise of Terrorist Campaigns* (Princeton: Princeton University Press, 2009); and Seth G. Jones and Martin C. Libicki, *How Terrorist Groups End: Lessons for Countering al Qa'ida* (Santa Monica, Calif.: RAND, 2008).

Conclusion

> The confrontation that Islam calls for with these godless and apostate regimes, does not know Socratic debates, Platonic ideals, nor Aristotelian diplomacy. But it knows the dialogue of bullets, the ideals of assassination, bombing, and destruction, and the diplomacy of the cannon and machine-gun.
>
> —*Military Studies in the Jihad against the Tyrants* (The Al Qaeda Training Manual)

> Even if Al Qaeda could be considered a Power [under the 1949 Geneva Convention], which we doubt, no one claims that Al Qaeda has accepted and applied the provisions of the Convention.
>
> —*Hamdan v. Rumsfeld*, US District Court of Appeals, July 2005

Emphasizing the continuity of international politics after September 11, Kenneth Waltz wrote that "[t]error is a threat to the stability of states and the peace of mind of their rulers."[1] A focus on terror and terrorism has tended to be favored over more deeply rooted examinations of divergent patterns of organization and associated behavior that create fear and profound unease. Investigating the sources of this brand of deviation and uncertainty advances our understanding of threats to order, both world order and the cognitive orders of leaders and other observers. Reorienting toward recognized modes of international interaction and familiar frameworks is a natural but inadequate reaction to these events. John Dewey wrote, "the prime function of philosophy is that of rationalizing the *possibilities* of experience, especially collective human experience."[2] International relations theory benefits when tempered with logics of possibility, which themselves generate collective responses that can be understood in the framework of international society. This concluding chapter has three main sections. The first two synthesize observations concerning

---

[1] Kenneth N. Waltz, "The Continuity of International Politics," in *Worlds in Collision: Terror and the Future of Global Order*, ed. Ken Booth and Tim Dunne (Basingstoke: Palgrave Macmillan, 2002), 353.

[2] John Dewey, *Reconstruction in Philosophy* (Boston: Beacon Press, 1948; 1920), 122.

244   Conclusion

transformation in international systems and the development of international society, respectively. The third considers the implications of those observations for the current challenges we face.

International system

This section focuses on whether the mechanisms and processes posited concerning system transformation were supported by observations in the case studies. It is clear that the main expected observations were confirmed in nearly all the cases, with important exceptions and qualifications. Additional observations and remaining, or newly raised, questions are also discussed.

Bucking the system: systemic change and system transformation

In previous conceptions of neorealism change occurred either in the surface structure (distribution of power and resources) or deep structure (ordering principle) of the international system. Severe shifts of the surface level could change ordering principle on rare occasions, resulting in consolidation or dissolution of power. The cases here demonstrated that lesser shifts in distribution, changes *in* systems, also are associated with processes that help account for changes *of* international systems. In each there was one or more dominant power that declined, creating conditions leading to changes in the composition of the system, that is, significant episodes of system change short of changes in the ordering principle, anarchy.

These chains of events occurred through two main modes. The first involved decline and retrenchment and its effects on the relationships between great powers and their lesser associates. The decline of the Fatimid Empire in its long struggle with the Abbasids and then Seljuk Turks was clear to its cadre of da'is, religio-political missionaries. A dynastic struggle was the pretext for division, but it is clear that the Nizaris set out on their own path, advancing their "new preaching," in response to their sponsor's increasingly decrepit condition. This is a case of both opportunity and compulsion, with an ambitious leader, Hassan-i Sabbah, sensing that his and his followers' fortunes were separate from the Fatimid base. The same pattern is shown in the case of the Barbary powers. The decline of the Ottoman Empire in the late sixteenth century left the increasingly powerful city-states to their own designs. Continued legitimation by association could not mask their independent status and freedom of action.

International system 245

The second mode consisted of the opportunities provided for expansion by the decline of major powers. The Mongols benefited from the decline of three major powers, the Jin dynasty, the Karakhitai, and the Khorezmshah. In this case there is convincing evidence that conditions of decline directly contributed to the early expansion of the Mongols and generated momentum for further conquest. The decline of the Soviet Union was the primary systemic trigger for the rise of Al Qaeda, whose leaders recognized the opportunities presented by the modern-day Persia's collapse. In each case the lesser power sensed an opportunity, a gap that had opened up in the surface structure of the system. The desire to ascend and expand is evident in at least three cases, with the Barbary powers seemingly intent on dominating the Maghreb and siphoning off the spoils of Mediterranean trade and coastal raids. According to Randall Schweller, "[p]redatory states motivated by expansion and absolute gains, not security and the fear of relative losses, are the prime movers of neorealist theory."[3] Indeed, at first glance, the behavior of these actors seems more in line with power aggrandizement than security seeking.

There is a distinction, though, between established powers whose survival is for the most part assured, and these actors who arose under conditions of extreme vulnerability. Security seeking and the aggressive accumulation of power are more aligned in such circumstances. There is no defensive positionalism since their positions are often defenseless relative to their more established rivals. Incentives for aggression are built in, but this does not mean that explanations for this aggression can be reduced to that precarious position in the system. The animus toward being dominated seems to accompany rather than substitute for an *animus dominandi*. In each case there was little or no accommodation to the rules of the system, and in three there was an explicit desire to adjust them by dominating it. These are the ultimate revisionist powers, altering not merely the distribution of power but also its fundamental configuration, revealing a status quo bias in neorealism more ingrained than assumptions about seeking power and security. It is not surprising that their goals and plans are contrary to the system they enter into, an observation that should be weighed when considering the role of ideologies in driving outcomes. What room is there for comporting to existing ideational structures, especially when adherence to those would mean being bound to a status quo that would leave them powerless and subjugated?

---

[3] Randall L. Schweller, "Neorealism's Status-Quo Bias: What Security Dilemma?" *Security Studies* 5, no. 3 (Spring 1996): 119.

246   Conclusion

Opportunity structure and the logic of dissimilation

The conception of opportunity structure employed here involves the relationship between systemically induced goals and institutionalized means. These means were further broken down as factors of protection, including manpower (skilled and unskilled), technics (tangible artifacts to produce force), and coercion-free space. The systemically induced goals were those posited in neorealism for all actors: some measure of survival, autonomy, and security, and perhaps beyond these. The availability of means, however, was anything but uniform for each of the actors under consideration.

What resulted was fairly remarkable adaptation to straitened resources through organizational innovation and deviation. Contrary to predictions in neorealism, in these cases necessity bred more invention than imitation. Extending logics assumed under neorealism, with its emphasis on the motive force of necessity, we found structural and associated behavioral deviation to be a relatively rare but real reaction to the constraints of anarchy. The Nizari Ismailis managed to construct a centrally directed, spatially dispersed "state within a state," and even had a franchise in the Holy Land. The Mongols scaled up their nomadic organization to a powerful, if relatively short-lived, empire. In so doing, they exhibited astounding and often cruel efficiency in identifying and distributing expertise and matériel throughout their conquered territories. The Barbary powers retained the antiquated city-state form while competing with the centralized territorial states of Europe and forcing a level of accommodation. Each was dissimilar in its organizational form and interaction in space relative to the major actors in their systems. This logic of dissimilation does not supplant the logic of anarchy but is a product of the same.

Systemic change was not the key determinant of resource availability. While the decline of major powers did affect the availability of resources in some instances (the labor pool and technical access for the Mongols most notably), there was no clear association of that availability with the outcomes of system change. In the case of the Mongols, while the availability of skilled and unskilled labor was affected by the decline of several major powers, this merely amplified their effectiveness and the rapidity of their expansion. In the cases of the Nizari Ismailis and the Barbary powers, decline arguably decreased access to the factors of protection, while for Al Qaeda deeper forces of globalization were at play in expanding possibilities.

One of the most striking conclusions in this systemic to system change sequence is what happened afterward. The historical cases under consideration all returned to systems characterized by unit isomorphism. But this observation and apparent vindication for arguments that foretell

International system 247

emulation has qualifications. First, this occurred only after a long period. The Nizaris lasted about a century and a half until their demise as a collective actor; not bad when considering both their original sponsors and primary adversaries, the Fatimids and Seljuks, respectively, were gone by that time. The shorter-lived Mongol Empire, depending on the starting date, still lasted around half a century, and undoubtedly made the most of its time. The Barbary powers lasted a whopping two centuries. This result is even more improbable given their combination of political instability and marginal resource bases, in addition to the antagonism of the great powers, their immediate neighbors, and each other.

The second caveat involves the ways in which these actors eventually met their end. With the Nizari Ismailis and the Mongols this was not consistent with neorealist predictions. Under the underspecified assumptions of emulation and socialization, it is competition in the international system that determines fitness. In the case of the Nizaris they outlasted dominant members of the system and only met their end due to a systemically exogenous actor, the Mongols. The Nizaris competed effectively, even as their initial expansive goals were checked. The Mongols were not only outside of that system but were irregular in configuration themselves, demoting the significance of imitation as the likely successful adaptive response. The Mongols were, to put it mildly, pretty potent competitors themselves. Despite minor setbacks that checked their expansion in the Near East and India, it was only after the empire had dissolved that they were defeated on the battlefield by the Mamluks. Internal contradictions were the culprit that brought the empire down, and led to the devolution into competing khanates. This outcome would be consistent with neorealist predictions if, somehow, pressures from outside competition led to its collapse, which was not the case. The case where internal distortions *and* competitive pressures led to being selected out of the system is the Barbary powers. But this, to reemphasize, took place only after a substantial amount of time.

Beyond providing one set of mechanisms that explain why homogeneous systems are not determinative outcomes, these observations suggest that such systems may represent a likely result and arguably could be considered an equilibrium condition. Establishing this would require a broader investigation of systems than is offered here. Others have ably cast doubt on the utility of limiting our examination to isomorphic systems regardless of whether they constitute natural end states.[4] Examining this small

---

[4] See Barry Buzan and Richard Little, *International Systems in World History: Remaking the Study of International Relations* (Oxford: Oxford University Press, 2000); and Georg Sørenson, "'Big and Important Things' in IR," in *Realism and World Politics*, ed. Ken Booth (London and New York: Routledge, 2011), 111–17.

248   Conclusion

sample alone does call into question the overall import of homogeneity as an equilibrium, as well as neorealism's emphasis on external competition as the primary generator for isomorphism. The long time frames for a return to that equilibrium, moreover, raise the question of whether the end states of homogeneous systems have diminished in their empirical richness and theoretical fruitfulness. This conclusion is even more compelling given our contemporary struggle with actors that refuse to conform to international norms of structural and behavioral homogeneity.

Logics of concealment and path-dependent deviance

Resource constraints and severe vulnerability contributed to behaviors intended to enhance prospects for survival. These behaviors were categorized under the label of "logics of concealment" and included hiding, deception, and dissimulation: the concealment of physical presence, intentions, and identities, respectively. Conventional actors exhibit each of these behaviors, but for these powers it is more the core or essence of their activities. One cumulative effect of these behaviors and the irregular patterns of interactions was a condition of heightened uncertainty in the system.

Each of the relatively weak actors examined here, the Nizari Ismailis, Barbary powers, and Al Qaeda, exhibited these behaviors. The Mongols, whose increasing power made them less and less vulnerable, did so in less appreciable amounts. Each of the weaker set used physical environments to insulate themselves from their stronger rivals. The rugged mountain ranges of Persia, the natural and manmade harbors of the Maghreb, and the badlands of Afghanistan and Pakistan, all provided a protective shell. Deception as a core behavior is most evident in the cases of the Nizaris and Al Qaeda, whose overall goals were clear but whose manner and means of achieving them were, and are, hidden. Dissimulation is also most evident in their actions, but also present in the case of the Barbary powers. False flags also had a prosaic purpose to avoid taxation, but this could be considered an additional benefit to other strategic and tactical advantages.

In each case where these behaviors were witnessed, the expected enhancement of uncertainty was also realized. It is clear that the enemies of the Nizaris lived in conditions of peril that could not be fully gauged. Merchants and coastal communities of southern and, for a time, northern Europe reeled with both fear and uncertainty that the menacing "Turk" would abscond with both their bodies and souls. Having obtained greater and greater levels of control, the Mongols exhibited these behaviors in insignificant amounts but still enhanced uncertainty through their odd behavior of advancement and withdrawal. That observation

International system 249

expanded our appreciation of the range of behaviors that magnify uncertainty beyond the more intentional logics of concealment. Al Qaeda's threat has been variably presented as both existential and trumped up. Is there any better marker than this of the heightened uncertainty its nature and actions have caused? While analysts differed over the extent of the Soviet threat, this was mostly (apart from ideologically addled fringes) a matter of over- or under-estimation. Uncertainty in the circumstances presented here was, and is, a condition of inestimable but ever-present danger. This ability to enhance uncertainty is a key advantage for otherwise overmatched adversaries, resulting in both overreaction and underreaction, unjustifiable fears and equally groundless complacency.

One interesting unanticipated observation was the extent to which behaviors that were, at least in part, derived from weakened and vulnerable conditions persisted far past their usefulness. They continued indeed even when they clearly reached negative utility. What can be termed "path-dependent deviance" is evident in each case. The Nizaris were effective in rattling their Sunni and Seljuk rivals, but also badly alienated their neighbors in nearby towns and communities. Threatening Möngke with assassination, if the sources are credible, was not overly wise and may have hastened their destruction. The Mongols found clearing areas of human populations a useful expedient due to their relatively small numbers, at least until they realized that they needed to tax people more than they needed to kill them. Massacres decreased, though reforms enacted did not cease the practice that so defines their historical image. The Barbary powers exploited the plump sea lanes as they continuously struggled to pacify their interiors, but the resort to sea-raiding later essentially guaranteed their exit.

Al Qaeda has exhibited any number of malign and abhorrent behaviors, but few as evocative as beheading. Potent and internet portable, these signals of resolve and (badly distorted) historical memory, though, have clearly not raised its broader popularity in the Islamic world.[5] Al Qaeda in Iraq's heavy handedness and atrocities led Zawahiri to attempt to reign in their partner organization. Confidence in bin Laden steadily declined after 2003 but remained disturbingly high among some segments of the Muslim world.[6] Nevertheless, the prospect of actual life under Al Qaeda

---

[5] As one 2004 report put it, "[r]egional public opinion has long become accustomed to car bombings and suicide attacks by Palestinian militants, but the videotaped beheadings appear to exceed the public's threshold for political violence." Charles Recknagel, "Middle East: Extremists Opting for Beheading as Weapon of Choice in Terror War," Radio Free Europe/Radio Liberty, June 24, 2004.

[6] Low double-digit favorability ratings for bin Laden and Al Qaeda have been the norm. See "Osama bin Laden Largely Discredited among Muslim Publics in Recent Years," Pew Global Attitudes Project, May 2, 2011.

250   Conclusion

rule cannot seem anything but exceedingly grim for all but a deeply misguided fringe of Muslims. The overall effects of the recent revival of beheading as a prominent tactic by ISIS cannot yet be determined. A short-term boost in recruiting is possible resulting from its interpretation as demonstrating toughness and resolve by potential followers. Long-term effects on efforts to generate wider public support, as opposed to short-term acquiescence, will likely be deleterious.

Blowback and the liability of newness

The puzzle of why some of these actors rise from marginal to systemic status while most aspirants remain stifled or expire was at least partly solved. Previous relationships with dominant powers in the system give actors key advantages upon entering, despite severe challenges to late entry into systems. This occurs through material assistance, protection, and legitimation in early developmental phases prior to asserting their autonomy. Legitimation may take place due to simple association or through the effectiveness of the group or particular leaders within it. In highly precarious circumstances, effectiveness in battle or organization translates readily into legitimacy at the unit level and in initial interactions with dominant powers, but is subsequently denied at the level of international society.

Each of the cases supports a significant role for these types of relationships and advantages. The highly skilled and ideologically schooled da'is provided the Nizari Ismailis a capable core of leaders when they decided to split. The networks established while serving Fatimid interests were then readily transformed to their own ends. Chinggis Khan's once-removed association with the Jin dynasty is somewhat obscured in the historical record. But it is clear that his vassal status under Ong Khan, who had a close Jin association, played a significant role in his ability to survive very dicey circumstances. The Barbary powers benefited from their close association with the Ottoman Empire. This included protection by janissaries, raw material for their fleets, and the legitimation derived from their affiliation with the Sublime Porte. The support provided by the United States, and its partners Saudi Arabia and Pakistan, was a factor in Al Qaeda's early development. The evidence suggests that the role of the United States was indirect, but could have been better conceived to benefit mujahedin factions that were not as adamantly anti-American. Another mitigating factor in that judgment, one that applies to each case, is that while support may have been a necessary condition for their success, it was not a sufficient one. There have been innumerable lesser actors that have received support who did not rise to any

International system   251

consideration. Other structural conditions, and probably unit-level factors, are necessary for this support to have any systemically significant effect.

The question remains as to why dominant actors foster possible future antagonists. In neorealism, foresight concerning the hazards of security cooperation with potential future rivals is supposed to hamper collaboration. Why are these dominant actors seemingly less sensitive to relative gains in these circumstances? There are a number of plausible explanations: (1) major powers do not see the potential of a future threat due to the relative power of the actor; (2) they do see the threat but it is overshadowed by the security concerns that led to the cooperation in the first place, including the policy of cooperation and shifting support among lesser rivals as a hedge to future threats witnessed in the Mongol case; (3) such a threat is seen as too far in the future to be concerned about; and (4) lack of understanding of the actor's intentions, rather than estimates of its relative power, leads to underestimation of risk. Concerning US support for the mujahedin, given a fairly quick glance at that episode, each explanation seems plausible and likely acted in some combination.

The lessons from these episodes are mixed regarding support for armed factions. The first consideration is that while support for the adjunct forces was instrumental in their rise to systemic status, other forces were more fundamental. Systemic changes, opportunity structures, and, perhaps, singular leaders, were also necessary factors. It would be overly cautious to say that all such support programs will likely lead to a significant *systemic* outcome as the odds are long. Some blowback may be realized, with small-scale attacks by elements associated with the groups, but a disruption of world order is not likely without the other factors in alignment. Nevertheless, the lesson of US support for the mujahedin, that immediate benefits need to be balanced with both short- and long-term risks, ought to be foremost in the minds of whoever designs and implements such programs. Those lessons may have been over-applied in the case of the decision-making concerning arming the Syrian resistance, which, according to critics, has been too cautious in trying to avoid enabling extremists and may have contributed to ISIS being able to out-maneuver its rivals.[7]

Role of individuals

Conspicuous in each of these cases is the role of individual leadership. Agency often plays a formative role in social movement theory concerning

---

[7] See Jeffrey Goldberg, "Hillary Clinton: 'Failure' to Help Syrian Rebels Led to the Rise of ISIS," *The Atlantic Online*, August 4, 2014.

252   Conclusion

the structure of political opportunities, and in international relations theory that emphasizes transformation. In these formulations there is a need for "entrepreneurs" who identify opportunities and act upon them. So the prominence of these individual actors, Hassan-i Sabbah, Chinggis Khan, the Barbarossa brothers, and Osama bin Laden, is consistent with the model. But questions remain whether these prominent individuals produced or were products of their environments and circumstances. This study emphasizes the material and structural constraints that actors face (from the material environment and vis-à-vis other actors), but also stresses that constraints may be conducive to variety. That sort of innovation takes acumen that goes beyond merely sensing opportunity, pointing to the likely key role of extraordinary individuals.

Of all the leaders, Chinggis Khan seems the most indispensable. His task was daunting, his organizational prowess was remarkable, and the results were unquestionable in their impact. There is a risk, though, in relying on historical depictions that elevate such leaders as key to the outcomes. Lacking a proper appreciation of the systemic contextual factors has led previous accounts to overemphasize personal qualities. It seems sensible in all of these cases that individual qualities of particular leaders were a necessary but clearly insufficient factor in the outcomes. That is a tentative judgment. The empirical record is warped in favor of exaggerating their role, and the likelihood of satisfying counterfactual experiments is low. Would the Mongols have been the Mongols without Chinggis Khan, or just another steppe tribe? We will have to guess. But without question there would be no Mongol Empire, nor a "Genghis Khan," without the systemic conditions he so ably navigated.

International society

In his examination of the transformation of international orders, Andrew Phillips highlights the role of disruptive forms of military violence, and the anxieties they create, in establishing new orders.[8] This study attempts to understand the mechanisms and processes that occur as the result of disruptive political-military forms and behaviors, and their role in spurring the reinforcement and adaptation (both in physical and ontological security) of existing orders. One key lesson drawn from the cases is the lack of a clear, practical distinction between processes of functional adaptation and identity formation in response to introduced heterogeneity in international systems. Another is the centrality of categorization in

---

[8] Andrew Phillips, *War, Religion, and Empire: The Transformation of International Orders* (Cambridge: Cambridge University Press, 2011), 47; 52.

International society 253

achieving the requirements, both functional and identity-based, of physical and ontological security. The "diversity and un-likeness" of these actors,[9] borrowing Buzan's characterization of non-state actors, extends beyond a lack of common cultural bonds, though such bonds contribute to both the collective and corporate identity formation that occur in response to their emergence. The following sums up observations that help round out our understanding of this set of mechanisms and processes spurring the development of international society.

Norms, uncertainty, and power

Do new norms and normative frameworks emerge in response to irregular interactions with deviating actors? The evidence presented here suggests that is not quite the case. Rather than norms generated to cope with conditions of uncertainty, as posited in the relief thesis, we witnessed dominant actors placing newly emerged dissimilar actors into *existing* normative frameworks. In a sense this is the reverse of the transmission thesis, at least in the short term. Instead of new norms developing, becoming generalized, and transmitting to other actors, the actors were placed into longstanding normative frames. This raises the question of whether the impact of these dissimilar actors, in heightening uncertainty or in the risks they pose, makes resorting to existing categories a necessity. Subtle formulations of inclusion and exception of actors and their activities seem far less likely when these actors are so unfamiliar or dangerous.

This sorting into existing categories occurred most clearly in two of the four cases, with the other two providing illustrative exceptions. The Sunni orthodoxy and their Seljuk overseers placed the Nizaris outside of the fold of rightful rebellion. While their numbers satisfied existing standards, their doctrine was deemed indefensible, making them apostates and unprotected from any enforcement restraints. Al Qaeda's acts quickly fell under existing norms against terrorism. These norms provided a ready reference reinforcing the group's criminality and were later extended to apply more widely to the international system and some of its members. States charged with complicity with terrorism fell under the same normative categories as the terrorists themselves, subjecting them to similar enforcement measures.

The Barbary powers are a case where the actor was initially *excluded* from the prevailing normative category. The distinctions between piracy and privateering were becoming clearer. The regencies were for the most part considered to be state-like enough to avoid designation as piratical, a

---

[9] Barry Buzan, *From International to World Society? English School Theory and the Social Structure of Globalisation* (Cambridge: Cambridge University Press, 2004), 58–59.

254   Conclusion

result primarily of state interest. Over time insecurity turned out not to be costly on balance, particularly to England and France, and indeed benefited them by harassing rivals and smaller naval powers. Once the regencies' power diminished and their usefulness waned, their status as quarrelsome but tolerable privateers evaporated.

This progression also addresses the issue of how interaction over time may reduce uncertainty. The initial interactions with the Barbary powers, around the first half of the seventeenth century, were marked by high degrees of uncertainty. But after initial efforts to root them out failed, and diplomatic exchanges began, the Barbary powers were tolerated and enjoyed a measure of recognition. The Mongols provide another exception where relative power affected the formulation and enforcement of norms, though the depiction of their rootless aggression later did affect weaker manifestations of nomadic organization. Reactions associated with each of the historical actors over time informed the development of future norms of partiality – against assassination, massacre of civilians, and piracy – though not through direct transmission or "passed on as the status quo from generation to generation."[10] Norms diffused, but only over the long term and only after being filtered through processes of identity formation, becoming more fixed over time as standards of civilization.

Invidious distinctions: the structural conditioning of "others"

The concept of ontological security helped our understanding of the dynamic between the functional requirements of categorization and those of identity formation. Jennifer Mitzen observed that deep uncertainty can be a threat to identity, making it difficult to act and maintain a self-conception. At the same time, ontological insecurity results in incapacitation and inability to confront dangers, highlighting the interdependence between the requirements of ontological and physical security.[11] That interdependence was borne out in this study, allowing for further elaboration of this relationship. Moving from estimable risk to uncertainty makes processes of identity formation even more central to the functional processes of categorization. Similarly, identity requires the sorting into categories that is a functional reaction in coping with uncertainty. Figure C.1 displays this relationship. What this dynamic underscores is the necessity for both neo-utilitarian and

---

[10] Andrew Schotter and Barry Sopher, "Social Learning and Coordination Conventions in Inter-Generational Games: An Experimental Study," Working Paper, New York University, November 2001, 3.

[11] Jennifer Mitzen, "Ontological Security in World Politics: State Identity and the Security Dilemma," *European Journal of International Relations* 12, no. 3 (September 2006): 345.

International society

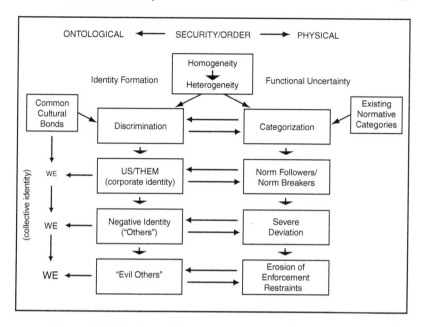

Figure C.1 Identity and functional uncertainty

constructivist frameworks in understanding underlying processes in the development of international society. Neither can be reduced to the other.

As systems change from conditions of homogeneity to heterogeneity, parallel processes of categorization and discrimination occur. Discrimination is part of the fundamental processes of identity formation that occur when collective actors encounter something unfamiliar. It establishes a self-conception through processes of common identity formation, which here encompassed collective ("we-feeling") and corporate ("us vs. them") identity formation. At roughly the same time, the functional requirements of coping with uncertainty are met. Since there is no defined set of probabilities, agents, in Frank Knight's words, "must take various and shifting groupings according to the purpose or problem in view, assimilating things now on the basis of one common property (mode of behavior) and now on the basis of another."[12] Identifying commonalities in the psychological sense interacts with identifying common properties in the analytic sense. Both processes establish categories that determine essential qualities and set expectations, key factors in adapting to uncertainty. These processes not only interact but intensify

[12] Frank H. Knight, *Risk, Uncertainty, and Profit* (Boston: Houghton Mifflin, 1921), 206.

256   Conclusion

each other. Sorting the environment into norm followers and breakers coincides with corporate identity formation. Valuation of actors and behaviors in such circumstances is likely to enhance corporate distinctions between "us" and "them," making negative identity formation and "othering" a more likely outcome. Conflict does not necessarily lead to an "other," but structural and behavioral deviation and cultural dissonance make this far more likely. Further intensification due to negative identity formation and severe deviation may lead to "evil othering." This process, in turn, is more likely to lead to circumstances where restraints on enforcing existing norms erode.

Mitzen employs ontological security to explain the persistence of disputes. Parties become wed to conflicts and regularized interactions as it satisfies their need for ontological security. It is not difficult to see how the processes outlined above, and the need for both physical and ontological security in the face of deviation, lead to conflicts where the adversary is seen not as useful but as baneful and worthy only of eradication. This helps explain exceeding norms for enforcement as a product of the intensification of intertwining processes of normative orientation and identity formation. Jef Huysmans points to the need for "fixing social relations into a symbolic and institutional order" in fulfilling the requirements of ontological security, and to the role of international society in not only "the elimination of enemies but ... the destruction of strangers, or more generally strangehood."[13] In this set of processes, the actual elimination of strangers is assisted through their cognitive transformation into irredeemable villains. This goes beyond Phillips' observation that constraints limit sociability among strangers, and creates a dynamic facilitating the strangers' destruction both cognitively and physically.

Appreciating the need to establish common properties in the flux inherent in conditions of uncertainty, it should not be so surprising that existing categorizations serve as a common reference. Similarly, common cultural bonds contribute to common identity formation. The fluidity of these processes was demonstrated in the case of the Mongols where they were first identified as saviors of Christendom and later transformed into messengers of Tartarus. This was a functional reaction to the condition of uncertainty assisted by a reservoir of cultural associations. This adaptability should not be confused with instrumentality: the intentional or even cynical application of categories. Fully ingrained beliefs aided provisional orientation and reaction. When this did not comport with the activities witnessed, other categories substituted. Whereas Buzan

---

[13] Jef Huysmans, "Security! What Do You Mean? From Concept to Thick Signifier," *European Journal of International Relations* 4, no. 2 (June 1998): 242.

International society   257

emphasizes the accumulation of solidarity from the functional processes operating in a system, in these cases common cultural bonds helped allow for the functioning in the first place. Most recently, in the struggle against Al Qaeda, the label "freedom-loving people" reflected a cultural bond that provided a reference point for distinguishing behavior that impinged on a set of common values and beliefs. In turn, this facilitated the categorization and enforcement seen as necessitated by the functional requirements for order.

Given that uncertainty and lack of familiarity play such prominent roles in the development of these categories and identities, how do varying and increasing levels of familiarity affect these processes? Are these actors considered dangerous things because we have little knowledge of them, or is a little knowledge more likely to exaggerate or misinterpret dangerous things? As indicated, it seems that both familiarity and lack thereof can breed contempt. The very familiarity with the Nizari Ismailis and the similarity of their doctrines – deviating but still within a range of Islamic thought – made sharp distinctions a necessity for the Sunni orthodoxy. Plausible associations that threatened core values and beliefs necessitated a strong distinction as apostates, i.e., worse than non-believers. The Nizaris' odd interactive modes made such distinctions even more necessary as they threatened both ontological and physical security.

The Mongols were initially so strange and foreign to Europeans that they could fulfill whichever cultural frames were plausible, including varying portrayals first as saviors and then as servants of the Antichrist. As the Europeans became somewhat more familiar with the Mongols, this limited understanding fed additional negative distinctions, ones that attributed to them a voracious, crude, and rootless nature. The case of the Barbary powers stands out since there were phases of relative ignorance and of fairly comprehensive interactions and understanding. Diplomatic relations with the powers regularized an irregular set of relations, paradoxically making their regular deviations part of an overall expected pattern. Yet much of the knowledge about the Barbary powers concerned captivity, and those real and distorted tales were more emotive and had a greater impact than the quotidian accounts of consuls. Early images of each of the historical actors, formed in the interaction of categorization and discrimination, turned out to be quite sticky. For instance, the collusion between the Barbary powers and the major European naval powers did not dilute their malign images over the long term. While such negative identities may be muted for a time, due to the intensification of the processes outlined above they are not likely to be fully revised or rehabilitated.

258   Conclusion

Might, rights, and rules: setting standards of civilization

The very stickiness of these categorizations and identities made their persistence over time more likely. Images of evil and subhuman beings with fantastic rituals and cruel demeanors became the source for ever-lasting negative associations. Over time, this study posited, norms would develop and become embedded as norms of partiality, benefiting the dominant members of international society. This element of the theory was not manifested in the cases directly through functional processes, but through their interaction with processes of identity formation. Norms concerning assassination had distinct sources not associated with its namesake, though that group was later employed to highlight its malign qualities. The same pattern holds true for the Barbary powers and piracy. Norms concerning piracy were rooted in interactions with lesser actors, and the Barbary powers were for a time excluded from that designation. Massacres like those of the Mongols were not uncommon, though perhaps not on the same scale, and a norm concerning the protection of noncombatants would come only later. In each case the negative imagery and valuation of the actors were later reassigned to reinforce those norms.

It is in this reassignment that standards of civilization were closely associated with images of historical "others." This firmed up the legitimacy of actors and activities in a modernizing international system where interactions were becoming standardized and power monopolized. Standards of civilization rooted in common identity provided boundaries for distinguishing actors that belonged to international society from those who did not. Considering the working definition of legitimacy, rightful membership and conduct in international society, the distinction between identity formation and normative designation fades in practice. Establishing membership in civilization, and in international society, requires identifying qualities and modes of behavior that make an actor worthy of participation. It is in these processes of categorization and discrimination that potent symbols from a distorted view of the past were instrumental.

This categorization and characterization coincided with the more aggressive investigation of the outside world during the Enlightenment. "From a perceived European 'center,'" Peter Hulme and Ludmilla Jordanova note, "writers began to speculate about the 'peripheral' parts of the world," providing the Enlightenment and European society with its "shadows."[14] Actors that operated in the shadows of systems, first as weak adjuncts and then often in the interstices, provided the raw material

---

[14] See Peter Hulme and Ludmilla Jordanova, "Introduction," in *The Enlightenment and Its Shadows*, ed. Hulme and Jordanova (London: Routledge, 1990), 7.

International society 259

for these imaginative interpretations. This imagery reinforced another European project of the time, the domination of the periphery. In so doing, it placed alien and weaker societies and their modes of resistance outside of the fold of civilization. Antagonism toward fanaticism, treachery, and mobility, combined with the elevation of stateness and valuation of human freedom to form civilizational standards. Al Qaeda would run headlong into each of these standards, contravening the limits placed on legitimate organization and behavior, standards that overwhelmingly benefit the dominant actors in the system. *This* clash with the *tenets* of civilization is what made its actions both so abominable and unexpected. Efforts to conflate Al Qaeda's origins and activities with a particular civilization are far less convincing.

These standards of civilization also make stark distinctions between certain types of violence. "Civilized warfare" requires an uncivilized "other" to mitigate its own horrors. Even before the atrocities of the twentieth century, there were concerns about "humanity's slide into barbarism," and the inability to distinguish barbarism from civilization.[15] The splendor of Caesar would be contrasted with the bloodthirstiness of Genghis Khan, even though both were exceedingly brutal. As the impropriety of Western "civilized" warfare increased, the West needed Genghis Khan to distinguish exceptional from routine acts of carnage. Earlier it needed the figure of the foreign and fiendish Assassin to add vibrancy and distance to the very old, very European practices of tyrannicide and political murder. The Barbary powers were perfect foils to depict German naval depredations, and even in this era provided false historical continuity due to their deviant violence and adherence to Islam.

The theoretical implications of this discussion reaffirm Daniel Nexon's conclusion that "[c]onstructivists and realists can enrich one another's understanding of international political processes without sacrificing either on the altar of the other."[16] A focus of this study has been to examine the ways in which insights from realism, particularly a variant of neorealism, and the English School could combine and be applied to a particular research problem. This was achieved without either losing their coherence as research programs, while each aided in compensating for the other's weaknesses. It also reveals that the potential affinities of realism and constructivism are not limited to classical realism.[17] While

---

[15] Joanna Bourke, "Barbarisation *vs.* Civilisation in Time of War," in *The Barbarization of Warfare*, ed. George Kassimeris (New York: New York University Press, 2006), 19.

[16] Daniel H. Nexon, "Realism and Constructivism," *Duck of Minerva* Blog, September 26, 2005.

[17] See Samuel Barkin, *Realist Constructivism: Rethinking International Relations Theory* (Cambridge: Cambridge University Press, 2010).

260   Conclusion

fundamental epistemological and methodological barriers remain, this does not prevent the careful application and combination of theories and concepts, which may be beneficial for both theory and practice when applied to real-world problems. Synthesis of research programs is not necessary to derive benefits. Analytic eclecticism requires only that the overlap and relative strengths of paradigms be appreciated and utilized. This should be coupled with a more general recognition that paradigmatic exclusivity is a prescription for regressive research programs in a world characterized by an expanding array of combinatorial possibilities, ideational and material.

International society, barbarism, and the "war of ideas"

In the years following the attacks of September 11, there was much discussion of engaging in a "war of ideas" as a means to counter Al Qaeda. Applying our ideas in order to influence outcomes has yielded, and likely will continue to bring, limited results. To the extent that we can affect perceptions, our emphasis should be limited to correcting misrepresentations while avoiding the appearance of meddling in intra-Muslim world debates, and, above all, not making major mistakes.[18] Promoting Western values such as democracy and individual freedoms has its salutary effects, but Western civilization means different and often decidedly negative things to a significant swath of the Muslim world.[19] The characterization of a clash of civilizations, which is a godsend for Al Qaeda and ISIS leaders, pits what many view as a corrupted Western society against a gang of deranged fanatics, not presenting the most palatable choice.

More emphasis should be placed on proliferating the raw material for the formation of norms and firming of identities than on any grand struggle of ideas. The primary generators of those norms and identities are not found in Washington, D.C. or London, but in the Muslim world itself. Steven Simon and Jeff Martini called for "marshaling" and "propagating" norms against Al Qaeda and the use of terrorism.[20] Many of their suggestions are sound, including supporting institutions to bolster

---

[18] Abu Ghraib did incalculable damage to the image of the United States and the West, while many point to the invasion of Iraq as a singular error. See Fawaz A. Gerges, "Iraq War Fuels Global Jihad," *YaleGlobal Online*, December 21, 2006.

[19] According to a 2006 poll, "large percentages in nearly every Muslim country attribute several negative traits to Westerners – including violence, immorality and selfishness." "The Great Divide: How Westerners and Muslims View Each Other," Pew Global Attitudes Project, June 22, 2006, 4.

[20] Steven Simon and Jeff Martini, "Terrorism: Denying Al Qaeda Its Popular Support," *The Washington Quarterly* 28, no. 1 (Winter 2004–05): 131–45.

International society, barbarism, and the "war of ideas"   261

segments of the Arab and Muslim world that hold consistent values, but the application of their proposals is compromised by long-standing US support for oppressive Arab regimes. There are also conceptual issues with their suggestions that have practical implications. Norms and identities result in large part from intersubjective understandings and are not readily marshaled or propagated. The discussion in the previous chapters of how certain norms evolved over decades, even centuries, and of their stubbornness in their selective diffusion, highlights that norms are not readily manipulated. Overstating the level of intentionality and precision in the development and application of norms exaggerates their utility as instruments of policy.

The case studies revealed that new norms are rarely applied when actors can be fit into existing normative categories. That has been the case with Al Qaeda, and to the extent this represents marshaling norms then this has had the effect of clearly demarcating their acts as beyond the pale. Where this falls short is in distinguishing the violence perpetrated by Al Qaeda from that of other actors. In many respects, by lumping Al Qaeda in with terrorist groups of lesser scope and scale normative judgments can be diluted, its actions being part of a broader set of irregular violence, some of which is viewed as legitimate by key constituents in the "war of ideas." There are significant segments of the Muslim world that either passively or actively support groups like Hamas. As objectionable as the goals and means of Hamas are, casting such a wide net – reinforcing norms concerning terrorism generally rather than specifying the aims and activities of Al Qaeda and its offshoots – is likely to have more modest effects. The efforts to counter each of these types of threat should be disaggregated and the measures to cultivate and reinforce norms and identities, to the extent they can be, should be actor-centric. Portions of the Arab and Muslim worlds, where the norms and identities we would hope to marshal would originate, *do* condemn Al Qaeda and hug Hamas.[21] Efforts in recent years to move away from universalizing the conflict, the broader "war on terror," are welcome yet have arrived late in trying to narrow its parameters.

So how do the United States and the West cultivate, rather than propagate, norms consistent with our values and interests? There may be more promise in shaping corporate identity, "us vs. them," in an effort

---

[21] Favorable views of Hamas in states with substantial Muslim populations in the Middle East, Africa, and Asia have been nearly double those of Al Qaeda, according to a Pew Research poll. Over a third of respondents in three Arab states (Jordan, Egypt, and Tunisia) were favorable toward Hamas, while views of Al Qaeda were favorable for 11, 15, and 9 percent in those states, respectively. See "Concerns about Islamic Extremism on the Rise in the Middle East," Pew Global Attitudes Project, July 1, 2014.

262   Conclusion

to reinforce and enforce norms, but this leverage is still quite limited. As the "war on terror" progressed, observers emphasized the potential positive influence of language, noting that "jihadist" is not necessarily pejorative in the Muslim world, and terms like *"mufsidoon,"* which in Arabic means "evildoer," would have more resonance.[22] Efforts to change the language used to describe Al Qaeda and its cohorts to coincide with valuations already present in the Muslim world would be a bit tardy, and perhaps patronizing. The potential effects of negative language engineering are more pronounced, and actively working to avoid those tendencies is probably more beneficial than relabeling in the hopes for unspecified salutary effects. Naming our adversaries, particularly attempts at severe negative identification, has in the past courted dehumanization, supporting and justifying policies that were ultimately counterproductive and often self-destructive.

In addition to moving away from the overly broad definition of the enemy, the Obama administration has sought to dispel Al Qaeda's association with Islam. President Obama elaborated this theme in his June 2009 speech in Cairo addressing the Muslim world, and his chief counterterrorism adviser John Brennan later reinforced it:

Describing terrorists in this way, using the legitimate term "jihad," which means to purify oneself or to wage a holy struggle for a moral goal, risks giving these murderers the religious legitimacy they desperately seek but in no way deserve. Worse, it risks reinforcing the idea that the United States is somehow at war with Islam itself. . . . Instead, as the president has made clear, we are at war with al-Qaida, which attacked us on 9/11 and killed 3,000 people. We are at war with its violent extremist allies who seek to carry on al-Qaida's murderous agenda. These are the terrorists we will destroy; these are the extremists we will defeat.[23]

Distancing Islam as a faith and tradition from the ideology and practices of Al Qaeda is a reasonable goal, particularly in the presence of ill-considered conflations like "Islamofascism" and absurd paranoid fantasists' warnings of "stealth jihadism." Terms like these reemphasize the effects of chronic uncertainty on ontological insecurity, engendering facile conceptions of a poorly defined threat. Jettisoning the terms "jihad" or "jihadist," however, may have more drawbacks than benefits. More recently, suggestions have been made to modify the self-professed name of ISIS, the "Islamic State," to emphasize its un-Islamic and non-state nature.[24] But avoiding or altering these labels in public discourse

[22] See James Fallows, "Declaring Victory," *The Atlantic*, September 2006, 69.
[23] John O. Brennan, "A New Approach for Safeguarding Americans," Address to the Center for Strategic and International Studies, August 6, 2009.
[24] Dan Bifelsky, "In New Front against Islamic State, Dictionary Becomes a Weapon," *New York Times*, October 2, 2014.

International society, barbarism, and the "war of ideas" 263

may effectively distance Al Qaeda and its ilk from one of their greatest transgressions, perverting venerated Islamic tenets to pursue power and justify violence. This risks diluting one of the arguments against Al Qaeda and ISIS that has the most potential to resonate in the Islamic world, that the groups do great violence not only to Muslims but to Islam itself.

Emphasizing the damage Al Qaeda has done to the Muslim world presents greater promise than language shifts that are likely to accomplish little. The focus should not be on "evildoers" but rather their evil doings, undoing Al Qaeda's self-professed role as a defender of the Muslim world.[25] Rather than attempts at norm propagation or engaging in rhetorical manipulation, enabling negative identification within reasonable bounds, easing but not unleashing norm enforcement, is the most promising avenue for shaping outcomes. This should avoid any focus on the West and its values as inherently good and worthy of emulation, favoring emphasizing that the enemy's acts are bad, making it worthy of marginalization and neutralization. Many in the Muslim world, including a share of the vast majority who do not support violence, see emulation of Western forms and norms as a recipe for subordination and decline.[26] Promotion of the West and its ideals may be more self-congratulatory than effective in helping bring about a more thorough rejection of Al Qaeda and radical Islamist militancy.

While the current conflict is not part of a clash of civilizations, the Muslim world is its own civilization, one fused with elements of Western civilization. This civilization has within it the values and beliefs to recognize Al Qaeda as a distortion rather than a reflection of itself, a monstrosity not only of international society but of Muslim society. Focusing on evil doings rather than "evildoers" entails cataloging and promoting their wide array of transgressions and atrocities. We do not need to invent detestable acts, like Belgian babies bayoneted by the Kaiser's Huns. After Abu Musab al-Zarqawi's bombing of three hotels in Amman, bin Laden's popularity plummeted in Jordan.[27] Blowing up a wedding party will do that, and it is imperative that the United States and other Western powers do more to routinely advertise and clearly depict Al Qaeda's brutality. ISIS's horrifying immolation of a Jordanian pilot, its ritual drowning of prisoners, and beheading of "sorceresses," have generated their own momentum for revulsion due to their extraordinary cruelty. We have a

---

[25] Al Qaeda's killing of Muslims is a key vulnerability that directly undermines this representation. See Alia Brahimi, "Crushed in the Shadows: Why Al Qaeda Will Lose the War of Ideas," *Studies in Conflict & Terrorism* 33, no. 2 (February 2010): 93–110.

[26] See Bernard Lewis, *What Went Wrong? Western Impact and Middle East Response* (Oxford: Oxford University Press, 2002).

[27] "The Great Divide," 3.

264   Conclusion

ready-made enemy that repeatedly makes its own case for extinction. Efforts to highlight this violence, by widely and energetically advertising the range of depraved acts committed in Islam's name, would seem to have been an obvious tactic, but had received little emphasis until recently.[28] Providing this raw material for negative identification holds far more promise than professions of Western merit and our enemy's intrinsic, as opposed to demonstrated, evil.

Focusing on the actions rather than suggesting an innate evil nature of these adversaries also helps prevent the processes that might allow for a return to the "barbarian option," unchecked exertion of power against alien enemies. Normative frameworks that do not leave off at states' edge should provide an effective bulwark, narrowing the legal expanse that served as a no-man's land and site of our own depravity exercised in the name of defending civilization.[29] The extension of protections for state-based personnel to others, preferably before they become "others," is one essential step. It is especially important if we consider that violence perpetrated from outside of and against the normative framework of international society and its rights and rules is likely to remain common, if not predominant. More routine deviation from legitimate forms of resistance may lessen the severity of the processes of extreme negative identification and subsequent norm transgression by established powers, as coping with the unfamiliar becomes more commonplace. But the experience of the post-9/11 reaction to novelty and deviance should not give us confidence that the same mistakes will not be repeated.

How do we temper our response without legitimizing means that weaker yet determined enemies employ? One reason that "terrorism" and "terrorist" are so clumsy analytically and normatively is that it is very difficult to declare the tactic of terrorism as inhumane without declaring terrorists inhuman. The use of "terrorist" as a moniker essentializes inhumane acts in the humans who perpetrate them. Delegitimizing means while standardizing treatment of combatants, state-based or not, has to be part of this effort. These measures must also be insulated to the extent possible from manipulation due to state interests. This recalls the machinations of the jurists who justified then condemned the acts of the Barbary powers as it served state needs, or further back to the exclusion of

---

[28] See Ali Weinberg, "Obama's Social Media Strategy against ISIS Falling Short, Experts Say," ABCNews.com, October 1, 2014.

[29] In November 2014, following a request from the UN body that monitors compliance with the Convention against Torture and Other Cruel, Inhuman, or Degrading Treatment or Punishment, the United States clarified that it would adhere to the convention's prohibitions "at all times, and in all places." "Statement by NSC Spokesperson Bernadette Meehan on the U.S. Presentation to the Committee against Torture," The White House, Office of the Press Secretary, November 12, 2014.

Confounding power 265

the "Batiniyya" by al-Ghazali. We need not go back that far into history when we recall the justification for torture against Al Qaeda prisoners by citing their non-inclusion in the protections of the Geneva Convention.[30] While allowances safeguarding those who commit detestable acts rankle some, by protecting "them" we are at the same time protecting and defining "us."

Conclusion: confounding power

This study focused on how certain actors under constrained systemic circumstances challenged the dominant actors who defined those systems. Through a combination of systemic opportunities, outside support, resourcefulness, and guile, they overcame the severely precarious conditions that accompanied their emergence. Despite these successes in establishing themselves as oddities within these systems, they still suffered from their divergent forms and behaviors. The Nizari Ismailis persevered, vexing their rivals, but their peculiarity and ambitions led them to creep to the edge of extinction. The Mongols experienced increasing organizational impediments and limitations as their scale increased, eventually succumbing to their internal contradictions. The Barbary powers reached a level of accommodation that allowed them to persist even as they weakened and European navies achieved the capacity to defeat them. Each actor eventually perished due to either external pressures (the Nizaris), internal contradictions (the Mongols), or a combination of both (the Barbary powers). Al Qaeda also seems likely to become a victim of both as its expansion to regions of instability has been accompanied, much like the Mongols, by fissures in its overall leadership's authority, and as it continues to wear down under external pressure.

How can those actors in the fold of contemporary international society hasten this process? Three senses of constraint, borrowed from Anthony Giddens, were cited in this study. These were material constraints (those dealing with access to materials), structural constraints (those dealing with other actors), and negative sanctions. While both material and structural constraints were demonstrated to lead to variety in international systems, they may just as easily, and indeed more often, suppress such deviation. Creating a severely straitened operational environment has been a key strategy in confronting Al Qaeda, involving a range of military, diplomatic, and legal means, with the denial of safe havens touching each.

---

[30] *The New York Times* has provided a valuable service in aggregating the memos that justify these measures. See "A Guide to the Memos on Torture," *New York Times*, 2005.

266   Conclusion

Will Al Qaeda fall apart like the Mongols, devolving into regional entities with a semblance of their progenitor's character, or hunker down and eke out an existence like the Nizaris? Though efforts to date to root out Al Qaeda completely have been unsuccessful, much, though certainly not all, of its effectiveness has been constrained. It seems unlikely that a Nizari-like strategy can be viable for long, even with the facilitating communications technologies that extend its reach and influence. ISIS's capacity to withstand meaningful military force is now being tested, though its Iraq-based predecessor's ability to survive years of withering attacks does give pause. For Al Qaeda, conspicuous successes in attacking Western interests are likely the only way to maintain support from its younger, socially disaffected following, particularly with the challenge posed by ISIS. Being bottled up and fomenting modest attacks by dubious surrogates does not seem to be an effective long-term strategy. Moreover, the United States possesses such technological dominance that an eventual Mongol-like routing as the Nizaris suffered remains a distinct possibility. That does not suggest the unthinking broadened application of force, which would be wasteful and counterproductive by its undermining of international society. An emphasis on restraint, however, does not preclude the use of force and utilizing the power that our technological and material dominance provides.

The combination of military, diplomatic, and legal measures will in time result in Al Qaeda's demise. How long this will take and in what form is uncertain, like much surrounding its activities. As discussed in the previous chapter, the idea of a "Long War" against "Islamic extremism" is a bad one due to its imprecision identifying the principal adversary and resulting amenability to prophetic self-fulfillment. How Al Qaeda ends, whether it evolves into barely recognizable fragments or disappears, will affect how easily we can discern its expiration. The potential for ambiguity concerning the level of threat and the overarching conditions of uncertainty, however, should not be used to justify continuing the scale and scope of current counterterrorism efforts. Nor does the inability of Al Qaeda to execute "spectacular" attacks justify fully reeling in those counterterrorism capabilities that have made such attacks less likely. These are dilemmas distinct from efforts against conventional adversaries, with continued uncertainty confounding our ability to know when, or if, to cease our efforts and how best to apply our power.

The actors examined in this study were "error makers" or "stochasts," deviating forms contending in the pitched competition of their respective international systems. These were confounding powers in the sense of bucking systemic pressures and constraints, as well as in their inscrutable modes and behaviors. They have also confounded by defying easy treatment in existing theoretical constructs. Their survival, persistence, and impact on their systems were not adequately accounted for in prevailing approaches in the study of international politics. This confounding required a broader founding of the logics of anarchy that better incorporated both the economy and the ecology of international systems, to appreciate the possibilities of international "life" that contravene ingrained patterns and expectations. Possibilities when they are not clearly estimable lead to conditions of uncertainty. Coping with such uncertainty and processes underlying the formation of identities, in tandem, have had distinct effects on the development of international society. These insights demonstrate the necessity for both intra- and inter-paradigmatic pathways to theoretical progress, opening the possibility of understanding a broader range of historical experiences, and, in turn, aiding in comprehending future theoretical and policy challenges.

Index

Abbasid Caliphate, 72, 76, 89, 90
  al-Mustazhir (Caliph), 92
  destruction by Mongols (1258), 124
  successor states, 71–74
abolition(ists), 194–97
  Vienna Declaration (1815), 196
Abu Bakr (Caliph), 95
Abu Geith, Suleiman, 224
Adams, John, 147, 194
Afghanistan. *See also* Soviet Union, 73,
  200, 203, 208–17, 222, 229, 231,
  241, 248
Al Qaeda. *See also* bin Laden, Osama;
  al-Zawahiri, Ayman; Azzam, Abdullah,
  2, 3, 4, 7, 9, 11, 18, 22, 108, 199–242,
  243, 245, 246, 248, 249–50, 253, 257,
  259, 260–66
  Africa embassy bombing (1998), 228
  Al Qaeda in Iraq, 225, 249
  Bayt al-Ansar (House of Supporters), 213
  far enemy vs. near enemy, 219, 220
  London transit bombings (2005),
  226, 238
  Maktab al-Khidamat (Office of Services,
  MAK), 213
  Ma'sadat al-Ansar (Lion's Den of the
  Supporters), 213
  regional affiliates, 225–27
  significance of, 1–2
  transatlantic airline plot (2006), 226
  USS *Cole* bombing (2000), 231
al-Din, Salah (Saladin)
  Ayyubid dynasty, 89
  perceptions by Europeans,
  Crusaders, 98
  relations with the Nizaris, 89
Aleppo, 87
al-Faqih, Saad, 220–21
Algeria, 154–55, 166, 218
  colonial intervention, 197
  Oran, 156, 167
  Tlemcen, 155, 157, 158

al-Ghazali, Abu Hamid, 92–94, 265
Algiers. *See also* Algeria, 151, 156, 157–58,
  159, 161, 164, 166–67, 168–70,
  173–75, 179, 184, 187–89,
  191–96, 197
Ali (Caliph), 82, 94
Alighieri, Dante (*Divine Comedy*), 100
al-Iraqi, Abd al-Hadi, 231–33
al-Mulk, Nizam, 76, 82
  Nizamiyya (madrasas), 84
  Siyasat-Nama, 77
al-Suri, Abu Musab, 219
al-Zarqawi, Abu Musab, 225, 263
al-Zawahiri, Ayman, 205, 214, 218, 220,
  221, 249
Amman (Jordan), 260
Anabaptists, 101
analytic eclecticism (theoretical pluralism),
  8–9, 260
anarchy, 6, 7, 10, 14, 21, 24, 25, 26, 31, 32,
  37, 45, 48, 51, 52, 55, 60–61, 69, 244,
  246, 267
  and necessity, 24
Angell, Norman (*The Great Illusion*),
  148
apostasy (apostate), 93–96, 173, 184, 185,
  225, 253, 257
  apostate regimes (Al Qaeda declared),
  219, 243
  takfir, declaring as, 93
Arab Afghans, 209–13, 217, 219
Armenia, 135
Arnold of Lubeck, 97
Aron, Raymond, 46
Ashcroft, John, 237
Attila the Hun (Huns), 67, 145–48,
  150, 263
Augustine (of Hippo), 178
Axelrod, Robert, 62, 63
Azzam, Abdullah, 213–14, 215
  al-qaeda al-sulbah (*al-Jihad* magazine),
  213–14

268

Index

Bacon, Francis, 101
Baghdad Pact, 202, 203
Barbarossa brothers, 157–60, 252
  al-Din, Khayr (Khizr), 157–59, 160
  Arudj, 157–58
  death of Arudj (1518), 157–58
  death of Khayr al-Din (1546), 160
  Hasan (son of Khayr al-Din), 163
Barbary powers. *See also* Algiers, Rabat-Salé, Tripoli, Tunis, 3, 5, 17, 18, 20, 22, 151–98, 236, 244, 245, 246, 247, 248, 249, 250, 253–54, 257, 258, 259, 264, 265
  agha (janissary commander), 166
  bey (regional governor), 166, 167, 169, 180
  beylerbey (military governor), 160–61, 163, 166
  captivity narratives, 184, 190, 191–92
  dey (ruler), 166, 167, 169, 187
  divan (officer council), 161, 166, 195
  number of captives taken, 152, 183–84
  origin of "Barbary", 154
  redemption (of captives), 185, 189
  regencies (label by European powers), 161
  renegades (runagate), 157, 173, 184, 190, 194
  September 11 analogy, 153, 259
  ta'ifat al-ra'is (sea captain guild), 161, 166
  triennial pashas period, 161
  ujaq (janissary power base), 161, 166
Barfield, Thomas, 110, 114, 117, 123, 126
Barkin, Samuel, 11–12
Barnett, Michael, 201, 202–3
beheading, 225–26, 249–50, 263
Benjamin, Daniel, 206
Berber (dynasties), 154–55
  Hafsids, 154, 157, 158, 160
Berend, Nora, 134
bin Laden, Osama, 210, 211–12, 213–14, 215–21, 222, 228, 239–40, 249, 252, 263
bin Laden, Muhammad (father), 204
Jaji (Afghanistan), Battle of, 213
Binalshibh, Ramzi, 223
Black, Jeremy, 102, 143
blowback, 35–36, 38, 250–51
  and Al Qaeda, 210–13, 250
  and the Barbary powers, 164–65, 250
  and the Mongols, 114, 116–17, 250
  and the Nizari Ismailis, 84, 250
Bonaparte, Napoleon, 147
Bosnia, 215

Brennan, John, 262
Brzezinski, Zbigniew, 212
Buell, Paul, 116, 118, 121
Buffon, Comte de, 144
Bukhara, 118
Bull, Hedley, 17, 41, 42, 44
Burke, Edmund
  and Algiers, 188–89
  and homogeneity, 46
  and the Nizari Ismailis (Assassins), 102–3
  Further Reflections on the Revolution, 103
Burns, Conrad, 238
Buyids, 72, 73, 75, 76
  "Iranian Intermezzo", 73
Buzan, Barry, 6, 10, 16, 23–24, 27, 41–47, 221, 253, 256–57
Byzantine Empire (Byzantium), 74, 75, 76, 78
  comparison with the United States, 216–17

Caesar, Julius, 145, 259
Carthage (destruction of), 149
Central Asia, 76, 111, 118, 121, 132, 208, 213, 215, 216, 220
Central Intelligence Agency (CIA), 210, 213
  Hayden, Michael (General), 237
  prisons, 240
Cerny, Philip, 29
Chechnya, 215, 229
Chinggis Khan (Temüjin, Genghis Khan), 22, 108–9, 113, 114–17, 119, 123–25, 130, 131, 141, 142, 145, 146, 147–50, 198, 252, 259
  born (c. 1162), 114
  death of (1227), 118
  relationship with Jin, 113, 115–17, 250
Churchill, Winston, 149
"Cinque-tetes, or the Paris Monster" (1798), 192, 193
Clark, Ian, 43–44
Clarke, Peter, 238
"clash of civilizations", 201, 205, 238, 239, 240, 260, 263
Cold War, 201, 202–3, 204, 212, 214, 216, 218, 221, 241
  "myth of the superpowers", 217, 219
Congress of Vienna (1814–1815). 180, 196
Connolly, William, *See also* abolition (ists), 56
Conrad of Montferrat, 99
conspiracy (charges of). *See also* United States, military commissions, 93, 232–33

270 Index

Constant, Benjamin, 147
constructivism, 7, 25, 48, 67, 255
  and neorealism, 11–12, 259
Crusader (Frankish) states and orders, 71,
  87, 88, 90
  Antioch, 87
  Edessa, 87
  Hospitallers, 87
  Kingdom of Jerusalem, 87, 99
  Templars, 87
  Tripoli (Levant), 87
Crusades, 76, 78, 96, 99, 102, 149

Daftary, Farhad, 79, 82, 83, 86, 96, 100
Damascus, 87
Dardess, John, 127, 128–29
Davis, Robert, 183, 185
Deudney, Daniel, 36
Dewey, John, 1, 243
Dodgshon, Robert, 39
dominance structures, 201, 219
Doran, Michael, 207, 224

East Turkestan Islamic Movement, 229
Egypt. *See also* Fatimid dynasty, 74, 76, 89,
  154, 156, 188, 189, 201, 202, 218, 220
  al-Qahira (Cairo), 76
emulation and socialization, 4, 6, 12, 13,
  23, 25, 26–28, 39–40, 48, 53, 60, 61,
  69, 125, 246–47
  and innovation, 28
England (Britain), 4, 152, 171, 172, 174–75,
  177, 178, 181, 183, 184, 185, 188, 189,
  190, 192, 196, 201, 202, 238, 254
  Anglo–Spanish naval expedition
    (1620), 174
  Charles II (King), 100
  defeat of Algerine ships (1671), 166
  James I (King), 185
  London, 226, 238, 260
  Oxford University, 100
  Rabat-Salé naval expedition (1638), 175
  Richard the Lionheart (King), 99
English School. *See also* international
  society, 10, 41, 42, 227
  and (neo)realism, 10, 13, 67, 259
Enlightenment, 101, 102, 106, 142, 152,
  186, 188, 190, 258
error makers, stochasts (actors as), 39, 266

factors of protection (manpower, technics,
  space), 33–34, 85, 246
Fatimid Empire, 74–75, 76
  al-Musta'li (Caliph), 79
  al-Mustansir (Caliph), 78, 79

da'is, 77, 78–79, 81, 87–88, 93, 244
da'wa, 74, 77, 79, 93
  decline of, 71, 78, 79, 84, 244
Ferguson, Adam
  and Algiers, 187
  and the Mongols (Tartars), 145
First Council of Lyon (1245), 99, 140
First World War
  comparison Germans and Huns, 67, 263
  German use of submarines (Barbary
    comparison), 198, 259
Five Dynasties and Ten Kingdoms
  (China), 110
France, 4, 5, 156, 158–59, 172, 175, 180,
  181, 182, 192, 196, 197, 254
  Francis I (King), 158
  French Revolution, 102–3, 106, 188–89
  Nice, 172
  Philip Augustus II (King), 99
Franklin, Benjamin, 190, 192, 194, 195
Frederick II (Holy Roman Emperor),
  99, 133
Frederick the Great (II, King)
  and Silesia, 187

Geneva Convention(s), 230, 243, 265
Genoa (Genoese), 154
  Doria, Andrea, 158, 160
Gentili, Alberico
  and the Barbary powers, 177–78
  and the Nizari Ismailis (Assassins), 104
Georgia, 135
Ghaffur, Tarique, 238
Ghaznavids, 73, 76
Gibbon, Edward
  and Algiers, 187–88
  and the Mongols (Tartars), 143–44
  and the Nizari Ismailis (Assassins),
    101–2, 107
  Decline and Fall of the Roman Empire, 143
Giddens, Anthony
  types of constraints, 31, 265
Gilpin, Robert, 10
globalization, 30, 200, 221–22, 246
Gobineau, Arthur de, 148
Godfrey (of Bouillon), 150
Gog and Magog, 135, 139, 141
Goguet, Antoine-Yves, 144
Gong, Gerrit, 65–66
Grotius, Hugo, 104, 146, 197
  and the Barbary powers, 178–79

Haiti (Saint Domingue, Haitians), 105, 194
Halliday, Fred, 46–47
Hamas, 229, 261

Index

271

Hamdan, Salim, 233, 243
Hamdanids, 72, 74
Hamdi, Yaser Esam, 233
Haqqani, Jalaluddin, 209, 211
Hartley, David, 192
Hasan, Nidal (Ft. Hood shooting), 239
Hekmatyar, Gulbuddin, 209, 211
Henry IV (King of France), 100, 104
Hodgson, Marshall, 81, 82, 83, 86, 90, 93
Holsti, Kalevi, 8
Hsi Hsia, 110, 112, 118
   destruction by the Mongols (1227), 119
Hume, David, 188
Hungary, 134, 136
   Béla (king), 133
   Mongol invasion (1241), 124, 133
   tatárjárás (Mongols compared to
     locusts), 134
Huysmans, Jef, 58, 59, 256

Ibn Khaldun, 144
Ibn Taymiyya, 206, 220
Iceland, 152, 173
   Reykjavik, 172
identity (identity formation), 3, 4, 7, 10–11,
   12, 14–15, 21, 22, 24, 25–26, 36, 37,
   41, 43, 44–48, 53–61, 62, 64–69, 71,
   72, 83, 90, 91, 92, 94–96, 97–98, 99,
   100, 103, 109, 132, 138–41, 145,
   152–53, 173, 182–86, 189–90, 192,
   197, 200, 231–32, 236–39, 248,
   252–58, 260–64, 267
   common/collective/corporate, defined,
     54–55
   homogenization ("others"), 56–57, 64,
     190, 229, 239
   maximization, 60, 64
   "others," "othering," "evil others", 3, 26,
     54–60, 64–65, 67, 68, 95, 132, 140,
     145, 189, 190, 199, 240, 255, 256,
     258, 259, 264
   "us vs. them", 55, 255, 261
   "we-feeling", 44, 55, 64, 132, 255
imam (imamate), 74, 77, 81, 102
India, 72, 126, 203, 208, 247
   East India Company, 17
   Thugs (Thuggee), 105
individual leadership (as factor), 6, 19, 35,
   108, 123, 251–52
interaction capacity, 222, 225
international society, 1–13, 15, 21–22,
   23–26, 41–48, 53, 55, 57, 61–69, 72,
   104, 106, 109, 152, 177, 190, 200,
   227–28, 235, 236, 237, 241, 243–44,
   250, 252–67

and homogeneity, 46–48
and legitimacy, 4, 10, 26, 42, 43–45, 47,
   61, 64, 68
"barbarian option", 66, 240, 264
defined, 42
pluralist vs. solidarist, 44–48, 61
standards of civilization, 4, 26,
   65–67, 68, 104, 106, 143, 150,
   153, 182, 197–98, 201, 241, 254,
   258–59
Iran (Persia), 72, 73, 76, 77, 78–79, 85,
   122, 154, 248
   Daylam, 72, 79
   Gilan, 72
   Iranian Revolution, 204
   Persia comparison with Soviet Union,
     216–17, 245
   Qomm, 78
   Quhistan, 82
   Zagros (mountains), 72
Iraq, 73, 77, 149, 237, 242
   Abu Ghraib (prison), 240
   Baghdad, 72, 76, 78, 90
   Baghdad sacked by Mongols (1258), 131,
     132, 140, 149
   Basra, 88
   invasion of Kuwait (1990), 204, 217
   Mosul 74, 75
Islamic Awakening (*al-sahwa al
   Islamiyya*), 205
Islamic State of Iraq and Syria (ISIS), 226,
   227, 237, 239, 242, 250, 251, 260,
   262–63, 266
Islamism (Islamist), 200, 205–7, 208, 209,
   215, 216, 217, 218
   radical Islamism, 205, 206–8, 209,
     212–13, 215, 220, 263
"Islamofascism", 262
Ismailism, 74, 78, 84, 85, 92
   batin and *zahir*, 77
   "black legend", 94, 96
Israel, 147, 205, 217, 220
   Six Day War (1967), 205
Italy, 156, 172
   Leghorn (Livorno), 172

Jackson, Patrick T., 12–13
Jackson, Peter, 126
Jaish-e-Mohammed, 229
Jamestown (Virginia), 195
Jamuqa, 116
   relationship with Temüjin (Chinggis
     Khan), 115, 117
Jefferson, Thomas, 104, 147
   and the Barbary powers, 194

272   Index

Jerusalem. *See also* Crusader (Frankish) states and orders, Kingdom of Jerusalem, 87
siege of (1099), 149, 150
"jihad," "jihadist" (use of terms), 262–63
Jin dynasty (Jurchen), 109, 110, 112, 113, 114, 119, 120, 126, 132, 245
decline of, 117–18
defeat by Mongols (1234), 118, 121, 124
establishment of (1121), 111
Jüyin (frontier auxiliary forces), 118, 120
Mongol invasion (1211), 118
relationship with Temüjin (Chinggis Khan), 115–17, 250
Juvayni, 'Ata-Malik, 70

Karakhitai (Western Liao dynasty), 111, 112, 245
submission to Mongols (1218), 118, 121
Katzenstein, Peter, 8–9, 15, 43
Kepel, Gilles, 215
Kerry, John, 149
Khitan (Liao dynasty), 110, 111, 112, 118, 126, 127
Khorezmshah (Muhammad), 112, 119, 121, 245
decline of, 121
defeat by Mongols (1221), 118, 121
King David, 134, 137
Kipchaks (Cumans, Polovtsi), 133
Knight, Frank, 51–52, 255
Knights of Malta (Maltese corsairs), 17, 159, 160, 168
Kowert, Paul, 56–57

Lashkar-e-Tayyiba, 229
Lattimore, Owen, 120, 124
Leslie, T.E. Cliffe, 23
Lewis, Bernard, 70–71, 78, 79, 85, 103, 239–40
liability of newness, 25, 35, 211, 250–51
Lieber, Francis (Lieber Code), 105, 231
Little, Richard, 10, 16, 27
logic of dissimilation, 3, 25, 31–36, 37, 38, 165, 246–48
logics of concealment, 3, 25, 36–39, 85, 137–38, 176, 248–50
Lord Byron, 151
Lorimer, James
Institutes of the Law of Nations (1883), 196–97
Lustick, Ian, 201–2

Maghreb, 72, 77, 153–57, 160, 165, 180, 201, 245, 248
and piracy, 157
political conditions of, 154–55
Mamluks, 90, 126, 156, 188, 189, 247
defeat by Ottomans (1517), 154
defeat of Mongols (1260), 124
Syrian Nizari submission to (1273), 89
Manchuria, 109, 110, 111
"Manchurian Candidates", 126
Mantran, Robert, 155, 166
Marlowe, Christopher (*Tamburlaine*), 184
Martini, Jeff, 260–61
Marx, Karl, 46
Massoud, Ahmed Shah, 210–11
Mather, Cotton, 195
Mawdudi, Sayyid Abu'l-A'la, 206
May, Timothy, 123
McCarthy, Joseph, 238
McSweeney, Bill, 3, 54, 106
Mearsheimer, John, 48–49
Mediterranean, 74, 75, 154, 155, 157, 158, 160, 162, 172, 190, 245
and piracy, 151, 152, 172
Mendelsohn, Barak, 235
Merton, Robert, 29–30, 32
methodology, 13–21
"actorhood," significance criteria, 16–18, 227
case selection, 16–21, 89
comparative process analysis, 13
conflict groups, 16–17
deviant cases, 19, 108
discourse analysis, 13, 15
historiography, improvements in, , 19, 21
Mitzen, Jennifer, 58–59, 254, 256
Mohammed, Khalid Shaykh, 199
Möngke Khan, 124, 128, 131, 249
death of (1259), 125
Mongol successor states, 124, 125
Ilkhanid, 124, 126
Mongols (Mongol Empire). *See also* Chinggis Khan, Möngke Khan, Mongol successor states, tribal federations, 3, 6, 18, 19, 20, 22, 70, 80, 86, 89, 90, 107–50, 151, 182, 189, 198, 206, 225, 226, 245, 246, 247, 248–49, 251, 252, 254, 256, 257, 265, 266
dissolution of (1260), 125–26
explanations for expansion, 119–24
Güyük (Khan), 124, 140
Karakorum (capital), 127–29
massacres by, 130–31, 149, 249, 258
mobile secretariats (*tanma*), 128

Index

273

Mongol polity united (*quriltai* of 1206), 117
Ögedei (Khan), 119, 124, 135
origins of name (Onon gol), 113
qaghan (great khan), 125, 127, 129, 135, 140
taxation by, 124, 131, 249
Montesquieu, Charles de Secondat, Baron de
and Algiers, 187–88
and the Mongols (Tartars), 142
Morgan, David, 71
Morocco. *See also* Rabat-Salé (Sallee Rovers), 154, 155, 173, 188
mufsidoon ("evildoer"), 262
Muslim Brotherhood, 207

Nasser, Gamal Abdel, 201, 202, 203, 205
Native Americans, 187
captivity narratives, 191–92
comparison with Mongols (Tartars), 147
Nazi Germany (Nazis), 148–49
comparison with radical Islamism, 207–8
neorealism (realism). *See also* Waltz, Kenneth, 3, 5, 6, 7, 10, 11–12, 13, 16, 24–28, 30–35, 39–40, 45, 48–53, 60, 67, 244–46, 248, 251, 259
and isomorphism ("like" units), 2–3, 23, 24, 26–28, 125, 241, 246–48
animus dominandi, 245
offensive realism, 33, 53
Nestorian Christians, 114, 134
Netherlands (Holland), 179, 188
Nexon, Daniel, 13, 38, 259
Nizari Fortresses (Iran and Syria), 79–81, 82, 85, 87
Alamut, 20, 79–81, 82, 85, 86, 88, 89, 91
Kahf (Syria), 89
Masyaf (Syria), 89
Nizari Ismailis (Assassins). *See also* Nizari fortresses; Sinan, Rashid al-Din; Sabbah, Hassan-i, 3, 18, 20–22, 70–106, 107, 150, 165, 181, 182, 226, 231, 239, 241, 244, 246, 247, 248–49, 250, 253, 257, 259, 265, 266
and suicide attacks, 18–19
and terrorism studies, 71
Assassin legends, 71–72, 96–100, 103, 106
Batiniyya (Batinis, Batinites), 77, 92, 93, 231, 265
Buzurg-Ummid, Kiya, 86
fida'is, 82, 87, 88, 97
Ibn Attash, 78
malahida (heretics), 92

"new preaching", 81, 244
"Old Man of the Mountain", 97–99, 101, 102, 104, 106
origin of "Assassins" (*Hashishin*), 71, 96–97
routing by Mongols (1256), 70, 80, 89, 247
takfir (declaring Nizaris apostates), 93
targeted killing by, 18, 71, 81, 82–83, 85, 87, 89, 91, 95, 98, 99
norms, 3, 4, 7, 9, 10, 12, 14, 15, 24, 25–26, 37, 41–44, 47–48, 53, 60–64, 65, 68, 90, 91, 92, 93–96, 97, 99–100, 105–6, 109, 131–32, 137, 138, 145, 152, 177, 181–82, 197, 200, 201, 219, 224, 227–36, 239, 248, 253–56, 258, 260–62, 263–64
defined, 43
enforcement (thesis), 62, 68, 95, 145, 182, 197, 234–35, 239, 253–56, 257
of partiality, 62–63, 65, 68, 105, 182, 232, 254, 258
relief (thesis), 62–63, 68, 95, 181–82, 235, 253
transmission (thesis), 63, 68, 95–96, 105–6, 138, 182, 253, 254
Nubians, 75

ontological security, 3, 12, 25, 26, 57–60, 63, 64, 250, 252, 253, 254, 255, 256
and Al Qaeda, 199, 224, 227, 240, 262
and the Barbary powers, 173, 190
and the Mongols, 109, 133, 138, 141
and the Nizari Ismailis, 71, 72, 83, 92, 95, 106, 257
Opp, Karl-Dieter, 62–63, 181–82
opportunity structure(s), 2, 13, 32–34, 38, 246, 251
and Al Qaeda, 211, 221–23
and the Barbary powers, 165, 170
and the Mongols, 122–24
and the Nizari Ismailis, 71, 85
defined, 29–30, 32
Robert Merton and, 29–30
transnational opportunity structures, 29
organizational form, 27, 32, 38, 40, 129
Ottoman Empire (Sublime Porte), 5, 17, 152, 153–54, 155, 156–57, 158–61, 163–65, 166, 174, 182–83, 185, 186–87, 189, 191, 250
Belgrade, fall of (1521), 156
decline of, 152, 161–63, 164, 165, 166, 170, 244
janissaries, 158, 161, 163, 164, 166, 167, 187, 188, 250

274 Index

Ottoman Empire (Sublime Porte) (cont.)
  Kapudan Pasha (fleet commander),
    158, 164
  Mehmed II (Sultan), 153, 154
  naval defeats (Malta, Lepanto), 157
  naval victories (Preveza, Djerba),
    156, 158
  pasha (title), 158, 161, 164
  Rhodes, fall of (1523), 156
  Selim I (Sultan), 158
  siege of Vienna (1529), 156
  Suleyman (the Magnificent, Sultan),
    154, 156

Padilla, Jose, 233
Paine, Thomas, 192–93
  Rights of Man, 192
Pakistan, 201, 203, 226, 248, 250
  Inter-Services Intelligence (ISI),
    209, 211
  Khan, Mohammed Ayub
    (President), 203
  Pashtunistan concerns, 203, 208
  support for Afghan mujahedin,
    208–11
pan-Arabism, 201, 202, 203, 204, 205
papacy, 17, 99, 133, 162
  Gregory IX (Pope), 99
  Innocent IV (Pope), 140
Paris, Matthew, 136
path-dependent deviance, 249
Phillips, Andrew, 12, 240, 252
Pichon, Stéphen, 194
piracy, 151–52, 153, 156, 157, 161, 167,
    168, 171–76, 192, 196, 198,
    235–36, 254
  Declaration of Paris (1856), 181
  "Golden Age of Piracy", 171
  norms against (vs. privateers), 177–82,
    189–90, 253–54, 258
Poland
  as "Tartar state", 148
  Mongol invasion (1241), 124, 133
Polo, Marco, 97, 98, 142
Prester John, 133, 134, 141
Pufendorf, Samuel, 146
Purchas, Samuel, 184, 195

Qutb, Sayyid, 206

Rabat-Salé (Sallee Rovers), 173, 175, 176,
    179, 185
Raymond (of Toulouse), 150
Raymond II (of Tripoli), 87, 99
Rice, Condoleezza, 229

rightful rebellion, judgment of (*Ahkam-al-
    Bughat*), 92–93, 94–95, 181, 231, 253
  shawka (sufficient numbers), 92, 94,
    95, 181
  ta'wil (plausible doctrine), 92–94
Rogers, Edward Coit, 195
Roosevelt, Theodore, 107, 198
Rubin, Alfred, 177, 178
Russia (Caucasus). *See also* Soviet Union, 4,
    132, 133, 139, 229
  Kalka, Battle of (1223), 133
  Kiev, fall of (1240), 133
  Mongol invasions (1222–1223, 1237),
    119, 124
Rye House Plot (1683), 100

Sabbah, Hassan-i, 78–80, 81, 84, 85–86,
    87, 97, 123, 244, 252
  death of (1124), 85
Sacy, Silvestre de, 103
Samanids, 73
Saracens, 97, 98, 134, 139, 140
Saudi Arabia (House of Saud), 201, 203–4,
    208, 210, 211, 217, 218, 219, 250
  Mecca and Medina, 204, 217
  OPEC oil embargo, 204
  relations with bin Laden, 211–12,
    217–18, 222
  support for Afghan mujahedin, 209–10
Sayyaf, Abdurrab Rasul, 210, 211
Schweller, Randall, 245
Scythians, 143, 151
Seljuk Turks. *See also* al-Mulk, Nizam, 21,
    73, 74, 75–76, 77–87, 91, 95, 241, 244,
    247, 249, 253
  Alp Arslan (Sultan), 76
  Barkyaruq (Sultan), 84
  Malik Shah (Sultan), 76, 82
  Manzikert, Battle of (1071), 76
  Muhammad (Sultan), 84–85
  Toghril Beg (Sultan), 76
September 11, 2001, attacks of (9/11), 7, 9,
    11, 153, 198, 199, 223, 224, 227, 229,
    233, 235, 236, 237, 243, 260, 262, 264
  9/11 Commission (Report), 221
  and international relations theory, 1
"shadow empires", 110, 126
Sherman, General (William T.), 148
Sicily, 152
  Palermo, 172
Sil, Rudra, 8–9, 15
Simon, Steven, 206, 260–61
Sinan, Rashid al-Din, 88–89, 97
  death of (1192), 89
"skulking way of war", 37

Index

275

Smith, Adam, 144–45
Smith, John Masson, 130–31
Somalia, 215, 217
Song dynasty (China), 110, 111, 112, 118, 132
Southeast Asian Treaty Organization, 203
Soviet Union, 202, 203, 208–9, 210, 213, 249
  Bolsheviks, 148
  decline of, 11, 200, 212, 214–19, 221, 245
  invasion (occupation) of Afghanistan (1979–1989), 200, 208, 211, 214
  withdrawal from Afghanistan (1988–1989), 213, 214, 216
Spain, 73, 152, 153, 155–56, 157–59, 162, 165, 172, 177–78
  Alicante, 172
  Anglo-Spanish naval expedition (1620), 174
  Cádiz, 172
  Charles V, 156
  Ferdinand II, 156
  Ferdinand (II) and Isabella, 155
  Moriscos (Spanish Muslims), 155, 157, 173
  presidios (outposts), 156, 158
  Reconquest, 155
"stealth jihadism", 262
Stryker, Sheldon, 54, 56
subsystemic dominance, 203
Sudan, 222
Sumner, Charles, 194, 195
  "Crime against Kansas", 105
  "White Slavery in the Barbary States" (1847), 195
Syria. *See also* Nizari fortresses, 71, 74, 75, 76, 77, 78, 126, 140, 251
  Nizari *da'is*, 87
  Nizari presence, 86–90, 91
system change, 3, 12, 14, 19, 21, 24, 31, 34, 38, 57, 67, 68, 77, 244, 246
systemic change, 3, 24, 31, 32, 34, 77, 244, 246, 251

Taliban, 212, 228
taqiyya (dissimulation of faith), 18, 223–24
Tartars, 133, 134, 139, 140, 141, 142, 143–46, 148, 183, 186–187
  applied to Mongols, 133
  comparison with Native Americans, 147
  "Modern Tartars", 206
  Tartarus (mythological hell), 133, 256
Temür (Tamerlane), 141, 142, 146, 148, 149, 150

Thies, Cameron, 39–40
Thompson, D'Arcy Wentworth, 23
Tibet (Kingdom of), 112
To'oril Khan (Ong Khan), 115, 116
  patronage of Temüjin (Chinggis Khan), 115, 116
torture, 230, 265
Toynbee, Arnold, 119–20, 151
treachery (and perfidy). *See also* United States, military commissions, 95, 99, 100, 150, 198, 199, 230, 231–32, 235, 240, 241, 259
Treaty of Aix-la-Chapelle (1818), 180
tribal federations (Inner Asian), 113–14
  Kerait, 113, 115, 117
  Merkit, 113, 114, 117
  Mongol, 113
  Naiman, 113, 114, 117, 118
  Tatar (steppe polity), 113–14, 115, 117
Tripoli (North Africa), 151, 154, 156, 160–61, 168, 170, 179
  Karamanli dynasty, 167
Tsarnaev brothers (Boston Marathon bombings), 239
Tunis(ia), 74, 151, 154, 156, 157, 158, 160, 161, 167–69, 170, 175, 179, 180, 185
  Husayni dynasty, 167
  mahalla (revenue expeditions), 167–68
  qa'ids (tax collectors), 167–68
Turgut (Dragut), 160
Turks (Turk), 146, 148, 183, 186, 189, 198, 248
  as label for Barbary inhabitants, 152, 171, 172, 173, 190
  "turning Turk", 185, 190, 238

Ullmann-Margalit, Edna, 62
Umma (community of Islamic believers), 94
uncertainty, 3, 7, 11, 12, 13–14, 24, 25–26, 38, 40–41, 48–65, 68, 69, 71, 90–91, 95–96, 100, 104, 134–38, 141, 173, 177, 181–82, 199, 225–27, 230, 234–35, 240, 243, 248–49, 253–57, 262, 266–67
  factors affecting systemic, 52–53
  vs. risk, 51–53
United Nations (UN), 228–29, 237
  Commission on Human Rights, 228
United States, 22, 149, 153, 171, 181, 190–96, 200, 201–4, 214–21, 222, 226, 228, 229, 230, 233, 235, 238, 241, 261, 262, 263, 266
  atomic bombings (1945), 149
  Barbary Wars (1801–1805 and 1815), 176

276 Index

United States (cont.)
  Bush, George W. (President), 230,
    234, 236
  Civil War (1861–1865), 148
  Dresden firebombing (1945), 149
  Eisenhower Doctrine, 202, 204
  Eisenhower, Dwight (President), 203
  Guantánamo (Bay, Cuba), 231,
    233–34
  Gulf War (1991), 215, 217, 220
  Iraq War (2003–2011), 149, 234
  military commissions, 230–33, 240
  Obama, Barack (President), 237, 262
  Philippine–American War (1899–
    1902), 105
  support for Afghan mujahedin, 208–13,
    250–51
  unlawful enemy combatants, 230,
    234
  Vietnam War (1955–1975), 149, 209
  Washington, D.C. 260
  XYZ Affair (1797), 192
Uthman (Caliph), 82

Van Bynkershoek, Cornelius, 179
Vattel, Emerich de
  and the Barbary powers, 179–80
  and the Mongols, 146

and the Nizari Ismailis (Assassins),
  104, 106
Venice (Venetian), 4, 154, 156, 162,
  174, 178
Voltaire
  and fanaticism, 101
  and the Barbary powers, 186–87
  and the Mongols (Tartars), 142–43, 144
  and the Nizari Ismailis (Assassins),
    101, 231
  Orphan of China, 142
  Philosophical Dictionary, 101
von Clausewitz, Carl, 148
von Hammer-Purgstall, Joseph, 70
  History of the Assassins, 103

Waltz, Kenneth, 12, 19, 26–27, 35, 40, 45,
  50, 57, 243
Watson, Adam, 42
Weber, Max, 30
Weldes, Jutta, 59
Wendt, Alexander, 54–55, 58, 65, 201
Wheaton, Henry, 147
William of Rubruck, 128, 139, 141
William of Tyre, 97

Yemen, 77, 204, 217, 218, 219
Yusuf Reis (Captain John Ward), 185